Friedrich Paulsen

Introduction to philosophy

Translated with the author's sanction by Frank Thilly

Friedrich Paulsen

Introduction to philosophy
Translated with the author's sanction by Frank Thilly

ISBN/EAN: 9783337056766

Printed in Europe, USA, Canada, Australia, Japan

Cover: Foto ©Thomas Meinert / pixelio.de

More available books at **www.hansebooks.com**

RODUCTION TO PHILOSOPHY

BY

FRIEDRICH PAULSEN

PROFESSOR OF PHILOSOPHY IN THE UNIVERSITY OF BERLIN

FIRST AMERICAN FROM THE THIRD GERMAN EDITION

TRANSLATED WITH THE AUTHOR'S SANCTION

BY

FRANK THILLY

PROFESSOR OF PHILOSOPHY IN THE
UNIVERSITY OF MISSOURI

NEW YORK
HENRY HOLT AND COMPANY
1895

Das Wahre war schon längst gefunden,
Hat edle Geisterschaft verbunden,
Das alte Wahre, fass es an.

GOETHE.

·PREFACE.

It gives me great pleasure to be sponsor to our public for Professor Paulsen's *Introduction to Philosophy*. For many years past young Americans have brought back tales from Berlin University of the wide-spread interest in Philosophy which Professor Paulsen's lectures were arousing there and of the great influence of his *Introduction* over students not pursuing a technically philosophical career. Two years ago these introductory lectures were published in the form of the present book. Professor Paulsen is a farmer's son, was born in 1846 in Schleswig-Holstein, took his Ph.D. degree at Berlin in 1871, became Privat-docent in '75, extraordinary-professor in '77, and full professor in 1893. The temper of his mind is essentially ethical, and philosophy for him is nothing if it do not connect itself with active human ideals. His most important publications besides the present one are on Ethics and Pedagogics. His *History of German Universities* has just been translated into English by Prof. E. D. Perry of Columbia College, and published by Macmillan, 1895. He writes a style of which even English readers must feel the euphony as well as admire the clearness, and which (unconsciously, no doubt, to the author) reveals his heart as much as it displays his technical mastery.

There have always been two ways of thinking about Nature. For Christianity, e.g., Nature is something opposed to the truer unseen world, a surface of recoil to which we must first die. For the more pantheistic systems the relation of Nature to the Unseen is not one of contrast but rather of less and more—there is but one world, partly seen

iii

and partly unseen, and its evolution is simple and direct.
'Now if we give the name of "naturalism" to any specimen
of the latter way of thinking that also asserts the universality of mechanistic determination throughout the universe,
the present *Introduction to Philosophy* may be briefly described as an attempt so to state naturalism as to make it
harmoniously continuous with religious faith. Professor
Paulsen does not believe in a philosophy that is only a
"philosophy of the human mind." The philosophic aim
until Locke's time was always to give as unified an account
as possible of all existence in the heavens above and on
the earth beneath ; and our author thinks that Philosophy
should never have taken anything less than this for her
ideal task. On this view it is impossible to separate philosophy from the natural sciences. But the natural sciences
left to themselves have more and more drifted towards an
atomistic materialism. For atomistic materialism, however,
the very existence of consciousness is inexplicable, and remains what has been called by one of Paulsen's colleagues
an "absolute world-riddle." The notion that the spiritual
must be something completely foreign to the primarily
real, and its connection with the real an absolute enigma,
is of course sufficient, as our author says, to stamp with inadequacy any theory that implies it. He accordingly substitutes for physical atomism an idealistic monism or mo-
dernized hylozoism which, being supported by inductive
arguments, is, to say the least, as "scientific" an hypothesis. The universe on this view is animated or
spiritual both in its parts and as a whole, and the nature
of Being is most reasonably to be conceived everywhere
after the analogy of our own immediately experienced life.
In this latter, feeling and appetency are more primordial
elements than conception and reasoning, so it is fair to suppose that the inner life of the infra-human parts of the
world is of a more appetitive or conative sort, whilst the
Soul of the larger totals (the globe which we inhabit and
the starry heaven itself) involving our rational souls, as it
does, also knows all that our reason lets us know and much
more besides. Psycho-physical monism has had a number
of advocates in recent years. I know none as persuasive

as Paulsen; for his statement is untechnical, undogmatic, classical in expression, and absolutely sincere. I should go so far as to say that his exposition of the naturalistic view as a whole is by the superiority of its form calculated to supersede all previous general statements, and to serve as the standard text for criticism by those to whom for any reason the view itself is repugnant.

Passing now to the religious side of the book, there can be no "conflict" between science and religion for Professor Paulsen, for their diverse assertions about the world relate, he says, to entirely different aspects of its being. The task of science is to trace the facts, that of religion is to declare the system of values which they form, or to measure their teleological expressiveness. Religious faith, an utterance of something in us that is deeper than the intellect, insists that the facts not only exist, but have worth or import, and that the order of Nature which science ascertains and describes is *also* a moral order. Such faith does not (when taken in its essential purity) undertake to establish special facts at all, but only to affirm a special sort of significance for such facts as it finds. Whether facts that exist have significance or do not have it is something that cannot be proved or disproved by argument. If one *feels* the significance, it is there; but it can only be affirmed or denied dogmatically, as it were; so that religion and atheism stand opposite to each other not as theories, but rather as expressions of the will, and differing practical attitudes of men towards life. The essential religious affirmation, according to our author, is confidence that the soul of the world (whose existence has been inductively made probable) is *good*—in other words, that the vaster and more eternal sort of Fact is also the more perfect sort of being. The belief that this attitude of faith may be one's most important vital function is also an expression of the voluntary life, and not a theory that can be scientifically refuted. One's question towards it is rather the practical question: Shall I keep it? or be shamed out of it? or perhaps spontaneously give it up?

There is a class of minds to whom Professor Paulsen's system will seem intolerably *loose*, and on that account re-

pugnant from beginning to end. The very charm and un-
technicality of his style will be accounted a crime by readers who believe that only what is *streng wissenschaftlich* can
be counted true. I myself should be glad to see the system
tightened in certain places, and am personally doubtful of
many propositions in which Professor Paulsen believes.
All these defects, however, are minor matters in my eyes in
comparison with the one immense merit of his work, which
is its perfect candor and frank abandonment of dogmatic
pretence. The besetting sin of philosophers has always
. been the absolutism of their intellects. We find an assumption that was the soul of Scholasticism, the assumption
namely that anything that is necessary in the way of
belief must be susceptible of articulate proof, as ram-
pant as it ever was, in the irreligious agnosticism of
to-day; and we find it moreover blossoming out into
corollaries, as, for instance, that to believe anything without such proof is to be unscientific, and that to be unscientific is the lowest depth to which a thinking mind
can fall. Now these assumptions necessarily make philosophy discontinuous with life, because biologically considered man's life consists for the most part in adjust-
ments that are unscientific, and deals with probabilities
and not with certainties. Professor Paulsen makes philosophy and life continuous again; so the pedants of both
camps among us will unite in condemnation of his work.
Life lies open, and the philosophy which their intellects
desiderate must wear the form of a closed system. We
need ever to be reminded afresh that no philosophy can
be more than an hypothesis. As a great contemporary
thinker, Renouvier, has said: "Toute philosophie qui ne
tient pas compte avant tout des incertitudes et des variations et des coutradictions de la philosophie, mais qui
s'entretient dans l'illusion de les supprimer pour s'en
affranchir, est, disons le hautement, un pur enfantillage,
auquel un homme ne doit plus s'arrêtér."

I frankly confess that it is the anti-absolutism of Professor Paulsen that pleases me in him most. I have said
nothing of the predominantly historic method of his exposition, which in the pages that follow is very happily and

instructively carried out. Professor Thilly has well performed the translator's task, and I may say that I have been using advance sheets of the first three quarters of the translation as a text-book in one of my courses, and that, in a long experience as a teacher, it is one of the very few text-books about which I have heard no grumbling.

I should be glad if these introductory words of mine could procure for the *Introduction to Philosophy* a readier reception by American and English students.

WILLIAM JAMES.

HARVARD UNIVERSITY, April, 1895.

TRANSLATOR'S NOTE.

WHAT prompted me to undertake the arduous, and usually thankless, translator's task was the desire to render a masterly book accessible to such lovers of philosophy as are not familiar with the German language. Nowhere will the student find a clearer and simpler presentation of the fundamental problems of philosophy than in Paulsen's *Introduction*, nowhere will he receive, in so small a compass, a more comprehensive knowledge of the views held by the great thinkers of mankind. And though he may not always accept the author's own solutions, he cannot fail to be stimulated and broadened by the suggestive reasonings contained in the following pages. To be sure, no one who is able to understand the original should rest satisfied with a mere interpreter. Translations are at best but soulless copies of living, breathing realities, and no man can ever hope to reproduce the peculiar charm that lies in Professor Paulsen's writings.

I am indebted to Professor James for his kind willingness to act as sponsor for the book. It seems appropriate that a man of whom we Americans are so justly proud should do this service for his popular colleague at Berlin.

My thanks are due to Professors Leo Wiener and H. T. Cory of the University of Missouri for the valuable aid they have rendered me. And I am especially grateful to my wife, who has faithfully assisted me in every possible way during the preparation of the work.

FRANK THILLY.

COLUMBIA, Mo., June, 1895.

PREFACE TO THE FIRST EDITION.

THIS book does not present a new philosophy. As the title indicates, it offers an introduction to philosophy. Its aim is to place before my readers what I have endeavored to impart to the hearers of the lectures delivered by me for a number of years under the same title. The volume will guide them in their inquiries into the great ultimate problems which the world puts to the thinking mind of man, and lead them to study the great thoughts which the spiritual leaders of humanity have proposed as answers to these questions.

A historical account might serve as such a guide. Or we might consider the problems and thoughts in the form of a discussion of these questions. I have chosen the latter method, or rather I was compelled to employ it, because it seemed to me to be the only possible method. No man can explain philosophical problems and their solutions unless he has himself taken an independent stand in reference to them. Nor can he do so without introducing his own views and judgments into the exposition. Hence I shall not merely set forth the problems together with their possible and historical solutions, but I shall at the same time attempt to convince the reader that my solution is the correct one. And so he will after all find a philosophy in these pages.

I desire to be candid as well as to assist the reader in taking a proper attitude towards the philosophy developed in the following work. I shall therefore outline its characteristic features at the very outset.

I characterize as *Idealistic Monism* the view towards which the development of philosophical thought seems to me to be tending, the direction along which the truth is to be found. The contrary conceptions by which this view is bounded and defined are *Supranaturalistic Dualism* and *Atomistic Materialism.* The former is the system of the church doctrine, the heritage of mediæval scholasticism which was handed down to the eighteenth century in the new scholasticism of Protestanism. It separates body and mind as two substances merely accidentally and temporarily conjoined; it seeks to hold apart God and nature as two realities foreign to each other. Atomistic materialism, however, is the philosophy which the mechanical explanation of nature, in vogue since the seventeenth century, regards as containing not merely its own ultimate premises, but the final notions concerning the world at large.

We may construe the whole history of modern philosophy as a continued attempt to overcome this opposition. Traditional supranaturalism opposes God to the world as an extramundane and anthropomorphic individual. It assumes that after having once created the world out of nothing this God continues occasionally to act upon it. Modern science has cut the very ground from under this view. The uniform reign of law in all natural occurrences is the principle of natural science. One domain after another has been made subject to this principle, and thus the thought gradually has come to prevail with irresistible force that all natural processes are to be considered as the results of uniformly-acting forces. Materialism believes that this notion is the final outcome of the scientific knowledge of things, and invests it with the dignity of a metaphysic. The whole of reality is nothing but a system of blindly-acting physical forces. The old supranaturalistic system defended itself against this view partly with the traditional weapons of ontological and cosmological speculation, above all, however, by aspersing and defaming the materialistic philosophy and even the modern sciences, whenever occasion seemed to demand it, as godless innovations, dangerous to the State and society.

Philosophy attempts to overcome this opposition *from within.* It everywhere attempts—and we may regard this attempt as the moving factor in the entire development of modern philosophy—*to reconcile the religious view of the world with the scientific explanation of nature.* Many will regard this as an attempt to square the circle. Perhaps the task somewhat resembles that undertaking. Approximate values only can be reached in the latter case. Nor is the problem ever completely solved in the former. At any rate, we must recognize it as a historical fact that the philosophical thought of the last three centuries has been tending towards this goal.

Modern science is its starting-point and precondition, while the universal reign of law in natural occurrences is its fundamental idea. Whatever is not in accord with this thought lies outside of the sphere of modern philosophy. Its second fundamental conviction is that the teaching of natural science concerning reality is not all that can be said of it, that reality is something else and something more than a corporeal world moved according to the laws of mechanics. Many different attempts have been made to determine what this something is or to prove that it cannot be determined at all. But everybody has at bottom acknowledged its existence. What is not in accord with this idea also lies outside of the pale of modern philosophy.

Both of these features are conspicuous in the two great currents in which the philosophy of the seventeenth and eighteenth centuries moves. The *rationalistic-metaphysical* course of development, whose chief representatives are *Descartes, Spinoza,* and *Leibniz,* recognizes the truth of the modern *physical view of the world* and then supplements it with a *metaphysical* view. The *empirical-positivistic* train of thought native to England, represented by *Locke, Berkeley,* and *Hume,* sets out from the same presupposition. Epistemological reflection, however, leads it to the belief that the physical view is not absolute truth, but an accidental view, a projection of reality upon our sensibility. In *Kant* the two views meet and interpenetrate in a very peculiar manner. But what is most important, from him we date the significant turning-point which aims to bring about a peace between the religious view of the world and the scientific explanation of nature by separating the religious disposition from the intellectual function and basing the former on volition.

The development assumes a peculiar form in the *nineteenth* century. The development of philosophical thought separates, in Germany at least, into three distinct epochs. The first epoch is given up to *speculative* philosophy. This is an attempt not merely to supplement the physical view of the world, but to overcome it altogether by explaining it in a speculative-metaphysical way by a spiritual-logical principle. During the second third of the century, after the failure of the speculative undertaking, philosophy lost confidence in itself and was subjected to popular contempt. Then the physical view gained the ascendency and expressed itself in a *materialistic* metaphysics which it regarded as absolute truth. This view largely prevails among the educated up to this day. It has of late taken hold of the masses, who are beginning to reflect on their condition. During the last third of the century philosophy has been awakened from its lethargy into new life, and has attacked the old problem : not to supersede or to overcome the physical view, but to supplement and complete it by a broader and profounder conception of reality—by metaphysics. *Fechner* and *Lotze* may be mentioned as the representatives of the older generation, *Lange* and *Wundt* as representatives of the new.

A closer examination of the philosophical state of the *present* and the direction which philosophy is taking leads me to make the following classification.

The philosophy of the present is :

(1) *Phenomenalistic - positivistic.* Its epistemological creed is : There is no absolute knowledge of reality, least of all in physics. The corporeal world is a world of phenomena. Hence in Germany it leans on Kant.

(2) It is *idealistic-monistic.* Its metaphysical creed is : In so far as we can attempt to determine the nature of reality, we must turn to the world of inner experience. In the evolution of mind we find the most intelligible, or rather the only intelligible, expression of the content of reality. The final thought to which the facts lead us is this : Reality, which is represented to our senses by the corporeal world as a uniform system of movements, is the manifestation of a universal spiritual life that is to be conceived as an

idea, as the development of a unitary reason, a reason which infinitely transcends our notions. In this respect it retains the general features of the cosmology of speculative philosophy, or rather of all idealistic philosophy since Plato.

(3) It is turning from an intellectualistic to a *voluntaristic* ҡ conception, especially in psychology. Here we may recognize first, the influence of Schopenhauer, secondly, the increasing importance of the modern biological view. This conception, however, is also coming to the front in metaphysics and in our notion of the universe. At this point it finds its support in the Kantian thought which assigns to the will its proper place in the view of the world. Protestant theology is also in a state of transition from intellectualism to voluntarism due to these influences.

(4) It is turning to an *evolutionistic-teleological* view. Modern cosmology and biology are exerting their influence on metaphysics as well as on psychology and natural philosophy. They are supported here by idealistic monism. They have also begun to pervade *practical* philosophy. Ethics and sociology, jurisprudence and politics are about to give up the old formalistic treatment and to employ instead the teleological method : purpose governs life, hence the science of life, of individual as well as collective life, must employ this principle.

(5) Finally, this element is connected with a characteristic that marks the entire philosophy of the nineteenth century and distinguishes it from the preceding period : I mean its *bent for history.* The older philosophy rests on the mathematical and natural scientific conception of reality ; it is abstract and rationalistic. Speculative philosophy begins with the interpretation of mental evolution; it then attempts to interpret nature historically, as it were, at least according to a logical-genetical scheme. The natural sciences have followed along these lines, and have in reality treated nature historically in the cosmological and biological theory of evolution. In doing this they are plainly working into the hands of philosophy, which has always endeavored to combine the physical and mental worlds into a consistent view of the whole.

Philosophy seems to me to be moving in this direction at present. At any rate, this is the direction in which the thoughts herein presented tend.

As was indicated above, modern philosophy finds itself in a predicament because of its intermediate position between the religious view of the world and the mechanical explanation of nature. Here, as everywhere else, the mediator is very apt to find himself *battling with two enemies*. On the one hand, philosophy is exposed to the attacks of supernatural theology. It is accused of undermining the doctrines recognized by the church and protected by the State. In the beginning the power of the state was regularly employed to suppress philosophical heresies, frequently with success. To-day this procedure is practically abandoned, at least on Protestant soil. It is true that such has been the case only for a short time, and that in many circles the inclination still exists to call out the police force against the philosopher. Who has not heard the accusation, even in the most recent times, that the social-democracy is not a social or political party, but a view of the world; that atheism is its dogma, and that the infidel professors are its instigators? And to this day, Catholicism adheres to the mediæval conception that it is the duty of the spiritual and temporal authorities to control philosophy and to suppress it, if the case demands. The only difference is that the temporal power is no longer so willing to proceed against heresy as of old.

On the other hand, philosophy is maligned by the representatives of a purely physical view of the world. "The philosophy professors," the most calumniated persons since Schopenhauer, are derided as priests of the second order, who are appointed to second the church in its struggle against Science, as people who are paid to confuse the youth by all kinds of obscure and abstruse discussions, in order to prejudice them against Science and to drive them into the arms of the authoritative creed.

It is not my intention to defend philosophy against these accusations, or to examine whether and how much truth may be in them. All I care to do is to show that they are due to the historical position which modern philosophy occupies. They will last as long as their cause lasts, that is, as long as the opposition between the church doctrine and science lasts. And as long as this hostility continues the church will oppose a philosophy which marshals the conclusions of science against the traditional doctrine, rather than oppose the scientific detail work which, by the very nature of the case, confines itself to a very narrow sphere and may easily avoid a conflict with the teachings of the church. And just so long will the other side suspect a philosophy of being untrue to itself that talks about limits of human knowledge, and concedes the right of a religious view of the world alongside of scientific research. And the stronger this opposition becomes the more difficult will the position of philosophy be. "Materialism is the necessary correlate of Jesuitism; the water in these tubes invariably stands at the same height." We find these words of Paul de Lagarde everywhere confirmed in history; they are true of Protestant as well as Catholic Jesuitism. The more rigorous the creed becomes, the more intense becomes the animosity of the opposition, and the more intense will be the animosity of both parties against philosophy. The Church persecutes her as the more dangerous champion of infidelity; radicalism regards her as an unreliable or faithless ally, who is in communication with the hostile camp. Philosophy will not find peace until science is reconciled with faith. By faith, however, we do not mean a system of dogmatics. Until then her task will be to stay at her post between the two hostile hosts, regardless of the missiles from either side, having as her shield a good conscience, as her motto, "Subject to no one but to Truth alone."

In conclusion, let me say a word concerning the manner in which I shall treat the subject. I have everywhere set myself two tasks : (1) to develop the philosophical problems and their possible solutions, and at the same time to present and to prove the solution which seems to me to be the correct one; (2) at every point to indicate, at least in outline, the historical development of philosophical thought. That both methods regularly lead to the same goal is most likely due to a kind of pre-established harmony. As far as I can see, every thinker has, on the one hand, regarded his thoughts as a solution demanded by the facts, on the other, as the goal of historical development, and has attempted to convince others of this truth. Of course the choice of the historically-significant points by which the direction of the development is determined ultimately and always depends on their agreement with one's own thoughts. Just as, according to the old saying, " Man is the measure of things," one's own thoughts are the measure of the thoughts of others.

I expect that the objection will be raised that I am too apt to ignore the differences that exist between the idealistic systems, or that I obliterate them by harmonizing them. It was not my intention to escape this objection. My concern was to point out historically the main features of this form of thought in its general outlines ; the differences necessarily fell into the background. The genius of Plato and Aristotle, Spinoza and Leibniz, Hume and Kant, Fechner and Lotze, is certainly not the same, and the differences between their philosophical systems are great ; they saw that themselves. And yet it may be expedient for the time being to disregard the differences and to emphasize the great features that they have in common. In geographical instruction we first place before the pupil charts which show only the main outlines of countries and oceans, the principal mountain-chains and the great water-courses. Special charts showing the smallest details would simply confuse him. It seems to me that the student fares similarly in the history of philosophy. If the history is presented to him at the outset with its endless great and little differences of views and arguments, helpless confusion easily results, and the end of it all is a frightful scepticism. He comes to believe that the history of philosophy teaches that every philosopher is opposed to the other and hence that the entire undertaking results in nothing.

In opposition to this view the historical suggestions herein presented aim to produce the conviction that the work of philosophical reflection which has lasted for so many centuries has not been in vain, but rather that it leads to a view of the world that is uniform in its main features and assumes a more pronounced shape as the years roll on. The history of philosophy is the road to truth as much as the history of any other science. Of course it is full of deviations and circuitous paths.

Should connoisseurs condescend to read this book and then come to the conclusion that they have not been repaid for their trouble, I shall not feel very much aggrieved. I have never in my life met anybody who was able to satisfy the connoisseurs, especially not in Germany that is so full of connoisseurs in all branches of knowledge. But let them not accuse me of having deceived them : an introduction is surely not written for connoisseurs.

Should this book come into the hands of my old students, I beg them to take it as a greeting from the author and in remembrance of hours that were once spent together. I also hope that here and there a reader of my *Ethics* will find in these discussions a desirable supplement to many thoughts simply suggested in that work.

FR. PAULSEN.

STEGLITZ, near BERLIN, Aug. 6, 1892.

CONTENTS.

INTRODUCTION.

BOOK I.
The Problems of Metaphysics.

CHAPTER I.

CHAPTER II.

BOOK II.

The Problems of Epistemology.

CHAPTER I.

THE PROBLEM OF THE NATURE OF KNOWLEDGE, OR THE
RELATION OF KNOWLEDGE TO REALITY . . . 344

CHAPTER II.

THE PROBLEM OF THE ORIGIN OF KNOWLEDGE . . 378

APPENDIX.

INTRODUCTION.

THE NATURE AND IMPORT OF PHILOSOPHY.

THERE was a time, and that time is not very remote from us, when the opinion widely prevailed that philosophy had outlived its usefulness, that the positive sciences had taken its place. Its *raison d'être* was conceded on the ground that it served as a preliminary stage to scientific knowledge, but it was held that we should no longer attempt to gain a knowledge of the world and objects by general speculation. Let philosophy eke out its existence as the harmless diversion of sterile minds that are not fitted for real scientific labor. Not all, however, who lay claim to scientific training ought to be required to busy themselves with philosophy.

We need not discuss the question whether philosophy is to some extent responsible for the discredit into which it fell about the middle of this century. It is probable on *a priori* grounds that this is the case. Nowhere was philosophy so slightingly treated as in Germany. In that country a period of neglect followed the reign of speculative philosophy. It therefore seems natural to infer a causal connection here, and to regard the contempt in which all philosophy was held as the reaction against the speculative philosophers and their disciples who, with their overweening pride, had given offence to scientific research no less than to common-sense. The German reader had allowed himself to be intimidated long enough by their austere manner, and had been imposed upon by their turbid profoundness. He had permitted speculative philosophy to characterize as shallow and to call in question whatever he happened to understand. But he finally took courage and resolved to despise everything that might remind him of his past humiliation. Had Hegel reached Kant's age he would himself have lived to see the reaction. Instead, others, like Fechner and Lotze, became the victims of an indifference which they had neither caused nor deserved.

Meanwhile a new era has arrived. Although the former contempt for philosophy has not wholly died out, we may say that this feeling is not so characteristic of the last third of the century as it was of the second. Philosophy is beginning to recover from the effects of public neglect. It is regaining the sympathy of larger circles and has resumed more friendly relations with scientific research.

This is as it should be. For, in truth, philosophy is not a matter that can outlive its usefulness. Nor is it the business of a few barren and abstruse thinkers, but the concern of all ages and all mankind. Indeed, we may say, philosophy is not something that one may have or not have at will. In a certain sense every human being that rises above the dull level of animal life has a philosophy; the only question is what kind of philosophy he has. Is it one rudely fashioned from a few stray fragments of knowledge and disconnected thoughts, or one that is the result of thorough and logical study, and founded upon a universal examination of reality?

The intellectual life of man is distinguished from that of the brute by his capacity to theorize and his ability to see things in their relation to the whole. The lower animal sees and hears, and, most likely, has ideas and recollections, but it does not reflect on them. They come and go as isolated facts in the natural course of events. They are significant only as motives for the will. In man, intellectual activity emancipates itself from necessity. Theoretical interest is aroused. He gathers and examines the elements supplied by perception; he does not rest until he has combined them into a systematic conception of the whole. Practice and technics are satisfied with a knowledge of details; theoretical interest is directed towards the whole. In this way philosophy arises. In the most general sense of the term, philosophy is simply the continu-

ally-repeated attempt to arrive at a comprehensive and
systematic knowledge of the form and connection, the
meaning and import of all things.

It is apparent that in this sense every nation and every
man, at least every normally-developed man, has a philosophy. The plain man of the people, too, has a philosophy.
His catechism may have supplied him with the fundamental
ideas of the same. He gives an answer to the question regarding the origin and the destiny of the world and man.
In this sense peoples living in a state of nature have their
philosophy also. Thus the Indian and the New Zealander
formed a conception of the universe and its spatial structure. They had an answer to the question concerning the
Whence and the Whither of things, and saw a rational connection between cosmic occurrences and human life. In
this interpretation, therefore, philosophy is a universal
human function. Philosophy is coextensive with mental
life.

1. The Relation of Philosophy to Religion and Mythology.

In the common usage of language the term philosophy
has a narrower meaning. We no longer speak of a history of
philosophy before the flood, as was commonly done formerly, nor do we designate as philosophy the contents of the
catechism or the ideas of savage tribes concerning the universe. All these we distinguish from philosophy as mythology or religion. It is certainly not my intention to remove or obliterate this line of separation, but rather to
try to define it and thus more closely to determine the
nature of philosophy. We can distinguish philosophy
from religion according to two principles of division, that
of subject and that of function. First, we may say, the
collective mind is the subject of the mythological conception of the universe ; the individual mind, that of philosophy.
Wherever we have philosophy, it is the product of individual mental effort. There is no philosophy without a
philosopher. For that reason it is named after him ; we
call it Platonic, Spinozistic, Kantian philosophy. Mythology, on the other hand, like folk-lore and language, is not
the result of the conscious work of an individual, it is the

product of a whole people. There is no inventor of language, nor an inventor of the primitive mythico-religious views of the world, the origin of which is intimately connected with language and poesy. Nowadays no one speaks of a founder of the Egyptian or the Greek religion. The Christian and Mohammedan religions have their respective founders; they, however, were not concerned with an original creation of conceptions previously unknown, but only with a reform whose aim was practical rather than theoretical.

Corresponding to this subjective difference there is a difference of function. Philosophy is the product of the inquiring and thinking mind; the mythico-religious conception of the world is the product of poetic fancy, which combines and supplements its data and brings them into relation with a transcendent world created by it. All astronomical and terrestrial phenomena are at times, though not consistently, conceived as the voluntary acts of transcendent powers that are well or ill disposed towards the ego, furthering or obstructing its aims. All explanations are in answer to the question concerning the Why and the Wherefore of things.

Philosophy, on the other hand, begins with intellectual apprehension and takes things as they are. Its main object is to discover the What and the How instead of the Wherefore. Hence it aims, first of all, to determine phenomena as such and their relations in space and time. In this manner, it attains to a knowledge of laws, and with the aid of this knowledge it attempts to explain objects in general with increasing certainty. This is scientific procedure. Philosophy is originally nothing more than the scientific knowledge of reality as distinguished from or opposed to the mythico-religious notion of the universe.

Hence it follows that there is a difference in the manner in which the individual forms his philosophy and his mythico-religious ideas. The individual is a participant in philosophy by an act of *thinking*, in mythology and religion by *faith*. A faith-philosophy is as much of an internal contradiction as a philosophizing religion. This is true even of the highest forms of religion, for the individual partici-

ates in them, not as a thinking and inquiring being, but
as the member of a people, of a historical community.
His religion is essentially his, as something he has received.
Even though the content of philosophy is not his direct
production, it appears as something obtained through his
own exertions, as something which he might have thought
out for himself in the first instance.

The relation between philosophy and religion thus outlined throws light upon a conspicuous fact in the history
of mental life, the fact that there is often a hostile opposition between the two. For the most part strained relations existed between the philosophy of the West, in its
two great phases of development in antiquity and modern
times, and the traditional conceptions of religion. Indeed,
this relation often becomes one of open hostility. The
best known example of such a hostile encounter in the
history of Greek philosophy is furnished by the sentence
and execution of Socrates as a contemner of the gods and
a corrupter of the youth. But this is not the only case
on record. The history of modern philosophy contains
scarcely a page that does not tell of both internal and
external conflicts. The champions and pioneers of modern
thought were all of them opposed and persecuted by the
official or voluntary custodians of tradition, and in turn
regarded themselves as the opponents of the reigning
system. I have only to call to mind Bruno and Galileo,
Descartes and Spinoza, Hobbes and Locke, Voltaire and
Rousseau, Leibniz and Wolff, Kant and Fichte. All of
these men were treated as foes. They were either persecuted and punished directly, or their writings were sup-
pressed and burned by the public executioner, or they were
hampered in their activity as teachers by all kinds of
restrictions and aspersions. The conflict has not come to
an end at the present day, even though the old weapons
have, for the most part, been discarded. Even in our age
a new philosophy is tested not merely as to its truth, but
also as to its agreement with the prevailing doctrine. If it
fails to pass this test, it is straightway rejected as reprehensible and dangerous.

The cause of this hostile relation is evidently to be

found in the close affinity between philosophy and religion.
The battle is one between hostile brothers or sisters.
The older sister demands the recognition of her authority,
the younger endeavors to emancipate herself from this
authority. She wishes no longer to serve as *ancilla theologiæ*,
but strives after freedom and independence. The conflict
ultimately amounts to a struggle of the individual against
the collective mind for freedom. At the outset, philosophy
invariably encounters the old conceptions of the world,
which are the products of collective thought. The universal
mind is older than the individual mind. On the primitive
stage of development the genus is everything, the individual the mere exemplar of the genus. In action and
judgment the individual is determined by customs, in
thought by the religious ideas and conceptions of the
community. The possibility of individual thought is far
removed from him. But in the course of development,
differentiation and individualization take place. The individual now has the courage to be independent, and with
this feeling arises the courage to have convictions of his
own. According to Aristotle it is wonder, according to
Descartes doubt, which is the beginning of philosophy.
Both states mean the same thing, namely, the awakening
of individual thought which has hitherto either been
silenced or lulled to sleep by universal opinions. The
traditional collective mind rebels against this doubt or
wonder and its endeavors to form its own ideas concerning
the world and things, as a strange and unheard-of presumption. Why can you not rest satisfied with the
recognized and traditional conceptions of your ancestors?
it asks. This is impious presumption on your part, which
it is my right and duty to suppress, the more so since every
departure from the universal modes of thinking simply
opens the way to a departure from custom or tries to
palliate the same.

The efforts of antiquity to resist philosophy lacked
coherence and consistency. The mythico-religious conception of the world had not developed a uniform system,
nor did it possess an external organization that might have
rendered it capable of defence and resistance. Philosophy,

therefore, soon became wholly free here. The case was different in modern times. The Christian religion assimilated so much philosophy during antiquity and the middle ages as to present a comprehensive system of its own, one that leaves no room for a free development of thought. In the church and its system of administration and instruction it possesses the external organization which enables it at once to observe deviations from its doctrine and to oppose them with combined authority. On this account the struggle was much fiercer and lasted much longer than in antiquity. The conflict is by no means ended yet, even though the fundamental demand is no longer made to subject philosophy to the ecclesiastical system, at least not on the Protestant side. Still, a tendency in this direction occasionally manifests itself. If the attempt to bring the theological faculties back again under the authority of the church should prove successful, we should presumably not have to wait very long for the attempt to subject philosophy to control. For the present, however, there is little prospect of that.

How will the conflict end? Will it last forever? Will it lead to an amicable settlement? Or will it end with the final defeat or destruction of one of the opposing parties?

The latter view largely prevails in our times. Religion, it is believed, is on the wane; philosophy and science have undermined its roots; the final outcome will be the supremacy of science.

I cannot altogether accept this view. In a certain sense, of course, it is correct: the old mythical conception of nature is doubtless on the decline. The belief in gods and demons that exist somewhere as individual beings and interrupt the causal nexus in nature by means of occasional encroachments is dying out and will not be revived unless, of course, science and philosophy should disappear in the West. It does not make any essential difference whether we presuppose many such beings or only one.

On the other hand, I do not believe that religion will die out with this belief. I do not believe that humanity will ever be satisfied with scientific knowledge to explain its inward relation to reality. Were man a purely intellectual being, he would content himself with the fragments of knowledge which scientific research gradually gathers together. But he is not mere understanding, he is above everything else a willing and feeling being. And religion is deeply rooted in this side of his nature. Feelings of humility, reverence, yearnings after perfection, with which his heart is inspired by the contemplation of nature and history, determine his attitude to reality more immediately and profoundly than the concepts and formulæ of science. Out of these feelings arises the trust that the world is not a meaningless play of blind forces, but the revelation of a good and great being whom he may acknowledge as akin to his own innermost essence. For in truth the real essence of every religious belief is the assurance that the true nature of reality reveals itself in that which I love and reverence as the highest and the best, it is the certainty that the good and perfect, towards which the deepest yearning of my will is directed, forms the origin and the goal of all things.

Inasmuch as this certainty does not come from science, science cannot destroy it. It has its roots, not in the understanding, but in the will. The understanding does not judge at all by means of the predicates good and bad, valuable and valueless; it distinguishes the real and the unreal, the true and the false. It is a registering machine of phenomena and is indifferent to their value. Man, however, is more than a registering machine of reality; consequently he has not only science, but also poetry and art, faith and religion. There is one item at least in which every man goes beyond mere knowledge, beyond the registration of facts. That is his own life and his future. His life has a meaning for him, and he directs it towards something which does not yet exist, but which will exist by virtue of his will. Thus a faith springs up by the side of his knowledge. He believes in the realization of this his life's aim, if he is at all in earnest about it. Since, however, his aim is not an isolated one, but is included in the historical life of a people, and finally in that of humanity, he believes also in the future of his people, in the victorious future of truth and righteousness and goodness in humanity. Whoever devotes his life to a cause believes in that cause, and this belief, be his creed what it may, has always something of the form of a religion.

Hence faith infers that an inner connection exists between the real and the valuable within the domain of history, and believes that in history something like an immanent principle of reason or justice favors the right and the good and leads it to victory over all resisting forces. From these premises another conclusion naturally follows. Man's historical life in turn is not isolated, it is a part of the general course of nature and cannot in any way be separated from it. If now the law prevails in the former sphere that truth is fundamentally and permanently victorious over falsehood, right over wrong, good over evil, in spite of the fact that the opposite seems to be the case, why should we not be permitted to extend this relation and believe in a power of the good over the whole of reality? Least of all, it seems, ought this idea to be contradicted by those who so emphatically affirm the uniform reign of law in the world, and assert that history is a part of the universal process of nature. Whoever believes in a steady progress in history, and at the same time regards the life of humanity as a part of universal nature, makes all the premises which must lead him to the belief that there is a meaning in all things, unless indeed he desires to reject his own conclusions. These premises will lead him to faith, not to knowledge and proofs. For the meaning of history, indeed the meaning of an individual life, is not a matter of knowledge and proof.

What can hinder us from holding this belief? Is it the weak arguments that have brought such discredit upon a good cause, and do we owe it to the understanding, which rejects these arguments, to abandon the cause itself? If so, we shall be forced to the strange confession that the final outcome and problem of science consists in showing that the belief that there is a meaning and a reason in things is nonsense and superstition.

Here the possibility is offered of a peace between science and faith, between philosophy and religion, the possibility of a real and permanent peace, not of a convenient compromise, of a compromise made at the expense of truth. Nor would this be a peace in which the parties merely tolerated or contemptuously avoided each other, it would be a peace depending on free and mutual recognition. The first step to such a peace is the precise definition of the problems. Above all, religion must cease to interfere with the business of science as it used to do. It must grant full sway to the investigation of natural and historical reality. It has no right either to limit such investigation or to dictate its results. Such a procedure would be fatal to science. Religion may recognize the claims of science without endangering its own existence. Science will never wholly satisfy the heart of man, nor will it ever thoroughly exhaust reality. This fact it will acknowledge more readily, the safer it feels itself against encroachments upon its own domain. At the same time science will confess its inability to supply the place of religion; it will admit that in addition to its own problem there is room for another which it cannot solve. Besides the question concerning the What and the How, man inevitably raises the question as to the Wherefore. It is true, philosophy has always attempted to answer this question as well. It surveys the whole of life, and attempts to determine its end or highest good. It surveys the sum-total of things, and attempts to grasp their relation to the highest good. But it is becoming more and more convinced that this undertaking cannot be accomplished with the means of scientific knowledge; that, as Goethe remarks, existence divided by human reason leaves a remainder. Hence the problem to interpret the meaning of things, not by concepts of the understanding, but by sacred symbols which satisfy the heart, is left to religion.

The historical relation between science, philosophy, and religion may be expressed as follows: Originally all three were one. Causal explanation, theoretical exposition, and ideal interpetration of reality are one and the same in religious mythology. The symbols of perfection serve at the same time as explanatory principles of nature. These two elements are not held apart, as yet, in scholastic theology and philosophy. God is the highest good and at the

same time the first cause which all sciences, astronomy
and biology no less than history, employ as the principle
of explanation. Increasing differentiation which governs
all historical as well as organic life has also led to a division here. Science has separated from religion and pursues
its aim, the description and causal explanation of reality,
regardless of the possibility of an ideal interpretation.
Religion offers faith its explanations, regardless of the possibility of a scientific construction. The formation of
dogmas, which pretended to be a conceptual construction
of faith, has stopped. Philosophy occupies an intermediate position between the two. Starting from the known, it
seeks, as a universal science, to answer the question concerning the essence and form of reality. It soon becomes
aware of the limitations of human knowledge. And the
insufficiency of this knowledge becomes all the more
marked when science inquires into the import and meaning
of things. It recognizes the impossibility of deducing the
form of reality from the assumed concept of its meaning,
and, conversely, of deducing the meaning underlying reality
from its form. The world is a mystery. It is left to religion, the custodian of all mysteries, to reveal to the heart
its hidden meaning.

The recognition of this differentiation is the condition
of peace. Whoever endeavors to impede this progress,
whoever strives again to subject science to dogma, or to
reduce faith to knowledge, wastes his efforts, and for his
part hinders the realization of a wholesome relation.

Is this peace near at hand? The signs seem to be
favorable. Philosophy has long ago offered the hand of
peace. It is the cardinal point in the philosophy of Kant
that knowledge and faith are different functions; both
are endowments of man's nature and capable of existing
side by side. The sum and substance of his undertaking
is to gain for each its rights: to protect knowledge against
the scepticism of Hume, faith against the dogmatic negation of materialism. In order to make room for faith, it is
necessary to remove the positive dogmatism of Wolffian
philosophy; for negative dogmatism stands and falls with
positive dogmatism. That is what Kant means when he

says : " I was obliged to destroy knowledge in order to
make room for faith." The knowledge in question is not
the knowledge of science, but the alleged knowledge of the
transcendent philosophy and theology of the schools,
whose orthodox form necessarily provokes heretical forms,
especially when it is protected by the State. Kant therefore regards it as far more consistent with a government's
wise regard for sciences as well as for society, "to favor the
freedom of such a criticism, by which alone the labors of
reason can be established on a firm footing, than to support the ridiculous despotism of the schools, which raise a
loud clamor of public danger whenever the cobwebs are
swept away of which the public has never taken the slightest notice and the loss of which it can therefore never perceive." (Preface to the Second Edition of the *Critique of
Pure Reason.*)*

After a transitory relapse into intellectualism, which
characterizes the reign of Hegelian philosophy, Kantian
philosophy again exerts the widest influence. It has
put an end to both speculative philosophy and dogmatic
materialism. Both of these attempted, though with different objects in view and in different directions, to destroy
faith by means of knowledge, and to render it superfluous. And philosophers are not the only ones in our day
who lean on Kantian philosophy. Physicists and physiologists do the same. It is true that each appropriates
something different from this philosophy. It is also true
that for many the appeal to Kant's theory of knowledge is
simply a shallow excuse for their thorough lack of positive
thoughts concerning God and the world. Nevertheless
we may assume that the present spread of Kantian philosophy, on the whole, proceeds from a desire to reconcile
science and religion on the basis of Kantianism.

The spread of Positivism in France and England is a
parallel to the spread of Kant's philosophy in Germany.
This school emphatically rejects the church's guardian-
ship over science. Yet, on the other hand, it acknowledges
with equal emphasis that knowledge is something relative,

* Max Müller's Translation, vol. i. p. 383.

and does not go to the bottom of things, and that we need something else to express another side of our inner life, the relation of our emotional nature to reality. Religion has always offered something to satisfy these demands. Upon this point Comte and Renan, Mill and Spencer, are at agreement.

On the side of religion we may welcome as a hopeful sign a movement that is rapidly gaining strength in Protestant theology. I refer to the attempt to give the dogma a new place and significance in church-life. A former view regarded the dogma as the expression of theoretical truths. These truths, it held, can and must be scientifically demonstrated by means of exegetical and historical proofs or ontological and cosmological arguments, or they can and must be interpreted by abstruse speculation. For the new movement, however, the dogma has the significance of a formula that does not bind the understanding as much as the will. It does not contain demonstrable predications of historical and natural reality, but articles of faith in values that are universally recognized, that satisfy the heart and determine the will. By rejecting scholastic philosophy Luther rejected the artificial union between faith and knowledge. The modern view follows his precedent. It seeks to free Protestant theology from the intellectualism of orthodoxy, from the intellectual mania for demonstration and system, which again controlled it soon after the Reformation, and to base church-life on the gospel of salvation by faith and charity.

Thus the two parties make advances to each other. All that seems to be necessary to establish peace is that the church decide to render openly and without reservation unto science the things that are science's. She has gradually consented, at least on the Protestant side, to render unto Cæsar or to the State the things that are of the State. We may presume that she will also consent to render unto the understanding what belongs to the understanding, that she will unconditionally cede to it the entire domain of natural and historical reality for free investigation, and admit that she has neither means nor grounds for opposing the knowledge gained by scientific inquiry. When that happens, philosophy and science will no longer regard faith as an encroachment upon knowledge, but will confess with Goethe : " It is the highest happiness of the thinking being to investigate what can be investigated, and silently to adore what cannot be explained." *

A radicalism that is absolutely hostile to religion and that is at present spreading among the masses is calculated to obscure this hopeful outlook. The hostile feeling which ₁was aroused among the educated a generation ago in consequence of governmental interference has now taken possession of the masses, who are socially and politically dissatisfied. Here, too, science is appealed to. Science has shown, they declare, that religion is nothing but a survival from the childhood of man, a survival which the political and social interests of the governing classes protect and preserve. The *bourgeoisie* was formerly under the ban of the same delusion. The hatred of the political *régime* and of the church in league with it was directed against religion, and made infidelity a political article of faith. Similarly atheism appears as the article of faith of the social-democracy. It is the catechism reversed. The old dogmatism was an enemy to science. The same may be said of this new negative dogmatism in so far as its own dogmas fetter the spirit of criticism and doubt. The term " anti-priests," which a leader of the socialistic party recently applied to certain hotspurs of the atheistic wing, is indeed very suggestive. Religion as such occupies an altogether neutral position in regard to political and

* In connection with what I have written above, attention has been called to the recent controversy concerning the *apostolicum*. It was pointed out that the prediction of an eternal peace had in this case again proved to be an illusion. I am not ready to give up hope so easily I did not expect the views which prevailed in theology a generation ago to yield the field without a struggle. Winter takes its leave with reluctance, and a few more snow-storms delay the coming of spring. But spring comes none the less. The old orthodoxy's campaign of protest does not shake my belief. Indeed, I perceive in this very fact a favorable sign. Did she not feel herself in danger, she would not be so anxious to post her sentinels on the walls. She sees that her days are numbered, that the youth are leaving her ranks, and her oft-repeated protests make her believe in the strength of her host. Thus she tries to scare her opponents and, if possible, to ward off the inevitable.

social parties. A belief in God is thoroughly recon-
cilable with the belief in humanity and the social brother-
hood of man, and only by the strangest misconception can
we attribute to Christianity a tender weakness for the rich
and well-born.   Of course, this misconception of Christianity is not original with social-democrats or exclusively
confined to them.

Nevertheless this hatred prevails and will show its
effects.   Religion can overcome it and prove its own truth,
not by hatred, contempt, and inquisitions, but by the
righteous fruits of justice and of love.   Christianity itself,
however, which has outlived so many revolutions of states
and changes in civilization, so many empires and peoples,
will also outlive the storms now threatening the European
nations.   Nay, who knows but that its deliverance from
the interests of the governing classes of society may be
the condition of a new and grand development of its life.

2. The Relation of Philosophy to the Sciences.

The rational conception of reality is, as has already
been pointed out, the starting-point common to the
sciences and philosophy.   Philosophy is science.   What
distinguishes it from the other sciences?

At first sight two views seem possible.   Sciences are
distinguished by their subject-matter and their form.   The
difference between philosophy and the other sciences
must therefore be sought either in the subject-matter with
which it is concerned or in the manner in which it
handles it.   Both views have been brought forward.   According to the former, philosophy has a field of reality of
its own that cannot be claimed by any other science.   In
a classification of sciences, therefore, philosophy occurs
as a separate science co-ordinated with the rest.   According to the second view, it has the same subject-matter as
the other sciences ; but it treats this in a peculiar way, and
is consequently distinguished from them by its method.

The latter view dominated the first half of the present
century.   It was the view held by speculative philosophy.
The whole of reality, it assumes, is capable of a twofold
treatment,—of philosophical and scientific, of speculative

and empirical treatment. In the two large fields of human knowledge, in nature and history, we have side by side natural science and natural philosophy, the science of history and the philosophy of history. The function of science is, by means of methodical experience, to acquire knowledge of the facts ; the function of philosophy, on the other hand, is, by a process peculiar to itself, to set forth the real essence and the inner connection of things.

This view disappeared when man lost faith in the speculative method. Our age no longer believes in the possibility of gaining an *a priori* knowledge of the meaning of reality by means of a dialectical development of concepts. As we know but one reality, so we know but one truth, and one road to truth—rationalizing experience. Thought without experience no more leads to a knowledge of reality than irrational experience. The philosopher has no royal road to knowledge. Pure speculation is in truth nothing but a distorted reflection of knowledge, and this knowledge is the result of experience, only its possessors will not admit it.

If there is no special philosophical method, then the second view alone remains—that philosophy is distinguished from the other sciences by its special subject-matter. This opinion now predominates. Many different attempts have consequently been made to stake out for philosophy a special domain. According to a view commonly held in our day, knowledge is the special object of philosophy. Kant has the merit, if we are to believe K. Fischer, of having procured for philosophy a secure place among the sciences, by obtaining for it a special field claimed by no other science, namely, that of knowledge. " Things constitute the object of experience ; experience, indeed the entire fact of human knowledge, constitutes the object of philosophy." *

---

* *History of Modern Philosophy*, III², 16. A. Riehl agrees with him in his inaugural address on Scientific and Unscientific Philosophy (now also in the work, *Der phil. Kriticismus u. s. Bedeutung für die positive Wissenschaft*, II, 2, pp. 1 ff.). That philosophy is unscientific which, after the manner of Greek philosophy, reasons about all things. That philosophy, however, is scientific which, since Locke, has taken its place by the side of the other sciences as a science of knowledge.

Others seek to distinguish philosophy from natural science by assigning to it the field of inner experience; they define it as mental science. This is done by Lipps in his work *Grundthatsachen des Seelenlebens* (p. 3). A. Döring, on the other hand, defines philosophy as the investigation of goods and values, distinguishing it from the other sciences, which deal with reality. In his work entitled *Philosophische Güterlehre* (1889), the need of such a definition is set forth dialectically and historically. An older, wide-spread view, which in a certain sense goes back to Aristotle, defines philosophy as the science of first principles or of the general fundamental notions and preconditions of the separate sciences.

In my opinion, these attempts to draw a line around philosophy, and to separate it from the other sciences, are also open to serious and well-founded objections. Philosophy is the science of knowledge, they say. Such a science, however, has another and an older name: logic, or the theory of knowledge (epistemology). Why should it exchange this name for another, and that, too, for one already having a different and wider signification? For, according to the common usage of language, logic, or the theory of knowledge, is *one* philosophical discipline out of many. And the same objection may be raised against the two other views. We are accustomed to designate investigations of mental life in its historical aspects as mental sciences in opposition to the natural sciences. Similarly, the investigation of goods and values is commonly called ethics, or forms a part of this science. Ethics, however, and the other mental sciences, do not constitute the whole of philosophy. They are, according to the common usage of language, parts of philosophy.

We shall perhaps, in a certain measure, be obliged to return to the definition which describes philosophy as the science of principles, a definition which Ueberweg, for example, places at the head of his *History of Philosophy*. Yet we cannot accept it as it stands. First, on account of its indefiniteness. At what point do the principles, the fundamental notions, with which philosophy presumably deals, end? At what point does the territory of the other

sciences begin? Shall philosophy treat of the essence of
matter, of force, of motion, of space and time? In that case
it must treat also of the general properties of matter and
the general laws of motion, and that would bring it right
into the field of physics. Shall philosophy deal with the
nature of the soul, of life, of the principles of law and
of the State? If that is so, where shall we draw the boundary-line separating philosophy from politics, jurisprudence,
biology, and psychology? Manifestly, the line can be defined only arbitrarily, not by means of concepts. What is
to be considered as a question of principle and what not,
will depend on one's standpoint. The principles of the law
of liens or of copyright are just as much principles as
those of the laws of ownership or of the State. Furthermore, whence shall philosophy derive its science of principles? The answer comes, Philosophy shall explain the
fundamental concepts which the empirical sciences fail to
investigate. But how shall it reach a knowledge of these
things? Shall it examine matter, employing the means of
observation and experiment? Why, these are the very
methods by which physics and chemistry seek to discover the essence of matter. If these are the only means
at the disposal of philosophy, then, obviously, the sciences
have no need of philosophy in order to discover what
matter is. They would scarcely be restrained by the objection that such inquiries transcend "the object, and consequently the nature and the definition, of an empirical
science." * What do we care, they would say, for this
arbitrary boundary-line drawn by other sciences? Has
philosophy a better way than the sciences to the knowledge
of the essence of things? If so, we should have to return
to the definition which we have just rejected.

What difference is there, then, between philosophy and
the other sciences? If it is distinguished from them
neither by a special method nor by a special subject-matter,
it must coincide with them.

Indeed, it is my opinion that this is the case. Philoso-

---

* Harms, *Philos. Einleitung in die Encyclopädie der Physik von Kar-
sten*, § 89.

phy cannot be separated from the sciences ; it is simply *the sum-total of all scientific knowledge.* All sciences are parts of a uniform system, of a *universitas scientiarum,* the subject-matter of which is the whole of reality. This never-completed system, which the ages are building, is philosophy. Each particular science investigates a definite portion or cross-section of reality. Physics considers reality in so far as it is corporeal, and manifests certain general modes of action; biology considers the processes of life which take place in this matter; psychology considers the real from another side, in so far as it is consciousness. We get philosophy by combining all the results of these sciences for the purpose of answering the question as to the nature of reality.

To speak figuratively, reality is a great riddle put to the human mind. ˙ Each of the separate sciences offers data for determining the answer. Philosophy is the attempt to solve the riddle, to find the key to the *mysterium magnum.*

The common usage of language also leads us to this conception. According to it, philosophy is not a separate science, but a sum-total, a system of sciences. We usually characterize logic, metaphysics, and ethics as parts of philosophy. We have but to go a step farther and say : Physics too, and chemistry and biology and cosmology, in˙ short, all sciences, belong to philosophy.

The objection will be raised, If all that is philosophy, then it is an impossible task. Who would undertake such a problem ? Who would profess to possess, or even to aspire to, anything like such a comprehensive amount of knowledge ? Would not he who attempted such a thing, to use Döring's words, raise dilettanteism to the rank of a profession ?

Before discussing this objection I deem it proper to show by means of a brief historical survey that the definition of philosophy formulated above is the only appropriate one from a historical point of view. All the intellectual efforts which have been designated as philosophy invariably aimed at a unitary and comprehensive knowledge of the world. To be sure, the definition of philosophy cannot

really be determined by history. The definitions of sciences
are definitions of problems, and must therefore ultimately
be construed as such. Perhaps all former attempts have
failed or aim at an impossible goal. Nevertheless such
a historical justification will protect our definition from
the reproach of being an arbitrary, individual definition.

The word philosophy is of Greek origin. It was at first
employed, not as a technical term, but as a word in general
use. The reader of Herodotus will find it in the well-
known story of Solon's meeting with Crœsus. Crœsus
welcomes the Athenian with the remark that the fame of
his wisdom and of his travels has already reached him,
"that thou, philosophizing, hast visited a vast part of the
world for the sake of reflection ($\vartheta\epsilon\omega\rho i\eta\varsigma\ \epsilon\check{\iota}\nu\epsilon\kappa\alpha$)." Evidently, the expression "for the sake of reflection ($\vartheta\epsilon\omega\rho i\eta\varsigma$
$\epsilon\check{\iota}\nu\epsilon\kappa\alpha$)" intends to explain the word "philosophizing."
What makes Solon a "philosophical" traveller is the sur-
prising circumstance that he does not, like the merchant or
soldier, pursue a practical object in his journeys. Thu-
cydides, Isocrates, and others use the word philosophy in
a like sense, to characterize a general theoretical education
as distinguished from the technical or practical one.*

When we speak of Greek philosophy at present we do
not usually have in mind Solon and the general culture of
the Athenians, but the galaxy of men headed, according
to an old tradition, by the Milesian Thales. Why is Thales
called a philosopher, and in what does his philosophy consist? We can answer in a word : He is a philosopher because he sets up a general theory of reality—the theory
that all things have arisen from water and will return to
water. It is a very simple theory, but none the less a
theory—a first attempt to explain all things scientifically.
The same is true of his successors. Not water, another
holds, but air or fire or the four original elements or atoms

---

* References in Ueberweg, *History of Philosophy*, at the beginning
of the first volume. Compare also the exposition of the definition of philosophy among the Greeks, at the beginning of Zeller's *History of Greek
Philosophy*. Let me also state that I have discussed the relation between
philosophy and science in the above sense in Avenarius' *Vierteljahres-
schrift für Philosophie*, vol. I, 15–50 (1876).

are the universal principles of reality. The philosophy of Heraclitus, of Empedocles, of Democritus are attempts to apply such thoughts universally. Of course, we cannot speak of the existence of special sciences alongside of philosophy at this period.

Besides, the name philosopher was not applied to these men until afterwards. They were originally called wise men (σοφοί, σοφισταί), or more especially, investigators of nature (φυσιολόγοι). The disciples of Socrates were the first to use the term in this sense. Plato and Aristotle and their associates and pupils call themselves philosophers. What does the word mean here? Plato defines it more closely by contrasting the philosopher with the sophist. What difference is there between them? Plato represents the sophist as a man who travels through the cities as an itinerant teacher for the sake of acquiring money by giving instruction in all the sciences and arts essential to culture, especially in rhetoric. His purpose is therefore a practical one. He journeys from place to place, not "for the sake of contemplation" (θεωρίης εἵνεκα), but as a merchant, as a dealer in knowledge. The pupil has the same practical end in view. He buys the knowledge in order to elevate his social position, in order to increase his influence and fortune. The philosopher, on the other hand, is a pure speculator: he follows no trade and seeks no gain; the knowledge of things is his sole object. Socrates is the typical pattern. It is the object of his life to search after truth, and to destroy error and illusion. It delights him, by free intellectual intercourse, to inspire beloved youths to a like aim. There is something of Socratic irony in the new expression. While the Protagorases and Gorgiases allow themselves to be called wise men (σοφοί, σοφισταί), Socrates and his disciples refuse to be regarded as possessors of knowledge. Lovers of wisdom is a less presumptuous title.*

---

* We may add that tradition traces this distinction back to Pythagoras. It is stated that he was the first to call himself a philosopher, declining the appellation of wise man. No one, he is reported to have declared, is wise except God. At the same time he is said to have regarded pure speculation as alone worthy of the philosopher. "Life resembles a spectacle.

Here, too, the relation between philosophy and science
remains the same. Philosophy is the comprehensive sum-
total of all true knowledge. The sciences do not exist outside and by the side of it; they are parts of it. Plato presents no systematic classification of the sciences. He
speculates on all things : on the nature of bodies, the form
of the cosmos, the nature of the State, of the soul, of pleasure, of love, of rhetoric, of knowledge ; all these constitute
his philosophy. Aristotle was the first to arrange all
knowledge into classes, and to discuss the separate classes
systematically : logic, physics, psychology, cosmology,
zoology, metaphysics, ethics, politics, economics, rhetoric,
poetics. All of these taken together make up his philosophical system, and outside of philosophy there is no
science in the real sense of the term. For history is no
science. All sciences concern themselves with the general
or with concepts. And in a certain sense mathematics has
no place in the classification, because reality is not its subject—at least not its immediate subject.

Such is the meaning of the term philosophy on its
native soil. The tendency towards universal knowledge
and the purely theoretical aim constitute its essential characteristics. Philosophy is an end in itself, not a means to
an external end, and indeed, in the opinion of Plato and
Aristotle, it is the ultimate and highest end ; man reaches
his natural or divine destiny in the complete knowledge of
existence. God has put him in the world in order that
he may reflect on and interpret his works.

Later, an element that had always been implied in it
became more prominent in the notion of philosophy.
Philosophy came to denote the knowledge of the final
ends of life, and to characterize the disposition of the sage
and his manner of life as determined by these ends. Still,
the element of universal knowledge, the insight into the
nature of all things in general, and of man in particular,
remains its essential precondition.

Some attend it in order to participate in the contests; others, to do business;
the best, to look on. So it is in life : the vulgar seek fame and money; the
philosophers, truth." (In Diogenes Laertius, *Prooem.* 8; VIII, 1, 6.)

The middle ages adhered to this notion of philosophy, defining it as the unity of scientific knowledge. The notion remained current up to the beginning of the present century. Let me give a few examples.

Two men are usually placed at the head of modern philosophy as the originators or first representatives of the two great modern schools of thought: the Englishman Francis Bacon and the Frenchman René Descartes. The latter is the founder of the rationalistic-metaphysical, the former the forerunner of the empirical-positivistic line of development. In both schools the conception of the relation of philosophy to the sciences remains the same.

Bacon distinguishes between historical and philosophical or scientific knowledge. The former occupies itself with the concrete and particular; philosophy or science, however, deals with general concepts. The former has its seat in memory, the latter is the work of reason. After referring revealed theology as a special mode of knowledge to a separate class, Bacon next divides philosophy or science into three branches, corresponding to the three objects of the understanding, namely, God, nature, man: into natural theology, anthropology (physical anthropology, embracing medicine; and psychical anthropology, in which are included all the mental sciences), and natural philosophy.* However inadequate this classification may be in other respects, it nevertheless shows that Bacon's aim is to include all scientific knowledge in the notion of philosophy. Only history (and poesy) is excluded, simply because it is not a science.

In exactly the same way Descartes embraces the whole of scientific knowledge under philosophy. His chief work embodying his system bears the title *Principia philosophiae.* The first book contains a short discussion of epistemological and metaphysical questions, the second, the

---

* De dignitate et augmentis scientiarum II, 1 : Historiam et experientiam pro eadem re habemus, quemadmodum etiam philosophiam et scientias. . . . Historia proprie individuorum est—philosophia individua dimittit, sed notiones ab illis abstractas complectitur.—III, 1 : Philosophiae objectum triplex—Deus, Natura, Homo. Convenit igitur partiri philosophiam in doctrinas tres ; doctrinam de numine, d. de natura, d. de homine.

principles of mechanical physics, the third, the cosmology, the fourth, a series of physical, chemical, and physiological explanations. We should perhaps primarily call such a work an encyclopedia of the natural sciences. In the preface he himself defines philosophy as the totality of human knowledge. As its main parts he mentions (1) metaphysics, (2) physics, (3) the technical sciences—among them in particular medicine, mechanics, ethics.*

This conception of philosophy remains unchanged in the subsequent development of the two schools of thought. Here are a few examples at random. At the beginning of his logic Thomas Hobbes defines philosophy as the knowledge of the causes of effects or phenomena which is derived by correct thinking. Its aim is, as with Bacon and Descartes, to further our ends by giving us power over things: *scientiam propter potentiam.* Its main divisions are: Mathematics; natural science, which really begins with Copernicus, Galileo, and Harvey; and the *philosophia civilis,* which in Hobbes's opinion is not older than the book *De cive.* As not belonging to philosophy, he enumerates theology, both revealed and natural; and history, natural history as well as political history—none of these being sciences.

John Locke likewise employs the term philosophy as synonymous with science. As its main branches he designates *Physica,* or natural philosophy; *Practica,* whose chief part is ethics; and *Semiotica,* the most important part of which is logic.† That he too regards natural philosophy as the principal part of philosophy, the preface to the

---

* Philosophiae voce sapientiae studium denotamus, et per sapientiam non solum prudentiam in rebus agendis intelligimus, verum etiam *perfectam omnium earum rerum,* quas homo novisse potest, *scientiam.* Philosophiae prima pars Metaphysica est, ubi continentur principia cognitionis; altera pars est Physica, in qua inventis veris rerum materialium principiis, generatim examinatur, quomodo totum universum sit compositum, deinde speciatim, quaenam sit natura hujus terrae, aëris, aquae, ignis, magnetis et aliorum mineralium. Deinceps quoque singulatim naturam plantarum, animalium et praecipue hominis examinare debet, ut ad alias scientias inveniendas, quae utiles sibi sunt, idoneus reddatur, quae ad tres praecipuas revocantur, Medicinam, Mechanicam atque Ethicam.

† *Essay on the Human Understanding,* IV. 21. In the preface we read: "Philosophy, which is nothing but the true knowledge of things."

Essay on the Human Understanding makes sufficiently plain. His only ambition, he says, is " to be employed as an underlaborer in clearing the ground a little " on which such masters as Boyle, Sydenham, Huyghens, and Newton have erected their lasting monuments.

The exact sciences employ the term in the same sense. Newton entitles his work *Naturalis philosophiae principia mathematica.* In a treatise written in 1695, the mathematician Wallis thus speaks of the foundation of the Royal Society of Sciences : " Our business was (precluding matters of theology and state affairs) to discourse and consider of philosophical enquiries, and such as related thereunto, as Physick, Anatomy, Geometry, Astronomy, Navigation, Staticks, Magneticks, Chymicks, Mechanicks, and Natural Experiments ; with the state of these studies and their cultivation at home and abroad. We then discoursed of the circulation of the blood, the valves in the veins, the venae lacteae, the lymphatic vessels, the Copernican hypothesis, the nature of comets and new stars, the satellites of Jupiter, the oval shape (as it then appeared) of Saturn, the spots on the sun and its turning on its own axis, the inequalities and selenography of the moon, the several phases of Venus and Mercury, the improvement of telescopes and grinding of glasses for that purpose, the weight of air, the possibility or impossibility of vacuities and nature's abhorrence thereof, the Torricellian experiment in quicksilver, the descent of heavy bodies and the degree of acceleration therein, with diverse other things of like nature, some of which were then but new discoveries and others not so generally known and embraced as now they are : with other things appertaining to what hath been called the New Philosophy, which from the times of Galileo at Florence, and Sir Francis Bacon (Lord Verulam) in England, hath been much cultivated in Italy, France, Germany, and other parts abroad, as well as with us in England." *

The old notion retains its meaning in the Continental philosophy which follows the leadership of Descartes. Spinoza understands by a system of philosophy the unitary

---

* Quoted by Huxley, *Lay Sermons, Essays, and Reviews* (1891), p. 4.

system of all scientific knowledge which corresponds to uniform reality, *Natura sive Deus.* He calls his main work, not a system of philosophy, but *Ethica,* because one main branch of philosophy, the *philosophia naturalis,* is not contained in it or is simply outlined in a few propositions of the second book. Leibniz, who is at home in all the fields of scientific investigation, in the historical investigation of sources as well as in mathematics and physics, has exactly the same idea of the absolute form of science or philosophy as Spinoza. He conceives it as a demonstrative system in which we operate with concepts by means of a system of signs as in arithmetic. In this sense he speaks in a certain place of an *Encyclopédie demonstrative.**

Christian Wolff, who was the first to formulate modern philosophy as a scholastic system, begins his treatise on the nature of philosophy at the head of his logic by distinguishing between historical and philosophical knowledge. The former establishes the What, the latter the Why. *Cognitio eorum, quae sunt vel fiunt, historica, cognitio rationis eorum, quae sunt vel fiunt, philosophica dicitur.* He who knows the bare fact (*nudam facti notitiam*) that water in a river-bed flows downward has historical knowledge. He, however, has philosophical knowledge who knows that this is effected by the inclination of the soil and the pressure of the upper particles of water on the lower. As a third kind of knowledge he adds mathematics, which determines the quantitative relations of things. For the rest, philosophy also employs historical and mathematical knowledge. The third chapter discusses the principal divisions of philosophy. There are three of these: Natural theology, psychology, and physics. Three normative sciences are added: Logic, practical philosophy based on psychology, and technology based on physics. Ontology is added as the science of the properties common to all existence.

It is evident, natural science everywhere constitutes the principal part of philosophy; nay, for some it forms the real essence of philosophy. Everywhere its mode of knowledge is the real form of all scientific-philosophical

---

* *Opera philos.,* ed. by J. E. Erdmann, p. 169.

knowledge. The endeavor is made to raise the mental sciences to the dignity of a science after the pattern of natural science. Thus, for example, David Hume makes this his aim in his *Treatise on Human Nature,* as the title expressly indicates.

This view has not changed in the nineteenth century. It is commonly accepted in England and France. I call attention to A. Comte's *Philosophie Positive* and to Herbert Spencer's *System of Synthetic Philosophy.* Comte does not regard the subject-matter of philosophy as differing from that of the sciences : philosophy is the universal consciousness of the condition, development, aim, and method of scientific investigation in its various branches. Comte considers it as his special task to raise the science of social phenomena to the rank of a positive science, a rank already reached by the natural sciences, astronomy, physics, chemistry, and physiology. This is the same aim which Hume sets himself in regard to the mental sciences. And manifestly Spencer's synthetical philosophy is on the whole modelled after the same scheme. He defines philosophy as the last and highest unity of scientific knowledge: "Knowledge of the lowest kind is *un-unified* knowledge ; Science is *partially-unified* knowledge ; Philosophy is *completely-unified* knowledge."* The author himself explains the absence of physics from his system, which includes psychology and biology, as a mere accident.

It is the nineteenth century which has brought confusion into the settled traditions. Germany for a time held to a conception of philosophy that completely distinguished it from science, nay, brought it into opposition to science.

The confusion begins with Kant. His starting-point is the distinction between knowledge *a priori* and *a posteriori.* By the former he means knowledge which reason may completely deduce from itself, whereas experience is needed in the latter case. The fact that judgments exist which are *a priori* certain, and yet have objective validity, forms the chief subject of argument in the first two main divisions of the *Critique of Pure Reason,* namely, in the

---

* *First Principles,* part II., chap. I. § 37, p. 134.

Æsthetic and the Analytic. Such judgments, Kant holds, we meet at the outset in physics. For example : The quantity of matter does not change. The effect is equivalent to the cause in the transmission of motion, etc. A systematic exposition of all judgments *a priori* would be metaphysics or philosophy in the genuine and true sense. The fact, says Kant, " that this distinction between the two elements of our knowledge, some of which are altogether *a priori* endowments of the mind, while others are the *a posteriori* results of experience,—the fact that this distinction has been overlooked even by professional thinkers," has for so long a time hindered the separation of philosophy from the empirical sciences.*

So this new definition of philosophy for the first time separated it from the sciences and made it independent of them. Of course, Kant did not mean to say that this *a priori* philosophy contained the whole of our knowledge, and that it had any reason to frown upon the empirical sciences. On the contrary, the propositions of "pure natural science," taken by themselves, contain no knowledge of reality whatever ; they are axiomatic propositions which acquire significance and cognitive validity only in so far as they serve to conceive the given manifold of sensibility. Taken by themselves, they are empty schemata of a possible experience. It is Kant's chief aim by means of his Critique to destroy real or transcendent metaphysics, the rational theology, cosmology, and psychology of Wolff, —and to put in its place a merely formal metaphysics.

An event, however, not unusual in history, occurred here. Expressed thoughts have effects and destinies never intended by their authors. Against his will Kant became the father of speculative philosophy. From the Kantian principle that the forms of thinking also constitute the general laws of nature, or of the totality of phenomena, the philosophy was developed which undertook to deduce the whole world, both nature and history, from the nature of presentation, by means of an immanent dialectical evolution of concepts. The fundamental conviction that a system

---

* *Kritik der reinen Vernunft*, Methodenlehre, 8. Hauptstück.

of absolute knowledge of reality can be produced by a new process of purely conceptual thinking, independently of experience and the empirical sciences, characterizes the philosophies of Fichte, Schelling, and Hegel. "The science of knowledge," says Fichte,* "absolutely ignores experience and pays it no regard whatever. It would have to be true even if there could be no experience at all, and it would be *a priori* certain that all possible future experience has to be governed by the laws established by it." He likewise declares, at the beginning of the *Characteristics of the Present Age*, "that the philosopher performs his task [here the interpretation of history] without regard to any experience whatsoever and absolutely *a priori*, and that he must be able to describe the whole age and all possible epochs of the same *a priori*."

Fichte presents us with an *a priori* deduction of history. Similarly Schelling gives an *a priori* construction of nature. Incidentally he vents his spleen against that "blind and thoughtless mode of investigating nature which has become generally established since the corruption of philosophy by Bacon and of physics by Boyle and Newton." †

In Hegel speculative philosophy reaches its completion. He constructs the whole of reality out of concepts. Reality and truth are one in his system. We have also the empirical sciences. They collect all kinds of knowledge about particulars, not *ex principiis*, from the concept, but *ex datis*, through external perception. Philosophy furnishes us with the true knowledge of reality. Its form, the dialectical development of concepts, is nothing but the subjective repetition of the objective process of the development of the idea, that is, of reality itself.

Never before had philosophy spoken in so proud a strain. Wholly relying on herself, she now dismissed from her service the sciences which were formerly her instruments. She had no further use for them; she had discovered a "royal road" to knowledge. Now she evolved the absolute knowledge of things out of herself. It is true, the

---

* *Grundriss des Eigentümlichen der Wissenchaftslehre*, § 1.
† *Ideen zu einer Philos. d. Natur* (1797), Works, I., Div. II. 70.

old conception is to a certain extent preserved even here :
Philosophy is the totality of all real scientific knowledge,
but with this difference—formerly scientific research, especially natural science, was included in philosophy ; now
it is excluded, as a pre-scientific procedure.

However, the supremacy of speculative philosophy was
not of long duration. Since the thirties its reputation
rapidly declined, and finally this school, and with it all
philosophy, fell into contempt. Many causes united to
make its fall sudden and destructive. The most decisive
cause was the attitude of opposition which it had itself
assumed against scientific research. Natural and historical
science, each of which had attained to vigorous growth since
the twenties, pushed speculative philosophy to the wall by
depriving it of the confidence and sympathy of the younger
generation. The latter amply repaid philosophy for all the
scorn which speculation had heaped upon scientific research. Philosophy is no science at all, it was said. In
fact it is not to be taken seriously at all. It is the sophistical practice of speaking of all things in general, with a
certain air of sense and reason. Its professors are jugglers
who produce all sorts of obscure and profound oracles by
the promiscuous use of general concepts, to the amazement
of a lot of idlers.

Philosophy was in a sad state. She had relinquished her
old possession, the totality of scientific knowledge, in order
to run after a higher aim, pure knowledge *a priori.* And now
the latter with its dialectic method had eluded her grasp.
Like the dog in the fable who snatched at the shadow and
lost the meat he had held in his teeth, she lost everything.
What did she do at this juncture? The proper thing would
have been to designate speculative philosophy as an incidental aberration, and to return to the old definition. The
claim of philosophy to possess a special method of acquiring knowledge of reality had to be relinquished. Hence
she was bound to return to the old conception of her relation to science.

This she failed to do. The cause is not far to seek. Her
representatives did not have the courage to return to the
old conception, which seemed to place them under great and

insupportable obligations. For by defining philosophy as the sum of all scientific knowledge did they not seem to imply that they possessed something like such knowledge themselves? And who was willing to expose himself to the derisive laughter with which such a claim would have been met?

The case was different in ancient times. The Greek philosophers would without reserve have made such professions. Indeed, Democritus and Aristotle would have said, we possess or seek something like a universal knowledge of things. Nor would the mediæval philosophers have shrunk from the demand implied in this notion. Albert and Thomas too, nay, every new-fledged *magister artium* just completing his *biennium*,—in the mediæval universities of Germany each master was obliged to lecture on philosophy for two years after graduation,—would have accepted the definition. He would have said: Indeed, I certainly believe that in so far as such an achievement is possible to man, I have familiarized myself with the sciences well enough to claim a knowledge of all of them in a certain degree. Have I not, in order to become a " master," made a thorough study of all the works of " the philosopher "? And now I am able and ready to explain any science that may be assigned to me either by choice, turn, or lot. (In mediæval universities it was not uncommon for lecturers to draw lots for books.) For that very reason I am called a master of arts, because I can teach them all, mathematics and astronomy as well as physics and metaphysics, logic and rhetoric, ethics and politics. Am I not myself a miniature copy of the first grand master, Aristotle? The doctor of philosophy of the sixteenth and even of the eighteenth centuries would have said the same. Melancthon also lectured on all the sciences which belonged to the curriculum of the philosophical faculty, and often described them in text-books that remained in vogue for a long time. As late as the last century, Christian Wolff taught mathematics and physics as well as logic, psychology, practical philosophy, and political science. Kant would scarcely have declined a chair of physics or of mathematics, astronomy or geography, if it had been offered to him;

he refused, however, the professorship of poetry, which involved the duty of giving instruction in Latin and German versification.

To us, all this seems strange and impossible. And as a matter of course it is impossible in our day. Scientific research has branched out beyond measure, and has become specialized during the last hundred years. The old *professio historiarum*, which was for the most part connected with the *professio poesëos* or *eloquentiœ* (called philology by us), and also with the *professio moralium*, has been split up into a dozen or more branches. The *professio* of the old *physicus* has been divided into as many or even more separate parts. Formerly, nothing less was expected of him than that he should be able to give information concerning all things in heaven and on earth. Now the field is divided into a number of departments that increase with every year. And each branch of science claims a man's entire energy, so that he is hardly able to watch the progress in the adjoining fields of learning. Nor do teachers any longer change their subjects for the sake of an advance in salary, as was commonly done in the last century.

The definition of philosophy has been fashioned by this state of affairs. It is no longer possible to be a philosopher in the sense of possessing the sum of all scientific knowledge. No one attempting such a thing could escape the judgment of the old lines:

> *Viele Dinge wusst' er freilich,*
> *Aber alle wusst' er schlecht.*

Hence a new definition of philosophy is needed, one that will make it possible for a man to be a philosopher. The first condition is that it do not include all sciences; above all, not the so-called exact sciences. This inclination on the part of philosophers is met by the desire on the part of the sciences to free themselves from philosophy. It is not regarded as a credit to a science to be reckoned among the philosophical sciences. Physics, chemistry, astronomy, physiology, and zoology regard themselves as independent sciences; they do not wish to belong to the domain of philosophy any more than philology and history, which were not included even in the old notion of philosophy. Nor are politics and economics or political economy any longer referred to the "philosophical" sciences. In short, all sciences that have succeeded in establishing themselves as independent branches have withdrawn from the old alliance, and no longer belong to philosophy. Philosophy has retained such disciplines as have not been able as yet to establish themselves as separate and independent fields of investigation, mostly such whose claim to be real sciences is questionable,—as for example, metaphysics, ethics, æsthetics, logic and epistemology, psychology (which would like to become an "exact" science, in which case it would most likely try to emancipate itself from philosophy), pedagogy, the philosophy of history, and all other branches on which "philosophical" lectures are delivered in German universities.

It was sought to unite these sciences, which really do not deserve the name of sciences, by means of a definition. And this gave rise to the definitions we have already mentioned: Philosophy is concerned with the *form* of knowledge as opposed to its matter; or, Philosophy is a *mental* science as distinguished from the natural sciences; or, It is the science of principles, and so independent of the science which deals with particular facts. These and many other unsound definitions, all of which are evidently mere makeshifts, were offered.

Now it seems to me, philosophy must take courage and re-establish its ancient definition. Philosophy is the sum of all scientific knowledge. History demands that we accept this definition. Tradition has so firmly established it that any other explanation would conflict with history and the common usage of language. Moreover, the nature of the subject itself demands it, as I intend briefly to show in the following.

The sciences are not an aggregate of parts accidentally heaped together, but a uniform whole. Reality itself is not an aggregate, but a uniform whole, whose members stand in a uniform and general relation to each other. The knowledge of reality is a similar unified system. This fact does not exclude differentiation—only differentiation does not mean separation and isolation, but a living relation of all the parts to the whole. We have a practical illustration of this relation in this, that each science needs the others as auxiliary sciences; isolated from them it cannot solve its problems. Every branch of natural science presupposes the rest; biology presupposes chemistry and physics; and conversely also, physics needs physiology; in optics and acoustics, for example, the boundaries overlap. Similarly, every branch of historical investigation presupposes the others. Nor can the natural sciences and the historical sciences dispense with each other. History presupposes geography; chronology, astronomy. Philology comes into contact with physiology. Archæology occasionally appeals to geology and geography for help. The reverse is true also. The natural sciences, although more independent than others, cannot do without the historico-philological sciences. It is customary now to class geography with the natural sciences; and rightly so. But it would lack an essential aid in dispensing with the science of history, which informs it of the changes which occurred on the surface of the earth during historical times. And so each science, being itself but a historical process of development, is obliged to refer to its own history, if not for the sake of systematic exposition, at least in order to give us a general idea of its position and importance within the whole of mental evolution. Note how much space the historical part occupies in Humboldt's *Cosmos.* The history of science is of especial importance in instruction, although this fact is not universally appreciated—not even in our universities. We may finally call attention to the fact that all sciences stand in relation to psychology and epistemology, and come into touch with one another in these fields. The idea of a unity of the sciences is therefore not an arbitrary invention, but a necessary thought. The ideal unity of an all-comprehensive system of knowledge corresponds to the unity of the cosmos. Philosophy is the historical name for this ideal unity. It is caprice to rob this concept of its name or this name of its old signification.

But the objection mentioned before is raised: In that case can there be philosophy? Is not the thing itself

made impossible by the definition? Who would have the
courage to profess to be a philosopher? And is not a
theory of the universe in itself impossible, at least for the
human mind? Thales may have undertaken such a task;
one's courage is greatest at the beginning of the journey.
But now, after the labor of two thousand years has shown
the extent of the undertaking, we have become more modest, and we are glad if here and there we gain a knowledge
of a portion of reality. We may answer: Doubtless philosophy does not at present exist as a complete and final
theory of the universe, nor will it ever be realized as such.
However, this does not destroy the correctness of the definition; the same objection may be made against any science.
Neither astronomy nor physics nor physiology exists as a
complete and final traditional scholastic system. The definitions of sciences are definitions, not of empirically-given
objects, but *definitions of problems.* And the validity of
these definitions depends on the proper characterization
of the problem, no matter what progress the solution may
have made. Indeed, even though the solution had not yet
been begun, the definition would retain its validity. It is,
one might say, adopting Kant's language, an idea, *i.e.,* a
concept, for which there is no corresponding object in empirical reality. The same holds true of the concept of
philosophy: it is correct and valid in so far as the problem of a unity of all knowledge is given.

Nor will the fact that no one can comprehend and possess all knowledge disturb us. By no means. Is there
any one in our day who can grasp all natural scientific or
all philologico-historical knowledge? And yet we speak
of philologists and historians and physicists, not as possessors of science, but as investigators of their respective
fields. We employ the name philosopher in the same way.
It designates a man who *strives* after a uniform and universal knowledge of things. This the well-chosen term expressly states: φιλόσοφος, a lover, not a possessor, of
knowledge. According to a well-known anecdote, Pythagoras desired to be called a philosopher (φιλόσοφος) in
order to avoid the presumption implied in the term sage
(σοφός).

Hence every scientific investigator is a philosopher, who is possessed of the idea of the unity of all knowledge, be his narrower field of investigation what it may—be it physics or psychology or astronomy or history. We shall not call him a philosopher who on principle confines himself to a narrow sphere, who knows nothing and cares for nothing except his codices and readings, his acids and bases, not because his field of research does not belong to the territory of philosophy (in this respect he could never escape being a philosopher), but because he has not the mental habits which make a philosopher of the investigator.

This, it seems to me, invests the name with its former signification and dignity. It was purely theoretical ends, and the universal aim of investigation, which among the Greeks distinguished the philosopher from a mere mathematician or physician. The same characteristic marks the philosopher of our day, in spite of the great changes in the aspect of the scientific world ; namely, devotion to pure speculation and the contemplation of the whole.

That this is what we mean by the term is seen from the way we use it commonly in our language. A man like Darwin, who makes the most careful and painstaking examination of facts, for whom nothing is too insignificant, but who traces their remotest relations and makes generalizations, we call a philosophical natural scientist. And in the same sense we call W. v. Humboldt a philosophical philologist and historian. Whoever, on the other hand, narrowly confines himself to a narrow field, whoever is familiar only with his special subject and cares for that alone— him we call an unphilosophical mind, perhaps also a trite empiricist or specialist. If he understands his subject, if by means of his implements he is able to supply science with valuable material, we shall esteem him highly as a useful artisan. Still we shall think that he is lacking in something, namely, in a higher, freer appreciation of things. It will make no difference whatever in what field he is employed—whether he occupies himself with mathematical formulæ or with syllogistic figures, whether he studies the fishes of Japan or makes psycho-physical experiments on apperception-time. One might write a history of philosophy without being a philosopher. It is not the content but the form which makes the philosopher.

Nor has the other meaning of the word entirely disappeared from our language. Whenever we see in a man great powers of concentration, and notice in him a certain retirement from the world and its aims, a certain lack of practical skill, a certain indifference to possessions and fame, we say, perhaps with a slight smile. He is a true philosopher. We can also understand the indignation with which Schopenhauer speaks of the degradation of philosophy to a craft. We could more readily forgive a chemist or a physician for making money out of his science.

Of late, philosophy is coming back to its old definition in Germany. Thus W. Wundt defines philosophy as the "general science whose business it is to unite the general truths furnished by the particular sciences into a consistent system." * The definition evidently presupposes the idea of the unity of all scientific knowledge. Wundt would not object to calling the complete system philosophy, nor would he object to the demand that the philosopher have not merely a smattering of knowledge, but also a working knowledge in some particular field. Fechner, Lotze, and F. A. Lange accept the same view; the unification of physical and mental facts into a world-system is the final goal, and the thorough study of the sciences is the road to this goal.

In returning to the traditional definition of philosophy we reject two errors which result from a wrong conception of it: the error that philosophy can exist without science, and the error that science can exist without philosophy.

The first error confused the age of speculative philosophy. Fruitless endeavors were made to spin philosophical systems out of a few very general concepts—sub-

* *System der Philosophie* (1889, p. 21). In this thoughtful and important work Wundt has undertaken to sum up our scientific knowledge as well as to develop its necessary preconditions and its final consequences. Metaphysics occupies the central position in it. Its object is not, like the particular sciences, to restrict the synthesis of facts, according to the principle of cause and effect, "to certain fields of experience, but to extend it to the whole of all given experience." (Preface.)

ject and object, nature and mind, being and becoming.
This error has almost entirely disappeared. We may find
the remnants of it in the opinion, which is occasionally
advanced, that a special study of philosophy is possible
without a study of the sciences—say by studying the history of philosophy. However instructive such a study may
be in itself, it cannot fail to be barren and empty unless it
is supplemented by scientific studies in other fields. The
true philosopher will deal with the things themselves. Even
if it be impossible for him to be an independent investigator
in all lines, he must make some field his own. In this way
alone will he go to work with a clear conscience; in this way
alone will he acquire judgment in scientific affairs and become able to gain an independent conception of the thoughts
of others and to use their investigations for his own purposes. He has a free choice of the field; it may lie within
the mental or natural sciences or at the boundaries of both
in physiology and psychology. As in the old proverb all
roads lead to Rome, so all roads in science lead to philosophy, only not the road through the air.*

In our times the other error that there can be science
without philosophy is more fatal. It is implied in the view
that philosophy is a special science, like every other science,
only not so well established; it is an airy science of things,
not capable of exact investigation. There are persons who
shun a contact with philosophy as though they feared
thereby to weaken their sense for the real. Physics, be-
ware of metaphysics! The advice is sound in so far as it
warns against hasty systematization, barren formalism,
and the confusion of metaphysical interpretation with the
physical explanation of phenomena. But it becomes unjust when it seeks to hinder the sciences from reaching
ultimate and universal principles in their respective fields,
and from harmonizing them with the final results of

* E. Renan, *Fragments philosophiques*, p. 292: "Philosopher c'est
connaître l'univers. L'univers se compose de deux mondes, le monde
physique et le monde moral, la nature et l'humanité. L'étude de la
nature et de l'humanité est donc toute la philosophie. . . . Le penseur suppose l'érudit et, ne fût-ce qu'en vue de la sévère discipline de l'esprit, il
faudrait faire peu de cas du philosophe, qui n'aurait pas travaillé une fois
dans sa vie a éclaircir quelque point special de la science."

other sciences. That would be equivalent to surrendering to popular metaphysics the problem of the general explanation of things, and at the same time deprive the sciences of their main motive. For we may say that ultimately all sciences have their common root in philosophy. If they are separated from this root they will wither away. The final object of every science is not the explanation of this or that particular phenomenon, not the knowledge of this or that particular field, but the knowledge of the whole of reality. The impulse to find an answer to the question concerning the nature and meaning of things in general originated scientific research or philosophy. The need of a division of labor led to its separation into different fields. It is not intended, however, that this division should isolate the sciences; it makes each particular one more efficient in performing its part in the solution of the universal problem. The theoretical interest, which forms the vital principle of every science, is measured by its relation to philosophy, and by what it can contribute to the solution of the problem of the nature of things. This becomes evident when we do not look to the personal feeling of the investigators so much as to the entire historical development of a science. What is it that places biology in the centre of natural scientific research at the present time? What impels it to make special investigations of the lowest forms of life microscopically and micrologically? The hope, apparently, of thus obtaining a clue to the great mystery of life and its development on earth. We should not care very much for the thousand forms of lichens and fungi, of monads and infusoria, as such. Within a narrow circle an interest for the infinitely small may deteriorate into a sport, but no science can be kept alive by that. Or take astronomy. With tireless diligence it gathers observations, registers the positions of hundreds of thousands of stars, calculates the paths of comets and of swarms of falling stars, discovers new planetoids and cosmic nebulæ, tests the intensity of light and the spectrum. To what end? Is it for the sake of the details? Certainly not. No, we hope in this way to gain a deeper insight into the constitution and development of the entire universe. If this motive

were to disappear, if this question ceased to interest us,
then our observations would soon be closed. Particular
facts may have practical or technical interest for us, as
the discovery of new combinations in chemistry. But the
theoretical interest, which forms the vital principle of a
science, is directed toward the general, and science becomes
philosophical.

The same conditions obtain also in the historical sciences. It is true, the particular events, especially those
which bear a direct relation to us, are of immediate
importance.   Still, here, too, the question concerning the
whence and the whither of all historical life is the vital
question. Should this question no longer interest us, historical investigation would languish. The same result would
ensue if we had a thoroughly satisfactory answer to the
problem.   In that case there would be no need of investigation.   The middle ages were in such a state. They possessed a philosophy of history satisfying all their demands.
Human life lay open to their view between creation and
the judgment day, divided into acts, like a mighty drama,
by the great events of sacred history. Consequently the
middle ages had no science of history; they knew all that
was essential and worth knowing. What was the use of
delving into insignificant and unessential facts? We are
not in such a blessed or unfortunate state, and therefore we
have become historians. We do not despise even the little
and the insignificant; we preserve every fragment of an
ancient papyrus or of an inscribed brick. These things
may perhaps, in their proper place, throw a light upon an
epoch of ancient life and thought, upon a period of an extinct language, and thus illuminate the path which our race
has traversed on earth.

In this sense we may say, philosophy is the central
fire, the sun, from which life-giving warmth radiates upon
all the sciences. The soil of investigation becomes arable
only when warmed by these rays. And the work of an
individual science will bring forth fuller and riper fruit
in proportion to the sunlight that shines upon its field.
Whoever, on the other hand, grubs and digs at random,
without due regard to light and warmth, wherever he may

happen to find a place, will reap scanty and unripe fruit. A science, however, that forgets its relation to philosophy or to the general unity of knowledge would, like a garden deprived of the sunlight, grow to leaf, and be without bloom and fruit. Or, to discard figures of speech, such a science would perish in consequence of barren subtlety or a senseless accretion of matter. Kant calls such erudition Cyclopean : it lacks an eye—"the eye, namely, of true philosophy, the eye suitably to use the mass of historical knowledge, the freight of a hundred camels." (*Anthropologie*, § 58.)

But what becomes of the professional philosophers if this view be accepted? Well, it seems to me, the term itself has a somewhat curious sound. It is just as though one should speak of professional blockheads. There are scientists with and scientists without philosophical minds. Physicists, astronomers, psychologists, biologists, historians, metaphysicians, sociologists, moralists, may all have such minds or not have them. Philosophy does not exist as a special profession. Nevertheless, should any one insist on defining philosophy as a separate branch, we should have to return to the Aristotelian distinction of a "first philosophy," or philosophy in the narrower sense. Its function would be the discussion of certain ultimate problems of reality ; it would be that which in our day is called metaphysics. And to this task would have to be added epistemological investigations, which are inseparably connected with ontological and cosmological problems. But if we thus wish to form a separate class for metaphysics and epistemology, and call them philosophy in the narrower sense, we are obliged immediately to add, that they can by no means be discussed separately and in isolation from the rest of the sciences. A *purus putus metaphysicus*—and the same holds true of the epistemologist—is a chimera or an empty babbler. The sciences alone, natural and mental sciences, furnish the material by means of which to judge of existence in general, and of the world as a whole. The sciences alone supply the occasion and the subject-matter for epistemological investigations. Hence it remains a settled fact that a man is the better fitted to be a "professional

philosopher," the more familiar he is with the two great
fields of scientific research—the mathematical-natural-
scientific and the philologico-historical fields.

Should any one, however, reply: "Professional philosophy" is a presumptuous undertaking, inasmuch as
no one can satisfy this demand, we should be obliged
frankly to admit it. Still, a few arguments might be
adduced for a less radical view. We have already remarked above that the formation of settled convictions
concerning problems which we characterize as metaphysical and epistemological is not a matter of free choice.
Every human being who rises above the mere needs of
brute existence fashions for himself some kind of metaphysics, some kind of conception of the nature of things, of
God and the world, of the relation of our knowledge to
reality. We must furthermore acknowledge that it is
better to concentrate one's attention upon these problems
than to leave them to convenience or to chance. It may
perhaps be regarded as presumptuous in a man to offer to
communicate to us the results of his reflections. It is the
same kind of presumption, however, that the poet shows
when he publishes verses expressing his innermost experiences and feelings. We might, however, with equal
right consider it as a kind of sacrifice on the part of a man,
not merely to impart the results of special investigation,
but to be ready to submit to public consideration general
views which are, by the very nature of the case, more
subjective and not so easily demonstrable. For does he
not thereby expose himself to public criticism and to a
kind of compassionate ridicule which tries to excuse his
weakness for speaking of things of which he has no knowledge—at least no professional knowledge? It is strange
that any one who values his good name should venture to
pose as "a philosopher by profession" in a time like ours
that uses the term *dilettante* or mere amateur, with the
intention of insulting a scientific author, and is easily con-
soled for its lack of a connected system of philosophy.

The fact, however, remains that such persons never die
out. Poets appear again and again, who, heedless of the
fate of so many predecessors, expose their intellectual

children to the dull curiosity and the scornful ridicule of the passers-by. Likewise there will always be men who, like old Christian Wolff, are ready to expose their "thoughts on God, the world, and the soul of man, as well as of all things in general," to the malice of the prudent, to the reprimands of the wiseacres, to the shrugs of the connoisseurs, and to the laughter of the multitude. Perhaps they may find consolation in the thought that they are not entirely useless to the community. If they accomplish nothing else, they do one thing at least—they call our attention to the ultimate aim of all investigation, which is to orient the human mind in the world of which it is a part. The sciences are apt to lose sight of this aim. Led from fact to fact, they finally forget their original purpose. The reverse of what befell the son of Kish, who set out to seek his father's asses and found a kingdom, happens to them. Science, which set out to seek a theory of the universe, is at last content and happy to find earthworms and quietly to dissect them. And whenever, like Faust, it begins to feel that there is something wrong with its critical endeavors or its *encheiresis naturae*, it straightway consoles itself with general phrases: Nothing is too insignificant for the true scientist; or, We are not yet ready for generalizations; the detail work must first be brought to a close.*

The metaphysician would cause that state of unrest which hinders science from lapsing into quietistic specialization. His function in the workshop of science would be to keep alive the idea of the ultimate aim of all investigation, perhaps also to exemplify in his own person the inadequacy of human power to reach this aim; or to show that

---

* The philologist Schleicher, who, let it be said, does not himself belong to the quietists, characterizes this tendency of our times in his little treatise on the Darwinian theory and the science of language: "We endure with the greatest tranquillity the lack of a philosophical system conforming to the condition of our acute and exact specialized sciences. For we are convinced that such a system cannot as yet be constructed, that we must postpone the attempt until we possess a sufficient amount of trustworthy observations and assured truths from all spheres of human knowledge." Who can help thinking of Horace's peasant, who stands at the bank of the river and waits until the water has run down?

"At ille
Labitur et labetur in omne volubilis aevum."

the human mind does not reach a final explanation of
things by way of science, but that faith and poetry have
their rights also. On the other hand, it would be his business to bring the influence of scientific inquiry to bear upon
our view of the world. If this is left undone, if science
remains in isolation, if there is no serious philosophy, obscurantism together with specialism will reign supreme.
This brings us to the definition which Kant calls the world-
definition of philosophy, in distinction from the scholastic
definition : " Philosophy, the science of the relation of all
knowledge to the essential ends of human reason."

Goethe, the poet-philosopher by the grace of God, portrays in his Tasso the character, the true gift, of the philosopher :

> Sein Ohr vernimmt den Einklang der Natur ;
> Was die Geschichte reicht, das Leben giebt,
> Sein Busen nimmt es gleich und willig auf ;
> Das weit Zerstreute sammelt sein Gemüth,
> Und sein Gefühl belebt das Unbelebte.

3. Classification and Fundamental Problems of Philosophy.

All possible scientific investigations may be looked at
from three points of view : they are concerned either with
the nature of reality, or the form of knowledge, or the
problems of conduct.

This gives us the old classification of the sciences customary in later Greek philosophy—physics, logic, and
ethics. Physics is the science of the nature of things ; logic,
the science which deals with the forms of knowledge ;
ethics, the science of goods and values, the problems of
conduct and the principles of judgment.

Indeed, this division marks the ultimate elements of
scientific reflection. The names, it is true, have undergone
a change of meaning. The term ethics alone is still used in
its old sense. The other two sciences, however, now have
a narrower signification. The term logic is now commonly
used to designate the examination of certain formal relations of conceptual thinking. The most general considerations of the nature, import, and origin of knowledge we
generally discuss under the head of epistemology.

The meaning of the term physics is still more narrowed. The Greeks defined physics as the science of the nature of things in general; it included the knowledge of the organic world and of psychic life. We have excluded from the concept of nature, first, the mental world; physics or natural philosophy is concerned solely with corporeal nature. By the side of it stands psychology as the science of the nature of mental life. Then the notion was still more restricted. Physics now constitutes but a part of the doctrine of bodies. The investigation of the most general modes of action of all material elements forms its field. Besides physics, we have chemistry, mineralogy, biology, etc., which deal with the special manifestations of bodies. In a measure we use the term metaphysics as the Greeks use the term physics. We mean by it ultimate and universal inquiries into the nature of corporeal as well as psychical objects; investigations which, based on the particular sciences, like physics and psychology, seek to gain a comprehensive view of the nature of reality. Indeed, the etymology of the term suggests this meaning—metaphysics, a science which goes beyond physics and its view of nature. It is true, this is not the original signification of the word. It was first used as the title of a work by Aristotle, which the author himself called "First Philosophy." It afterwards received the name metaphysics from its place after the treatise on physics in the collection of Aristotelian writings. We shall therefore employ the word in the following pages to designate all attempts to reduce our knowledge of objects to the most general views of the nature of reality. We may specify as its real and ultimate object, the unification of the physical and mental worlds, or, what amounts to the same, the harmony of the causal and final view of reality.

After what was said above concerning the possibility of philosophy, I see no need of discussing the question whether such a science is in any way possible or not. The epistemological-positivistic view denies the possibility of metaphysics. Metaphysics, it holds, must be looked upon as a great historical aberration of the human mind; the positive sciences and the theory of knowledge exhaust the sphere of the knowable. To be sure, if by metaphysics is meant the science of objects which lie beyond all possible experience or the *a priori* explanation of reality in a conceptual system, then it has seen its day. But metaphysics in the sense specified above will never die out. The attempt to find an answer to the ultimate questions which are put to the human mind by reality will be repeated as long as theoretical interest impels man to reflect. It seems immaterial whether these attempts be called science or not. That the subjectivity of the thinker plays a greater part here than in mathematics or physics, may be admitted without reserve; also, that the progress in the history of metaphysics is not so continuous as in the history of the exact sciences. Notwithstanding all this, however, it must be acknowledged that the problems which are usually called metaphysical are actually put, and that such investigations form a field of their own. These questions may also, it is true, be settled in the theory of knowledge; indeed we might also, if we chose, assign them to psychology or to physics. Every classification of the sciences is ultimately accidental. But I cannot at all see the propriety of depriving these investigations of their relative independence, and of discussing them incidentally in a different connection. Thus if we consider these questions in the theory of knowledge, they will be looked at from an unfavorable and false point of view.*

In each of the three great branches of philosophy the inquiry leads to a few ultimate fundamental problems. I shall first give a brief and connected exposition of them. The discussion of these problems will constitute the subject-matter of the subsequent chapters.

The examination of reality or metaphysics leads to two ultimate questions, which I call the *ontological* and the *cosmological* or *theological* problems.

The ontological problem is expressed by the question: In what does the nature of reality, as such, consist? A

---

* The reader will find suggestive remarks concerning the necessity and object of metaphysics in J. Volkelt's *Einführung in die Philosophie der Gegenwart* (1891), with which work my own book has much in common.

simple answer to this question does not at first sight seem possible. Reality does not appear to us as something homogeneous. Different sciences show us a wholly heterogeneous reality. Physics regards it as body which occupies space and moves in space; all its efforts tend to reduce natural phenomena to the regular movements of particles occupying space. In the mental sciences we meet reality ⌐ as something entirely different; here it appears as something sensitive, presentative, thinking, feeling, striving, willing. Psychology deals with processes of consciousness, phenomena which we can neither see, nor touch, nor measure, nor at all conceive as processes occurring in space.

What is the relation of these two forms of reality to each other? Does reality consist of two entirely different kinds of existence? Or can these two forms, the physical and the psychical, be reduced to one?

The different answers to this question lead to the different metaphysical standpoints which are designated by the terms *Dualism, Materialism, Spiritualism* or *Idealism.*

Dualism is the name of the view which holds that there are two heterogeneous kinds of reality, two kinds of substances—corporeal and mental, extended and thinking substances. This solution of the ontological problem has at all times seemed most satisfactory to common-sense.

Philosophy always reveals a tendency to overcome *Dualism* and to reach *Monism.* The reasons therefor are obvious. The unity of reality is so great and absolute, that it seems to repudiate the view which would regard it as composed of two entirely heterogeneous elements. In addition to this, thought tends to a simplification of reality. To explain things means to reduce the manifold phenomena to simple principles.

The desire for unity may be satisfied in two ways. Either, we can explain the mental processes by the bodily states, and say: Body and motion constitute reality as such; states of consciousness are mere phenomenal forms of processes which are in themselves physical. This is *Materialism.* Or, we can explain physical phenomena by states of consciousness, and say: Mental processes constitute reality as such; the physical world is a mere phenomenal form of this true reality. This is *Spiritualism* or *Idealism*.

A fourth possibility remains. We can say that we are by no means able to know the nature of reality as such. The two forms, the corporeal and the spiritual, are our first data. We assume, however, that they are but different manifestations of one unattainable reality. This view might be called *Agnostical Monism*.

The second great problem of metaphysics is the *cosmological* or *theological* problem. It is expressed by the question: What conception shall we form of the connection between all things? What is the form of reality as a whole? *Atomism, Theism,* and *Pantheism* are different answers to this question.

At first sight reality appears to be a plurality of independent objects. Each of these, it is true, is related to others, but each exists independently and by itself. This view is consistently thought out in *Atomism:* Reality is an aggregate of many independent, underived, and imperishable elements. By combining them in various ways we get, as it were, objects of the second order, popularly called things. Atomism or pluralism is not necessarily material. istic; in the monadology of Leibniz we have a spiritualistic form of it.

Here, too, philosophy has at all times shown a tendency to overcome plurality and to reach a unity. The unity and harmony of the world appears to be so great that it cannot be conceived as the result of an accidental confluence of entirely heterogeneous elements. The monistic view of the world exists in two forms. Either, it derives the unity and harmony of things from the action of an architectonic intelligence operating according to a uniform plan: this gives us *Theism.* Or, it seeks a still more thoroughgoing unity, and maintains: Reality is a single, unitary being, a substance; plurality is but the systematic arrangement of the parts of this unity: this gives us *Pantheism.* Philosophy is led to this latter conception from two sides. The notion of God leads theological speculation to it. If God creates all things out of nothing, as monotheistic theology claims, then he is in truth the sole being, and all

objects are through him and in him; they cannot exist
independently, outside of him or in opposition to him.
On the other hand, the concept of nature directs physical
speculation towards the same idea of the unity of essence.
If all things are universally and uniformly correlated, then
all processes are joined together into a single, comprehensive process—the unitary structure of the world. This
gives us the notion of unity in all change, the notion of the
unity of substance.

The theory of knowledge leads to two ultimate problems—the problem of the *nature* and the problem of the
origin of knowledge.

The first problem is expressed in the question: What is
knowledge? Different answers are given by *Realism* and
Idealism or *Phenomenalism*. Realism beholds in it an adequate copy of reality; in true knowledge objects appear as
they exist in reality, only they are not reality itself. Idealism regards this conception as impossible; how can knowledge be a copy and, as it were, a repetition of things?
Knowledge is an inner psychical process; how could there
be similarity between it and external objects? And even
if such similarity did exist, we could not know it; we cannot get outside of ourselves and compare our ideas with
the objects.

The second question is: How does knowledge arise?
This question also gives rise to an antithesis that runs
through the entire history of philosophy—the antithesis
between *Empiricism* and *Rationalism*. Empiricism derives
all knowledge from perception: Experience is the sole
source of knowledge, and experience consists of the combination of percepts. Rationalism, on the other hand, asserts: All really *scientific* knowledge presupposes another
principle that cannot be derived from perception. Universality and necessity, to be found in the most absolute form
in mathematics, and aimed at by all sciences, can never
arise from experience, which reveals only what happens in
particular cases, not what happens universally. Real science originates in the understanding, which forms concepts
and follows out their relations in conformity with the inner
uniformity peculiar to it.

The investigations of ethics culminate in an ultimate question of principle: What is the final ground of all distinctions of worth, in particular of those between human actions and dispositions? Two opposing views exist. The one asserts : They are grounded on the effects which actions have on life; that is good which produces favorable effects, that is bad which produces unfavorable results upon the life of the individual and the society of which he is a member. This is the *teleological* view. The other, which may be called the *formalistic* view (it is also designated as the *intuitionalistic* in distinction from the *utilitarian* view, the name given to teleological ethics in England), holds: Good and bad are absolute qualities of modes of conduct and dispositions of will, which can only be perceived and recognized, but not derived and proved. If the first opinion is correct, a new question arises : By what content of life can we distinguish favorable from unfavorable effects? What is the highest and final aim of human activity? If the answer is, Feelings of pleasure or happiness, we have *hedonism.* If, however, the aim is sought in an objective form and activity of life, we have a view for which there is no traditional term. We might call to mind the origin of this conception in Aristotelian philosophy, and name it *energism.* The highest good consists in the exercise of all virtues and capacities, especially the highest.

BOOK I.

THE PROBLEMS OF METAPHYSICS.

Ich gebe aber etwas auf den ursprünglichen Naturinstinkt des Menschen und glaube, dass nichts wahr sein kann, was nicht auch gut ist zu glauben, am wahrsten aber das, was am besten. Freilich auch in dem, was man für gut hält, kann man irren, aber einmal muss doch ein Punkt kommen, wo der Mensch sich selbst glaubt.

—FECHNER, *Zendavesta*, Preface, xiv.

CHAPTER I.

1. Historical Orientation.

POPULAR opinions form the starting-point of all philosophizing. This is true of the development of thought in the race as well as in the individual. It is proper that a work aiming to introduce the reader to philosophy should set out from these.

Common-sense takes note of the visible and tangible objects around it, and gives the following answer to the question concerning the nature of reality as such : The corporeal world is the real world. This view is not necessarily materialistic. Materialism is a product of scientific reflection. In addition to bodies, common-sense recognizes also a different reality, the soul. There is something in living bodies which is not body, at least not real body. No language, perhaps, exists that has not a word for what we call soul, and that does not attribute reality and essentiality to this soul. The origin of the idea of a soul as a separate existence is, perhaps, to be sought in the following facts. An important and striking difference appears in bodies, the difference between living and lifeless bodies. The former possess voluntary movement, while the latter have not the power of motion; they require an impact from without. The popular inference is that the ground for this difference must lie in the fact that there is a something in the living body that wills and moves, is sensible and feels : that is, the soul.

That this soul is a separate, independent essence, and not a mere force or quality, is inferred from another fact—one that exerts a profound influence on primitive thought: the phenomenon of death. At death, the living

53

body loses the property which distinguishes it from lifeless bodies; it becomes insensible and motionless. How does this happen? What takes place in death? The body remains what it was a moment ago; externally it is undiminished and unchanged, only it has lost its power of motion. The obvious conclusion, therefore, is that that which moves it, the soul, must have left it. Hence, the soul must be incorporeal, else we could see it depart; and it is an independent being. Its separation from the flesh and its continued existence prove this. For the experience of all peoples agrees in the belief that the soul does not perish at death; it can again appear and act. Everywhere anthropology discovers ancestor-worship, a sure sign of the belief in the existence and perpetuity of the departed soul. No one troubles himself about what does not exist. Moreover, the notion is also common to primitive stages of civilization that the soul can temporarily separate itself from the body even during life. The body lies motionless in sleep, but the soul is not inactive; it sees, hears, feels, and at times experiences wonderful things. It dreams, we say. Primitive thought, however, interprets the fact differently: the soul leaves the body in sleep and sets out on a journey of its own, hence it experiences those very things which we call dreams.

The primitive conception of the nature of the soul is about as follows: It is like the breath; it is visible, but not tangible, having the form of the body, like the real substantial shadow of the body. The connection between life and breath is evidently the reason why so many languages designate the soul as a breath ($\psi v \chi \acute{\eta}$, animus). It might be defined as a substantial image, or the existent vision of the body, without corporeality, impenetrability, and weight. Thus Homer describes the departed souls or spirits; so the mediæval painter portrays them; and the superstitious believer in ghosts imagines them in the same way. At the same time these spirits have power to haunt as well as recollection and feeling, though in a changed and weakened form.

If we wish to refer the ontological view of popular thought to a class, we shall have to call it *Vague Dualism.*

Bodies constitute the real reality, but alongside of them there exists a reality of the second order, bodily beings without real corporeality, that are both active in the bodies as efficient forces, and also exist for themselves as departed spirits.

The philosophical conception of reality is, as was mentioned before, characterized by the tendency to *Monism.* It is the fundamental impulse of philosophic thought to derive reality from one principle, to reduce the different forms of being to one original form. Two kinds of ontological monism result, according as we proceed from the facts of the external, visible world, or from those of the inner world; namely, *Materialism* and *Spiritualism.* The former asserts: Bodies and movements constitute the original form of reality; these also explain the facts of perception, thinking, and willing. *Spiritualism* or *Idealism,* on the other hand, asserts: The facts of inner life as presented in self-consciousness are the first and only reality; thoughts cannot be conceived as products of matter, while matter may be conceived as the product of thought; the corporeal world is phenomenal.

We meet these two ontological theories at the outset of Greek philosophy in two forcible and bold thinkers, Democritus and Plato. The former reduces all reality to atoms and the void. Minute, indivisible, but extended bodies constitute the original elements of reality; by means of their motion all natural occurrences may be explained, the heavenly as well as earthly processes, and among the latter also the manifestations of life, including perception and thinking. Plato, on the other hand, was the first European philosopher who had the courage to think out the following thought logically: Bodies are not only not the true reality, they are not real at all, not in themselves real; they are manifestations of something else. Reality as such is spiritual in its nature; the world as such is a system of real thoughts (ideas). Mind apprehends this true reality in conceptual thinking, whereas sensuous presentation cleaves to the copies of the ideal world, to the corporeal objects or phenomena which are not realities, but which originate and decay and are scattered through space.

Aristotle again comes nearer to the popular view. In his discussion of philosophical problems, he often begins with the conceptions of popular language, and is prone to return to them in his conclusions. He dislikes the abrupt and one-sided conceptions of the great seclusive thinkers. His philosophy has the strong and weak sides of a philosophy of mediation. His ontology is a dualism that inclines to idealism. At the beginning of the second book of his work on the soul, he defines the essence of the soul : it is the form of an organic body. The definition reminds one of the popular notion. It has a deeper meaning, it is true ; the soul is not a shadowy outline of the body, not the external, stereometric, but the inner, functional form, the operative and formative life-principle. All that distinguishes a living organism from a lifeless body is activity of soul : development, metabolism, spontaneous movement, sensation, desire, thinking, and rational volition. The functions of an organic body cannot be derived from the particles of matter composing it; they are the activities of a special principle of life, and that is the soul. This makes the body what it is. Matter furnishes only the potentiality of life, as wood furnishes the potentiality of the bow; marble, of a statue. But form alone fashions the real statue out of the possible one. In the same way, the soul makes the living body out of organic matter. It is evident, form is the essential, matter the accidental and secondary element of these two principles; the former is the real essence of the object, the latter the medium. Matter as such is the entirely indeterminate and intangible potentiality; it is through form alone that it becomes a determinate, formed, tangible reality. And in the mind of God, who is not potentiality but pure form or pure thought, matter finally disappears altogether. It may be said, however, that Aristotle does not develop the logical consequences of this latter idea as Plato did. There is no system of philosophy that approaches the popular conception of things more nearly than this explanation, which is based on the principles of form and matter, force and potentiality. The abruptness of Platonic idealism has been weakened in it so as to make it acceptable to common-sense. We may assume that this change made it available as a scholastic system for so many centuries.

Modern philosophy follows the paths which the great Greek thinkers have marked out : dualism, materialism, and spiritualism are the recurring fundamental forms.

It begins in Descartes with the most logical expression of dualism. Body and soul are two wholly non-comparable forms of reality. Body is a being whose only attribute is extension, soul a being whose only attribute is thinking or consciousness. *Corpus = res extensa, mens = res cogitans;* these are the two great definitions underlying the entire Cartesian philosophy.

The new definition of body is the older one of the two. A new principle was introduced into natural science by Galileo: Motion neither originates nor is lost. Just as a body at rest remains at rest unless acted on from without, so a body in motion continues that motion *ad infinitum* in the same direction and with the same velocity. It is true, the Aristotelian-scholastic philosophy of the middle ages did not assume the origin and decay of bodies themselves in the natural course of things. But it did not deny the disappearance of motion any more than common-sense does. Why should it? Is it not a matter of the most common experience? In like manner, then, why should not movement that did not exist before be originated, say, by the activity of the soul? Descartes appropriates the modern Galilean conception. The quantity of motion, he claims, is constant in the world ; it can neither be increased nor diminished. Motion is simply transmitted through contact, *i.e.*, by pressure and impact. This gives the axiom : All natural states are without exception to be explained by pressure and impact, also the vital processes in the organic body ; *philosophy is the mechanics of vital processes.* The corresponding negative formula is : The soul is no natural-scientific principle of explanation. The physicist as such knows nothing of its existence ; he becomes untrue to his science when he follows the example of the schools and derives nutrition, growth, and organic movement from it.

A purely *spiritualistic psychology* is the reverse of mechanical physics and physiology. If states of bodily life

cannot be explained by means of the activity of the soul,
then, of course, the explanation of thought from physical
processes is equally impossible. Motion produces motion,
but it can never produce a state of consciousness, otherwise it would disappear in this state, that is, cease to exist
physically. This contradicts the first axiom of physics.
However, since the reality of thought cannot be doubted,
for it is the most certain fact of existence, it is necessary
to assume a separate principle entirely different from
body, that is, mind (*mens*). Thus modern philosophy, proceeding from mechanical physics, begins with the most
thorough-going dualism. It is true, in this it was preceded
by scholasticism, whose presuppositions were different, but
which assumed the existence of purely spiritual substances.

Dualism, however, is not the last word of modern philosophy. Nay, dualism logically carried out naturally
reduces itself to monism. We can tell the exact point at
which dualism changes into monism. It is the question
concerning the correlation of the two kinds of reality. The
fact remains that regular relations exist between bodily
and mental states. Feelings and volitions correspond to
voluntary movements; sensations and perceptions correspond to the excitations of the sense-organs. How is this
relation to be conceived if, according to the principles of
the new mechanical physics, it can no longer be thought
as reciprocal action? Spinoza answers: We must determine it as *identity*. Body and soul are not absolutely
different; they are really the same thing, looked at from
different points of view. A state of movement and a state
of consciousness are at bottom the same process, seen at
one time from without, at another from within. This
relation runs through the whole of existence. Reality,
which forms one single, unitary being, one substance, be it
called nature or God, unfolds its essential content in two
forms—in the form of a corporeal world (*sub attributo extensionis*), and in the form of a world of consciousness (*sub
attributo cogitationis*). This explains the fact of a regular
relation without interaction. A *parallelism* of such a nature
exists between the physical and the psychical worlds that
every state or process (*modus*) occurs in both: what occurs

in the corporeal world as movement (*modus extensionis*) appears in the world of consciousness as sensation or idea (*idea, modus cogitationis*). Interaction is out of the question : the two kinds of processes exist *alongside* of each other, not *through* each other. Each of the two worlds, the physical and the psychical, forms a closed causal system. And this parallelism is a *universal* one : there is absolutely no state of consciousness that has not its corresponding state of movement, and, conversely, there is absolutely no state of movement in nature that has not its corresponding state of consciousness. All things, as Spinoza once expressed this logical conclusion, are animate : *omnia quamvis diversis gradibus animata.* The corresponding converse reads : All souls are incorporated.

The metaphysical system which Spinoza outlined in the few brief propositions of his *Ethics* might seem to one surveying the development of modern thought as a whole, as the accomplished solution of the problem. More and more does modern thought gravitate towards this view, most perceptibly in philosophy. Of late, however, the physiologists and biologists also approach it, sometimes, indeed, without clearly seeing its consequences.

We shall discuss this fact more at length in what follows. In the present connection I should simply like to call attention to one thing: Such a parallelistic monism may be turned in two directions, in the direction of materialism and in that of idealism. Natural scientists, who busy themselves with the corporeal world, are inclined to pursue the former path. Hobbes may be regarded as their philosophical leader. Philosophers prefer to interpret this notion in an idealistic sense. Leibniz follows this course. Certainly, he says, extension and consciousness are the two great forms of existence, but they are not equal expressions of the essence of reality ; the mental world defines the true nature of reality more adequately. The ultimate elements of reality, the monads, are, taken by themselves, beings of spiritual nature ; desire and sensation are their original determinations ; extension is a secondary and accidental quality, a manifestation rather than a true mode of being of reality.

Epistemological reflections at the same time lea↓Berkeley in the same direction. The nature of body may be resolved into elements of perception. This view is gaining more and more adherents as epistemology grows in importance. It has been at the very foundation of German philosophy since Kant forced upon the latter the critical reflection on the nature of knowledge : the corporeal world is the manifestation of the same reality which reveals its real nature in the mental world. Thinkers so opposed, nay, even so hostile to each other as Hegel, Schopenhauer, and Beneke agree in this. We might perhaps designate this metaphysical conception, which has since prevailed in philosophy, as a parallelistic monism in an idealistic key. In addition to it, we have also, it is true, especially in natural-scientific circles, monism in a materialistic key. The pure epistemologist prefers to remain on the standpoint beyond which Kant himself would not go : the corporeal world and the mental world are different manifestations of reality as such, which we cannot know, but may assume as a homogeneous unity. This would be the standpoint of agnostical monism, which Herbert Spencer occupies.

So much for the historical orientation. We now enter upon the real consideration of the problem. I shall begin with an exposition and critique of the materialistic view which poses as the real scientific conception, and proclaims itself as the result of the natural-scientific investigation of modern times.

2. Materialism and its Arguments.*

We designate that ontological theory as materialism which answers the question relating to the nature of reality as follows : Reality as such is body ; its attributes are extension and impenetrability ; its primary and essen-

---

* The excellent work of F. A. Lange, *Geschichte des Materialismus und Kritik seiner Bedeutung in der Gegenwart*, 2 vols., 3d ed., 1877 (English translation by E. C. Thomas, 1892). The reader will find in this work a most careful historical exposition of the nature of materialism and the conditions of its development in the history of civilization. Its relations to the natural sciences, to theology and to the church, as well as to society and its aims, are set forth in all their bearings. A biography of this excellent man has recently been published (1891) by O. A. Ellisen.

tial form of activity is motion. These principles can and must explain all processes in reality, in particular also the so-called states of consciousness.

The latter point, the reduction of psychical states to physical states, forms the real thesis of materialism. The arguments in its behalf are about as follows :

Experience discloses the fact that psychical processes occur only in most intimate connection with physical processes. As far as we can know, only organic, or rather only animal bodies are possessed of conscious states, and these appear to be connected particularly with the action of the nervous system. Hence it follows that science must seek the cause of the former states in the peculiar quality of these bodies. Psychical processes are to be regarded as functions of the nervous system.

Common-sense drew a different conclusion from the same fact; it inferred, as was shown in the preceding chapter, that animals possess a special something, a force or an essence that effects these processes. That is the answer, says the materialistic philosopher, upon which pre-scientific thought universally hits. Wherever it perceives a group of characteristic phenomena, it assumes for their explanation a special power or an essence. Thus primitive thought refers the phenomenon of the thunderstorm to a god of thunder, who has his seat in heaven, the phenomenon of disease to powers of disease.—Like primitive thought, a natural philosophy that was long prevalent explained the rise of water in the pump by the notion of the *horror vacui*, the processes of organic life by a special vital force. And after the same scheme, the states of consciousness are explained as manifestations of a separate principle, the soul. Of course, this does not help us in the least; soul is nothing but a *vis occulta*, a force or essence assumed *ad hoc*, but otherwise unknown, like the *horror vacui*. To explain thought by means of a soul is just like the explanation which the learned doctors of the school in Molière's play give for the fact that opium puts one to sleep : it has dormative powers.

Science, materialism continues, differs from the prescientific mode of thought in this, that it explains phenomena, not by means of essences and powers, but by means of other antecedent and simultaneous phenomena. Explanation in natural science means to state the law according to which a given phenomenon is connected with other phenomena, so that the entrance of the one may be foreseen from the appearance of the others. Thus scientific meteorology explains the thunder-storm by inserting this phenomenon into a larger group of homogeneous phenomena. In other words, it recognizes lightning as an electric spark, and then searches after the conditions of its origin, *i.e.*, the processes which precede and accompany electrical expansion and discharge in the atmosphere.

Science has the same task to perform in relation to states of consciousness. It has to seek their uniform antecedent and concomitant phenomena in order thus to determine the lawful relation of these phenomena. The antecedent and concomitant phenomena, are, as experience shows, physiological processes in the brain and nervous system. Accordingly, it is the business of science to substitute for the pseudo-science " psychology " and its pre-scientific principles, " soul " and " psychic forces," the natural-scientific explanation. Scientific psychology is physiology.

This gives us the formal principle. As regards the matter itself we may go further and say : The so-called states of consciousness, proclaimed as peculiar and unparalleled states, are in reality nothing of the kind. Science can see in them only peculiarly modified movements ; psychical states as such, regarded objectively, are nothing but physiological processes.

This fact may be proved logically as follows. The highest principle of all modern natural science is the principle of the conservation of energy : The sum of real motion and of motive force is constant. Motion is transferred and transformed, mass-motion is turned into molecular motion, active energy is transformed into potential energy, but it is preserved without loss and may be recovered from it. Now we have the following two cases. Movements are introduced into the nervous system from without ; air-waves proceeding from a sounding-bell strike the auditory nerve and arouse a physiological process in it that may be shown to be carried to the central organ by means of the nerve-fibres. We are not able as yet to pursue this process to its end, but we may assume that it does not altogether vanish. Simultaneously, as we know from another source, a sensation occurs : a sound is heard. We conclude: The sensation is nothing but the nervous process produced in the central organ by the peripheral excitation.

The reverse of this also happens. I stretch out my hand and grasp an object. Physiology explains the process: A contraction of muscular fibres is the immediate cause of articular movements ; the contraction itself is due to an impulse conducted by the fibres of the motor nerves, which we can trace back into the central organ. At that point the impulse cannot as yet be physiologically explained. However, here too it happens that simultaneously in another quarter a psychical process, an excitation of the will accompanied by feelings and ideas, is observed. We conclude : The psychical process is in itself a physical process, namely, the same which must be presupposed as the cause of the innervation of motor nerve-fibres. For natural science must insist positively that a physical effect must have a physical cause. Should we grant that a mere intention as such, a mere conscious state, can cause a movement, we should thereby surrender the fundamental principle of natural science. Then there is no telling what would happen. If a mere thought can move a brain-molecule, it can just as easily transpose mountains or turn the moon from its path ; the one thing is just as intelligible or unintelligible as the other.

This argument, which, as was seen, depends on the presupposition that the so-called states of consciousness are inserted into the physical chain of organic life, may be strengthened and made more plausible by biological and cosmological considerations.

Reference is made to the facts of comparative anatomy. They disclose a thorough-going parallelism between the development of the nervous system and soul-life. Brain and intelligence show a corresponding increase in their growth throughout the advancing stages of animal life. Man heads the animal kingdom in intelligence as well as in the size and internal development of his brain, especially of the cerebrum. Although the weight of his brain is not absolutely the greatest, the brain of the elephant, for example, being three times heavier than his own, still it is greater in proportion to his body. The weight of his brain amounts to about one fortieth of his total weight, while in the case of the elephant the brain-weight does not come within one five-hundredth of the whole weight. It is true, there are birds whose relative brain-weight even surpasses that of man, but these are evidently exceptional cases, to be explained by the abnormal lightness of the bird's body. And it is an unquestionable fact that the human brain far excels all animal brains in the size and internal development of the cerebrum, the real organ of intelligence.

The same parallelism recurs in the human race. The development of the brain and the civilization of the races run parallel. And we may infer from the numerous measurements of the cranial capacity of great men that even within the confines of a single race a brain-development surpassing the average corresponds to superior mental endowment, whereas idiocy and microcephalism or arrested growth go together. Hence, all these facts seem to say : The soul is the brain.*

The same intimate connection between brain and mind is disclosed by physiological and pathological experiments and observations. Every disturbance or injury in the brain produces disturbances in mental life. If layers of the animal brain are removed, or certain parts destroyed, certain psychical functions will disappear. Accidental injuries will cause the same effects in man. In all works on psychiatry numerous observations are to be found on psychical disturbances due to external injuries of the brain. When a fragment of bone penetrates the brain, the psychical effect is not only a disturbance of the intellectual activity, but also a complete change of character. The patient becomes suspicious, reserved, obstinate. The removal of

---

* A brief collection of the most important data of physical anthropology will be found in the second chapter of O. Peschel's excellent *Völkerkunde*.

the fragment of bone is followed by the disappearance of
the psychical change. So in old age diminution of mental
activity invariably takes place, often to the extent of loss
of judgment (*dementia senilis*). The anatomical examination
reveals that waste and degeneration of brain-matter is the
cause. Every mental disease, that is the conviction of
modern psychiatry trained in natural-scientific methods, is
brain-disease, whether the latter can be disclosed by the
anatomical investigation or not. Therefore, the brain is the
soul.

The *cosmological* reflection leads to the same view. There
was a time, modern cosmology teaches, when no organic
life existed on the earth, hence no psychical life, no so-
called states of consciousness. Yes, there was a time when
there was no earth. What we now call our planetary system was in primordial times an immense gaseous or nebu-
lous mass. By rotating around its axis this mass formed a
swelling at the equator. In consequence of the continued
shrinking of the mass, the latter became separated from the
central body as a ring suspended in mid-air, and this developed into an independent body by disruption. This
process was repeated and thus arose the system of the
planets revolving around the sun as the central body. The
earth is one of these planets. Originally a fiery, liquid
drop of cosmic matter, it gradually cooled off until a hard
crust was formed, and the aqueous vapor was condensed
into water. Not until then could organic life arise. Life
first appeared in the most primitive form in minute protoplasmic particles. These gradually assumed an inner
structure; cells arose having a sac and nucleus, and the
ability to propagate by means of fission and to develop into
a complicated system. Together with the progressive differentiation of the parts and their transformation into
heterogeneous organs, the external differentiation, the
growth of manifold forms of life, also took place. Finally,
man was evolved from one branch of the ramified animal
kingdom. He acquired an ever-increasing supremacy over
the other members, so that when he began to reflect
on his descent, a relation with the lower world seemed
utterly incredible to him, and he invented a more distin-

guished origin for himself. Natural science has destroyed this dream; it shows that he did not enter in perfect form into a completed world awaiting his coming, as a son of the gods, but that as a child of the dust he strove upwards, painfully struggling for existence with brothers of equal rank. Countless generations, of which no history tells, have passed away, until at last, in the struggle for existence, his entire organization, and in particular his brain, has developed so far as to enable him to become the exponent of historico-mental life.

Such was the past of mind on earth, the only mind of which we know. And its future?

Cosmic physics, it is said, does not leave us in doubt. Life and mind have had a beginning; they will also come to an end. The time will come when the sun will no longer shine from the heavens. The amount of heat which it has is not infinitely great. Inasmuch as its heat is constantly expended without being replaced, it must finally be exhausted. Long before this will have happened, the earth will be congealed. The sun's heat is the source of all movement and life on its surface. A comparatively small diminution of the supply is sufficient to destroy organic life; ultimately the whole earth will congeal into a motionless, rigid mass.

Such reflections are well adapted to give one an overpowering impression of the littleness and insignificance of life. As a loaf of bread is covered with a coating of mildew, with a world of living plants, so too the earth is at any given moment of its long development covered over with a world of living organisms; and among them man appears as a variation of these forms. After a brief bloom, this world sinks back again into the nothingness from which it came. One thing alone remains: eternal matter and the laws of its motion. Between the infinite past when there was no life and the infinite future in which there will be no life, the moment of the present and of life emerges—a moment only, though we measure it by millions of years; and at this moment a small portion of infinite matter reveals that wonderful phenomenon of phosphorescence, as it were, which we call self-consciousness or mental life—a brief interlude which, however great and important it may seem to us, is none the less an altogether insignificant accident in the history of the immense universe. Matter and motion are the realities, and the strange guise in which motion for a moment appears is as nothing to the universe —"the brief play of a day-fly floating above the ocean of eternity and infinity." *

3. The Practical Consequences of Materialism.

I shall preface the examination of the theoretical value of the view just presented with a few general remarks.

---

* Ludwig Büchner *Kraft und Stoff*, 16th ed. (1888) p. 239 (tr. by Collingwood, 4th ed., 1884). This work may still be viewed as the typical exposition of the materialistic view of the world in our popular philosophy, although the author himself repudiates the designation of his standpoint as materialism. Not unjustly ; for his fundamental notions are so indefinite and at variance that they might be brought almost under any metaphysical category. The only points which stand out in relief are these : Neither God nor ends exist in nature, nor is there a special soul-substance with immortality and freedom. One may regard the book of little worth philosophically considered ; one may regard its manner of treatment and its style as unsatisfactory; yet the fact remains that since 1855 it has been bought and read by the German public in sixteen editions, that it has also been translated into thirteen languages, in which again it has been bought and read in numerous editions. It can therefore undoubtedly lay claim to being a characteristic phenomenon of the second half of our century, for a time is characterized more by the books which it reads than by those it writes. In its youth the book circulated particularly among the educated middle classes who were at outs with the church and its creed ; it has long since penetrated into the lower strata of society ; it is now the working tool of the itinerant social-democratic agitator. In answer to the question, To what merits does the book owe its wide circulation and influence? we may emphasize two points: First, it offers a mass of scientific knowledge stated in popular form ; secondly, it shows contempt for the church, theology, and the creed. For the former the reader is justly thankful, while the latter gains for the author confidence and sympathy : he appears as the protagonist of honest men in the righteous struggle against falsehood, obscurantism, narrowness, and injustice. This is a fact highly suggestive to everybody, whatever be his attitude to the church and religion. A more recent and equally successful book—Max Nordau, *Die konventionellen Lügen der Kulturmenschheit* (13th ed., 1889)—is likewise suited to arouse reflection. This book is conspicuous neither for its contents nor form ; it contains nothing but the assurance repeated a hundred times that our whole life and thought is a lie. But this very circumstance will puzzle a future age more fortunate than our own, let us hope; for what made the work so attractive? will be asked. Did it really express the self-consciousness of its age?.

First, a word concerning the tendency of materialism to depreciate the spiritual, and to regard it with a certain contempt as an unimportant and unessential secondary effect of nature.

I believe that however great or small the part may be which so-called mind plays in the world, it is at all events the only thing of immediate worth and significance to us. Were it absent, the world would become meaningless and indifferent to us. Let us imagine a world without life and soul, without sensation and thought, without mind and history, a world of which nothing could be said except what astronomy and physics know of it. And now suppose a man should enter it, knowing nothing, but endowed with a perfect understanding, and suppose a most learned astronomer should accost him and begin to explain everything to him, the particular planets, their mass and their motion, giving him a detailed account of their physical and meteorological occurrences. He would, perhaps, listen for a while with interest. If, however, the astronomer should go on taking up new world-systems and explaining them in the same manner, the listener would at last become impatient and ask: Well, then, what is the use of it all? What does it mean? And if he should receive the answer: Nothing; all this constitutes reality, and beyond that nothing can be said of it; he would turn away perplexed and disappointed, and say: Well, if that is really all that can be said of the world, I have learned enough and will trouble you no further. Nor would a materialistic philosopher behave differently. He, too, is ultimately interested, at least practically interested, in the fact that brain-phenomena and their subjective reflexes are found in the world, and form the wonderful process which we call historical life. At least in practice; for he, too, practically considers all things as instruments and means of expression of mind; for him, too, body is the organ and symbol of the soul; all of his interests are centred in the mental and historical sphere. But he has also a purely theoretical interest in mind as the centre of all things, even though he demonstrates that the presence of spirit is an insignificant datum in the cosmic evolution. If this datum were absent, the planets would have no more meaning for him than the grains of sand which are the sport of the winds and waves on the ocean's shore.

That mind is to mind the object of greatest interest in the world is clearly shown by the division of scientific labor into the two spheres of reality, nature and history. If we were to banish from our libraries everything that pertains to the mental life of man, everything that belongs to history and philology, politics and morals, theology and philosophy, sociology and jurisprudence, medicine and technics, we should have left a very modest remainder. Or, suppose we should strike out of our large voluminous encyclopedias and lexica the same subjects, retaining only what pertains to astronomy and physics, chemistry and mineralogy; the remainder would fill a small thin volume. And this will most likely always be the case. The human mind will ever regard the human mind as the most important object of reality.

My second remark will consider the question concerning the consequences of materialism for morality and mode of life. The view is widely circulated that materialism has consequences dangerous to morality. In destroying religion, it is held, it also destroys morality and faith in ideals; its practical conclusion is: Virtue is an empty dream, conscience a freak, and the moral law the invention of priests; true wisdom consists in enjoying life and getting what we can get.

I do not believe that this view can be accepted, at least not in the form in which it is stated. A man's conduct is not determined by his metaphysical ideas concerning the nature of reality, but essentially by natural impulses, temperament, education, and condition in life. If, however, there is any connection between theoretical and what is called practical materialism, it is brought about, not because a man's metaphysics determines his life, but because his life determines his metaphysics. An empty and low life has the immediate tendency to produce a nihilistic conception of life; its features are a low estimate of life and its destiny, a depreciation and scorn of the nobler phases of man's nature, a loss of reverence for moral and spiritual greatness, disbelief and derision as regards all ideal aspirations. And such a nihilistic view of life naturally tends to a materialistic philosophy. It will welcome the "results of science" that nature as well as history is the play of meaningless chance, that blind forces combine atoms and carelessly scatter them again at the next instant. Conversely, an active and honorable, a good and great life naturally tends to an idealistic metaphysics; it is exalted and pacified by a view that represents its highest aims and ideals as the underlying forces of reality. From the striving after great ends grows the belief in the supremacy of ideas, in the governance of Providence in the historical life of man, and this belief finds a theoretical basis in the thought that reality as a whole is founded on ideas, that the world is the work of God.

These tendencies are not always victorious. There are plenty of righteous men who accept a materialistic metaphysics, and there are, on the other hand, men who hold an idealistic-philosophical or ecclesiastical creed, not only of words but of reason as well, and yet are guided by low sensuous-egoistic motives in their mode of life. Still, the fact remains that a man's mode of life generally has a tendency to gather around it great ideas, as was indicated above. As far as he is able, every man seeks to interpret the meaning and import of life and reality according to the deepest experiences of his individual life.

To be sure, a man's view of life also reacts on his view of the world. The will becomes surer of itself by creating a world of ideas in accord with it. And above all, a great and sudden change in one's ideas may exert a considerable influence on one's mode of life. A young man, impressed with the teachings of the church at home and at school, enters into new surroundings. In the factory, in business, at college or in the university, he comes in contact with enlightened comrades, he becomes acquainted with the popular scientific literature in which nature and history are treated from the standpoint of opposition against superstition and priestly dominion. And now the scales fall from his eyes. Why, all that they have crammed into my brain in childhood is fraud! The world is eternal; man is but a highly-developed animal species ; moral laws and the hereafter are inventions of priests to scare the stupid. Such a revolution in the world of ideas cannot but react on life. The newly-enlightened youth will continue to philosophize : Since there is no God and no hereafter, I can do as I please ; whatever pleases me is permissible. Why, the very persons who insist so strongly that " the masses " keep their religion do not act otherwise in their private lives. And now he begins, at first not without inner struggles, to do what was prohibited by religion and morals. The violation of inherited morality and the contempt for conscience become for him the proud signs of freedom and enlightenment.

That this actually happens cannot be doubted. It is repeated around us a thousand times a day. Perhaps there are few men in our time who have been spared such a line of reasoning. But, it is to be added, that does not make the reasoning true. The rejection of the moral law is not the *logical consequence* of a materialistic theory of reality, but rather the result of a *false notion of the nature of morality*—the notion, namely, for which our system of education is partly responsible, that morality is nothing but a collection of arbitrary commands and prohibitions, imposed upon us by a supramundane arbitrary ruler. Where such a notion prevails, the renunciation of the belief in the existence of this arbitrary ruler is, of course, accompanied by the repudiation of his alleged commands. But this notion is false. The moral law is not foreign to our nature ; it was not imposed upon us by a despot, as the Continental embargo was imposed upon European nations at the beginning of this century, hindering the approach to a thousand goods and pleasures. It is rather the law of our own being. Moral laws are natural laws. We may assign to them a transcendental significance or not ; they are, first of all and at all events, natural laws of human life in the sense of being the conditions of its health and welfare. According to the natural course of events, their transgression will bring upon nations as well as upon individuals misfortune and destruction, while their observance is accompanied by welfare and peace.

There is nothing in the metaphysical concepts of materialism to contradict this statement. Experience, which acquaints us with other natural laws, acquaints us also with these. Whoever disregards the laws of statics will see his structure fall to ruin, he may think of these laws what he will. Whoever transgresses the laws of medicinal dietetics will pay the penalty with indisposition and disease, whether he believes in the validity of these laws or not. Similarily, whoever violates the laws of morality will pay for it with his own life's happiness, regardless of what he may think of them. Whoever disregards the duties which he owes himself, whoever abandons himself to intemperance and dissipation, destroys the fundamental conditions of his own welfare. Whoever surrenders himself to idleness and love of pleasure, expecting in this way to find his happiness, will ultimately perish in satiety and disgust; that is a biological law of human nature as well as the other law that successful activity is followed by pleasure, and that capacities grow through exercise. Finally, whoever disobeys the commands of social morality disturbs the life of others, and suffers for it himself as a social being. Whoever treats his surroundings inconsiderately, haughtily, and meanly, arouses aversion and hatred and the behavior corresponding to these feelings, his views concerning the nature of moral laws to the contrary notwithstanding. No one exists, however, to whom these things are altogether indifferent; there is not a man in the world who can do without the love and the confidence of his fellows, to whom distrust and hatred are not painful in themselves and destructive in their consequences. And even if any one should succeed in perpetrating wrong and baseness, undiscovered and with impunity, he could not escape the reaction: the fear of discovery would remain. For it is a strange fact that the man who has something to conceal always believes himself to be watched and seen by others. Consciousness of guilt makes a man lonely. And should any one succeed in shaking off all relations with others, he would not be secure against one—the judge in his own heart. Blinded by passion, he may momentarily delude himself into the belief that he has torn out his conscience by the very roots ; it will come again some day and audibly speak to him. When the passionate desire is satisfied, when recollection and reflection reawake, or when, with increasing age, strength and courage fail, then the image of past deeds arises before the soul and causes anxiety. There is perhaps no man who could look back upon a life full of emptiness and baseness, full of falsehood and cowardice, full of wickedness and depravity, with feelings of satisfaction. At any rate, it would not be advisable for any one to make the trial. The lives of so-called men of the world and their female partners, or of blacklegs and scoundrels, little and big ones, are not apt to be described at length and openly either by themselves or others. Should it be done, and perhaps it would not be a useless task, it is not likely that any one would lay aside the book with the feeling: that was a happy and enviable life. And if such a life had achieved an apparent success, if it had committed everything and enjoyed everything with impunity, nevertheless it would not easily strike an observer as a beautiful and desirable lot.

Hence, as long as the world is what it is and human nature remains what it has been, the moral laws will remain in force, whether we conceive reality as composed of atoms or immaterial substances or what not. The only problem which materialism can put to itself in this connection is this: to explain with the means at its command facts that are indisputably given. If it is in the right, if soul-life is a function of the brain, it will be obliged to explain the laws of morality as well as those of logic as a peculiar organization of the human brain ; it will have to show how such and such a structure of the cortical substance, such and such constitution of certain ganglionic cells, is the cause of such and such strivings and feelings, such and such judgments of the behavior of others and of self. Let the biologist add how this arrangement, no less than the other arrangements of the organic system, acts for the preservation of the individual and the species. And turning to the practical, let him endeavor to found upon his physiological knowledge of the brain a gymnastics or dietetics of the "moral ganglia," of the "conscience-area," in order at last to establish pedagogy upon a "scientific" basis.

Until that is done, the materialist will have to content himself with his "provisional" laws. There is no reason why he should not do so. The invalidity of the moral laws is absolutely no logical consequence of the view that all reality is body or function of body. It may be that now and then materialistic writers betray a tendency to speak of morality and conscience with a certain contempt as things with which "science" has no occasion to deal. This tendency to treat slightingly or to ignore altogether facts which one's own theory finds hard to explain is universal. That is accidental. Ancient materialism, which, to begin with, is more philosophical, *i.e.*, more universal in its speculation, than the materialism of modern physicians and physiologists, makes morals its very aim. Ignorance alone can claim that the morality of Democritus or Epicurus has anything in common with a morality of licentiousness. It leads to a discipline of the heart.

Furthermore, let us remark in conclusion that to attack an antagonistic theory on the ground of its dangerous consequences invariably creates a bad impression. It arouses the suspicion that we fear a theoretical examination. We do not extol a view as good as long as we think that we are able to prove its truth. And after all, when we come to think of it, error alone is dangerous ; things are what they are ; how can true ideas concerning them harm us, or false ones benefit us ?

4. Critique of Materialism. Parallelistic Theory of the Relation between the Physical and the Psychical.

Let us now turn to the examination of the theoretical value of the materialistic theory. Is the assertion true that all reality is corporeal or the manifestation of corporeality ?

I must confess at once that I cannot be convinced of the truth of the statement. This view may satisfy the purposes of natural science ; it is not adequate to explain reality in general.

In philosophical circles its insufficiency is usually set

forth in our day by means of epistemological considerations. Kant has been regarded as the absolute vanquisher
of materialism. He is represented as such in F. A. Lange's
History of Materialism, for example. Schopenhauer also
praises him as such. Kant, he declares, has indicated the
great truth: no object without subject, while the absurd
undertaking of materialism consists in the attempt to derive the subject from the object.

I do not wish to enter upon this line of argument at
this point. I shall return to it in discussing the epistemological problems. Let me say, however, that I share the
view that dogmatic materialism is overcome by epistemology. It shows that bodies, far from being the only absolute
reality, have no absolute reality at all. Bodies have relative
existence only, namely, phenomenal existence; they exist for
a subject organized in a certain way. Their entire essence
is a content of perception: a body is black or white, soft
or hard, has form and extension, occupies space and is impenetrable. All these qualities belong to it in relation to
a subject with sensibility and intelligence. Without a
tongue, no taste; without eyes, no light and no color; without sensibility and understanding, no space and no body;
without subject, no object. This is a conception of whose
truth every man reflecting on these things must be convinced. Schopenhauer gives a clear and logical illustration
of it in the form of a dialogue between Subject and Matter,
as follows. Matter argues: "I exist, and outside of me there
is nothing. The world is my transitory form. You are a
mere result of a part of this form and altogether accidental.
A few moments and you are no more. But I remain forever and ever." The Subject responds: "This infinite time,
during which it is your boast that you exist, is, like the infinite space which you occupy, simply my idea, in which
you are presented, which apprehends you, to which you
owe your existence." *

Such a view is well fitted to surprise and, perhaps, to
agitate one, but it will hardly produce a lasting conviction. Whoever meets it for the first time, will have the

* *World as Will and Idea,* vol. II. chap. 1.

feeling that he has simply been taken unawares. Yes, he will say, that is easily said, and perhaps it is difficult to refute it, but that does not make it true. It remains a truth that the world existed before me and my presenta-- tion ; that sun, moon, and stars were here before I existed to see them. As soon as we look upon the world of·objects again, the belief comes back with overpowering force that it, the solid world of bodies, constitutes reality, and that its existence is independent of the presenting subject. As Antæus regains his strength by coming in contact with the earth, so materialism regains its strength by coming in contact with perception. That may be a weakness of common-sense, which stands aghast at abstract thinking, and perhaps Meynert is right when he says that "a man's ability to conceive or not to conceive the unreality of the world created by the activity of his brain, is one of the surest tests of his intellectual capacity."* Still, it would not be wise for any one wishing to produce a·real conviction of the insufficiency of the materialistic theory of reality to stop at epistemological considerations. Materialism origi- nated and is at home on the soil of metaphysics or natural philosophy. Whoever wishes to overcome it will have to seek it out here. We shall look at it from this standpoint.

The thesis of materialism is the proposition : States of consciousness are functions of matter ; they can be ex- plained physiologically as functions of the nervous system, as results of the nervous processes. Has this assertion any foundation ?

Of late, objections have been urged against it from the *physiological* side. It is absolutely impossible, it is said, to explain states of consciousness by states of motion, and that is exactly what a physiological explanation ultimately amounts to. Du Bois-Reymond is the illustrious spokes- man of this wing. In the oft-mentioned treatise *Über die Grenzen des Naturerkennens* he argues : Physical processes are without exception to be explained physically, and here there is no limit to the possibility of explanation ; there are many things as yet not explained, but none is

---

* *Psychiatrie* (1884).

inexplicable in itself. The explanation of vital processes, of the origination of the first organisms, with the means of natural science is not, in principle, impossible. But with the first element of consciousness, with the most primitive sensation, something arises which eludes natural-scientific explanation. "Consciousness cannot be explained by its material conditions. The astronomical knowledge of the brain, the highest which we can reach, reveals nothing in it except matter in motion. By no discoverable arrangement or movement of material particles can a bridge be built into the realm of consciousness." He concludes with the emphatic declaration : "In reference to the riddle of the corporeal world, the natural scientist has long ago learned to confess his *ignoramus* with manly resignation. Looking back upon the past road of victory, he is inspired with the secret thought that where he is now in ignorance he might, at least under certain conditions, know, and perhaps will know at some future time. But as regards the riddle concerning what matter and force are and *how they can think*, he must once for all make up his mind to render the much harder verdict *ignorabimus*." *

---

* *Ueber die Grenzen des Naturerkennens* (7th ed., 1891), pp. 40 ff. A second lecture, *Die Sieben Welträthsel*, delivered in 1880, gives the history of the former lecture of the year 1872 and continues the discussion. I enter upon a closer examination of these views because they have aroused such attention among natural scientists and have been discussed so frequently. We may regard them as typical examples of a mode of thought which is very common to these circles. The English physicist Tyndall had shortly before expressed a similar view in a lecture delivered in 1868 before a congress of natural scientists. Let me append the graphic sentences in which he embodies his thought : "The passage from the physics of the brain to the corresponding facts of consciousness is únthinkable. Granted that a definite thought, and a definite molecular action in the brain, occur simultaneously; we do not possess the intellectual organ, nor apparently any rudiment of the organ, which would enable us to pass, by a process of reasoning, from the one to the other. They appear together, but we do not know why. Were our minds and senses so expanded, strengthened, and illuminated as to enable us to see and feel the very molecules of the brain ; were we capable of following all their motions, all their groupings, all their electric discharges, if such there be ; and were we intimately acquainted with the corresponding states of thought and feeling, we should be as far as ever from the solution of the problem, ' How are these physical processes connected with the facts of consciousness ?'" (*Fragments of Science*, Scientific Materialism, pp. 419 f.)

These reflections have been regarded as a refutation of materialism, and perhaps they are meant as such. They seem to me, however, to be inadequate for that; they miss the real point where materialism is vulnerable, or at least strike it only at random. Materialistic philosophers might answer the objection as follows: According to his statements, the disputed point between us and the author of the *Grenzen des Naturerkennens* is simply, whether states of consciousness *can be explained* by material conditions or not; we affirm the question, he denies it. On the other hand, we both agree that consciousness is *dependent* on material conditions; he, too, considers himself far above " dogmas and time-honored systems " with their belief in a special soul-substance; he, too, says that "in a thousand cases material conditions affect mental life." To his unbiassed view there appears no reason to doubt that sense-impressions are actually "communicated to the so-called soul" (p. 45); the hypothesis forces itself upon him "that the soul arose as the gradual product of certain material combinations" (p. 47); he finds no fault with Vogt's "figure concerning secretions" "for considering the activity of the soul as the *product* of material conditions in the brain. The mistake lies in supposing that the nature of the activity of the soul can be explained as clearly by the structure of the brain, as secretion might be explained from the structure of the glands if our knowledge were sufficiently advanced" (p. 50). Hence he does not call in question the fact of conditionality, but only its conceivableness; we know *that* movements occasion states of consciousness, only the *how* remains an eternal enigma.

Perhaps, the materialistic philosopher might proceed, that is the case. *How* the molecules manage to think, that we do not know, and perhaps will never know. Is there anything unusual in this? Does natural-scientific explanation anywhere consist in stating *how* the cause sets about to produce the effect? Physics explains many phenomena by the law of gravitation: the falling of the stone, the flow of the brook, the rise of the balloon, the flow and ebb of the ocean, the motion of the planets. It does it by showing that all these movements are included in the general formula of the law of gravitation. But does it show *how* bodies at all attract each other, or *why* they tend to move toward each other according to that formula? Not at all. Just as little does chemistry explain *why* such and such elements combine in such and such proportions, or why they unite at all. Chemistry, too, informs us only concerning the *that*, not the *how* and *why*. Nor is the case different in mechanics. *How* a body manages to transfer its motion to another body which it strikes, mechanics does not explain; it simply reduces the actual occurrences to a law. Hence, to *explain* a phenomenon in natural science means nothing but to find a formula which embraces the case, by the aid of which it may be foreseen, calculated, and, under certain circumstances, brought about. Du Bois-Reymond holds the same view. What force is, or what is the origin of motion, is for him as much of a transcendental problem as the essence of matter.

Therefore, the materialistic philosopher might conclude, we can neither expect nor demand a different procedure in the explanation of states of consciousness. They are explained in the sense of natural science, when we succeed in reaching formulæ according to which their occurrence can be foreseen because of other processes, say of certain physiological processes in the brain. If we knew that such and such processes in the cells and conducting fibres are regularly followed by such and such ideas or feelings, of such and such a quality and intensity, we should know all that we care to know as scientific investigators. Not to know *how* the physiological process succeeds in producing a sensation cannot trouble us, as long as we do not know how one movement produces another. There is no theoretical reason why brain-physiology should not succeed in reaching such formulæ. It is very doubtful whether this will actually occur, whether it will ever be able to explain the movements of brain-molecules by which a certain sensation or a certain thought-process is effected. But granting the mere possibility of such a procedure, the possibility of a physical explanation of states of consciousness is also granted, in the same sense in which the word explanation is generally used in natural science.

In this way, it seems to me, materialism can escape the aforesaid objection.* If the objection is to have any real weight, it must be stated in different terms. We should say, and that is most likely the import of the objection, there can be no formulæ which correlate physical and psychical occurrences in the same way in which movements are correlated in the laws of mechanics. Or in other words: *No causal relation obtains between physical and psychical processes. States of consciousness are neither effects nor causes of physical occurrences.†*

Here we have the beginning of the end of materialism. The beginning only, it is true.

In order to prove this assertion, however, it will be well, first of all, to hold materialistic philosophers to a more exact declaration of principles. We find them regularly using different statements in the same sense. These statements may be reduced to two fundamental forms: first, states of consciousness are effects of physical states; secondly, states of consciousness as such, or objectively considered, are nothing but physical states of the brain. These formulæ are constantly used by our materialistic writers indiscriminately. Thus Büchner somewhere explains psychical phenomena as *effects* of brain-action. It is immaterial to us *how* they arise from material combinations, he says; it is sufficient to know "that matter in motion acts on the mind through the mediation of the sense-organs and causes motion in it, and that this in turn produces material movements in nerves and muscles."

---

* Büchner hints at such a conception. *Kraft und Stoff*, p. 316.

† Incidentally Du Bois-Reymond himself establishes this formula. Among the passages quoted above which represent thinking as the *product* of material "conditions," statements are also found in which the impossibility of regarding it as the *product* of physical causes is expressed. "Motion can produce motion only, or transform it back into potential energy. The mechanical cause completely disappears in the mechanical effect. The mental states accompanying material occurrences in the brain are, as far as our understanding is concerned, without a sufficient cause. They stand without the pale of the causal nexus" (p. 45). The meaning evidently is: without the pale of the *mechanical* causal nexus, with which alone the "Laplacian mind" is familiar. During the last century every physicist would have made such a distinction. We cannot neglect philosophy with impunity.

Right beside this statement, however, we find the other:
" Thought can and must be regarded as a special *form of
the general motion of nature,* which is as peculiar to the substance of the central nerve-elements as contraction is to
the muscles, or the motion of light is to the world-ether."
And this, he continues, is not merely a demand of logic.
It has of late also been proved experimentally—by the experiments, namely, which make plain that psychical states
or intellectual motion require time for their occurrence.
" The necessary conclusion follows that the psychical act
or act of thought occurs in an extended, impenetrable, and
composite substratum, and that such an act is, therefore,
nothing but a form of movement." He also attempts to
prove his point by the fact that the arrival of a sense-im-
pression in the brain " at once arouses there an immediate
increase in temperature." This, therefore, proves that
psychical activity is and can be nothing but the radiation
in the cells of the gray cortex of a movement initiated by
external impressions." Other experiments are calculated
to enlighten us as to the nature of such motion—the experiments, namely, which show " that the electricity generated
in the nerves is diminished, or wholly vanishes, as soon as
the nerve exercises a physiological function. This proves
beyond doubt that nervous force or nervous activity is
identical with transformed electricity." *

---

* *Kraft und Stoff*, pp. 295, 297, 300 ff. One should read through the sections on brain and soul, thought and consciousness, in order to see the
frightful confusion in his fundamental notions. There are three kinds of
conceptions concerning the relation of thought and movement, which are
tangled into an inextricable snarl. 1. Thought is motion. 2. Thought is
the *effect* of motion. 3. Thought is indissolubly *connected* with motion ;
" thought and extension can be regarded only as two aspects or manifestations of one and the same unitary being " (p. 300), the real nature of which
is as yet unknown to us (pp. 3, 316). *Influxus physicus,* Parallelism, Identity, and the popular conceptions, Spinoza, Kant,—all these stagger around
like drunkards. No wonder that such a man should, on every page of his
book, defame the " philosophers " as persons who are skilled in the art of
bringing confusion into the simplest and clearest notions by means of a mass
of high-flown empty words !
    Vogt mentions as soporifics " speculative-philosophical " books. Per-
haps it would have been well for him, had he at some time or other resisted
the influence of these drugs and paid some attention to what Spinoza and

A Danish philosopher has recently offered a materialistic theory of the emotions with the same double formula.*
According to the common view, the emotion of fear, for
example, arises as a purely conscious state; this causes a
series of physiological processes, pallor, trembling, etc.
The physiologists reverse the process: the emotion is not
the cause but rather the *effect* of the bodily state, that is,
the effect of a physiological process in the vaso-motor
system. Or, expressed differently: Emotion really consists
of functional disturbances of the body. The popular view
" that the modification of the mental state constitutes the
real emotion, real pleasure or grief, while the bodily states
are merely secondary phenomena, which, though they are
never absent, are nevertheless unessential as such," is rejected. Instead, it is shown that the purely psychical emotion is a superfluous hypothesis. " What the mother feels
who mourns for her dead child is in reality the fatigue and
languor of her muscles, the coldness of her anæmic skin,
the inability of her brain to think clearly and quickly. All
this becomes evident from the consideration of the cause
of these phenomena. Take away from the frightened person the bodily symptoms, let his pulse beat slowly, his gaze
be firm, his color healthy, his movements quick and certain,
his thoughts clear; and what then is left of his fright? "

If materialism resolutely adheres to the second formulation of its thesis, it is absolutely irrefutable. The proposition, Thoughts are in reality nothing but movements in
the brain, feelings are nothing but bodily processes in the
vaso-motor system, is absolutely irrefutable; not because it
is true, however, but because it is absolutely meaningless.
The absurd has this advantage in common with truth, that
it cannot be refuted. To say that thought is at bottom
nothing but a movement is to say that iron is at bottom
made of wood. No argument avails here. All that can be
said is this: I understand by a thought a thought and not

Kant have to say on the subject. He would, perhaps, have escaped the
confusion which is so manifest in his own writings. See *Physiologische
Briefe*, 4th ed. 1876, p. 354.

   * C. Lange, *Über Gemüthsbewegungen*, translated into German by
Kurella (1887).

a movement of brain-molecules ; and similarly, I designate
with the words anger and fear, anger and fear themselves
and not a contraction or dilation of blood-vessels. Suppose
the latter processes also occur, and suppose they always
occur when the former occur, still they *are* not thoughts
and feelings. Turn it which way you will, you will never
find thought in movement. The common man knows
nothing whatever of the motion in the brain or of the vaso-
motor process, but he knows what anger is, and what
thought is, and he means these, when he speaks of them,
and not something else of which the physiologist alone
knows or thinks he knows. Or will the physiologist stop
talking of thoughts and feelings after his science will have
acquired more exact information concerning the bodily
processes, and will he, instead, speak only of what they are
at bottom and in reality or objectively considered, that is,
movements ? Will he, in case he should happen to fall in
love, no longer confess his love, but mention the corresponding vaso-motor processes or, in the words of Tyndall,
discourse on the right-handed spiral motion of the molecules of the brain ? Does that tell the whole story ? How
nonsensical !

Hence, in order to make argument at all possible, materialism must first relinquish the formula : Thought is
motion. Thought *is not* motion, but thought. It is, however, possible that it bears some uniform and determinable
relation to motion. Should experience show this to be the
case, the problem would be to ascertain the nature of this
relation.

Two forms of the relation between physical and psychical occurrences are conceivable after we have excluded the
relation of identity. We can have either a causal relation
or a relation of mere coexistence in time. Since the seventeenth century the two rival philosophical theories have
held to these two conceptions concerning the relation of
body and soul. I mean the theory of *interaction* (*influxus
physicus*) and the theory of *occasionalism* or *parallelism*. We
are obliged to choose between the two. Unless I am mistaken, materialism will decide for the former view : States
of consciousness are *effects* of bodily states ; whereas its

physiological critics mentioned above, incline to the theory
of parallelism, without, it is true, really carrying out the
thought consistently.

We must first elucidate the two conceptions. Let us
imagine with Leibniz the skull of an animal or man to be as
large as a mill. Suppose one could walk around in it and
observe the processes in the brain as one can observe the
movements of the machinery and the cogging of the wheels
in the mill. What brain-processes would the observer expect to see according to each of the two theories?

The adherent of the parallelistic theory must evidently
expect the following. The physical processes in the brain
form a closed causal nexus. There is no member that is
not physical in its nature. One would see as little of
psychical processes, of ideas and thoughts, as in the movements of the mill. A man crosses the street. Suddenly
his name is called ; he turns around and walks toward
the person who called him. The omniscient physiologist
would explain the whole process in a purely mechanical
way. He would show how the physical effect of the
sound-waves upon the organ of hearing excited a definite
nervous process in the auditory nerve, how this process
was conducted to the central organ, how it released certain physical processes there which finally led to the innervation of certain groups of motor nerves, the ultimate result of which was the turning and movement of the body in
the direction of the sound-waves. All these occurrences
together combine into an unbroken chain of physical processes. Alongside of this, another process occurred of
which the physiologist as such sees nothing and needs to
know nothing, with which, however, he is acquainted as a
thinking being who interprets his percepts ; there are auditory sensations, which aroused ideas and feelings. The
person called heard his name ; he turned around in order
to discover who called him and why he was addressed ;
he perceived an old acquaintance and went to greet him.
These occurrences accompany the physical series without
interfering with it; perception and presentation are not
members of the physical causal series.

The case would be different if the theory of interaction

were correct. The adherent of this theory must expect the physical process to be interrupted at certain points—at such, namely, at which psychical occurrences enter as members of the causal series. If nervous movement is the cause of the sensation, it must vanish as such, and, in its place, sensation must appear. The motion of the ball A has as its effect the motion of the ball B, that is, the first motion disappears, and in its stead there appears an equal definite motion of the second ball. A motion produces heat, that is, the motion vanishes, and in its stead there appears a definite amount of heat. The same would have to happen in our case : instead of a lost movement there would appear a sensation, or an idea of definite intensity and quality, as its equivalent. The idea is not, however, an object of external observation ; ideas and feelings cannot be seen as such or be discovered by the methods of natural science at all. For the physicist there would then be a break in the causal chain ; a link would be wanting from the physical series.—Should our materialistic philosopher refuse to grant this, holding that the idea in turn is also something physical, some form or other of motion, he would thereby, of course, prove untrue to his hypothesis and go over to the parallelistic theory. For, if he were right, the natural scientist would, of course, be concerned only with the physical, and could ignore the fact that the process has as its concomitant a state of consciousness. The physical effect and not the sensation as such would then be the equivalent and effect of the physical cause.

These are the two possible conceptions. Which of them is true ?

This question being a question of facts can be decided only by experience. In themselves, both views are conceivable. Has experience settled the matter ? I think no one will claim that final observations have been made by which either one of these conceptions would exclude the other. Perhaps they will never be made. Observations and experiments are powerless in the presence of these unapproachable and most complicated processes of organic life.

Nevertheless, the natural scientist will not long be in

doubt as to which notion to choose. He will say that the
analogy of combined experience leads him to assume a
continuity of physical processes even in this case. He
would regard it as a presumptuous and impracticable demand to assume that motion is transformed, not into
another form of motion, not into potential physical energy,
but into something that does not exist at all physically.
Transformation of motion or force into thought, into pure
states of consciousness, would for the natural-scientific
view be nothing but the destruction of energy. Similarly,
the origination of motion from a purely mental element,
for example from the idea of a wish, would in physics be
equivalent to creation out of nothing. Consequently he
would be forced to accept the parallelistic theory instead
of the other which assumes a causal relation. Perhaps the
materialistic metaphysician will, in order to escape this
dilemma, go over to the parallelistic hypothesis. Rather
than give up the law of the conservation of physical energy,
he will in the end abandon the formula: States of consciousness are effects of the physical organization. What
hinders us, he will say, from conceiving them as concomitants of brain-processes? In that case the relation between
them would remain essentially the same : mental processes,
though not incidental effects, are incidental reflexes of
physical processes. Nay, perhaps he will say: This is exactly my view of the matter. The brain-process is the objective element; sensation, idea, and feeling, the subjective
reflex. We read in Büchner: " Thought and extension,
two aspects or manifestations of one and the same unitary
being " (p. 300) ; " Mind and nature are at bottom the same " ;
" Logic and mechanism are the same, and the reason
of nature is at the same time the reason of thought " (p.
127). In what follows we shall, therefore, accept the theory
of parallelism. We beg the reader to bear this in mind as
we proceed to discuss the consequences of this view.*

---

* That this is Spinoza's solution of the problem was already mentioned
above (p. 58). But it must be added that he himself confused this thought
with another. He straightway substitutes for metaphysical parallelism an
epistemological parallelism, or at least employs the parallelism of the physical and psychical worlds solely in order to obtain what turns out to be an
altogether unsatisfactory solution of the epistemological problem : How

5. The Consequences of the Parallelistic Theory. Panpsychism.

Two propositions are contained in the theory of parallelism: (1) Physical processes are never effects of psychical processes; (2) Psychical processes are never effects of physical processes.

The first proposition implies that the living body is an automaton. It is distinguished from the machine by the infinite complexity of its composition, but all its operations are ultimately explicable by the same fundamental forces which the natural scientist generally employs. There are no exceptions to the rule ; even the most complicated movements of living bodies, the most skilful works and acts of man, can be explained without regard to mental processes,

thought and being happen to coincide. He thinks he can solve it by identifying logical consequence and mechanical causation on the ground of this parallelism. Leibniz took up the thought, without thus distorting it, and more logically developed its biological as well as psychological consequences. He extends soul-life beyond the boundaries of consciousness ; and, on the other side, beyond the limits of the animal world. The founder of psycho-physics, G. Th. Fechner, revives this view in our time (a brief exposition of the fundamental concepts in *Zend-Avesta*, II. 312 ff.). W. Wundt also accepts it (*System der Philosophie*, pp. 582 ff. See also the concluding chapter in his *Physiologische Psychologie*). An intelligent discussion of the question from the same standpoint will be found by the reader also in H. Höffding's *Umrisse der Psychologie*, 2d ed. 1893, pp. 71 ff. (tr. by Mary Lowndes). There are also philosophers who adhere to the principle of interaction between the physical and psychical realms. H. Spencer, for example, evolves states of consciousness from movement (*First Principles*, § 71). Lotze occupies a peculiar position. In principle he holds to the possibility of interaction. On the other hand, by adopting universal spiritualism and pantheism, he finally renders superfluous the reasoning which he had employed in defending the theory of interaction.

The physiologists and psychiatrists find it difficult to reach a consistent view. They deny the possibility of mind acting on body, and thus approach the parallelistic hypothesis. But, on the other hand, they cannot muster up the courage to accept this theory's conception of the effects of body on mind, and hence they do not get beyond the conception of the *influxus physicus;* that is, they are caught in the meshes of the materialistic view : Soul-processes are reflexes and effects of bodily states. The lectures of Du Bois-Reymond, quoted above, are typical examples of this attitude. Or take H. Maudsley (*Physiology and Pathology of Mind*). Spinoza is often quoted by Maudsley, but the author deceives himself when he believes that his views coincide with the thoughts of that acute and logical thinker.

solely as mechanical reactions of a peculiarly-fashioned bodily system upon such and such physical excitations. A dog pursues a rabbit : he is determined by scent and sight, as it were. The movement is to be explained purely physically, not otherwise than the movement of the sun-flower which turns to the light, or of the planet which rotates around the sun. Action and reaction are more complicated in this case, but they are present in both as purely physical manifestations, and are to be explained by the methods of physical science. An author writes a book ; a builder has a house built by the help of a hundred work-men ; a general fights a battle with a hundred thousand soldiers. The omniscient physiologist would explain all these processes, as physically conditioned, by the organiza-tion of the respective bodies, their nervous and muscular systems, and, on the other hand, by the nature of the external stimuli. He would explain the author of the *Critique of Pure Reason* just as he would explain a clock-work. In consequence of this particular arrangement of the brain-cells and of their interconnections with each other and the motor nerves, certain stimuli exciting the retina and the tactile nerves of the fingers had to occasion certain move-ments, which are in no wise different from those of a writ-ing automaton or a music-box. Not the slightest allusion would be made in his illustration to thoughts and the like. The physiologist might know that some such process occurs, but he would neither wish nor be allowed to make use of it in his explanation. Thoughts are as little able to make fingers move as to turn the moon from its orbit. It is not to be expected that such an omniscient physiologist will ever exist; the action of the brain-molecules which accompanied the intellectual labor of the *Critique of Pure Reason* will never find its Newton. Yet it would have to be admitted that the action of the molecules and not the thoughts are the sole causes of the movement by means of which the written characters were set down on paper.

But that is nonsense, common-sense will say, and per-haps a physiologist or two will agree with it. No autom-aton can accomplish such a feat; such things cannot be explained without thought and purpose. Well, in that case, we are manifestly compelled to return to the theory of interaction and all its difficulties : Motion originates from something that does not exist physically at all, and motion is transformed into a purely mental element. One or the other; there is no other alternative.

However, as regards the inability of the body to perform such automatic movements, we may say with Spinoza that no one has ever discovered the body's limits. He refers to somnambulists, who perform the most complicated movements without consciousness and thought. In our day he would, perhaps, have referred to hypnotic processes, to the post-hypnotic effects of suggestion, for example. Orders are given to a person during hypnotic sleep to enter a certain house on the next day at noon, and to wave his pocket-handkerchief out of the window. He knows nothing of the command ; he does not remember what happened to him in the hypnotic state, and yet when the hour comes he proceeds to carry out the order. How else can this process be explained than by assuming that the words of the hypnotizer have produced a certain arrangement of the brain, so that, when the clock strikes, a series of movements is released just as in the alarm-clock when the hand passes the time set for alarm? It is not surprising that infinitely more complicated movements take place than can be performed by our machines. The 500 or 1000 million cortical cells, which in turn are composed of countless and exceedingly complicated and heterogeneous chemical molecules, and are connected with each other by innumerable paths, can surely accomplish more than the few wheels and levers in our machines. And though our physiologists are as yet at sea in reference to them, still an immense field is opened to our imagination. This, however, we must make clear to ourselves : If the mind participates in these processes as a cause, it does so without knowledge. It effects the movements of the writer's fingers, for example, surely not by knowing the nature and position of the nerves and muscles, but in some absolutely mysterious manner. The soul moves the limbs, is equivalent to saying : I do not know how the body is moved. By no means can movements be explained by conscious purposive action of the mind, guided by a knowledge of the means.

The entire corporeal world is thereby unreservedly placed at the disposal of natural seience. It may declare: For me, reality means nothing but body; all processes in nature can be explained by the means at my command, exclusively as movements and motive forces of material elements. I do not need the hypothesis of a soul, or a mind, or a God, formerly employed by physics; the causal series nowhere shows me an element that does not fall within the physical world. Nay, if such factors were placed at my service from other sources, I should neither wish nor be able to make any use of them.

This is one side of the matter. I believe materialism itself has reason to be satisfied with these statements.

We now turn to the other side, to the second proposition which was characterized above as a consequence of the parallelistic theory : Psychical processes are not effects of physical processes. It is but the reverse of the first proposition, just as reasonable, just as evident as that. If thought can be the effect of movements, there is no reason whatever why a movement should not be the effect of a thought. Let us examine the consequences of this proposition. I fear the metaphysician of materialism and the physiologist will find them hard to swallow. Yet I do not see how we can get around them.

I hear the sound of a bell. That is the effect, says common reflection, of the vibration of the air; the excitation of the auditory nerve is the cause of the sensation. That is impossible, says our theory ; a sensation is a psychical process, and cannot, therefore, be the effect of a movement. Of what, then, is it the effect ? For we surely all assume that it is an effect, not an isolated process independent of the causal law. Even those who believe in free-will regard sensations as caused. Hence, what causes the sensation ? A state of consciousness preceding it in the mind of the hearer ? Apparently not, for it follows upon any state of consciousness whatsoever. The cause must, therefore, be sought outside of the states of consciousness themselves. Are we then forced back to the air-waves which proceed from the sounding bell; or is there still another possibility?

There is, indeed, still another possibility. It is the hypothesis of Spinoza and of Fechner, the hypothesis of *universal parallelism.* No psychical process without concomitant movement, no process of movement without a concomitant psychical process. If we accept this hypothesis, it is evident that we shall overcome the difficulty. Then we shall say: The movements which proceed from the bell have as their sole effects nervous excitations and brain-states. Sensation, on the other hand, is the effect of the inner processes accompanying these vibrations.

Let me add, however: We have no knowledge of these inner processes; movements are given, not their psychical accompaniments. The latter are given only at one point, in self-consciousness, whose states we conceive as phenomena accompanying the processes in our nervous system. The external world, on the other hand, is given to us only from the physical side, as a corporeal world in motion; the inner side is an addition of thought. Practically, therefore, this hypothesis does not effect any change in our conception of these processes; we shall continue to say: Sound-waves occasion the sensation of sound, the prick of the needle occasions pain. Only when we desire to go to the very bottom of things, shall we declare once for all: Such statements are in reality inexact modes of expression; the proposition ought really to assert: Processes which are unknown to us, but whose physical equivalents are physical or chemical processes, are the causes of these psychical states. Our hypothesis is, to use an old comparison, like the Copernican theory in this respect. We first get a clear conception of the real state of affairs, and then go right on speaking of sunrise and sunset in the usual way. We do the same here. Two sides of reality are coextensive with each other; for every fact in the one there is a corresponding fact in the other; the psychical processes α, β, γ correspond to the physical processes a, b, c. A causal relation exists between the members of the same series. Since, however, there are breaks in both series, we substitute for them the members of the corresponding series.

Our view of the processes does not, therefore, undergo any practical change because of our hypothesis. It is easy to see, however, that it would have important consequences for our conception of the world. It would lead us to an *idealistic view of the world.* For one thing is evident : if the physical and psychical sides of reality are coextensive, we shall say : The psychical domain is the representation of reality as it is by itself and for itself ; the physical side, on the other hand, is degraded to a mere external phenomenon. In this connection, the advance from Spinoza to Leibniz is inevitable.

What about this conception? Is it more than a mere subterfuge, to avoid the difficulty of interaction between soul and body? Is it really a credible view of the nature of things? Can we take the notion seriously that some inner processes or other run parallel with all bodily processes? This is evidently the cardinal question of ontology. The answer to the question concerning *the extent of soul-life* is the point at which metaphysical conceptions of the world really diverge.

The popular mind, and with it the conception prevailing among physicists, makes short work of the question concerning the extent of mental life. States of consciousness are concomitants of brain-processes. Animal bodies are the only bearers of psychical life ; all other bodies are mere bodies.

It is plain that in this answer we do not get beyond the confines of a materialistic world-view. Conscious states remain isolated secondary processes of nature; they are, in the eyes of the natural scientist, strange and perplexing anomalies. He cannot get rid of them; their existence, indeed, is indisputable, but they make him uneasy : without them the system of bodies in motion, which he calls world or nature, would be entirely transparent and rational; they force upon him that unfortunate *ignorabimus.* His only consolation is that these conscious states are of no consequence after all; at least, they do not interfere with the course of nature. Nor is great importance to be attached to these isolated and insignificant processes from the cosmical point of view.

If this disposes of the matter, materialism essentially gains its point, even on the assumption of the parallelistic theory.

The philosophers, however, have never been willing to abide by this settlement of the question. They have always shown a tendency to attribute greater importance to the processes under consideration. From the beginnings of Greek philosophy to our day, the philosophical, that is, universal view of reality has gone beyond the physical-astronomical notion, and has regarded it as necessary to associate with reality in general and in particular, an inner, ideal, mental principle. Plato and Aristotle, Spinoza and Leibniz, Schelling and Schopenhauer, Lotze and Fechner, however else their thoughts may diverge, all agree that the mental element does not play the part of an isolated side-issue in the world ; that, on the contrary, *everything corporeal* points to something else, an inner, intelligible element, a being for itself, which is akin to what we experience within ourselves. Whoever shares this conception that mind has the importance of a universal and cosmical principle of reality, sides with *Idealism*, however else he may explain the matter to himself.

In what follows I shall not attempt to prove the truth of this conception. Proof in the field of metaphysics is a delicate matter. But I wish to offer a few reflections that seem to urge us to such a world-view. They may, if they mean nothing else, serve as *rationes dubitandi* against the obstinate dogmatism of popular opinion and of the physical conception of the universe.*

---

* I should like to call the reader's attention to a little treatise of Fechner's, *Ueber die Seelenfrage* (1861). In the title, Fechner calls the treatise "a journey through the visible world to find the invisible world." No one who has attempted such a task has accomplished it with greater success than he. In a remarkable degree Fechner unites the circumspection of the natural scientist with the careful foresight of the philosopher and the emotional fancy of the poet. The extent of psychical life is the central problem of his philosophy. He treats it especially in *Nanna, oder über das Seelenleben der Pflanze* (1848), in *Zend-Avesta, über die Dinge des Himmels und des Jenseits* (3 vols., 1851) ; he touches upon it in the *Elemente der Psychophysik* (2 vols., 1860), and gives a comprehensive, very intelligible, and pertinent exposition of his view in the above-mentioned little work *Ueber die Seelenfrage*. A final and definite exposition of his philosophy, in its oppo-

First of all, let us consider the guiding principle. How can we at all decide as to the presence of psychical processes? The answer is self-evident. We become immediately aware of our existence only at one point, namely, in our self-consciousness. I can never know through immediate observation that, besides the sensations, ideas, and volitions which I experience in myself, similar processes occur in the world. What my neighbor feels and thinks, I do not know by observation, but by inference; all that I see is a physical phenomenon. I see movements and gestures, hear sounds which proceed from a body like mine, but I see no feelings and ideas; and no microscope or telescope can help me to see them. The feelings and ideas I add in thought by inferring from the analogy of the bodily processes which I see, the existence of analogous mental processes, which I do not see.

How far may this inference be extended? The popular view answers, as was said before : As far as animal life extends. Animals are animated beings; all other objects —metals, stones, plants—are not animated : they are mere bodies. At the most, plants might possibly be considered as having souls, but not seriously. The plant-soul is a dream of childish fancy.

This view claims to be the self-evident and only possible view, but I am inclined to think that its assurance exceeds the force of its arguments. Indeed, it is purely arbitrary.

In the first place, how far does the animal world extend? Is it separated by a fixed boundary from the rest of the

---

sition to materialism and dualism, is given in *Tagesansicht gegenüber der Nachtansicht* (1879). Fechner's conception is intimately related to Schopenhauer's, whose philosophy has as its central dogma the thesis : That which is presented to our thought as the corporeal world is, as such, psychical in its nature, namely, will. In Schopenhauer's works, particularly in the little treatise *Ueber den Willen in der Natur*, we find numerous passages from natural-scientific writers who, unwittingly and even against their will, testify to the truth of his view. Fechner excels Schopenhauer especially in the clearness of his insight. He sees that the assumed inner world cannot serve as an explanation of the physical world ; in the world of bodies, only physical principles of explanation are valid. There is a universal tendency in Schopenhauer to misapply the metaphysical principle, the will, to the explanation of nature. Schopenhauer, on the other hand, excels in his voluntaristic psychology. We shall return to this point later on.

corporeal world, particularly from the vegetable kingdom? Common opinion presupposes this. It divides the corporeal world into three distinct kingdoms, in accordance with old scholastic concepts—into animal, vegetable, and mineral kingdoms. But modern biology has obliterated these fixed lines ; here, too, it is confronted with the proposition that nature makes no leaps. Though the animal and vegetable kingdoms differ greatly, they approach each other very closely on the lower stages of development. There are numerous lower forms of life which have the characteristics neither of true animals nor of true plants. A separate group, the group of the protista, has been formed for them, an intermediate kingdom in which plant and animal meet. If there is no fixed boundary-line between the animal and vegetable worlds, if we are obliged to regard them as two branches grown on one stem, the question is forced on us : Are plants also bearers of psychical life ? Everybody concedes an inner life to animals, even to the lowest forms, however far removed they may be from the higher forms. We cannot, without being arbitrary, refuse to admit that the protista, the plant-animals or animal-plants in which the animal world gradually vanishes, also have an inner life. Hence the inference is obvious : Just as there is no fixed line of demarcation between the animal and the plant worlds, so there is no fixed limit to psychical life. Soul-life may extend over the entire organic world.*

---

* E. Haeckel, *Natürliche Schöpfungsgeschichte* (8th ed., 1889 ; English, *Natural History of Creation,* 1892), pp. 414 ff., inclines to the belief that primitive life is found in plantlike organisms. "Zooplasm was evolved from phytoplasm by division of labor, since only phytoplasm can arise directly from anorganic combinations by the influence of sunlight." Animal organisms arose as follows : Some of the first living forms began to assimilate organic matter and then lost the faculty of nutrition by means of inorganic matter (425, 431). According to Wundt, however, (*System der Philosophie,* pp. 503 f., 334 f.,) the simplest forms of life are to be regarded, as far as their functions and the metabolic process are concerned, as the simplest forms of animals. From these, plants branched off as chlorophyll-producing organisms. This distinction is immaterial for our purposes. The psycho-physiological studies of M. Verworn (1889) offer interesting observations on the soul-life of the protista. He attributes the fundamental forms of psychical life, sensation and will, although without real conscious-

While this possibility will be generally admitted, yet it is not proper for science to play with possibilities. It demands facts. Can we adduce them here?

I believe we can, only we must not expect the soul-life of a plant to be shown to us. In the case of man and the lower animals, we content ourselves with inferring analogous inner processes from the analogy of physical vital processes. Why not make the same inference here? For after all, a convincing proof cannot be given in the former case either. A man cannot be forced by logic to grant the existence of psychical life to infusoria, worms, frogs, and rabbits, if he regards the analogical conclusion as too uncertain. But if he admits this mode of inference without reserve in the latter case, and we all do it, there is no reason for excluding it in the case of plants. For plants manifestly show a far-reaching analogy with animals in visible vital processes: in nutrition, growth, cellular structure of elementary forms, reproduction by means of forms which separate from the parent organism. Development and death are common to both plants and animals. Language, too, universally speaks of life and death in plants as well as in animals. Why should there not be a correspondence between the visible and the invisible processes? To deny that there is, would, to say the least, require some proof. Indeed, we might say with Fechner: as a house is meant for an inhabitant, so a living body is meant for a soul. There is something strange in the unreasonable demand that we regard an animal body, a horse or a dog, as a soulless automaton, a view which is attributed to the Cartesians. Nay, such a body without a soul would strike us as something ghastly and full of terror. And shall we regard it as self-evident that plants are mere empty casings?

The reply is heard: That is merely a vague and trifling analogy. If so, let some one point out what is wanting in the analogy that would justify the inference of an inner life. With what functions, with what marks that are lacking in plants, is inner life connected?—Reference is made to the

---

ness, to the protista, on the ground of their movements : reactionary movements following stimuli are signs of the same psychical concomitants that are experienced in the most developed form in ourselves.

absence of a *nervous system* and *a brain.* Fechner answers:
Neither have the lowest animals a nervous system. Besides, the syllogism is worthless. It is formulated on the
plan : Horses, dogs, and cats have legs, without which they
cannot move ; therefore creatures without legs cannot
move. Snakes and worms contradict the syllogism. If
these can move without legs, plants may have psychical life
without nerves.

But, says the doubter, plants lack the power of spontaneous movement which we observe in all animals. Really ?
Does not the plant turn its buds and leaves to the light,
does it not send its roots where it finds nourishment, and
its tendrils where it finds support ? Does it not close up
its petals at night or when it rains, and does it not open
them in sunshine ? Do not many plant-germs move freely
about in water, whereas animals in the first stages of em-
bryonic development betray nothing of the power of free
locomotion possessed by the developed animals ?—But, the
doubter replies, these are not spontaneous movements, but
mechanically-conditioned reactions upon physical stimuli.
—Well, did we not agree in the last section to regard all
processes in the animal body as purely physically conditioned ? Do not physiologists and materialistic philosophers insist upon this very fact, that the spontaneous
movements of animals are not explained by means of sensations and feelings, but as physically-conditioned reactions
of a given body upon given stimuli ?

To be sure, there are differences between animals and
plants, and these differences we do not wish to deny;
they become conspicuous enough in the higher stages of
development. Besides the difference in metabolism, a
difference which Wundt emphasizes is particularly marked:
in the growth of the plant the principle of homogeneity
and co-ordination of the elementary organisms prevails,
while in the animal world the principle of differentiation
obtains. (*System der Philosophie,* p. 508.) Fechner's
statement is evidently in line with this : The plant
develops outwardly ; it pushes to the surface ; with its
thousand leaves and buds it seeks the approach to light
and air, while the trunk or stem lignifies on the inside or

becomes hollow, and is preserved only in so far as it is needed for support. The animal, on the other hand, shuts out the external world by means of skin and hair, scales and covering, and develops inwardly, where the many vital functions and organs are unfolded. Contact with the external world is confined to a few places, and the whole body is concentrated and centralized in a narrow space,— in the nervous system.

But difference is not an argument against psychism as such. It may be conceived as indicating a difference in inner life also, it may mean that plants possess a peculiar inclination to receptivity and decentralized extensity, whereas the psychical life of the animal shows more spontaneity and centralized intensity. Fechner finds the same difference between animals and plants that exists between the psychical life of man and woman, only that it is infinitely intensified and deepened on the higher stage. It does not matter what we think, for in reality all endeavors to infer the inner life of plants from their external appearances are at best feeble attempts. And it must be remembered that we do not fare better with the interpretation of the psychical life of animals, particularly of the lower animals. When it comes to that, we know very little about the inner experiences of a jelly-fish, or the feelings of a caterpillar or butterfly. But Fechner is, in my opinion, perfectly right when he says that the same reasons which induce us to infer an inner life, which we do not see, from a bodily life, which we do see, hold for all organic life, for plants as well as animals. Although it is usually held : *Probatio incumbit affirmanti,* one feels inclined to say here : The burden of proof rests on him who denies the validity of the analogical syllogism. He must show why it is not valid here, otherwise his negation is arbitrary.*

_____

* How arbitrary the discussion of this question is, is clearly seen in the case of W. Volkmann (*Lehrbuch der Psychologie,* i. 99). He considers the extension of psychism to plant-life as "inexpedient." Even though certain remote analogies with the instinctive movements of animals cannot be denied to plants, still the uncertainty of the question admonishes us "rather to disregard the remote analogies than to give up our precise definition of the soul." As though it were a matter of moment, at all events to save the "definition of the soul," which was intended by Herbartian psychology to

The further question arises at the conclusion of this discussion : Have we reached the end, is the parallelism between physical and psychical processes limited to the organic world ?   Or is there any meaning in the statement of the philosophers mentioned before, that it holds universally ; that wherever physical processes are given they point to an inner being ?

Let me suggest a few facts which may at least show that the question is not as absurd as at first sight it seems to popular thought.   The organic and inorganic bodies form, not two separate worlds, but a unitary whole in constant interaction.   There is no difference in substance ; organic bodies are composed of the same ingredients of which inorganic bodies consist.   The carbon, nitrogen, hydrogen, and oxygen of which a plant or animal body consists are identical with the substances found in inorganic constructions.   Matter, therefore, is capable of organization, and this organization is a state of unstable equilibrium, in which the particles of matter continually change, the form remaining the same.   Organic bodies constantly give off and take up matter.   After a certain space of time, a complete change of matter has taken place ; new elements now appear as the bearers of organic and psychical life.—Furthermore, new animal and plant bodies are constantly arising.   A few handfuls of grain placed in the earth yield a bushel of wheat ; a pair of mice left alone with the wheat soon change it into hundreds of living and feeling animal bodies with souls.   Whence came these souls ?   Did they pre-exist somewhere, and did they suddenly pass into the bodies prepared for them ?   Or, if this conception repels the natural scientist, did they arise by the division of the parent soul ?   What a strange and unintelligible notion !

And how did soul-life originate to begin with ?   Modern biology is forced to the assumption that organic life had a beginning on earth, and that the first creations arose from inorganic matter, spontaneously, through parentless genera-

embrace " only man and the most highly-organized animals," rather than to extend the definition to meet the facts.   Neither the human nor the animal mind would suffer should we attribute soul to plants.   An inadequate definition alone would suffer.

tion. Whence did psychical life arise? Is the first feeling in the first protoplasmic particle something absolutely new, something that did not exist before in any form, of which not the slightest trace was to be found before? That, of course, would be an absolute "world-riddle"; it would mean a creation out of nothing, and would baffle the natural scientist as much as if he were expected to believe that the protoplasmic particle itself was created out of nothing. But why does he not reject the inconceivable in the former case just as he does in the latter? He assumes that organic bodies arise from pre-existing elements. Entering into new and more complicated combinations, these bodies are enabled to perform new and astonishing functions. Why does he not make the same natural assumption in this case as well, and say that an inner life was already present in germ in the elements, and that it developed into higher forms? Indeed, hylozoism is a conception which almost irresistibly forces itself upon modern biology. We ought not to blame Haeckel for having the courage to accept it as a necessary presupposition. Even Büchner has accepted it; he assumes "that not merely physical but mental forces dwell in matter, and that these manifest themselves whenever the necessary conditions concur" (p. 66).

Still, the objection is urged: Is it not inconceivable that lifeless, rigid matter should be the bearer of psychical life? And is not the very condition absent here, from which alone our previous discussion inferred an inner life, namely, an analogy between physical processes and those of our own body? Do we not miss here all spontaneous activity, all activity coming from within?

It seems to me that we are ourselves responsible for this inconceivability, because we have formed an arbitrary conception of matter. Having once defined matter as an aggregate of atoms, of absolutely hard and rigid little blocks that are moved without being determined from within, by pressure and impact only, we naturally find it inconceivable that matter should be determined from within and should move by inner impulses. But what compels us to form such a concept? Surely not the facts.

They show us none of those absolutely rigid, inert, passive atoms, awaiting an impact from without. On the contrary, they show us parts of matter with spontaneous activity issuing from within. This activity is not necessarily isolated; it is related to its environment. A drop of water falls to the ground. What pushes or pulls it? Its weight or the law of gravitation? That, however, is nothing but the subsequent formulation of its behavior. In falling, it assumes the shape of a sphere. What compels the parts to arrange themselves in such a way? It falls upon a stone and runs over the surface or penetrates the infinitesimal crevices of its structure. Is it forced to do this from without? Its temperature falls below the freezing-point: the parts of our drop are arranged in the form of a pretty ice-flower. Are they pushed into this form by some external force? We see nothing of the kind; they arrange themselves entirely spontaneously into that form, and just as spontaneously return to the liquid condition when the temperature rises. Or, they come in contact with a piece of iron; this is soon covered with a yellow rust: its elements have freed themselves from their previous combination, and unite with the oxygen and hydrogen of the water to form a new compound, hydroxide. Here, too, nothing whatever is seen of an external compulsive force. Chemists speak of attraction, a term with which physicists, too, have been familiar since Newton's day. Thus the facts, as it were, extort recognition, at least a verbal recognition, even from the reluctant and the dissenting.

Spontaneous activity everywhere! Your inert, rigid matter, movable only by impact, is a phantom that owes its existence, not to observation, but to conceptual speculation. It comes from the Aristotelian-scholastic philosophy, which, after having completely separated all force or form from matter, left the latter behind as something absolutely passive. Descartes gets it from this source; it was a concept convenient to his purely mathematical conception of physics: Matter is without all inner determination, pure *res extensa*, whose only quality is extension. Modern natural science has utterly discarded the idea of such absolutely dead and rigid bodies. Its molecules and atoms are forms of the greatest inner complexity and mobility. Hundreds and thousands of atoms are united in the molecule into a system that preserves a more or less stable equilibrium by the mutual interaction of its parts, and at the same time is quickened by other movements—by such as are felt by us as light and heat, and others, which appear in electrical processes. And this system, in turn, is in constant interaction with its immediate surroundings as well as with the remotest system of fixed stars. Is it then absurd to ask whether we have, corresponding to this wonderful play of physical forces and movements, a system of inner processes, analogous to that which accompanies the working of the parts in the organic body? May not attraction and repulsion, of which physics and chemistry speak, be more than mere words; is there not an element of truth in the speculation of old Empedocles that love and hate form the motive forces in all things? Certainly not love and hatred as men and animals experience them, but something at bottom similar to their feelings, an impulsive action of some kind.

Philosophers have always shown a weakness for this thought, and that too, not merely fantastic dreamers, but such cautious thinkers as Spinoza and Leibniz, Fechner and Lotze, and, among contemporaries, Wundt; all of them, men who cannot be accused of being antagonistic to a natural-scientific or mechanical conception of things. It is worthy of notice that this thought is beginning to find acceptance even among natural scientists. Permit me to offer a few examples.

In his thoughtful treatise on the limits of natural scientific knowledge (reprinted in the appendix to the work, *Die mechanisch-physiologische Theorie der Abstammungslehre*, 1884), the botanist C. v. Naegeli positively embraces the theory of panpsychism. He holds that, just as there is no absolute chasm between organic and inorganic matter, there is none between animate and inanimate bodies. The natural scientist must assume that that which appears in the more complicated forms is contained in germ in the elements. The analogy existing between physical phenomena makes it necessary to assume the presence of inner processes. "Sensation is clearly connected with the reflex actions of higher animals. We are obliged to concede it to the other animals also, and we have no grounds for denying it to plants and inorganic bodies. The sensation arouses in us a condition of comfort and discomfort. In general, the feeling of pleasure arises when the natural impulses are satisfied, the feeling of pain, when they are not satisfied. Since all material processes are composed of movements of molecules and elementary atoms, pleasure and pain must have its seat in these particles. Sensation is a property of the albuminous molecules; and if it belongs to these, we are obliged to concede it to the other substances also. If the molecules possess anything even remotely akin to sensation, they must have a feeling of comfort when they can obey the law of attraction or repulsion, the law of their own inclination or aversion; a feeling of discomfort, however, when they are compelled to make contrary movements. Thus the same mental thread runs through all material phenomena. The human mind is nothing but the highest development on our earth of the mental processes which universally animate and move nature."

Fr. Zöllner expresses the same thought. In a treatise on the general properties of matter (in his work, *Ueber die Natur der Kometen,* 3d edition, pp. 105 ff.) he discusses the preconditions essential to an understanding of nature. He finds that sensations offer us the alternative "either forever to forego the possibility of understanding nature, or hypothetically to increase the general properties of matter by adding such a one as will bring the simplest and most elementary occurrences in nature under a process of sensation uniformly connected with them." He finds that we restrict the faculty of sensation to more highly-organized matter, merely because the material for our induction is by far too insufficient. "If by virtue of more finely-developed sense-organs we were able to observe the molecular movements of organized groups of a crystal which has met with violent injury at some point, we should probably reject our judgment as uncertain, or at least as very hypothetical, that its movements occur absolutely without simultaneously arousing sensations." He amplifies this thought as follows:

"All acts of natural beings are determined by the feelings of pleasure and pain, and in such a way that the movements within a distinct field of phenomena seem to pursue the unconscious purpose of reducing the amount of pain to a minimum." In all material processes, either potential energy is transformed into active energy, or the reverse occurs. If we assume that the former occurrence is connected with pleasure, the latter with pain, then a diminution of pain would take place whenever the amount of collisions in a system in motion is reduced to a minimum. And the tendency would have to be in that direction, if feelings are to have practical significance.

The circumstance which impels us to this view from the natural-scientific side is the fact that we cannot tear the organic and inorganic worlds apart; they form one unitary whole. Since biology has rejected vital force as a special principle alongside of physical forces in organic bodies, life had to be assigned to the elementary parts of which the organism consists. There is now no longer any fundamental difference between the two forms of the corporeal world. Ultimately the same forces act in inorganic as well as in organic bodies, only in the latter case they appear in extremely peculiar and intricate combinations. Nor is there any difference in the form of the activity : all bodies are moved by inner forces, but on occasion of an external stimulus. In the case of organic bodies, we are in the habit of emphasizing the inner force, on account of the difference that obtains between the stimulus and the effect, while in the case of inorganic bodies we emphasize the external cause. But there is no essential difference. When the excitation of the auditory nerve causes an animal to start up, the act is as much a mechanical effect of purely physical causes as when a billiard-ball in motion sets another in motion by impact. If, now, the movements are accompanied by sensations in the one case, no reason can be seen why they should not be, in the other.

Indeed, an old prejudice simply hinders many physicists from seeing this. Du Bois-Reymond most emphatically rejects the notion of vital force : the particles of matter in the organisms have no new forces; the same forces are active here that are active elsewhere. Hence "the division between the so-called organic and inorganic worlds is wholly arbitrary. Those who try to uphold it, who present the erroneous doctrine of vital force, under whatever form or deceptive guise it may be,—such men, let them rest assured of it, have never advanced to the limits of our knowledge." * It seems to me, we shall not wrong the celebrated physiologist, if we maintain that the limits of our knowledge of nature are not to be found even where he has set them with his *ignorabimus*. If he is right in his assertion that no new forces are added in the living body, he is not right in saying that an absolutely new, hitherto unheard-of element enters into existence with the first sensation of an animal body.

In addition to these natural-philosophical reflections other reasons impel us nowadays to the theory of panpsychism, namely, the epistemological considerations which have begun gradually to undermine the old naïve realism even among the physicists. If bodies are phenomena, the representations of reality in our sensibility, which do not as such possess absolute but relative existence, the question arises, What is that which appears, in itself? Or does it possess relative existence only? Is the corporeal world a pure phantasmagoria in my consciousness? No one has ever believed or will ever believe that. Hence, that which appears to us as a body must be something in and for itself. What is it in itself? That we cannot know, replies Kant. But in *one* respect at least we know it: everybody knows something about himself; he knows what he is; he knows, besides, that he appears to others and to himself as an organic body; he knows himself as a feeling, willing, sensible, thinking being. And this it is that he calls his real self, and from this standpoint he interprets the world outside of himself: analogous phenomena point to analogous inner being. To every body which, like his, appears as a relatively complete system of phenomena and activities, he ascribes a relatively complete inner life like his own. We all attribute soul to

* Du Bois-Reymond, *Reden*, II. 17.

man and to animals. The philosopher says that there is
no reason for stopping here, nay, no possibility of it; for
the assertion that certain objects are merely bodies leads
to the untenable theory of illusionism. At the same
time, he has the courage to express the parodox: All
bodies are animated: *omnia, quamvis diversis gradibus, ani-*
mata. A plant is a living being, hence a psycho-physical
system; a cell is, in a certain sense, an independent living
being, hence the same holds true of it; a molecule is a
relatively complete system of corporeal phenomena, a
plurality of parts most intimately correlated, and inter-
acting in manifold ways, and, at the same time, a whole
related to its surroundings. This system of bodily processes will have to be interpreted as pointing to a system
of inner processes. We cannot imagine this inner world
in concreto, but we construct it graphically in outline as
coextensive with the physical world.

I shall touch upon another point in this place, and shall
approach it from another side later on. Is there a higher,
more comprehensive psychical life than that which we experience, just as there is a lower one? Our body embraces the cells as elementary organisms. We assume
that in the same way our psychical life embraces the
inner life of the elementary forms, embracing in it their
conscious and unconscious elements. Our body again is
itself part of a higher unity, a member of the total life of
our planet, and together with the latter, articulated with a
more comprehensive cosmical system, and ultimately articulated with the All. Is our psychical life also articulated
with a higher unity, a more comprehensive system of consciousness? Are the separate heavenly bodies, to start
with, bearers of a unified inner life? Are the stars, is the
earth an animated being? The poets speak of the earth-
spirit; is that more than a poetic metaphor? The Greek
philosophers, among them Plato and Aristotle, speak of
astral spirits; is that more than the last reflection of a
dream of childish fancy? *

---

* It seems that there is a historical connection between the Earth-
spirit in Goethe's powerful drama, which embraces heaven, earth, and the
lower world, and the planet-souls of Greek philosophy. It is brought

It would be presumptuous foolishness to treat of these subjects in dogmatic definitions and arguments. Still, it seems to me, a negative dogmatism is equally out of place. To him who knows the earth solely from his globe as a pasteboard sphere, or from his book as a huge lump with a fiery, liquid interior and a thin rigid crust,—to him, of course, the question itself will seem ridiculous and absurd. On the other hand, he who lives in the real world himself, will not, if he is at all endowed with a little imagination, find it so difficult to conceive the world as a large animated being. Fechner's whole soul is given to that thought. With ever-changing expressions he urges his contemporaries, at last to awake from their sleep and to contemplate objects with a clear eye. Does not the earth really live a universal life ? Are not all its parts, the liquid interior and the firm crust, the ocean and the atmosphere, comprehended into a great whole whose parts interact in manifold ways and yet in harmony ? Ebb and flow, day and night, summer and winter, are they not life-rhythms, similar to those which the individual life experiences, or rather, do not animals and plants with their little rhythmical vital processes take part in the great life of the earth ? Is not the life of the earth mirrored in their sleep and waking, their bloom and withering, their origin and decay ? Forsooth, the earth is not merely a point of support, on which living beings, like grains on the barn-floor, accidentally meet each other, but the womb from which they proceed. The animal and plant worlds are products of the earth, they remain members and organs of its life as much as cells are members and organs of the body. The geologist interprets the history of the earth from the traces of the organic beings which it produced in every epoch ; the geographer describes the earth by means of the most characteristic living forms in every zone. These determine the impression which the

---

about by the fantastic cosmological speculations of natural philosophers of the sixteenth century like Paracelsus and Agrippa of Nettesheim from whom Goethe-Faust gets the astral spirits and the entire magical-spiritualistic conception of nature, or with whom he shares these views as a contemporary.

earth makes on the mind, and in a considerable measure
also determine its very shape. Their life is a partial process of the total life; matter runs in a continuous stream
through the organic bodies. Why should not the being
which produces all living and animated beings and harbors
them as parts of its life, itself be alive and animated?

Of course, such reflections will make little impression
on one whose mind is not open to the inner life of things.
He will say: Show me the brain and the nerves of
the earth, and I will believe in its soul. Indeed? If the
earth-body had a particular brain of its own besides all
animal brains, and eyes and ears, and a heart and stomach,
and arms and legs, and skin and hair, then would you take
it for an animate being? But consider what an absurd
thing such an earth would be. An animal needs a mouth
and a stomach; the earth as a whole does not need them,
for it does not need to take up substances from without. An animal needs eyes and ears, in order to pursue its
prey and to escape its pursuers; but the earth neither pursues nor is pursued. The animal needs a brain and nerves
in order to adapt its movements to its environment; the
earth finds its way through the universe without such help.

But, you say, its motion is apparently purely physically
conditioned; it obeys the law of gravitation with uniform
periodicity. What else should it do? What motion would
be more fitted to obtain for it what it needs: light and
heat in different amounts and in rhythmical periods, in
order to develop and to mature the life peculiar to it? Or
ought it to wander hither and thither, and at times lie idle
like an animal? Please do not ask it to do what is contrary to its nature and cosmical position. It surely has
diversified and irregular movements enough on its surface,
—movements occurring in air and water, in plant and animal
bodies. It has regulated its relations to the external world
in the most beautiful and becoming manner. Or does the
uniformity of movement as such exclude the hypothesis
that that which is moved is the bearer of states of consciousness? If so, there is no such thing as an animated
body for our physiologists, and especially not for the materialistic philosophers among them, for do they not strenu-

ously insist that all vital processes must be reduced to the uniform movements of the smallest particles?

I shall forego any further elaboration of this matter. Whoever wishes to pursue the subject will find in Fechner's *Zend-Avesta* a most helpful guide. In ever-changing figures he represents to the reader the earth as a unitary being, in which, as in every organic body, plurality and unity inter- penetrate and condition each other. "The earth is a crea- ture combined into a unitary whole in form and substance, in purpose and effect, self-sufficient in its individuality, complete in its cycles, relatively independent of other sim- ilar but not identical creatures, evolving itself out of itself under the stimulus and co-determination of an external world, producing out of its own fulness and creative power an inexhaustible manifoldness of effects now recurring reg- ularly, now baffling calculation, developing a system of inner freedom in its passage through external necessity, changing in particulars but permanent as a whole, like our body. Nay, it is unspeakably more : it is that complete All of which our body is but a member, it is that permanent all of which our body is but a transitory part, it is to it what the whole tree is to a single twig, a permanent body to a perishable, small organ." (*Zend-Avesta*, I. 179.)

Fechner, of course, is fully aware of the fact that these thoughts are not matters of scientific knowledge. We can- not explain the organic life of a planet like that of a plaqt, or describe its inner life like that of a man. Such expositions are but indefinite ideal conceptions, which we can never hope exactly to define or to supply with a con- crete content. This is no place for real scientific work. Still, they have their value : they remind us that the astro- nomical-physical speculation is not the final and highest view of things in general, even though it is the highest con- ception which we can reach in scientific work. And in a certain sense, they are suited to bridge over the chasm between scientific and religious views. For, if the heavenly bodies as such are bearers of a unified psychical life, in which the psychical life of all partial beings is contained as a factor, we shall have to go a step farther and regard them in turn as members of a larger whole, of a cosmical,

universal life. The old conception of a world-soul is the
natural keystone of this entire cosmology. Every corporeal system is the bearer or body of an inner life ; the universal system is the body or phenomenon of God. It is
true, our knowledge does not grasp him : faith determines
his essence with objective symbols. Still, this view destroys the negative dogmatism of a purely physical view of
the world.

Kant had the same object in view. By explaining
nature as a phenomenon, he wished to clear the way for a
belief in a Supreme Being which manifests itself in nature.
But he ignored the intervening stages, he scorned to start
out from the given world. The sharp distinction which he
makes between phenomenon and thing-in-itself completely
demolishes the bridge between knowledge and faith. Fechner rebuilds it; he proceeds from the nearest and best
known, from the I and its two aspects, soul and body, and
advances steadily to the highest and most remote.

These are the consequences to which the parallelistic
theory of the relation between the physical and the psychical is led. And thus, the materialistic view is overcome,
—overcome, it is true, not in the sense of being altogether
false and groundless, for it is surely not that. Its demand
that everything that exists be explained physically is perfectly well founded, and this demand the view presented
by us fully satisfies. The physicist must still assume the
universe to be a physical nexus embracing the whole of
reality. Materialism, however, is vanquished, in so far as
it now appears to us as a one-sided view of existence that
can and must be supplemented. All corporeal reality
absolutely and universally points to an inner world like
the one which we experience in ourselves. And we will add:
The nature of reality, as it exists in and for itself, manifests itself in the inner world, which, to tell the truth, is
immediately given to us only at one point, in self-consciousness. Outside of that, we reach it by interpretation,
which is always uncertain, and beyond the animal world
we must depend on analogy and on an idealistic symbolism. The corporeal world is at bottom but an accidental

concept, an inadequate representation of existence in our
sensibility.

This is the fundamental conception of *Idealism.* From
the times of Plato to the present, it has been universally
characterized by the two propositions : The corporeal world
is phenomenal; that which appears in it is something akin
to our own inner life.

Why is it that this view, which is so acceptable to philosophers, appears so strange and incredible to popular
thought?

The most immediate reason is, without doubt, that popular thought is governed by sense-perception. That alone
is real which is seen : what is not seen does not exist. Such
is the pattern according to which all its conclusions are
drawn. The same is true in the case at hand. We see
the outside : the inside we do not see; we must add it
in thought. Wherever this inference is forced upon us by
the facts, we make it; but wherever mere abstract considerations invite us to draw the conclusion, popular thought
soon drops the thread. Popular thought instinctively
rejects the demand that it pass in thought beyond what is
given to that which the facts themselves suggest, as a fantastical presumption, disturbing its peace.

In addition to this inertia of thought, there are positive
obstacles which block the way to the idealistic view.
These are, above all, false ideas of the nature and metaphysical constitution of psychical life. The following two
sections will attempt to remove them.

**6. The Nature of the Soul. Intellectualistic and Volunta-
ristic Psychology. The Unconscious.**

The popular conception of the nature of mind is deficient in two respects. It has a false idea (1) of the *metaphysical constitution of the soul,* (2) of the *phenomenological
content* of soul-life. I shall consider the second point first.

Two kinds of psychical processes are to be found in
self-consciousness: ideas and volitions. Accordingly, we
ascribe to soul two phases, *intelligence* and *will.* As manifestations of intelligence we consider: sensation, percep-

tion, presentation, and thinking; as manifestations of will: striving, impulse, desire, willing, and action, with their accompanying emotions.

In German psychology, the old dichotomy has been replaced by a trichotomy, thinking, feeling, and willing, which is not, as I think, favorable to a correct understanding of psychic phenomena. This is not the place for a detailed discussion of the subject; I simply remark that it is impossible to separate feeling and willing from each other. On a primitive stage of development they are one: there is no feeling that is not at the same time a will-impulse, and no volition that is not felt in consciousness as feeling. Only on the highest stage of psychical life, in man, does a partial separation of feeling from willing occur. The æsthetical feelings are almost entirely devoid of will-impulses, that is, pure emotions without impulse. And to a certain extent, the will is determined without the presence of feeling: the rational will can determine its activity by means of ideas of purpose, without and in opposition to sensuous impulses.

If we adhere in principle to the dichotomy, the further question arises: What is the relation between the two sides of psychical life? Are both of them original, or is one of them to be regarded as the primary and radical activity, to which the other attaches itself as a secondary development? Popular thought inclines to the conception that presentation is the first and really characteristic function of the soul, while feeling and desire appear as an incidental and secondary element, which occurs in some cases as a secondary effect of the presentative process. Whatever presentation characterizes as good or bad, the will sets out to desire or to avoid. Psychology, too, frequently holds this conception, which I shall call the *intellectualistic* view. Herbart carried it out systematically. His psychology is an attempt to derive all states of consciousness from ideas and their relations. Ideas are, in his opinion, the original elements of mind; they persist, attract and repel each other, obstruct each other and combine like the elements of the corporeal world. It is the province of psychology, he believes, to formulate the laws governing the action of these ideas, and to explain the other processes by means of them.

Of late, psychology tends more and more to consider will as the primary and constitutive function of mind; intelligence, on the other hand, as a secondary evolution. Schopenhauer is the leader of this movement. He sees in will the fundamental function of the mind, which cannot be derived from presentation, but originally arises without presentation or intelligence, as a blind craving or impulse; only as development advances, does it learn to use intelligence as its instrument.*

I have no doubt whatever that Schopenhauer with his wonderful power of clear and penetrative intuition is a better guide here than Herbart with his piercing acuteness, bent upon conceptual analysis and synthesis. Only so long as we confine our attention to the processes in the developed human consciousness, can it appear as though presentation were the real content of consciousness, which

---

* Schopenhauer discusses this fundamental dogma of his philosophy in the second book of his main work : it is the ingenious intuition of his youth. All his writings aim to apply the principle to all the fields of reality. A very clear exposition of the thought is given in the little treatise on *The Will in Nature.* Modern psychology, which is more partial to biological views than its predecessor, is gradually approximating Schopenhauer's view. In this connection, Wundt deserves special mention. Like Schopenhauer, he regards the original activity of the soul as impulse, and everywhere emphasizes the intimate connection between psychical processes (including presentation) and will.—An acute discussion of the mental life of animals from the same point of view is found in G. H. Schneider's work, *Der thierische Wille* (1880). We may also point out that, in a certain sense, Schopenhauer's theorem of the primacy of the will is anticipated by Kant's doctrine of the primacy of practical reason. It is the reaction against the view which overrated intellect, science, and theoretical culture, a view that had dominated modern times since the epoch of the so-called restoration of the sciences. To this great reaction, which begins with Rousseau and culminates in Romanticism as the reaction against Enlightenment, both Kant and Schopenhauer belong. The latter becomes the exponent of the metaphysics of Romanticism by his doctrine of the absolute irrationality of the world-principle.—We may also suggest that the great changes in theology, or in the conception of the essence of religion, are most intimately connected with this reaction. Rational theology or the speculative philosophy of religion and intellectualistic psychology belong together, like positivistic theology and voluntaristic psychology. The recent change of front in theology towards Positivism is connected with the voluntaristic psychology of our times.

is only occasionally interrupted by emotions and volitions. When we turn our attention to the whole living and animated world, it soon becomes evident how secondary is the part of intelligence by the side of the will.

Within the lower animal world, no one will be apt to regard the functions of the presentative side as forming the essential content of consciousness. We cannot speak of intelligence at all in the lowest forms of animal life. A jelly-fish, a polyp, or an infusory, certainly does not present anything to itself or think. It knows nothing of itself or of the external world. Blind craving determines its vital activities : scarcely otherwise than blind forces determine motion in the inorganic world. As the water-drop falls, that is, moves towards its goal, the earth's centre of gravity, by the shortest road and with definite velocity, without knowing anything about the earth and the law of gravitation, or, as its parts group themselves according to a definite pattern in crystallization, without an idea of the geometric law ; so the living being acts and moves, almost with the same certainty, towards its goal,—the preservation of individual life and of the species. In neither case is the objective aim at the same time a subjective purpose. The animal knows nothing about itself and its life-conditions; nor does it know anything about its offspring and species. Impulses and emotions are the inner concomitants of vital processes, not foresight of aims and insight into means.

Gradually, in the progressive series of animal life, intelligence is grafted upon the will. As the organism and its functions become more complicated, as the relations to its surroundings multiply, sense-organs and a nervous system come into existence, and as their inner side we assume sensation and perception. Instinctive movements are then subjected to the guiding influence of perception. True, the aim is not foreseen, nor is the activity recognized and selected as a means. The bee knows nothing of the brood and of winter, and has no insight into the processes of nutrition; she is guided in all her activity, in her search for blossoms, the construction of her cells, the feeding of her offspring, by perceptions and traces of recollection, which are represented physiologically as nervous processes and dispositions. In higher animals, memory is evolved with brain, which first makes possible a primitive presentative life. Not only the perception of the present, but also the presentation of the past and the future now exerts an influence on volition; and, with this, deliberation and choice ensue.

In man, at last, thinking is evolved: the ability to operate with abstract ideas. While the animal consciousness does not, as far as we can make out, rise above concrete associations, man, with the help of language, in which the whole race objectifies its thought and renders it communicable, gains such mastery over perception that he separates himself from it as a self, and opposes it to himself as an object. Self-consciousness and objective consciousness of the universe are correlatives. At the same time, he surveys his life as a whole with an enlarged consciousness, and in a measure determines its content by means of thoughts, guiding ends, and principles. The will appears here as saturated with intelligence; a rational will has been evolved from animal impulses.

Hence, if we survey the development as a whole, we can say: The will is the original and, in a certain sense, constant factor of soul-life; at the end of the series, we find it directed towards the same great aims as at the beginning— preservation and evolution of individual life and of the species. Intelligence is the secondary and variable factor, which in the course of development is imparted to will as an organ.

The same relation between will and intelligence is observed in the evolution of the individual, which obeys the law of modern biology that the ontogenetic development repeats the phylogenetic one. Every human being enters the world as a blind will without intellect. The nursling is all will; forceful impulses express themselves in violent movements; the acts are accompanied by vivid organic feelings; but the presentative side is still altogether wanting: the movements are blind reflexes and instinctive movements. But soon intelligence unfolds itself, beginning with the exercise of the senses. The touch sense begins to act; it first assumes the guidance of movements; tactile sensations produce certain movements of the head, then also of the hand; and soon the other senses follow. With memory and recollection in the form of recognition, presentation begins to evolve; at last speech and thinking arise, and this gradually becomes the highest, regulative principle of action. Hence here, too, will is the primitive, radical function, intelligence the instrument grafted upon it in the course of life.

Schopenhauer finds his proposition confirmed by a psychological investigation of the developed human soul. The decisive fact is that it is the will and not the understanding which gives to life its purpose. It is the business of the understanding to discover the ways and means to the end at which the will aims. Every living being manifests itself as a concrete will, determined in such and such a way, directed towards such and such a life, towards such and such a series of developments and activities. An eagle or a lion is will directed towards this particular kind of life: he desires it absolutely, not because of a knowledge of its worth. Likewise man: he, too, desires to live a specific life absolutely, not because of a preceding knowledge of its worth. As a concrete will, determined by his descent from this particular people and this particular family, he enters into existence. Knowing nothing of life and its content, this germinal will keeps on generating new impulses; they follow each other like the impulses of a plant: the impulse to walk, to climb, to speak, to play with horses and soldiers, or with dolls and clothes, to build or to cook, to hear and to tell stories, and to see and to understand things. Then at last, at the end of boyhood, the love for the other sex suddenly breaks out as a new unheard-of impulse, and for a time constitutes the fundamental theme of inner life. Gradually the impulses of manhood force themselves into the foreground: work and acquisition, position and fame for himself and his children, become the great topics of a man's life, until finally, involution begins and death closes the account. This entire evolution is not effected by the activity of the foreseeing understanding; no one first plans his course of life and his development, and then carries out his plan after the understanding has

recognized its excellence; but he experiences things and
is himself surprised how it all comes about. It is true, in a
sense, man anticipates his life and his ideas. The boy or
youth is inspired with an ideal, with a mission, which helps
to determine his development and activity. The ideal,
however, is not a product of the understanding, but of the
will which contemplates itself in its ideal. The understanding fashions no ideals, nor has it any feeling for
ideals; it knows only the categories: real and unreal;
worthy and unworthy are categories of the will. He whose
will is not susceptible to the ideal is not influenced by his
idea, be it ever so clear. The idea will act only on him, the
fundamental tendency of whose will is in harmony with his
ideal.

The primacy of the will, which is shown by the entire
content of man's life, is also revealed at every stage of
intellectual life. Everywhere the understanding is an instrument in the service of the will and surveys the environment in order to discover how the will may reach its
end in the best and easiest manner. Interest, that is will,
universally manifests itself as the predominant element in
the world of ideas and its movements. This is a favorite
point in Schopenhauer's reflections. What is it that constantly occupies the understanding of the multitude? The
great business of espying advantages and warding off dis-
advantages. Purely theoretical interest is foreign and unknown to them. Where the will is not concerned, the
understanding is at a loss what to do; they are "bored."
Flying from tedium, they seek excitement for the will in
society; gossip and calumny serve their purpose, and
when that topic is exhausted, gaming must come to their
rescue and fill out the idle hours with such trifling excite-
ments for the will as are provided by the shifting chances
of gain and loss. Only in a few men does the intellect at
times free itself from the dominion of the will, and in isolated cases we observe the strange phenomenon that the
theoretical interest in objects altogether forces the practical interest into the background: this is what makes the
genius. Hence geniuses seem to the multitude to be
eccentric or insane; for what is insanity but not to see or

to ignore things that everybody else sees and seeks, and
to observe, instead, other things which the world does not
see ?

It is true, Schopenhauer's eloquence exaggerates the
truth, and he is sensible of it when he says elsewhere that
theoretical interest is not wholly wanting in any man; indeed, the interest in metaphysics, religious or philosophical, is essential to man.   Still, he is undoubtedly right in
holding that even ideas invariably receive their impetus
and direction from the will.   This is universally true.   The
will governs perception by determining the attention; it
chooses among the stimuli which indiscriminately strike
the senses and arouse sensations.   But that only enters
consciousness, or at least mainly that, which stands in
friendly or hostile relation to our purposes or problems.
The will governs the memory.   We forget what does not
concern us; we remember what is of lasting importance to
the will.   The will governs the course of our ideas; our
thoughts constantly gravitate towards the momentary centre of gravity of our interests; we think of what is near
and dear to us, or hateful and threatening.   The will constantly influences the judgment; it determines the weight
and importance of things and occurrences, reasons and
proofs.   In practical affairs, all this is obvious: as soon as
interest or inclination has decided, reasons are straightway
discovered which justify the decision.   But the will also
constantly exerts its influence on the theoretical judgment.
Think of the interpretation of history !   There is no important event of which there are not as many views and
expositions as there are parties to consider it.   Take the
history of the Reformation or of the French Revolution !
Nay, even Cæsar and Pericles are still subject to this law !
This shows what a decisive influence the will exerts on
the construction of one's entire conception of the world.   It
may be said, the will is the architect who determines the
form and style of the building; the intelligence simply
executes the plan.   Religions very clearly exemplify this
truth.   They universally mirror the will which creates
them ; the deepest disposition of a people is objectified in
the nature and will of its gods or its God.   In philosophy,

too, this circumstance reveals itself. I shall return to this subject later on.

This, then, is the conception of soul-life to which we are carried by biological and psychological and historical considerations. The original fact of every soul-life is a concrete, definitely-determined will. The original form of the will is the impulse, whose bodily expression is an organic system with active tendencies. In consciousness, the impulse is felt as a craving, on a higher stage as desire for a definite exercise of life. If the craving or desire is satisfied, a feeling of satisfaction arises, otherwise a feeling of discomfort; in pleasurable and painful feelings, the will becomes aware of itself, of its direction and of its momentary condition, as well as of its relation to its environment. Out of feeling, knowledge is gradually evolved. Sensation is anticipated organic feeling. The sensation of taste anticipates the feelings which accompany the introduction of a certain food into the body, and thus becomes an adviser of the impulse for food ; smell which scents the prey from afar may be designated as taste acting at a distance. The senses of hearing and of sight stand in an analogous relation to the sense of touch ; they are, as it were, forms of touching at a distance. The sense of touch informs the will of its immediate surroundings, while hearing and sight bring it into relation with the more remote surroundings. They direct movements in the sense of adapting them to attain what is favorable and to avoid what is injurious, only that the eye is the searching pursuer, the ear the listening watchman. Sensation and feeling are usually distinguished as follows : the latter is a purely subjective modification of our condition, while the former is the symbol of an objective element. The distinction is a good one. Nevertheless, the objective element is not altogether absent in feeling; every feeling of pleasure or of pain is not merely pleasure and pain in general, but a definite feeling with a specific content. And, on the other hand, the subjective element is never wholly absent in sensation; it is contained therein as an accentuation of feeling, which points to its origin in feeling.

Finally, presentation and thinking are a further development in the same direction. They still further extend the relations of the will to its environment, above all by including also what is distant in time. We might, indeed, define understanding as the faculty of seeing in the given element that which is not yet given, the faculty of anticipating future phenomena from present phenomena, on the ground of observed connections, in order to use them as motives for present decisions.

This is the way in which a voluntaristic psychology would describe the evolution and nature of consciousness. Schopenhauer bases his idealistic metaphysics on such a psychology. Indeed, I do not doubt that it is better fitted for the purpose than an intellectualistic psychology. Whoever regards presentation and thinking as the fundamental functions of the soul, will always find it impossible to conceive plants as psychical beings, or to consider the movements of inorganic bodies to be signs of psychical processes. But if acts of will constitute the original form of psychical processes, acts of will without presentation and without self-consciousness, then the great chasm which separates the thinking being from natural forces no longer exists. Then we may assume that just as a system of impulses with corresponding feelings runs parallel with the vital processes in animal bodies, a similar but less highly developed inner life corresponds to plant-life; and furthermore, that something akin to this appears in the spontaneous movements of inorganic bodies, in chemical and crystalline processes, in processes of attraction and repulsion. And, perhaps, common opinion will now discover that it came very near this view, when it ascribed forces to all bodies alike as their inner essence; and defined force as a tendency to definite activity, and hence identical in its general form with an unconscious will.

Let me add a remark concerning the relation of psychical processes to *consciousness*. Are psychical processes always conscious processes, or are there also *unconscious elements in psychical life?* *

---

* Cf. Wundt, *System der Philos.*, 551 ff. A mass of facts from the field of unconscious psychical life is given by E. v. Hartmann in the first volume of *The Philosophy of the Unconscious*, where the outlines of a history of the doctrine of the unconscious are also to be found.

As far as I can see, no psychology can help but affirm the latter question; it must confess that the conscious elements make up but a small portion of psychical life. The processes in consciousness may be compared to the waves which ruffle the surface of a pond. Only a small part of the entire mass of water immediately takes part in the motion of the waves. Yet the whole mass conditions the waves and helps to determine the size and velocity of the motion. Similarly, the processes of consciousness are based on an unconscious or, if we choose, sub-conscious psychical life which bears them, from which they rise, and by which their action is determined. Popular language universally and naively assumes this; it constantly reckons with such an unconscious element. We speak of a man as possessing a thorough knowledge of the ancient languages, not meaning, of course, that he is constantly conscious of his vocabulary and grammar, which would be an impossibility. We mean that he possesses them unconsciously, but that they are always effective and could, if necessary, be called into consciousness; just as he possesses muscles and nerves, without always using them. And in like manner, we speak of hopes and fears, of inclinations and aversions, as constant though not always conscious constituents of psychical life, whose existence is proved at every moment by the nature and the direction of the conscious feelings and desires.

How are we to conceive of such an unconscious psychical life? How can knowledge or willing exist, when it is not in consciousness?

Physiologists endeavor to make the matter clear to us by saying: Unconscious ideas are not present as ideas; an unconscious idea would be an idea that is not presented, a contradiction in terms; but they are present as dispositions of the ganglionic cells of the cortex. If an excitation proceeding from a sense-organ is transmitted to the brain, it is accompanied by a conscious process, say, by perception. When the excitation is past, the conscious state as such completely vanishes, but a trace of the physiological process remains behind as a permanent alteration of the excited cells. That is really the unconscious presentation.

If the area of the nervous substance, thus predisposed, is re-excited by some excitation or other from within or without, the presentation becomes conscious again. In this way, physiologists hope to get around the disagreeable concept of an unconscious presentation, and still to retain what is an indispensable condition of understanding conscious processes.*

No objection can be raised against the physiological explanation as such. We may accept it as certain that a permanent alteration of the nervous structure is brought about by excitations. On the other hand, however, this does not settle the matter, at least not according to the parallelistic theory of the relation between the psychical and the physical, which we have established. We cannot avoid attributing psychical existence to the unconscious elements of the soul. We could not grant that the excitation in the nervous system was the conscious state itself. As little can we now admit that the definite organization of a ganglionic cell is an unconscious presentation, or that it can take its place. Unless we are willing to relinquish our general view at this point, we are obliged to say : Nervous modifications have physical effects, not psychical ones ; they may determine the course of re-aroused nervous excitations, but not the nature and the course of presentation. Psychical effects presuppose psychical causes ; if these causes are not in consciousness, we must define them as unconscious psychical elements and these must therefore exist; for, *non entis nullus effectus.* But, whoever undertakes to explain the processes of the association and the reproduction of ideas by means of neural paths, can also derive

---

* Among physiologists it is especially the Englishman Maudsley who in his *Physiology and Pathology of Mind* dwells on the indispensability of assuming an unconscious psychical life, and then declares : The unconscious elements are arrangements of the brain. From this he infers that a psychology which does not operate with such brain-arrangements is worthless. So he finds fault with J. S. Mill for continuing to employ the old worn-out introspective method instead of the objective physiological method. I should like to know how much a person who studies it only from the writings of the brain-physiologists would know of the mental life of man. As far as I can see, brain-physiology as yet contains nothing but problems; it presents no solutions, not even physiological solutions, much less psychological ones.

all psychical processes from processes of motion, and con-versely. He returns to the theory of the *influxus physicus*.

The question, however, *How* can an "unconscious" pres-entation exist, might be answered: Not otherwise than a sound which is not heard, or a color that is not seen, or a body that is not perceived by any one. Everybody as-sumes that a brain with nerve-cells and their arrangements exists in his skull, although neither he himself nor any one else has ever seen it. He is convinced that one might see it under certain circumstances, and, therefore, he says: It exists. If the existence of ganglionic cells and their mod-ifications consists in *the possibility of being perceived*, we may say: In this, too, consists the existence of unconscious ideas, in the possibility of becoming conscious. They are potential inner perceptions, just as the aforesaid physical elements are potential external perceptions.

We can also say, however, and perhaps that is the most suitable way of conceiving the subject: The unconscious is not an absolutely non-conscious, but only a less conscious state, a conscious state that is perhaps completely im-perceptible. For from every point we are led to assume quantitative differences in consciousness. Two occurrences are simultaneously perceived : with rapt attention I watch a race and at the same time occasionally notice the sport of the flies in the air. The perceptions relating to the former occurrence are undoubtedly more intensely conscious. Similarly, there are gradual differences in unconsciousness, if we are permitted to use the term. An event which vividly excited me a quarter of an hour ago is now no longer in my consciousness; I am thinking of other matters. Still, its after-effect remains behind in the mood which it aroused, and this event is immediately called up into consciousness again by the aid of some association or other. It is no longer a conscious element, yet not as unconscious as an occurrence that happened to me three months or ten years ago, which I can recall only with effort and which I re-member very indistinctly or perhaps not at all. And in addition to this, we may remark that the intensity of con-sciousness not only differs for the separate elements, but that it also fluctuates as a whole. Moments of clear and comprehensive consciousness alternate with those of narrow and dull consciousness. There are daily fluctuations corresponding to vegetative processes. To these must be added the fluctuations which accompany the development of life as a whole. Consciousness rises from a minimum at the beginning of life to a maximum, which is reached, say, when the body is fully matured, and then declines, slowly at first, then rapidly. Accordingly, we may say : The unconscious is not something which does not at all exist for consciousness; it is the less conscious in its different gradations down to complete imperceptibleness. Psychical life is made up of the sum of conscious and unconscious elements. The processes in consciousness are at any given moment determined by the co-operation of all elements, from the most conscious down to the completely forgotten, which, however, in so far as they have determined the condition of psychical life, have not become altogether inefficient and unreal.

Should a physiologist, however, find difficulties in the physiological interpretation of this view, believing that consciousness can arise as a concomitant, only upon an excitation of brain-cells, and that unexcited paths are not bearers of states of consciousness in however weakened a form we may conceive these, I should reply : What hinders us from thinking that all the cells of the cortex are constantly in activity ? Indeed, we are carried to such a notion from all sides. A ganglionic cell is doubtless not to be looked upon as an atom at rest, but as the bearer of a system of the most diverse, never-resting internal movements. Disintegration and integration, interaction with the neighboring and more remote surroundings, constantly take place, and in every activity the inner constitution and organization of the cell is expressed. A reduced amount of consciousness would thus correspond to the reduced activity. I should think that this view would be the very thing for the physiologist. The other conception that only a few elements have psychical existence, would seem to me to be harder to explain. If the physiological processes in the cortex are at all accompanied by psychical states, we must expect an exceedingly complicated play of

such states and not merely the few processes which constitute the thin "thread of presentation" spoken of by psychologists. Or shall we say that at a given moment of time only
some cells are excited and in action, the rest meanwhile
lying idle and inactive, like grains of sand on the beach?
And if that is inconceivable, why should their excitation
have no psychical effect?

Impartial reflection cannot leave us in doubt that
psychical life at any given moment exhibits a highly-
diversified and complicated mass of more or less conscious processes, and not merely the scanty monomial series
which, as some psychologists maintain, is all that the
"narrowness of consciousness" will allow. I am seated in
a theatre, watching the performance of a play. Numerous
psychical processes are enacted simultaneously, appearing
in consciousness with more or less intensity. I have
auditory sensations; they occur in long series. Those become most prominent which I apprehend as the speeches
of the actors and translate into ideas and thoughts, but besides these I also hear the footsteps on the stage, the
rustle of the clothes, and my own as well as my neighbors'
movements. Simultaneously with these perceptions, an
equally complicated series of visual sensations arises. I
survey the entire stage with its decorations and settings, I
see the motions and the mimic play of the actors. The foreground is filled with the heads and hats of the persons in
front of me: these, too, I see to the extent of being attracted
by any conspicuous movement. The two series run parallel, not in such a way that their members relieve one
another intermittently, but each series is complete in itself,
even though certain members, now of the one, now of the
other, preponderate in consciousness. The two series form
the basis of the main series, which has most consciousness
and impresses itself most deeply: the series of ideas pertaining to the drama itself with its action and characters. At
each moment that group of ideas occupies the foreground
which is suggested by the particular speech or answer
heard at this particular time. However, not merely the
word or sentence just uttered is present in consciousness;
besides this, all preceding occurrences are present with

diminished intensity. Indeed, the separate word or sentence as such has no definite meaning at all, it is understood only because it is comprehended as a part of the whole, as the speech of a particular person to some other person on a particular occasion. A consciousness that could hold only one idea at a time would not be capable of comprehending even a speech, much less a play. At the same time, diverse feelings are present in my consciousness: feelings of tension or tedium, of exaltation or contempt, of æsthetic satisfaction or of discomfort. Nor are these interspersed with the members of the perception and presentation series; they constitute an independent combination which gains more or less prominence in consciousness. Finally, the constant background of this play of conscious states is formed by a mass of tactile and muscular sensations, by means of which I become aware of the position, attitude, and movement of my body and its parts. They are accompanied by an equally great number of common feelings, which hardly enter consciousness as isolated states, but which, in their totality, as common or vital feelings constitute the basis of an entire world of feelings: fatigue and languor, or freshness and elasticity, feelings of satisfied comfort pervading the entire system, or disturbing feelings of heat or cold, of exhaustion or satiety and indisposition, etc.

All these states are simultaneously in consciousness, and in addition to that, they are accompanied by the consciousness that they belong to this individual psychical life. I am always aware of who I am, whence I come, in what position and surroundings I live, what tasks and duties I have to perform. This knowledge is not a separate object of attention or reflection, but yet it is present as something that is always at hand, present in every conscious state as the ego.

Consciousness represents such a content at any given moment. A large number of elements are simultaneously conscious; though, of course, not equally conscious. A narrow group always occupies the centre as the most conscious; around it are grouped the rest, the intensity of whose consciousness rapidly diminishes in the beginning.

The constellation, however, lasts but a moment; the maximum of consciousness is, as it were, movable; like a wave it runs over the many elements, raising now this, now that element to the highest point.

With Wundt we may compare the content of consciousness to the content of the field of vision. A large mass of objects is simultaneously in the field of vision; a small portion of them occupies the point of clearest vision and is seen with greatest distinctness; the others are also seen, but with a distinctness which diminishes with their distance from the point of clearest vision. When we look at an open book, we survey the entire page with its characters; we see also the surroundings, the table, and the objects lying on it, until finally, at the margin of the field of vision, the images of the objects become entirely indistinct. Nor do we see the page and its letters with equal distinctness. If we fix the eye upon a particular letter and try to recognize the adjacent letters without moving the eye, we shall find that we can scarcely see the third or fourth letter on either side of it with clearness. The rest are seen only as an indistinct mass, except that we can distinguish, say, a big letter by itself, or a word printed in heavy type, or half a line, without, however, recognizing the separate characters. But the eye when left to itself will not remain fixed on one point; passing over the lines, it brings the separate characters upon the point of clearest vision in rapid succession, but for a moment only, and thus obtains a distinct image of the whole.

The same is true of consciousness. Here too, we have a wide field of vision, filled with numerous elements, containing a fovea, which is occupied at every moment by a narrow content; around it are grouped the other contents presented with rapidly-diminishing distinctness, until the outlines gradually vanish at the margin. Here, too, the fovea is movable; it hurries over the objects, raises up one after another, and thus obtains a view of the whole. As there are different degrees of illumination in the field of vision dependent on the amount of light that strikes an object so there are degrees of intensity in consciousness.

7. The Nature of the Soul, its Metaphysical Constitution, and its Seat in the Body.

In circles that do not accept materialism, something like the following conception of the essence of the soul prevails. The soul is a simple, unextended, immaterial substance ; as such it is absolutely persistent and imperishable ; it is the bearer of forces by which it effects states of consciousness ; and, finally, it is situated at a certain point in the brain, at which point it exchanges effects with the body. This view, as Wundt shows,* is the teaching of Wolffian philosophy, which dominated general culture during the Illumination, and goes back to Descartes. In this respect, as well as in other points, Descartes' philosophy has prevailed in spite of Spinoza and Kant. Its advantage lies in the fact that it is within easy reach of popular thought and its convenient notions.

I share the conviction of Fechner and Wundt that this view is not tenable or even possible. There is no persistent, immaterial substance existing for itself. The essence of the soul consists in psychical life ; if we subtract the psychical processes, no substance remains behind. The soul-atom is nothing but the survival of a worn-out metaphysics.

Our epistemological reflections will bring us back to the notion of substance later on. In this place, I have only the following to say. The immaterial and persistent soul-substance is not an object of immediate perception, neither of inner nor of outer perception. Changing states and processes only are given in self-consciousness ; the persistent substance is an addition of thought. What forces us to make this addition ? The advocates of the theory say : The immediate necessity of our thought obliges us to do it. A sensation, a feeling, or a thought cannot exist by itself any more than a movement ; these presuppose a bearer, and that is the substance. States of consciousness, however, cannot be attached to a corporeal substance. Try, in your imagination, to attach a feeling or an idea to an atom or a group of atoms, and you will see the impossibility of the task.

---

* In the essay: *Gehirn und Seele*, in his Essays (1885), pp. 89 ff.

The indivisible will not stick to the extended and divisible. Consequently, we are obliged to assume an unextended or simple substance as the bearer of psychical life. In this way alone does its inner unity become conceivable and intelligible.

It is doubtless true that a feeling or a thought cannot be attached to an extended body. But now make the same attempt with unextended substance; try to imagine the idea, for example, of the Tower of Babel, or of Darwinism and its Relation to Religion and Morality, as attached to an unextended substance. I believe you will feel the impossibility of the task. Perhaps it will be said: Of course the relation cannot be made plain, it is only thinkable. A substance without extension cannot be imagined. Well, then, I should like to know in what the content of this substance consists. In immateriality and simplicity? These are pure negations that deny but do not affirm anything. We cannot make realities out of negations. Or does the content consist in feeling and thinking themselves? But, according to the theory, feeling and thinking are mere accidents, passing activities of the soul-substance, and what we desire to know is what the latter is in and for itself. Or does the essence of the substance consist of its accidents? Good; then we agree; then, indeed, we have reached the view: The essence of the soul consists in its life, consists in its feelings and thoughts alone.—Or, is the soul-substance an unknown something or other, eternally remaining behind the scenes, something to be determined neither by intuition nor thought, a "thing-in-itself?" If that is so, I should like to know what such a wholly unknown something or other can do to create feelings and thoughts that cannot exist for themselves.

We shall, therefore, stop at what we know : the soul is a plurality of psychical experiences comprehended into the unity of consciousness in a manner not further definable. We know nothing whatever of a substance outside of, behind, or under the ideas and feelings.*

---

* Wundt (*System der Philosophie*, pp. 289 ff.) gives an excellent illustration of how impossible it is to apply the concept of substance to the soul. The concept of substance originated in the realm of the corporeal world, and here

It is not to be assumed that such reflections will succeed in at once convincing common-sense and its metaphysicians of the superfluity of the soul-substance. Common-sense will continue to say : A feeling can neither
exist nor be conceived without some one to feel it, and so
an idea presupposes a substantial subject that has it and
presents it. Common-sense is not in the wrong, only it mis-
understands its own demand, which it seeks to satisfy—
but fails to satisfy—by means of the notion of substantiality. What the demand really implies is this : A presentation or feeling *never appears in isolation,* but always and
only *in conjunction with an entire psychical life.* Such is its
place in the world; it belongs to it as a necessary member
of this combination. Nothing will hinder us from saying,
according to the traditional usage of language : The soul
has ideas and thoughts ; in it, feelings and desires are
aroused. We mean by this exactly what everybody understands by it, namely, that these particular thoughts and
feelings arise in this particular combination of individual
psychical life, and that their consciousness embraces the
consciousness of the entire combination. Nor will anything hinder us from saying : The soul is the substance
which produces and supports the separate states; to be
sure, for were it not for this entire psychical life, this
particular sensation or idea would not exist either. Furthermore, the whole is relatively persistent in relation

it has a definite, assignable meaning : the atoms are the absolutely persistent substratum of the material world, unchangeable in quantity and quality.
All change is to be referred to the alteration in the arrangement and motion
of atoms : that is the maxim of natural science. If we transfer this notion
to soul-life, we either annihilate the notion or destroy life. The soul is not
unchangeable and persistent, like the atom; on the contrary, it is in a state of
constant inner change ; it never returns to its previous condition unchanged,
like the atom which severs its connection with a compound. Hence, the soul
cannot be called a substance in the same sense as the atom. If, however,
we insist upon it, as Herbart does ; if we define its essence as a simple and
absolutely unalterable quality, and regard ideas, thoughts, and desires as
mere accidental manifestations of substances which are conditioned by the
changing external relations, and do not affect its inner essence, we destroy
the soul. Then " everything in our inner experience that possesses reality
and existence becomes an empty semblance, and, as a recompense, we retain
the worthless shadow of a substance whose complete emptiness is com-
pensated for by its absolute persistence."

to its parts. But if you imagine that we need a bearer
for this whole, that we need an immaterial and simple
soul-substance, in order that the whole may not be without support, let me ask the question : Would not such a
substance in turn also need a support ?   It seems to me,
very much so.   How a Herbartian " reality " can hold its
own has always struck me as the greatest among the
mysteries of metaphysics.   If a " support " is to be found
for soul-life, it must be sought, not in an isolated rigid
block of reality which is " posited absolutely," but in
the comprehensive whole from which, on which, and in
which it is.   God is the substance, and outside of him
there is no substance ; nay, outside of him there is absolutely nothing that can exist and be conceived by itself.
Those, however, who cannot relinquish the notion of
psychical substantiality ought to ask themselves how they
would conceive of God.   Would they regard him too as a
simple substance that must have its seat at some point
of the universe, as the soul is situated at a point in the
body ?   Or does God's essence not need a " real " to which
to attach itself ?   In that event the human soul will not
need it either.   But we shall return to this subject later.

Let me add another remark.   The clumsy soul-atom
of common-sense is in line with its equally clumsy notion
of the constitution of matter : Matter consists of minute,
absolutely hard, rigid, inert, qualitatively indeterminate
particles.   This, of course, is a conception that makes
the thought of *panpsychism* seem absurd indeed.   Do you
really mean to say, common-sense asks, that in each one
of these minute, extended atoms there is also an unextended
soul-atom ?   Of course, this is no more absurd than the
attempt to find a seat for the soul-atom in the endless
medley of ever-changing atoms which compose our body.
It appears to me, however, that the aforesaid notion of an
atom is worth just as much and just as little as the notion
of the unextended soul-substance.   Natural science has no
more to do with the former than psychology has to do with
the latter.   What science presupposes is ultimate elements
from which to proceed in its explanations.   It does not concern science whether these elements are absolutely ultimate,

indivisible, inwardly rigid, indeterminate, extensive quantities or not, any more than it concerns arithmetic whether the units used in calculation are absolutely ultimate and indivisible unities or not. On the contrary, it will say, nothing prevents us from regarding every unity in turn as a plurality; each unit has ten tenths, and each tenth may again be divided into ten tenths, *ad infinitum*. In the same way the atoms, with which natural science deals as with units, may at times be regarded as complex, articulated systems with internal movements. The speculations of modern chemists estimate the number of molecules in a cubic centimeter at twenty trillions, their diameters at less than a millionth of a millimeter, the weight of a molecule of oxygen at the fourth part of a quadrillionth of a gram.* It is evident, when once we get so far away from everything that we can picture to the imagination, nothing can keep us from again dividing the parts of these parts in the same way. It merely depends, however, on whether the necessities of a conceptual explanation of the facts demand it. We are not hindered from continuing this division and articulation any more than the astronomer is hindered from going right on in extending the universe. Analysis deals with the infinite as well as synthesis. The atom as an absolutely hard and rigid particle does not belong to scientific research but to metaphysics, and, in truth, to the same dull and sluggish metaphysics that puts forward the notion of the soul-substance.

  From this point of view, we shall now attempt to answer the old question concerning the *seat of the soul*. Let us first make plain to ourselves the meaning of the question. It is obvious from our conception of the essence of the soul, as indicated above, that we cannot speak of a seat in the sense of a space, or a place in space, in which the soul is supposed to be. In space, there are bodies; in space, movements take place, not states of consciousness. It is meaningless to say, a thought or a feeling is here or there, and extends through this or that part of space. Thoughts are not in the brain; we might as well say they are in the

─────────────────

* L. Meyer, *Moderne Theorien der Chemie*, 5th ed. (1884) pp. 131 ff.

stomach or in the moon. The one statement is as absurd as the other. Physiological processes occur in the brain, and nothing else. Now, if the soul is nothing but a unity of psychical life, it cannot of course be located in space any more than thoughts can. The meaning of the question concerning the seat of the soul can, therefore, only be this : With what bodily processes are psychical processes connected ? In the fourth section, we were led to the view that a relation of parallelism obtains between bodily and psychical processes. This parallelism has nothing whatever to do with a local concurrence ; it simply means : when a definite psychical process occurs, a physical process simultaneously takes place, which may be characterized as a concomitant phenomenon or as a physical equivalent of the psychical occurrence. The question as to the seat of the soul, therefore, means : What are these processes and where do they take place ? Throughout the whole body or in a part of the body, in the brain or, finally, in a single part of the brain ?

Popular opinion inclines to the view that the whole body is the seat of the soul; it is present everywhere in the body, for the body has sensation at every point.

Perhaps there is more truth in the notion than our physiologists are willing to admit. Indeed, I believe that we are ultimately driven to it. At first sight, of course, the facts urge us to a different view. Even our daily experiences, which could not have escaped popular thought, show that different parts of the body differ in their importance for psychical as well as for bodily life. The loss of an arm or a leg is not fatal, nor does it diminish our psychical existence ; while the destruction of the heart or brain results in bodily decay and in the cessation of psychical life. Apparently, this is the fact which has invariably impelled men to seek for a special seat of the soul in the body, and to locate it in the superior organs. A division of the soul itself into different forces, aspects, or parts, corresponding to the different functions, then leads to their distribution among the different bodily organs. In the Platonic psychology, we have such an ingenious classification : Thought is situated in the head ; the higher spiritual will, which manifests itself in specific human emotions, in the heart; the sensuous-animal impulses are placed under the diaphragm. In modern times, anatomical and physiological investigations have brought us to the view, so current in our days, that the psychical processes are most intimately connected with the nervous system, especially the brain. Contact with the surface of the body, excitation of the sense-organs by physical stimuli, does not, as our common self-consciousness testifies, immediately effect a sensation at the stimulated point. The latter is produced only in case the excitation is transmitted to the brain by intact nerve-fibres. If the path is interrupted, if the nerve by which the centripetal excitation is transmitted is severed, the peripheral excitation no longer arouses a sensation. Likewise, spontaneous movement ceases when the nervous connection between a limb and the central organ is broken. Hence, the conclusion is, the brain is the seat of the soul.

Finally, the metaphysical theories which make of the soul a simple substance in reciprocal relation with the body, lead to the attempt to assign to it a seat in a narrow region, preferably at a single point of the brain, where it receives the effects of the body and whence it acts upon the body. Descartes takes the lead in this matter, and the entire eighteenth century, following in his steps, inclines to the same view. During the age of critical and speculative philosophy, this conception, together with the idea of the soul-substance, was temporarily abandoned. Herbart and his school, as well as Lotze, raise it to its former dignity.*

---

* Following Herbart's example (*Psychologie als Wissenschaft*, II. 461), Lotze (*Medizinische Psychologie*, pp. 115 ff.) is inclined to locate the soul in the *pons Varolii*, through which numerous brain-nerves pass. He does not regard it as essential to his assumption to have a specially-formed physiological organ for the reception of all conducting nerves ; it is enough if they all converge into a nervous parenchyma that does not offer any further resistance to the universal distribution of the excitations, and therefore allows them safely to reach the substance of the soul. What keeps him from locating it in the cortical matter of the hemispheres, as seems most plausible to modern physiologists, is the extent and bilateral symmetry of the cerebrum, to which he simply assigns the task of maintaining the functional activity of the nerves as a force-producing apparatus. A discussion of the question from the standpoint of Herbartian metaphysics and psychology is to be found in Volkmann, *Lehrbuch der Psychologie*, I. 76 ff.

The last-named efforts to discover a single point in the brain at which alone the soul is supposed to be immediately present or to act, rest, it seems to me, on metaphysical reasons only, not on the facts of psychology or physiology. They are based on the presupposition that the soul is a simple, unextended substance. Now, inextension means non-spatiality, yet the imagination ever strives to represent it as a point and then demands for this a localization in space. But by abandoning the soul-atom, we at the same time abandon the necessity of localizing the soul at a point. If the soul is nothing but psychical activity in general, there is no occasion for letting the physical concomitants take place at one point or within a limited region rather than in any area of corporeal life, be it large or small. It is hard to understand why Lotze clings to the theory that the soul is situated at a point in the brain after he has abandoned the rigid soul-atom of the old spiritualism which is its presupposition. For he, too, conceives the soul as a "living unity of consciousness which comprehends itself." *

We therefore exclude metaphysics from the solution of the question. Psychology and physiology remain. It is immaterial to the former, as such, what view is advanced. The unity of consciousness and the non-spatial character of psychical life as such by no means imply the simplicity and inextension belonging to the mathematical point. Self-consciousness has no immediate knowledge whatever of accompanying nerve-processes. Physiology alone is cognizant of them. Physiology, however, is doubtless more inclined to the notion that the concomitant phenomena of psychical processes extend over a large territory. Laborious and painful investigations have gradually succeeded, at least in some respects, in establishing uniform relations between psychical functions and definite brain-areas. Thus, limited areas of the cortex may be pointed out, whose functions condition the different sense-perceptions and their recall, speech and the understanding of speech. Such facts are not, of course, subject to direct observation, but

---

* See his last controversy with Fechner, *Metaphysik*, p. 480.

experiments with animals and pathological investigations
with human beings show a regular parallelism between the
destruction of certain localities in the cortex and the disturbance or cessation of certain psychical functions. It is
the most plausible interpretation of these facts to say that
the physiological functions of such parts are the physical
equivalents of the corresponding psychical processes.
True, the assertion might be made that these parts are
but the intermediate conditions of excitation for some point
or other which has not yet been discovered. What assertions, however, might not be made in this field? There
are as yet no physiological reasons for such a statement.
The physiologist is constrained to explain even the simplest
psychical processes, like an act of recognition or an act of
will produced thereby and resulting in a spontaneous
movement, as an extensive nervous process in which numerous elements equally share; and there is no reason why he
should connect the psychical process with the functioning
of one of these elements rather than with that of all the
rest.*

It is furthermore plain that a Herbartian soul-reality
would be a great stumbling-block to physiologists in other
respects. What is its relation to metabolism? As far as

---

* Meynert attempts to illustrate such nervous processes as, for example,
accompany a visual perception and the attendant defensive impulse (*Psychiatrie*, 1884, 145 ff.). Results of experimental observations on dogs and
monkeys in Munk, *Die Funktionen der Grosshirnrinde* (2d ed., 1890). These
experiments seem to have established that the destruction of certain portions of the cortex results in the cessation of certain psychical functions.
Thus, the extirpation of the posterior apex of the occipital lobe results in
the loss of the ability to recognize known objects, and in such a way that
the destruction of one side of the lobe destroys the sight of the eye on the
opposite side. The dog sees, but he does not recognize what he sees.
Gradually the faculty of vision is acquired again; he learns to "see" again,
that is, to infer the nature of the object from his visual sensation.
Although there is still much obscurity here, and although the successive
occupation of the cells by memory-images, the temporary emptiness of cells
by which the reacquisition of memory is supposed to be conditioned, the
unfolding of a series of associations in consequence of the reflexive excitation of a series of cells, etc., are so far nothing but physiological speculations (which remind one strikingly of Beneke's speculative psychology);
yet it is intelligible why such facts should irresistibly impel the physiologist to assume the extended localization of psychical functions.

the physiologist can discover, psychical life never consists of a permanent stock of elements, but of elements in constant charge. Is the psychical "reàl" an exception, does it alone persist, while the other "reals" are in a state of constant flux? And how is it related to birth and death? Is it a constant element that reaches such a high stage of development because of its privileged position? And what becomes of it when it is deprived of its surroundings by the death of the body? Finally, it is worthy of note that the older attempts to find a point in the brain, the destruction of which would result in immediate death, have all proved futile. The ganglion of life assumed by Flourens does not exist; the patient survives the destruction of any portion of his brain, if it is not too extensive.*

After all this, it is plain enough that the tendency predominates among physiologists to accept the extensive localization of psychical processes. A nervous process in more or less extended portions of the brain, particularly of the cortical substance, corresponds to every psychical process. Can we stop here—or must we stop here? Or is it expedient to go further and to return with Fechner and Wundt to the old conception that the entire living body is the seat of the soul—that the entire unified bodily life is the physical equivalent for the entire unified psychical life? I believe we are driven to such a view.

In the first place, the thorough-going unity of corporeal life suggests it. Where is the boundary-line of soul-life, if we are not allowed to locate it at a single point? It seems hardly possible to select a fixed territory within the nervous system, and to associate psychical accompaniments with the excitation of this alone, denying them to similar occurrences outside of the same. And the nervous system in turn is so intimately connected with all the vital processes in its physiological functions, in its nutrition, that it must appear arbitrary to isolate the nervous system as the organ of psychical life. Indeed, if we once begin to rule out parts of the body that stand in no immediate relation to soul-life, but serve as its external instruments only, we

---

* Fechner, *Elemente der Psychophysik*, pp. 399 ff.

shall gradually be reduced to the monadological view. This would regard the bones and ligaments and muscles as nothing but an external mechanism, which the soul employs not otherwise than as levers or pulleys. The nervous system alone is the bearer of psychical life. But not the peripheral nerves : they evidently serve merely as paths of transmission, hence as external instruments. The central organs of the nervous system alone remain as bearers of psychical life. Not altogether, however; for the fibres most likely function as conductors, hence they, too, belong to the external mechanism. The ganglionic cells, especially the large masses of the cortex, remain. But what hinders us from continuing our line of reasoning and saying that the ganglia too, in turn, serve only as means? For do not experiments and pathological investigations show that not a single part of the brain is indispensable to psychical life or incapable of being replaced? It is said that under certain circumstances the degeneration of the whole of a hemisphere occurs with no considerable loss to the soul; hence the hemisphere itself is simply an external and not indispensable means. And how are we to conceive the relation of the two hemispheres to soul-life? Would we not also have to expect two regular series of psychical processes, if these hemispheres were the immediate bearers of psychical life, that is, if states of consciousness immediately corresponded to the physical states in them? Hence it seems advisable to regard the life of the body, including the nervous system, as nothing but a system of external means, as a mechanism, which the immaterial soul employs in order to enter upon manifold relations with its surroundings.

We, therefore, seem to be reduced to an alternative. Either we must regard the entire body, including the nervous system, as a system of means external to the soul, or we must regard the entire body as the visible expression or physical equivalent of soul-life. The division of the body so as to make certain portions only, say the cortical substance of the brain, bearers of psychical processes, can hardly be considered as a satisfactory account. If now the previously-mentioned reasons hinder us from

returning to the former view, we must make up our minds
to say : The physical equivalent of psychical life is the
sum of physiological vital processes ; a psychical element
corresponds to every physical one; the parallelism is
thorough-going. To be sure, I repeat, the parallelism is
not a local one : I do not intend to say that wherever a
physical process takes place, there too a psychical process
occurs. That is a meaningless statement. But an ideal
parallelism occurs. A penetrating understanding having a
thorough insight into all bodily occurrences as well as
into all inner processes, would be able to point out for
every process in the body a corresponding process in the
soul, be it conscious or subconscious. For such a penetrating understanding would indeed view psychical life, not
as a thin chain of conscious ideas, but as an infinitely-
complicated diversity of simultaneous conscious and less
conscious or subconscious processes. Corresponding to
the uniform action of the bodily vital processes with their
innumerable auxiliary processes, we should have a system
of psychical life of equal complexity and corresponding
gradations of consciousness.

Biological and evolutionistic considerations seem to
point to the same view: We find no nervous system in the
lowest forms of animal life to which we attribute psychical
life. The body of the protista has no particular centre at
which to locate the soul. The entire body appears as an
accumulation of homogeneous and homo-functional organic
substance. Upon division, every part becomes viable and
exercises all and the same functions which the whole performs ; it reacts upon stimuli, assimilates food, builds a
shell, etc. "There is no unitary psychical centre in the
body of the protista. Every infinitely small piece of proto-
plasm is the seat of psychical processes." * If organic
matter originally possessed psychical life at every point, it
is hard to see how it could have entirely lost this quality
later on. The centralization of the physical vital processes
on higher stages of development is accompanied by the
transformation of the functions of the parts, but not by

* M. Verworn, *Psycho-physiologische Protistenstudien*, p. 211 .

their destruction. Is it not possible that the same happens in the psychical sphere? The physical life of every animal being invariably begins in the form of a cell. Why should not its psychical life also originate from an elementary form?

The obvious objection that we have no actual knowledge of such a universal correspondence, and, moreover, that thousands of bodily processes are without accompanying conscious states, may be answered by referring to our former exposition (pp. 120 ff.): not every element belonging to psychical life is necessarily an object of self-perception in consciousness. Consciousness constitutes but a very small part of the entire soul-life, which we are nevertheless obliged to presuppose in order to explain the processes in consciousness. Unconscious or subconscious states most likely correspond to the bodily processes which are not accompanied by conscious psychical processes. The vegetative processes, the intra-organic processes occasioned by the constantly-recurring metabolic changes taking place in all parts of the body, and the corresponding ganglionic excitations of the sympathetic nervous system, have some minimal feelings or desires as their psychical equivalents; but these remain below the threshold of consciousness; only a summation of all of them enters consciousness, perhaps in the form of common feelings or organic vital feelings, or rather constitutes the background of all conscious states, which is for the most part hardly perceptible. Only under certain circumstances do individual feelings of this group attain to such a degree of intensity as to enter consciousness. It occurs regularly when disturbances of some kind or other reach a menacing intensity and demand relief: thus in the feelings of hunger, thirst, fatigue, suffocation, or in feelings of satisfaction, if the demand is satisfied. In this case, we should assume, a corresponding physiological process takes place in the central nervous system, while, as a rule, the processes of metabolism occur within narrower limits and do not affect the brain.

On the other hand, collisions between the body and its external environment generally arouse nervous excitations which are transmitted to the brain. When the surface of the body is touched, the ends of sensible nerves are always excited and these excitations are carried to the central organ. The sense-organs are particularly prominent points on the surface. A complicated apparatus conducts the slightest excitation, for example one caused by ether-waves or vibrations of the air, to the brain. Not all of these excitations are accompanied by conscious psychical processes; the thousands of tactile and muscular excitations which are constantly aroused in the entire periphery, for the most part remain below the threshold of consciousness. They exist, as is shown by the position and movement of the body; when they are absent, movements become uncertain; they can also be brought to consciousness at any time, as soon as attention is directed towards them, but as a rule they remain subconscious. In like manner, thousands of sense-impressions which at every moment enter through the eye and ear remain subconscious; as a rule we see and hear only what is related to our present interest. If the problem has no relation whatever to the external world, if we ponder over an abstract theme, or indulge in reminiscences, we neither hear nor see anything at all, for the time being. That is, the nerve-excitations and brain-processes are present even then, nor are psychical equivalents absent; we become aware of this fact when we are suddenly awakened from our dreams : we remember quite distinctly that we really heard such and such sounds, the sound of a bell for instance ; we even succeed in counting the strokes subsequently. But they could not, under the circumstances, rise into consciousness.

Evidently this is an arrangement that is beneficial or, rather, essential to the vital economy of higher animals : the intra-organic contrivances do not, as a rule, excite the cerebro-spinal system, and, similarly, their psychical equivalents remain beneath the threshold of consciousness. On the other hand, the relations with the external world are represented by nerve-excitations which are regularly transmitted to the central organ, and their psychical equivalents approximate consciousness. Of course, the preservation of the animal essentially depends upon whether it responds to the external environment with the appropriate reaction : the adaptation of its movements to the occurrences of the external world is for an animal the great problem of life. We may liken the animal body to the body politic. The inner processes which pertain to metabolic change, the economic activity of the different individuals, their family-life,—all these take place within the narrowest sphere; they do not enter the universal consciousness. True, taken all together, they are constantly present as the substratum of universal consciousness ; the countless little sorrows and joys experienced by the different individuals constitute the vital feelings of a people, as it were. On the other hand, a nation is extremely sensitive to contact with the external world. Every boundary-incident is discussed by all the papers, and a thousand eyes are constantly watching the state of the international relations in diplomacy.

The cerebro-spinal system has the function to regulate the external relations of the organism. Its peripheral terminations are sensitive to the slighest contact with air- and ether-waves. Nerve-fibres, which represent isolating paths of transmission, carry the excitations intact to the central organ. This, in turn, represents a system of organs which acquire permanent arrangements occasioned by nerve-excitations. By means of these paths, which, looked at from the psychical side, make up memory, the nervous process in the central organ (psychically, the apperception), as well as the reaction (the decision), is, upon subsequent excitation, determined. Concentration upon these contacts and reactions presupposes an isolation against intra-organic excitations ; or, psychically expressed, the origin of a world of ideas, the evolution of a mental life, presupposes a certain isolation of consciousness from the organic feelings.

The evolution, then, must be explained in this way. On the lowest stage of animal life, sensibility to stimuli is distributed equally over the entire body. Contact at any point provokes a local or general reaction of consciousness ; every process is accompanied by some psychical equivalent or other, which we interpret by analogy with our own soul-life as feeling and desire. In the same manner, the intra-organic processes are accompanied by corresponding psychical processes. A disconnected and undifferentiated plurality of such incidental processes is the form of the lowest stages of psychical life. With progressive develop- ment, the relations to the external world become more and more manifold and complicated, the problem of self-preser- vation demands more and more manifold and subtle adap- tations of behavior to the conditions and occurrences of the external world. The nervous system is developed as an organ for this function. Its sensibility to excitations from the external world becomes more and more intensified and differentiated, while in the other parts of the organic sub- stance this sensibility diminishes. With the centralization of sensibility, that of the reactionary movements keeps step. The central organs of the nervous system are a regu- lative apparatus of control that limits the faculty of reac- tion originally belonging to the entire organic substance.— The process of psychical evolution runs parallel with the evolution of organic life. The organic feelings are gradu- ally pushed into the background by the development of sensation and memory; the play of ideas begins, conscious- ness in the proper sense arises, which cannot be conceived without referring a psychical element to a whole.

I have reached the conclusion of this entire discussion. If we identify psychical life with conscious thought, we reach the point to which the Cartesians were led by their definition of the soul as a *res cogitans:* we are obliged to deny soul to animals; indeed, to all subhuman beings. If, on the other hand, conscious presentation and thought do not make up the whole of psychical life, not even in human beings, if there is a subconscious soul-life beneath the surface, then nothing can hinder us from assuming the existence of a soul-life in which a consciousness like human consciousness is never reached. Self-consciousness presup- poses world-consciousness with extensive recollection, yes, race-memory—that is, historical consciousness. The ego has self-consciousness in the real sense, only as a his- torical being. We cannot ascribe such consciousness to animals; not even the most sagacious animal could tell the history of its life. The soul-life of animals is most likely like that which we find in ourselves beneath self-conscious thought and willing. As we gradually descend the scale, we find that the presentative side gradually vanishes, the memory becomes narrower and narrower, perception scantier and scantier. At the same time, the will gradually loses the form of anticipating ends, of conscious craving or desire, until finally nothing is left over as the content of soul-life except a momentary impulse, which is aroused by contact with the environment. Inner processes like these would have to be assumed as the concomitants of all movements, even of those beyond the limits of organic life.

In this way we establish an *idealistic* or *spiritualistic ontology* in opposition to the materialistic one. It rests essentially on the parallelistic theory of the relation between the physical and the psychical, and upon the voluntaristic psychology. It culminates, however, in the monistic solution of the cosmological problem, to which we now turn.

CHAPTER II.

1. Facts and Hypotheses.

THE question concerning the essence of reality consti-tutes the ontological problem. The cosmological problem is the question concerning the relation between the parts and the whole of reality. I shall first state the facts which suggest the question.

To popular opinion the world appears as a plurality of independent objects, each of which has an existence inde-pendent of all the rest. True, they are not totally indiffer-ent to each other ; they stand in relation to, and act upon, each other. Nevertheless, this relation of interaction is unnecessary to the existence of each element as such.

If we look at the matter a little more closely, we shall discover a few further facts that are worthy of notice. In' the first place, things act and are acted upon, not occasion-ally only, but *constantly* and *universally*. Every portion of existence bears a constant reciprocal relation to every other portion. Physics teaches this. A brick falls from the roof. We say, the earth attracts it with a force corre-sponding to the mass. That means : its motion is deter-mined, at each moment, by the relation of all its parts to all the parts which constitute the body of the earth. If the mass of the earth were smaller, or a part temporarily in-active, the motion of the brick would be a different one ; on the moon, it would fall with less, on Jupiter, with greater velocity. Likewise, all parts of the brick act upon the earth by impelling it to move in the direction of the com-mon centre of gravity. The motion of the stone is, there-fore, a part of a universal motion which it and all the parts

145

of the earth together direct towards a common centre, the centre of gravity of the system. At the same time, this system bears a similar relation to a greater system. Every change that occurs in the former, the slightest transference of the centre of gravity, reacts upon the motion of the entire planetary system. And the latter in turn interacts upon a wider circle, the system of the milky-way, for the explanation of which, it must be confessed, we lack the data. Hence, all mass-particles that coexist in space make up a unitary system possessing a uniform motion, in which the movement of every part is contained and determined as a partial movement.

The same system which comprehends all movements in space into an all-embracing unity, also combines them into a unity in time. The brick was thrown from the roof by a storm. The current of air is the effect of the difference in the heat of different parts of the earth's surface. This cause in turn is itself an effect of previous circumstances, of cloudiness, precipitation, ocean-currents, the structure of the earth's surface and its motion, and so on, without end. Had a perfect arithmetician been able exactly to estimate the masses and their position and motion in reference to each other at any remote point of past time, he would also have been able to foresee the occurrence of this particular event, at this particular time, and in this particular place, just as the astronomer predetermines, to the very second, the appearance of the moon in the eclipses.

We are therefore driven to the statement: All motions in infinite time and infinite space really form a single motion; the corporeal world is a unitary system possessing one great single movement, to which all the separate movements are related as parts to the whole. Or, in the words of Leibniz: "Every body is affected by everything that happens in the entire world, so that a man seeing everything would know from each particular object everything that takes place everywhere, as well as what has taken place and will take place: he perceives in the present that which is remote in time and space." (*Monadology,* § 61.)

A second fact, conspicuous in the constitution of the

world, is the *reign of universal law.* So great is the homogeneity of elements, that the behavior of all of them may, at least in certain respects, be expressed by simple formulæ. The laws of mechanics or the law of gravity are, so at least physics and astronomy assume, the exact expression of the behavior of every mass-particle that exists anywhere in infinite space or acts at any time in infinite time. Any particle might be substituted for any other one of equal mass without effecting any change in the world-process. This homogeneity of all the parts of reality is evidently not a necessity of our thought ; it would be altogether conceivable,—indeed, on the presupposition that the world consists of many absolutely independent elements it would be a plausible assumption,—that these parts exhibit all kinds of differences in behavior. In that case, natural science in the modern sense of the term would not be possible, perhaps it would not be possible in any sense. That such homogeneity exists is a lucky accident for our mode of thinking.

A third significant fact must be added : the *cosmical organization* of reality. The great unitary system which we call world displays a tendency to a peculiar arrangement of its parts, the tendency, namely, to organize itself into smaller, relatively independent systems possessing an equally relatively independent unity of motion. The most comprehensive system that we can survey is our planetary system ; it is itself a partial system, relatively complete in itself, of a system of a higher order, and in turn organizes itself into smaller unities, the heavenly bodies, which again are themselves in part cosmical systems with many parts, planets with satellites and rings. Each of these parts, like the entire solar system, exhibits cyclical motion and unitary development ; each heavenly body moves in periodic revolutions on its own axis and around the central body ; at the same time it passes through serial stages of development which have a uniform history. We are able to sketch, at least in outline, the history of the earth's evolution. Upon the earth in turn, the only heavenly body with which we are more closely acquainted, we meet reduced copies, as it were, of those cosmic unities, that is

organisms. Like microcosms, they repeat the evolutionary
laws of the macrocosm; they represent small, unified
organized systems having a series of periodically-recurring
changes: circulation of the blood, respiration, metabolism,
generative changes, all of which are included in a unitary
total development (birth, growth, old age, death). Everywhere these changes occur within a relatively-complete
unity, but they are always related to the movements in the
larger system: plants and animals adapt themselves with
their cyclical vital processes to the cyclical motions of the
earth; generative changes generally follow the changes of
the seasons, that is, the motions around the central body;
the activities of life and metabolism are intimately related
to the changes of night and day, that is, the motion of the
earth around its axis. Finally, physiology again resolves
the living bodies into smaller unities, into cells, which in
turn exhibit the same microcosmic character in miniature.
And chemistry at last shows that all bodies, organic and
inorganic, consist of small systems, of molecules, which are
in turn explained as composed of presupposed parts, of
atoms. Here the analysis rests for a while, leaving it to
the future to construe these atoms as composite systems.
Thus natural science represents reality to us as a cosmos
unified and organized throughout.

It is easy to see that the *mental world*, as far as we
know it, reveals the same trait; here too, unity and
organization are the prominent fundamental features.
There are no isolated elements in the historico-mental
sphere any more than in the physical world. Rather, they
are all combined into the unity of a historico-mental
life. Take any individual life you please. Its contents
cannot be described except in relation to the historical
whole. The whole history of the age and the entire past
are contained in it, while its effects influence the entire
future. A biography of Lessing cannot be written without
the appearance in it of Frederick the Great and Voltaire,
Göze and Gottsched, Leibniz and Spinoza. But each of
these men in turn is also related to contemporaries and
predecessors; the entire historical world of the seventeenth and eighteenth centuries exerts its influence; and

it would be caprice to select any detail and to represent it by itself. And the development of modern times,
again, is most intimately connected with the Renaissance
and the Reformation, with the middle ages and antiquity;
and in Grecian history, antiquity comes in contact with the
Orient. All these factors are the presuppositions of the
mental content which we call the life of Lessing. We see,
the historico-mental sphere forms a unity like the physical
world : all in each and each in all !

The tendency to form smaller circles, relatively complete
in themselves, shows itself here also. Humanity organizes
itself into peoples, each one of which forms a unity of mental life joined together by the unity of language, in which
the mental content objectifies itself. The peoples in turn
are organized into tribes, these into provinces, the provinces into separate localities, the localities into families,—
each of these groups, a unified, relatively independent
sphere of life, having its own history and peculiar mental
content. The ultimate unities consist of individuals, in
each of whom the larger spheres exist as specialized forms
of inner life, occurring in this way but once.

Reality, therefore, represents, as far as we can see, a
unitary, organized system governed throughout by laws : a
cosmos. That is a fact. And now the question arises, How
shall we interpret or construe these facts? How does it
happen that the world is not a chaotic plurality of elements
absolutely indifferent to one another, for that, too, would
be conceivable? What is the explanation of the cosmical
nature of existence, the organization and concentration of
all things into one great correlated system ?

There are three attempts to solve this problem, three
cosmological hypotheses : *Atomism, Anthropomorphic Theism,* and *Pantheism.*

Atomism (which is not necessarily materialistic, for a
monadology consistently carried out is atomism) assumes
that the semblance of unity arises through the merely
accidental juxtaposition of original elements absolutely
independent as such. An original inner connection between
the atoms does not exist at all. But inasmuch as they,
although indifferent to each other, move in empty space

and meet each other, those transitory combinations arise which we call objects and connections between objects. And since infinitely many elements move promiscuously in infinite space and in infinite time, all possible combinations must become real for a time.

Anthropomorphic Theism asserts, on the other hand : It is not conceivable that the unity, organization, and arrangement of reality is a result of accident or of motion following blind law. The form of the world can be explained only by the action of an architectonic intelligence acting according to ends, anticipating the organization and course of the world in thought.

Pantheism, finally, assumes the principle of unity as a principle immanent in the world. Reality is a single being ; not the unity, but the plurality is the illusion. Or, the elements of reality are not independent objects whose sum constitutes the whole. They are elements determined by the whole, immanent determinations or modifications of its essence.

2. Atomistic and Teleological-theistical Explanation of Nature.

I shall begin my examination of the rival hypotheses with the exposition of the antithesis between the atomistic and the theistic hypotheses. And I shall present this antithesis, first of all, in the form in which it has for thousands of years dominated human thought, that is, without regard to the change effected in the problem in our century by evolutionistic biology and cosmology. These are the two conceptions which are still most acceptable to the popular thought of to-day. Atomism is prevalent in natural-scientific circles, while anthropomorphic theism flourishes in the circles influenced by the philosophy of the church. Let me add at once, however, that the doctrine of the church essentially differs from the view which I designate as anthropomorphic theism in this, that it assumes no independently-existing matter, that it regards God, not as the architect, but as the creator of the world out of nothing. In this respect it approximates the third concep-

CII. II.] THE ATOMISTIC AND THEISTIC HYPOTHESES. 151

tion, the pantheistic one, so closely that it cannot be separated from it in thought. A being that creates all the rest out of nothing is necessarily the only independent or really existing being. Objects that are created and preserved by him have no independence in relation to him ; they are, in relation to God, activities or determinations of his essence. The omnipotent being can do anything but give his creatures independence over against himself, unless, of course, he should be able to make them uncreated beings.

Anthropomorphic Theism, to begin with its exposition, rests on some such argument as the following. It is called the *teleological* argument.

Wherever we find a plurality of elements which are independent of each other, as far as their existence is concerned, so arranged that their co-operation regularly produces a rational or valuable result, we assume that the arrangement of the parts has been effected by an intelligence which desires the result as an end and brings together the parts as means to this end. In a clock, for example, there are many parts : wheels, pegs, jewels, hands, face, spring, so conjoined that their co-operation produces a uniform motion of the hands, and thus the clock becomes an appropriate instrument for measuring time. Whoever knows its purpose and sees the arrangement of the parts, at once infers with certainty that this object is a product of art and design. And if he were to find a clock or but the fragment of a cog-wheel on an uninhabited island, he would forthwith say : Men have dwelt here ; chance has not arranged these elements in this way, but human purpose.

Well, the same is the case with nature as a whole. We have not witnessed the first arrangement of the parts, but everywhere we meet products of nature which so resemble products of human art and purpose that we are driven to infer a similar origin, the activity of an architectonic intelligence. This is particularly true of living beings. In structure and function they resemble very complicated machines. The parts—bones, muscles, ligaments, nerves, vessels, heart, lung, blood, stomach, skin, hair, etc.—are so conjoined that their interaction produces the effect which

152 THE COSMOLOGICAL-THEOLOGICAL PROBLEM. [BOOK I.

we call life and recognize as rational and valuable, nay, as the presupposition of all values. And each of these parts is again composite and exhibits the same wonderful adaptation of many parts in order to make possible a function essential to the whole. Take the eye. First we have the retina with the terminations of the optical nerve-fibres —wonderfully complicated formations, as the microscope shows, capable of being excited by those extremely slight shocks, light-waves, and to conduct their excitations over the nerve-fibres to the brain. Such general sensitiveness to light would, however, be of little value in orienting us in the world, if sharply-outlined images of objects were not thrown upon the retina. This is effected by the optical apparatus in front. The entering light-rays are so refracted by the cornea, lens, and vitreous humor as to draw a sharp, reduced, reversed image of the object upon the retina. The movable screen or iris with its central opening, the pupil, which wards off the scattering rays which would otherwise enter the margin of the lens; the black pigment covering in the orbit of the eye; the complicated muscular and nervous system by means of which the eye can accommodate itself to the different distances of objects, as well as its ability to move in all directions in the socket, complete its utility. This so important organ is finally protected in the most careful manner; imbedded in a bony cavity of the skull, it is further protected against all kinds of accidental injuries by lids, lashes, and brows.

What meets us here is a thousand times repeated in the organism. Every system of organs displays the same ingenious combination of a plurality of parts into an instrument whose activity furthers the preservation of life, be it of the individual or of the species. The more deeply anatomy and biology penetrate into the structure and functions of the body with new methods of investigation, the more wonderful the phenomenon appears. The complication becomes greater and greater, the organization more and more thorough-going, the development more and more diversified. In the same measure, our wonder increases at the harmony between the parts and the whole, the adaptation of the whole to its environment. Each advance in the extension and concentration of knowledge brings biology to a deeper insight into the inner unity of the plan which governs the development. " Like an architect of nature," Trendelenburg, the renewer of Aristotelian teleology in our century, admiringly exclaims, "Cuvier outlines the means and the form of construction of an animal species from the idea of its purpose." * A few fragments of the skeleton of an extinct animal species suffice to acquaint the master with the plan of the whole, and enable him to reconstruct the animal's form and functions before our very eyes.

How did the living beings arise? Now they arise through generation and growth; the form is derived from parent-individuals by heredity. But how did they arise originally?

The question is answered by atomistic materialism as follows: By a spontaneous concurrence of atoms that move according to general physical laws. In the infinite succession of blindly necessary movements, all possible arrangements of the elements must be realized, among them incidentally also those which exist in plant and animal forms. Thousands of combinations may, perhaps, have fallen to pieces again, but finally such too had to be formed as were able to preserve and to propagate themselves.

Is that conceivable? the teleologist asks. Or, if conceivable, is it possible to believe that such a process has actually taken place? So then, at some point of time, at some place or other, here upon the naked earth or in the slime or in the water or in the air, all the elements met which make an eagle or a shark or a lion? There stands your lion, a happy conflation of atoms, provided with skin and hair, with eyes and ears, with teeth and claws, with heart and arteries full of circulating blood. Let the boldest fancy attempt to picture the process. And consider: at the same lucky moment, the same accident had to make a lioness, and that too, in the same place, for otherwise the happy chance would still have been in vain! And of course it had to make also a beast to prey upon, a gazelle, or bet-

---

* *Logische Untersuchungen,* 2d ed., 1862, II. 8.

ter, a pair of gazelles, or rather a number of such pairs, enough for food, until a fresh supply was produced.

We shall have to confess, if that is not incredible, then nothing in this world is incredible. And the matter does not become any the more plausible by letting the parts arise separately, as Empedocles suggests: arms and legs arise without a trunk, eyes and ears, without a head, and then these meet, and in case they fit into one another, they combine permanently. Aristotle is wholly in the right when he opposes this view with the thought: the whole exists before its parts; the parts evolve within and out of the whole, and can arise in no other way. The smallest hair will not grow except on a body to which it belongs, even if you shake the atoms together ever so long. And now we are even to believe that the hairs on a lion-skin, after having originated singly, after hundreds of thousands of them had been whirled through the world singly,—that one day these hairs suddenly came together on a skin, each inserting itself into its pre-established hole! Why, it would be a hundred times easier to believe that once upon a time, say perhaps in consequence of an earthquake, thousands of fragments of stone were so polished and shaken together as to produce a Doric temple and at another time a Gothic steeple, or that some one shaking millions of types out of a big bag had finally succeeded in getting them to fall together in exactly the right way to form an Iliad or an Æneid.

Indeed, Aristotle does these views no injustice when he compares them to the delirium of drunken men, and praises Anaxagoras for advancing the thought that it is reason through which order is brought into chaos, and for placing us upon the ground of a rational and conceivable view.*

There is nothing new and surprising to us in this thought of Anaxagoras. It seems plausible to us, and many a man of to-day will regard it as trivial. But in those days it was a discovery. The gods of the popular

---

* Aristotle, *Metaphysics*, I. 4 (984b, 15): νοῦν δή τις εἰπὼν ἐνεῖναι καθάπερ ἐν τοῖς ζῴοις καὶ ἐν τῇ φύσει τὸν αἴτιον τοῦ κόσμου καὶ τῆς τάξεως πάσης, οἷον νήφων ἐφάνη παρ εἰκῆ λέγοντας τοὺς πρότερον.

Grecian mythology were not creators or formers, but creations of the world. That the world might be the work of
a mind was a conception originally altogether foreign to the
Greeks. What makes Greek philosophy so attractive to
the man who studies it with historical appreciation is the
very fact that he perceives in it how the human mind
gradually begins to wonder at the world. The common
man is not surprised at objects; he has been familiar with
them from his earliest childhood; what is there so wonderful in them? That the sun, moon, and stars rise and set,
that plants and animals are born and grow,—well, that was
always so; what is there so wonderful about that? The
philosopher is the first to be astonished. Or rather, as
Plato and Aristotle observe, the beginning of philosophy
dates from the time when some one was astonished at and
began to reflect about what everybody had hitherto regarded as a matter of course. How did the firmament
arise, and what was the origin of plants and animals?
With these questions concerning the origin of the big and
little worlds, Greek philosophy begins. And the first
answers are the above-mentioned attempts to explain
nature by the specific qualities and movements of original
elements.

It was Anaxagoras who first became aware of the inconceivability of these views. The more clearly and definitely they were formulated, and they were so formulated by the philosophy of the atomists, the more distinctly their impossibility became apparent. And hence,
in the face of the mathematical uniformity of the world
and the eternal order of the heavenly motions, Anaxagoras, for the first time in the Greek world, expressed the
happy thought: From mind alone can order come. Plato
and Aristotle took up the idea; it is the cardinal point in
their view of the world. Not blind movement, but the
power of a thought directed towards the good gives to
objects their form and reality, pervading them universally.
Of course, " another " must also be presupposed which, on
the one hand, receives these " thoughts," on the other, however, hinders their perfect realization—an *irrational* factor
beside the rational one : that is, matter. And thus the diffi-

culty which is involved in the new theory is presented: How is thought related to matter? Whence the power it exerts upon the latter? Has the cosmical reason eyes and ears like the human workman? Trendelenburg expresses (*Log. Unt.*, p. 74) the difficulty as follows: " Nowhere in nature do we observe the point at which thought lays hold of force and employs it for its ends, nor can speculation discover it anywhere. The theory which seeks the inner purpose places the ideal in the real, but it still lacks the knowledge of how the ideal finds its way or enters into the real. In human affairs, the purpose controls the executing hand, and this initiates the real occurrence. In the case of the natural occurrence, the analogy breaks down at this point, and into this breach in knowledge the doubt enters which regards ends with suspicion. It is not impossible," he adds with resignation, "that our knowledge will be enlarged; for the present it is enough to know what we know and what we do not know."

Indeed, it is this "breach in knowledge" through which doubt has entered again and again and disturbed the teleological theory of nature. An explanation by means of a thought, whose existence cannot be proved empirically, and whose efficiency cannot be construed physically or physiologically! It is not strange that the natural scientist was at a loss what to do with it and therefore found himself reduced once more to the mechanical explanation. However improbable Empedocles's explanation of the origin of organic beings may seem, it is nevertheless an attempt to represent the process to intuition. By waiving a conception that may be rendered intelligible to the imagination, the teleological hypothesis waives a natural-scientific explanation altogether.

In this way we get the *dilemma of the mechanical and teleological views of nature* which runs through the whole history of philosophy. In ancient philosophy, the school of Epicurus renews the atomistic-mechanical-natural philosophy of Democritus in opposition to the idealistic-teleological speculation proceeding from Socrates. In modern philosophy, the prevailing interest for natural science is a point in favor of the former view. With the establishment of the new cosmical and physical conceptions in the sixteenth and seventeenth centuries, a strong aversion to the teleological explanation of nature made itself felt, and this feeling scholastic philosophy, the legacy of the middle ages, aided by the church dogma and Aristotelian philosophy, found it hard to suppress. The same feeling exists as a tendency in Bacon and Descartes, while in Spinoza, who absolutely rejects the teleological explanation of nature, it reaches its climax. Then a reaction sets in again. In the eighteenth century, the teleological conception of nature is in the ascendant. In the popular philosophy of the times in Germany and England, the explanation of nature by the design of a supranaturalistic reason was perhaps . carried out more naïvely than ever before. This is due, on the one hand, to the general conciliatory character of the age, which is exemplified by the two philosophical leaders, Leibniz and Locke. Another circumstance, however, also contributed to it. The little world, the world of living beings, offered a far more obstinate resistance to the mechanical explanation than modern science had expected in the first delirium of its triumph. One must read Descartes's physiological treatises in order to appreciate how confidently philosophy, equipped with the new principles, approached the explanation of vital processes, convinced that it must succeed before long in discovering every mystery of life by revealing its mechanism. Instead, anatomy and physiology continued to unearth newer and more profound mysteries, especially with the aid of the microscope. How helpless we stand to-day before the mechanism of the nervous system, whose activity Descartes finds it so easy to explain! Thus it happened that though the natural scientists did not exactly accept the teleological view, they nevertheless let it pass for want of a better. Even as late as the first half of the nineteenth century, the atomistic-mechanical conception of nature seems almost extinct. Vitalistic-teleological notions, such for instance as Trendelenburg (not to mention speculative philosophy) entertains, prevailed even among natural scientists.

Indeed, if we had to make our choice between Empedocles and Anaxagoras, the decision could hardly be in doubt. That animals and plants should have accidentally arisen, once upon a time, by the falling together of the parts, is and will remain incredible. That was felt even by such critical thinkers as Voltaire and Hume. However little they were inclined, as a rule, to make concessions to the theological philosophy of the time, the denial of ends in the organic world and the purely mechanical explanation nevertheless seemed to them a hopeless matter. Of course, the weakness of the teleological view did not escape them either. And so they found themselves confronted by an insoluble dilemma.

It is the modern biological conception, whose most recent development is connected with Darwin's name, which seems to offer the only escape, at least from the most immediate and perplexing difficulties. However, before I enter upon this subject, I should like to make a few criticisms on the old teleological argument. Even in our day the matter possesses an interest that is not merely historical.

3. Critique of the Teleological Argument.

Let me introduce the critical discussion with a general remark concerning the value of the teleological argument for religion and metaphysics.

The real thing which the argument ought to prove is the proposition : The formation of the corporeal world cannot be explained without assuming a cause that operates according to design. The tendency still exists in many circles to regard this argument as a part of the philosophical substructure of theology, or even as an indispensable support of the belief in God, and hence to view a criticism of it as an attack upon religion.

It seems to me, religion is not at all interested in these cosmological speculations. Religion does not rest upon a hypothesis concerning the origin of living beings, any more than it rests upon a definite idea of the astronomical form of the world. Its concern with such matters, if it has any at all, is only with the objective truth and subjective truthfulness of our knowledge. What is dangerous to it as well as to all things human is the alliance with error and falsehood. The church ought to have learned so much at least from her unfortunate conflict with modern cosmology in the seventeenth century, that it is under no circumstances advisable for her to affiliate with any scientific system. When the church made the Aristotelian-Ptolemaic cosmology an article of faith, she applied the axe to the roots of her faith. Every blow that struck the false theory also struck the church. The same effect is bound to ensue if the church declares a certain biological view as a part of her doctrine. The persons who see in Darwinism the final destruction of religion well illustrate this fact. By removing the Mosaic account of creation, and Adam and Eve, they say, Darwin has, at the same time, made superfluous for biology, "the hypothesis of a God" which cosmology had long ago abandoned. From youth they have been taught to regard the existence of God as proved and assured by the teleological argument; now they no longer have confidence in the old proof and consequently reject the thing itself. Nothing is more dangerous to a good cause than false arguments.

It seems that Darwin himself underwent the same experience. He lost his religion when he lost his confidence in Paley's evidences. He says: "The old argument from design in Nature, as given by Paley, which formerly seemed to me so conclusive, fails, now that the law of natural selection has been discovered. We can no longer argue that, for instance, the beautiful hinge of a bivalve shell must have been made by an intelligent being, like the hinge of a door by man."* "At the present day," he continues, "the most usual argument for the existence of an intelligent God is drawn from the deep inward conviction and feelings which are experienced by most persons." Formerly he was led by feelings such as those just referred to, to the firm conviction of the existence of God and of the immortality of the soul. The grandeur of the Brazilian forest, he says, used to inspire him with religious awe. "But now the grandest scenes would not cause any such convictions and feelings to rise in my mind. It may be truly

---

* Charles Darwin's Life, ed. by his son, Francis Darwin, p. 63.

said that I am like a man who has become color-blind."
In another passage he mentions the fact that his love for
poetry has gradually disappeared—a proof of the withering
effect which continual scientific investigation may exert
upon the soul! His state was, however, evidently precon-
ditioned by the original intellectualistic bent of his religious
convictions, formed by his early instruction. He has a
feeling of having been cheated by false theories and proofs,
and therefore looks with distrust upon the entire church.
This is an every-day occurrence. Consequently it is a vital
question for the church to assume a proper attitude towards
science. The mutual distrust existing between science and
the church is fatal to her. The proper attitude for her,
however, does not consist in always accepting the latest
theories, but in making herself altogether independent of
scientific and philosophical theories. What I offer, she must
say, is valid, whether Copernicus or Ptolemy, Darwin or
Agassiz, is right. The gospel is and has no system of cosmology and biology, it preaches the kingdom of God which
is to be realized in the heart of man. It does not rest upon
unexplainable natural events and miracles, but upon the
experiences of the heart which finds in it peace and blessedness.

Indeed, I am convinced that nothing in our time is so
dangerous to the belief in God and his kingdom, at least
in scientific circles, as the attempt to foist anthropomorphic theism upon the understanding, as a scientifically
necessary theory of the universe, by means of antiquated
arguments that conflict with natural-scientific investigation.
(It will be seen later on in what sense anthropomorphic
theism has been and always will be possible.) Ignorance
was ever a weak support; to attempt to cling to it looks
like a tendency to obscurantism, which makes ignorance the
basis of clerical domination : *nam sciunt, quod sublata igno-
rantia stupor, h. e. unicum argumentandi tuendæque autoritatis
medium, quod habent, tollitur* (Spinoza, *Eth.*, I., Appendix).

The teleological argument which tries to pick flaws
in the physical explanation of nature in order thus to
prove the need of assuming non-physical causes is not a
fit support for religion. Nor is it a fit support for an

idealistic philosophy, for a true teleological conception of the universe. It simply leads to the denial of all ends in reality. The natural philosophy which in our times insists upon the insufficiency of the physical explanation appears solely as an ally of "indolent reason," which it is the primary business of scientific investigation to repudiate. It is the legitimate triumph of Darwinism that it wrested from the *ignava ratio* the territory which she considered most peculiarly her own, the field of vital phenomena, and opened it to scientific research. No one rejoices at the defeat of the idea of design as such, but those of us who have theoretical tendencies cannot but welcome the overthrow of the *ignava ratio*.

Let us not be deceived! Natural science will never again be decoyed from its path, which seeks a *purely physical* explanation of *all* natural phenomena. There may be a thousand things which it cannot explain now, but the fundamental axiom that these too have their natural causes and therefore a natural-scientific explanation, will never again be abandoned by science. Hence the philosophy which insists that certain natural processes cannot be explained physically without a remainder, but necessitate the assumption of a metaphysical principle or a supranatural agency, will have science for its irreconcilable foe. The two can live in peace only on condition that philosophy absolutely refrain from interfering with the *causal explanation* of natural phenomena, and allow natural science quietly to finish its journey. But would this mean that there is no place for philosophy? Would a metaphysic find nothing more to do, would the completion of the natural-scientific explanation exhaust our theoretical interest in reality? I think not. For now a new question arises. What does it all *mean?* If astronomy had completely explained the cosmical processes by physical laws, if biology had completely revealed to us the origin and mechanism of organic vital processes, the question would remain, What is the meaning of this entire play of forces, what is that which meets us in the thousand forms and movements of the corporeal world? Or is nothing else involved in it, is the corporeal world the whole of reality, and does the physical explanation dispose of everything? Concerning this point we have already come to an understanding in the preceding chapter on the ontological problem. Perhaps we may say : There never was a man and there never will be a man whom such an explanation can really satisfy. Natural-scientific thought does not really desire to deny the existence of another, say of an ideal factor of reality in addition to the physical elements, in materialism ; it rejects the employment of this ideal principle as a physical explanation. There is no opposition whatever between the mechanical explanation and the idealistic interpretation as such. The conflict arises only when the idealistic interpretation strives to take the place of the causal explanation, and to render it superfluous.

To use an illustration : Suppose we had a sheet of paper with characters printed on it. It suggests two questions. How were the characters on the paper produced? and, What do they mean? The first question is answered by a description of the machinery and work in a printing-office ; the other by an exposition of the thoughts which are expressed by these characters. The two answers may exist side by side, and one cannot be substituted for the other. The same is true of our knowledge of nature. The physical explanation is necessary, but it does not settle everything ; the question concerning the meaning remains. On the other hand, the endeavor to discover the meaning cannot take the place of the causal explanation. Should the attempt be made, the natural scientist must repudiate it and say : That is not at all what my question called for ; what I desire to know as a natural scientist is not the meaning, but the process employed in producing the signs, the mechanism of the printing-establishment, as it were. It would be a foolish misunderstanding on the part of the metaphysician to believe that he can answer the question by referring to thought ; still more foolish would it be were the natural scientist to feel himself called upon to deny to these signs all thought or significance.

Hence : *Everything must occur and be explained physically ;* and *Everything must be considered and interpreted metaphysically.* This is the formula on which physicists and metaphysicians can agree. We need not discuss how large a remainder is left over in both cases and on which side it is the greater. The hostility between the two is due to their tendency to encroach. On the part of the natural scientist it manifests itself as a tendency to negate the metaphysical altogether : Only the physical exists ; reality has no other side than the one facing me. On the part of the metaphysician it appears as the tendency to wrest from the scientist as much of nature as possible, and to reserve it for metaphysical explanation only.

And here we are obliged to confess that the metaphysicians have invariably betrayed a strong and almost irresistible desire to interfere with the physical explanation, thereby provoking materialism absolutely to repudiate metaphysics and to posit the physical world as the only absolute reality. This propensity appears in the shallow and garrulous *natural theology* of the last century, in which the discovery of the " utility of things " or of the "purpose of the creator " was to serve for an explanation. It also appears under a different form in the haughty and scornful Speculative Philosophy which, though generally recognizing empirical science as a mental activity, regards it as an inferior mental activity, and takes occasion to discipline and correct science. For had she not fathomed it all ? And, if she only thought it worth her while, she certainly could explain the causal nexus of things. We find the tendency, however, even in such philosophers as have formed a true conception of the relation between physical explanation and metaphysical interpretation. This may be said of Schopenhauer, for example. His view concerning the relation between physics and metaphysics is, in general, the one indicated above. But at the same time, he is ever ready to meddle with the business of the physicist, that is, to replace a deficient physical explanation with a metaphysical one. There is really no causal relation between the metaphysical element (the will) and the physical one. Such a relation obtains between objects, but not between a thing-in-itself and its phenomenon. " We have as little right to appeal to the objectifications of the will as to the creative power of God, as a substitute for the physical explanation. For physics demands causes; the will, however, is never a cause." "The aitiology of nature and the philosophy of nature do not conflict with one another, but exist side by side, considering the same object from a different point of view." At other times, however, he concerns himself with phenomena which, in his opinion, the physicist cannot explain: the vital processes, for instance. He is indignant at the "stupid denial of vital forces" and the attempt "to explain phenomena of life by physical and chemical forces, and to let these in turn originate from the mechanical action of the matter, position, form, and motion of imaginary atoms." "Let us suppose that this could be done; then everything would, of course, be explained and fathomed, nay, finally be reduced to arithmetical calculations, which would be the holiest of holies in the temple of wisdom." Metaphysics here cries a halt to physics, to the aitiology of nature, in order to take the matter in hand herself.*

Welt als Wille u. Vorstellung, I. §§ 24 ff. (tr. by Haldane and Kemp, 3 vols. 1883–86). Compare also the passage in *Wille in der Natur* (section on Comparative Anatomy) (tr. in Bohn's Library) in which he corrects Lamarck by means of metaphysics. Lamarck, he says, was not able to conceive the development of living beings except in time-succession; because of his ignorance of Kantian epistemology, the thought never struck him that the will of the animal as a thing-in-itself is outside of time and yet determines its structure and organization. This also explains Schopenhauer's interest in all kinds of abnormal phenomena, animal magnetism, clairvoyance, sympathetic cures, etc. Physics is powerless here, but metaphysics can explain things by a will that is not bound by space and time, and hence the phenomena in question confirm the theory. In this way it happens that even Schopenhauer's philosophy is discredited by natural scientists who find much else in it to attract them.

The physicist is repelled by the same circumstance in the *Philosophy of the Unconscious*. It, too, refers to the gaps in the physical causal nexus and then introduces the metaphysical principle of the unconscious. v. Hartman himself, let it be said, has a very clear conception of the relation between physics and metaphysics. In his treatise, *Das Unbewusste vom Standpunkt der Descendenztheorie*, which he first published anonymously, he places himself wholly on the standpoint of natural science: all natural processes are physically conditioned. In the preface which he added to a new edition of the treatise, now appearing under his name (*Philos. des Unbew.*, 10te Aufl. III. 40 ff.), he makes the following remark concerning the weakness of his original position: The philosophy of the unconscious needs correction in this, that it underestimates or wholly overlooks the mechanical relation in its exposition. He should not have said that

Let me make a few critical remarks on the teleological argument. It maintains, as we have seen, that certain phenomena of nature, especially the organic formations, cannot be explained purely physically. Their similarity to products of human art and design is so great that they can be explained only as a system of means and ends which owes its arrangement to an intelligent being. And, therefore, since these formations are inseparably connected with nature, the whole of it must be regarded as the work of intelligence.

If the proof is not to confine itself to merely denying the possibility of a physical explanation, if it is to become a positive theory of existence, then it must solve two problems: (1) It must reveal the *end* which that intelligence had in view; (2) it must show that nature is an *appropriate system of means* for realizing that end.

As far as the *end* is concerned, we shall content ourselves, for the present, with the statement which all teleology ultimately makes, that it consists in the welfare of living beings. " God created everything for the sake of living beings, and these for their own welfare." Thus S. Reimarus defines the purpose of things in his teleological philosophy of nature, which was so highly esteemed in the last century.*

Now, how about the *means?* Does nature appear to the impartial observer as a system of means to this end? I fear, it would be a hard task to force such a view upon any

---

he overlooked it, but that his philosophy made the insufficiency of mechanical causation a proof that the unconscious is a necessary principle. Now that he is better informed why does he retain this unfortunate standpoint? Because "the question is of secondary importance only " ? That is a strange excuse on the part of a man who lays such stress on his agreement with natural science. Can it be that he finds it hard to repudiate the work which gave him such sudden fame, even though he has outgrown much that it contains? His pessimism is in the same predicament. At any rate, he shows a tendency in his later writings to treat it as a detachable piece of the system, the rejection of which would be no more equivalent to the abandonment of the system itself than the rejection of the view that the unconscious element expresses itself not only *in* but also *alongside of* the natural process.

* S. Reimarus, *Die vornehmsten Wahrheiten der natürlichen Religion* (3d ed. 1766, p. 300).

one who is not already convinced of it. First, consider the procedure of nature in the production of living beings. Does it resemble human purposive action? If, in order to shoot a rabbit, a man were to discharge millions of gun-barrels into all possible directions at random, would anybody call this an expedient way of killing rabbits?* Well, the procedure of nature in the production of living beings is not altogether unlike this. She places thousands of germs into the world in order to bring one to complete development. A single female fish lays hundreds of thousands of eggs a year. If all these germs were to thrive, develop, and leave the same number of offspring, all streams would in a few years be filled with fish. But such is not the case; nor is the earth full of hares or rabbits, though the offspring of a single pair would, as has been figured out, in a few years amount to millions if all were preserved. The reason for it is that of a thousand vital germs but one remains alive; the others perish during the different stages of development from a lack of favorable conditions of growth, though they are in themselves capable of life. Destruction is the rule, preservation and evolution, the exception. Popular reflection overlooks this fact; it sees only the favorable cases. The unfavorable ones are not noticed, that is all. It is just as in a lottery, where there are a thousand blanks to every prize. The blanks are forgotten, while everybody talks about the great prize. Hence the probability of winning seems great. Still, we should not have a very favorable opinion of the logic of the man who undertakes to prove that the lottery is a suitable way of acquiring a fortune. Well, it would be the same kind of logic which the surviving fish and rabbits or their philosophical advocates would employ in order to prove that nature is an institution whose purpose it is to produce fish and rabbits. Cicero's mariner was a better logician. He was exhorted to insure himself against shipwreck by votive offerings to Poseidon. His attention was called to the many votive tablets hanging in the temple. He answered with the question: And where are the tablets of those who have perished?

---

* The illustration is found in F. A. Lange, *Gesch. des Mat.*, II. 246.

A Darwinistic defender of teleology might, perhaps, answer: An excess of vital germs is necessary to maintain the struggle for existence by means of which the form is enhanced. Good. But now observe the manner in which death reaps its harvest. The cholera comes. It mows down the old and the young, wise men and fools, the healthy and the sick, the sound and the maimed, without making any great distinctions. It may be that on the average the strong and the prudent prove themselves somewhat more capable of resistance. Nevertheless we must confess that it is a very clumsy and unreliable procedure,—this method of mechanical averages whose teleology, when measured by human standards, is not of a very high order.

Or consider the facts which Haeckel collected under the title of dysteleology. Of what value to the organism are certain useless or injurious formations like the vermiform appendix, which, as far as we can see, is of no use to any one, but the cause of agonizing ruin to thousands?

Or look at the facts which might be called geographical or cosmic dysteleologies. It is plain that if the teleological philosophy of nature undertakes to explain the structure and organization of living beings by appealing to a cosmical or supramundane intelligence, it must also deduce the form of the earth, and finally, the entire cosmic system, from the purposes of that intelligence. Is there a *teleological geography?* Can there be such a science? It is true, there are parts of the earth's surface which are admirably suited as habitations for living beings. But there are, none the less, large areas which appear to be entirely useless for such a purpose. We may even leave out of account the extensive polar zones and the great oceans. The former might perhaps be justified as being cosmically necessary, the latter as having a teleological use for the climatic conditions of the continents. Besides, they are not devoid of living beings themselves. But what is the use of the enormous desert stretching across the two great continents of the Old World? Could not Sahara have been left out? It certainly might have been omitted without any great trouble. If the gulf which cuts into the northern coasts of Africa had been carried a few hundred miles farther, making a second Mediterranean Sea, something like the Baltic Sea in Europe, with a long line of coasts; if in addition to that, the mountains of this shapeless continent had been placed and grouped differently, a whole new world would have been gained. We admire the configuration of Greece and Europe, but it seems as though all art and care had been exhausted upon them and little or nothing had been done for the immense expanses of country in Asia, Africa, and Australia. It may be that a more perfect insight than ours can solve the riddle. Here, however, we have to do with a proof, with a theory, and such a theory can be constructed, as Hume somewhere says, not out of what we do not know, but only out of what we do know.

And how about *teleological cosmology?* Are the other heavenly bodies, or even the other planets of our system, suitable habitations for living beings? Or have they been neglected like the continents just mentioned? We have no means of answering the question. Suppose now some one were to deny it? Suppose he could make it appear probable that at least some of these bodies are not adapted to support life, that our earth owes its life to its fortunate position, and that the other planets, though having as great an excess of organizable matter as the earth, cannot produce life on account of a lack or superfluity of solar heat or because of other conditions? No one can furnish such a proof; the forms and conditions of earthly life are not conditions of life in general. Nor can any one prove the opposite; and hence it follows that it is not insight but caprice to assert that the universe is a structure arranged for the purpose of sheltering living beings.

If we expose a glass containing a vegetable infusion to the air, a mass of living beings will be generated in it within a short time, a mass of infusoria, which take their name from the infusion. Biologists tell us that the germs of such beings are diffused all over the atmosphere. When they find a favorable soil, such, for example, as a vegetable infusion presents, they come to life. If these animals were natural philosophers, they might reason as follows: Our existence is possible only through the special composition and temperature of the great ocean in which we are fortunate enough to live. It must, therefore, be assumed that our ocean and its further surroundings, if there should be such, were made by a creator who desired that we should live. If, however, these animals were to learn that at the very moment in which a favorable current of air blew them into the glass of water, millions of equally viable germs dropped by the side of it and perished, would they still adhere to their teleological philosophy? And should we, if they did, praise their logic?

So the matter stands with the solution of this part of the problem, the demonstration that nature is a system of means adapted to living beings. We turn our attention to the assumed *end.*

It is true, no human teleology can discover it except in the existence of living beings. Without life, the world would be absolutely indifferent and unintelligible to us. The problem of the teleology of design would therefore be to show that our living world exactly answers the highest purpose and represents the absolute good. It will have to show that the thousand different animal and plant forms are requisite to the realization of the best possible world. Has anything like that ever been done, or has it even been attempted? The interpreter of a play is able to show us the inner necessity of each person, of each action, of each scene, of each line in the drama. Has any one in the same way revealed the inner necessity of every animal and vegetable species? Has it been made plain that something would be wanting if any particular species had been omitted?

Or is that not necessary? Are the meaning and worth of each form self-evident to us? Do we immediately feel that reality is enriched by it? Manifestly not. We should soon be at an end, were we to try to enumerate the forms of life, especially of animal life, whose value our feelings concede without further question. The number of species which give us pleasure and are valuable is small compared with the infinite number of beings that are completely indifferent or repulsive and obnoxious to us. The

destruction of the thousand forms of creeping things would
not hurt our feelings in the least. No one but the zoolo-
gists, and among these only the specialists, would notice
the loss. Nay, numerous forms of life cannot be contem-
plated by us without abhorrence and dread. I simply call
to mind the parasitic existences which subsist in or upon
the bodies of other beings. How human feeling regards a
large portion of the animal world is shown by the circumstance that their origin was once naïvely attributed to the
devil. The church doctrine extricates itself from the difficulty by inserting between God and nature, as it now exists,
the fall of man, with which ruin came into God's creation.

Well, all those creatures which popular zoology classi-
fies as vermin, a term not expressive of high regard, were
created by nature with the same care as others. The
suctorial organ of the bedbug is, so the initiated assure
us, a real wonder of technics. It is plain that we are
obliged to draw the same conclusion from this as from the
structure of the human eye. It is also plain, however,
that we are thus placed before a new and immense riddle:
How can a mind of whose technical knowledge we must
have so high an opinion attach any importance to the
existence of such creatures?

Perhaps some one will remonstrate, saying: It is immaterial whether *we* are able to understand the value of these
formations or not. This mode of thinking is a survival of
the narrow view of the old *anthropocentric* teleology, which
derived the worth of everything from its relation to man.
A different way of looking at things has long been prevalent among sensible men, namely, the idea of *immanent*
teleology. This does not inquire into the utility or value
of a species for man, but considers every creature as an end
in itself. Existing for its own sake, its existence is justified
if it finds satisfaction in its being.

Let us suppose it were really so. Then we should
have to prove that inner organization and external environment universally constitute a system of means whose end
is to render the existence of living beings satisfactory or
happy. Has the argument been made? Can it be made?
I do not believe it. Nay, it would not be difficult to repre-

sent the facts in such a way as to suggest that the Creator was indifferent to this end.

The life of all animals is a constant struggle for existence, *i.e.*, for the conditions of life. For the great majority the struggle probably results in defeat long before the animal's inner vitality is exhausted. Of a thousand germs perhaps not one is developed, and of a hundred developed beings probably not one dies a natural death. The rest meet with a violent end in consequence of some unfavorable external circumstance, hunger and frost and all kinds of accidents, above all in consequence of a dreadful calamity : the animal becomes a prey to its enemies. That is not an exceptional case for which some excuse might be found, but the rule. It is the lot of most animals to serve as food for others : their life is a continual escape from and defence against stronger pursuers or little parasitic enemies. Why do such things happen if satisfaction or happiness is the end ? Why not enable all animals to subsist in some other way, by vegetable diet or by the immediate assimilation of inorganic substances in suitable combinations ? Why make them dependent on their fellow-creatures ? Why make the living bodies themselves the fostering soil for the enemies that devour them ?

The impartial biologist will perhaps see the facts in an altogether different light : pleasure and pain are not ends and evils, but means to the preservation of life. The animal is impelled by pain to escape injury and destruction, enticed by pleasure to seek what is useful and tends to preservation. And as far as I can see, the biologist would add, nature employs both means without preference. If, however, one of them is to be preferred, it is most likely pain rather than pleasure. Consequently, the end at which nature aims seems to be the preservation of life, and furthermore, the preservation of the species rather than that of the individual. The production and preservation of specific types is, therefore, the actual purpose of nature.

This would again place us before the riddle, How can the existence of all these forms of life be the end of a mind similar to our own ? To answer the question by saying that every animal is an end in itself, simply means to count on a person's stupidity and to put him off with an empty phrase. If we simply regard reality as we find it, as the absolute end, then, of course, it does not require great skill to show that nature is a system of means perfectly adapted to the realization of this end. If the pebbles on the seashore are "ends in themselves," then we can prove from them that the order of nature is the product of a mind operating according to design. Then, of course, the entire earth had to be so constructed, the ocean had to be so moved by wind and weather, the sun and moon had to be moved exactly so as to let these particular waves, having this particular force and direction, strike each stone. Otherwise it could never have assumed the exact shape which it now has. In view of these facts, I must confess that the old anthropocentric teleology is still preferable to its supercilious rival, the teleology of immanency. Here at least we get an intelligible if not satisfactory answer to the question concerning the universal end. The immanent argument tries to put us off with a mere word : end in itself.

This leads us to the question : How about the end and its realization in the field in which we perceive things most distinctly and make the surest judgments—in the world of man? Can it be that *the teleology of history* has been more fortunate in solving the problem than the teleology of nature? From times immemorial, nations and individuals have seen in the fate which they experienced, in the victories which they achieved, in the defeats which they suffered, in the fortunes as well as the misfortunes that befell them, the influence of the gods, the finger of Providence. Has the philosophy of history succeeded in transforming this *belief* into scientific *knowledge?*

The problem of a teleological philosophy of history is identical in form with that of natural teleology. It would first have to set forth the end of historical life and then show that the course of history is the direct road to that end.

In answer to the question concerning the goal, we get general statements like these : The purpose of history is the perfect development of the idea of man or humanity, the evolution of all their powers and dispositions into diverse and harmonious forms; or the introduction of reason into nature; or a life full of virtue, wisdom, love, and happiness,—in short, heaven on earth. Granted. But now we expect to see the perfect life concretely represented, to see the contour filled out; we expect a description of the rise of different nations, for the perfect development of humanity does not exclude a plurality and diversity of peoples; we also expect to get a clear idea of the perfect form of the religion of each nation, of its philosophy and science, its literature and art, its social and political institutions, its family life and its education. Or is that an impossible undertaking—impossible not only because our knowledge or our imagination is unequal to the task, but also because there can be no such goal, because life, at least life on our earth, consists of movement and is not a state of rest? Then the problem would be to prove that the course of history itself has absolute worth in all its parts, to show how each part is ingeniously combined with the whole, just as in an opera or a drama each part is conditioned by an intelligible inner necessity. Each particular element would then be a means to the end and a part of the end.

Hence the mere statement of the problem shows that it cannot be solved. Such a philosophy of history would have to show, not that each nation had to live in this particular climate, in this particular environment, in this particular proximity to other nations, in order to experience what it experienced and to become what it became—for it is self-evident that the Greeks would not have been the same people had they been cast on the shores of India, nor would the Mongolians have been the same had they been cast on the shores of the Ægean Sea—but it would have to show how such an environment, such contact with other peoples, such fortunes, have made its historical life as complete and rich in content as possible. It would have to show, for example, how the perfect development of German history, the highest evolution of the German spirit, was conditioned by the proximity of Germany to France and Russia, by the Thirty Years' War and the division of Poland, by the invention of printing and the distillation of brandy, and how it was likewise necessary that the ascension of Charles V.

to the throne should coincide with the beginning of the Reformation, Lessing's death with the appearance of the *Critique of Pure Reason* and Schiller's *Robbers*.

Let us leave out of account the speculative philosophy of history which imagines that it solves the problem by enumerating the peoples and ages according to a certain scheme, and by labelling each with a catchword to signify that it has passed through the dialectic process. Outside of this, very little has been attempted. Particular events of importance have been selected and brought into relation with their historical conditions as means and ends. Thus it has become customary to look upon the Roman Empire as a providential preparation for Christianity, and upon the humanistic movement as a preparation for the Reformation. Luther philosophized in a similar strain: No one knew before why God made languages; now it is plain to every one that he did it for the sake of the gospel. It is true, without such coincidences, history would have been different. Would that have been a misfortune? Was the temporary agreement of Luther with Hutten and the other enemies of the "obscurantists" a blessing? Who can say so? Surely no one can tell what would have happened had the factors been partially changed. We may say: The historical course of events, as it actually proceeded, was not the only possible one; but we cannot compare the possible with the real and say: Of all possible ways this was the best. Suppose the Peasant War had taken a different turn; suppose Columbus's ships had been sunk, or Charlemagne had been slain by the Saxons; or suppose the Straits of Gibraltar were closed and, on the other hand, that the Isthmus of Suez were a navigable channel; and the whole history of European nations would have been changed! Whether for better or for worse, who can tell? We may *believe* that all has turned out for the best, and a natural instinct which impels us to accept the actual as the necessary and the usual as the good, leads us to think so, but we cannot *prove* it. It is a mark of narrow-mindedness, which sees nothing in the lap of possibility beyond what actually exists, to hold that we can. It is the conviction of the happy, self-conceited speculative method, which prides itself on possessing in its concepts the world-moving forces called "ideas," and holds that the latter make use of the contingent facts of existence, be they what they may, without being deflected from their pre-established course.

It is furthermore worthy of notice that two opposite conceptions are formed of nearly all events that have brought about great historical crises. The one regards the occurrence as good, the other regards it as an evil. Take the Reformation as it is viewed by Protestants and Catholics. In one case, it is regarded as the deliverance of the German people from degradation and bondage; in the other, as the beginning of all disorder and dissolution, from which the church is again making a desperate effort to save us. Or take the account of the French Revolution as it is given by democrats and royalists. Or let the history of the Jews be written by Canaanites, the history of Spain by Saracens, the history of England by the peoples whom she has trodden under foot and crushed, in all parts of the world. The same events would, on the whole, be recorded, but with opposite signs—a proof that in evaluating these facts we are dealing, not with objective knowledge, but with subjective feelings.

Nevertheless, there is a certain agreement in the interpretation, and that is due to the circumstance that history is ultimately written by one side, by the surviving victors namely. The dead tell no tales. The same is true of those who are defeated in internal conflicts. If the counter-Reformation had been successful, the history of the Reformation would live in the memory of men in some such way as the Anabaptist movement. So it happens that by favoring the victor and bringing about the present state, history looks like a series of divine interpositions. If, in addition, it happens that the curtain of the future is painted with one's own hopes and ideals, then it is no wonder that things harmonize and that the whole of history seems to be the direct road to a predetermined goal.—It is this very circumstance which permits the theological philosophers of history to forget the strange ending of the history of the Jewish people. According to the old view, divine Providence is most conspicuous in the fortunes of this nation;

nay, we have in holy Scripture the authentic story of the way along which God led his chosen people. He chooses the country and the neighboring peoples for their surroundings; he inspires their judges and prophets, and gives them personal instructions; he is constantly taking a hand in their destinies, and helps them with miracles,—at the Red Sea and in the camp of the Assyrians before Jerusalem, for example; for centuries he inspires men to preach and prophesy the coming of a Messiah: and the end of the whole story is that when the Messiah appears, the people repudiate him, to be themselves repudiated by God as stiff-necked.

The impossibility of a teleological interpretation becomes even more evident in the life of the individual. At all times a man's own lot has been the ultimate and deepest cause of the individual's belief in a governing Providence. Significant crises in life depended on apparent accidents; an unforeseen issue suddenly led him out of calamity and oppression; even disagreeable occurrences finally produced wholesome effects. You see that it was not your foresight which gave your life a happy turn, and you say reverently : "What is man, that thou art mindful of him, or the son of man, that thou visitest him?"

But if you try to transform this faith into knowledge, countless difficulties and doubts assail you. Of course, everything that happened contributed to bring about the present state. But is it the best possible condition? Does your whole life correspond to your ideal? Was not a more perfect, higher, purer realization conceivable? And what of those who foundered in the sea of life altogether? Or are there no such men? To say so would be to fly in the face of facts. What was the trouble? Did the governing hand fail to come to the rescue? Or will you have the boldness to say : The conditions of life and fortunes they experienced were the best that the failures could have had; it is their own fault if in spite of them they did not live a righteous and successful life; any change in the circumstances of their education or of society would have resulted in still worse failure?

I do not believe that any one will undertake to defend

this view. If we can see anything in the facts, it is surely this. There are few natures so hopeless that no conditions of life could have made their lives bearable. In many cases it seems obvious to us that the individual's failure to develop properly was not due to his will and nature, but to unfavorable circumstances, either to extreme poverty and abject conditions, or to the abundance or dearth of serious problems to impel and stimulate the will, or to the dull indifference of his surroundings, or to the cunning seduction of wicked companions.

Hence it is impossible to get an insight even into the teleological necessity of an individual life. Faith may, at the end of the course, look back upon the intricate paths over which it has been led and thankfully adore a higher governance, but to speak of knowledge here would be presumption. Religious feeling pronounces the same judgment. It exclaims: "How unsearchable are his judgments, and his ways past finding out! For who hath known the mind of the Lord, or who hath been his counsellor?" And to this confession of ignorance it forthwith adds the confession of faith: "Of him, and through him, and to him are all things: to whom be glory forever." (*Rom.* xi. 33 ff.)

After what we have said, it will not be necessary to enter upon a detailed discussion as to whether the tele-, ology of history would be more successful if it were to substitute general happiness for the objective conduct of life in the sense of human perfection as its goal, and were then to show that the facts are means to this end. *One* fact will suffice to show how little such a view agrees with the sentiment common to mankind and hence with truth. The two religions which have the most followers, Christianity and Buddhism, are, in their origin at least, religions of salvation. They promise, not happiness, but deliverance from evil; not by means of civilization and the satisfaction of all needs, but by deliverance from desire, by deliverance from the will to live, from the pursuit of worldly goods, wealth, honor, and lust. Their judgment on the pleasure-value of worldly life is unanimous: life is suffering, sin and misery form the content of life of the natural man. According to Christian views, our terrestrial life is teleologically justified only by the fact that it bears a relation to a higher life, to the life beyond. It has meaning and import, not as an end in itself, but as a period of preparation and probation for eternal life. And this means, at the same time, that a scientific teleological interpretation of human life is not possible; the supramundane life is not an object of science but of faith.

Later on, it is true, Christianity entered upon closer relations with the world, and a Christian philosophy sprang into existence. It was then that a teleological philosophy of history arose on Christian soil and interpreted historical life as tending to the above-mentioned transcendent goal. Such a confusion of the transcendent and the empirical elements is, however, characteristic of the entire development of science while the latter was under the overmastering influence of the church. We may also concede that the teleology of history has never reached a system formally more complete than the philosophy of the church: heaven and eternal happiness the great goal of historical life; the earth its temporal scene of action; its central point the incarnation of God and the foundation of the kingdom of heaven on earth; all past ages leading up to this great central event, the entire future determined by it and imbued with it; the whole course of history bounded by the creation on the one side and the judgment-day on the other—indeed, such a simple and grand philosophy of history that we cannot look back upon it, in our helplessness, without a feeling of envy! What are Hegel's or Comte's barren abstractions compared with this concrete, living conception? Of course, we must console ourselves! The simplicity with which the middle ages jumbled together the elements of faith and knowledge is not ours. We also lack the narrowness of their field of vision. Their cosmic theory was destroyed by modern astronomy. Similarly, their historical theories, which were materially determined by the history of the old covenant and, since the Christian era, by the history of the church, have been overcome by historical research begun by humanism. Our field of vision has been infinitely extended by the most recent philologico-historical and biological investigations. Not the caprice of human thought, but the facts themselves, have burst the frame of the old system. It is futile to join the fragments together again into a teleological demonstration.

Let us sum up. Neither natural nor historical teleology has the value of a scientific theory. No serious philosophy can doubt this truth since the abandonment of the geocentric and anthropocentric view of the universe. All proofs that aim to force the understanding to recognize in the cosmos the operation of a spirit acting according to design fall infinitely short of the object of scientific argument.

But what, in spite of all, continued to turn men's thoughts into the same old channel was, especially, the absolute helplessness of natural philosophy in reference to the question concerning the first origin of living beings. It seemed incredible that, once upon a time, a lot of atoms should have been accidentally jumbled together so as to form such beings. And hence only one other explanation appeared to be possible.

It is true, this did not help the natural scientist in the least. The theory never possessed the worth of a satisfactory explanation or even of a practical hypothesis. To explain phenomena in the sense of natural science means to represent them as the natural and uniform effects of known forces. Now intelligence is, in truth, a known agency, that is, in the form in which it appears in human beings and animals. But it is by no means known as a cosmical agent. The natural scientist who is told that plants and animals were originally created by an intelligence will at once answer: Show me the nature of this intelligence and the way it acts; show me where, when, and, above all, in what manner it created organic beings. If you cannot do that, if you cannot get beyond the general proposition that a mind has been at work in the organization of the world, then I can do nothing whatever with your statement. Such a force, which is assumed to have been operative once, but of whose nature and mode of activity nothing whatever is known, is emphatically a *vis occulta*. In my opinion, therefore, it is utterly immaterial whether you answer the question concerning the first origin of

living beings by saying: A mind created them, we do not
know how, nor do we know anything further of the essence
of this mind; or whether you say: We do not know how
they originated.

And he might add: You say that the blind forces of
nature can create no living being, but I see daily that
they can. I place a seed of grain in the earth, and a stalk
grows out of it. The hen lays an egg, and, after a few
weeks of brooding, a chicken is hatched. True, I cannot
explain in detail all the forces and effects which take part
in the process, but this much I seem to observe: that deliberation and mental activity are not concerned in it, either
in the formation of the seed or in the production of the
egg or germ, or in the hatching or growth. If blind forces
are at present able to transform given matter into living
seed, and from this in turn to produce a living being, why
not originally? Or if the co-operation of an intelligence
was necessary then, why not now as well? If so, you are
certainly obliged to say: We cannot understand the growth
of the chick in the egg; hence it is necessary to assume
an intelligence, a mind that even now combines together
the particles of matter in all the thousand eggs and germs,
which are daily produced, in such a manner as to form
living beings. And then it will also be necessary for the
same mind to effect the movements of the parts in the living body. For we cannot expect blind forces to accomplish the task, whereas the intellectual powers of the living
beings themselves are apparently not the cause. What
does the chick just hatched know of muscles, nerves, and
digestion? Nay, how much does the physiologist himself
know about them?

4. The Theory of Evolution.

A new epoch in the treatment of the problem begins
with the establishment of the modern biological conception
of our age. The theory of evolution offers an escape from
the dilemma. It gives the natural or spontaneous origin
of living beings a form in which it is conceivable. It assumes, as is known, that animals and plants did not suddenly arise from inorganic matter as perfect beings, in the

forms in which we now behold them; it regards them
as the products of a long process of evolution. Not only
individuals but also species have their development. From
one or a few original forms with simple structure, diverse
and complicated formations gradually arose through the
co-operation of external and internal causes. In so far as
this view is able to adduce a long list of facts in its proof,
it is the first hypothesis which satisfies the formal demands
of a scientific explanation. The former theory, which
assumed that animal and plant species owe their origin to
an intelligence acting from without, is thereby finally overthrown as a natural-historical theory—overthrown, not by
being refuted, but, like every worn-out hypothesis, removed
by the entrance of its legitimate successor, the better
theory.

The first to apply the notion scientifically was the
French biologist Lamarck, in his *Philosophie Zoologique*
(1809). The thoughts of the contemporaneous German
natural philosophers, Schelling, Oken, and Goethe, moved
along similar lines. Exact science at first assumed a coy
demeanor towards such extravagant hypotheses. At first
the soil had to be better prepared. This was accomplished
particularly by the development of geology and palæon-
tology. The numerous extinct forms of life which were
gradually discovered made it certain that the organic
world had undergone great changes in the course of time.
The new facts were so many more obstacles in the way of
the old anthropomorphic hypothesis; they necessitated the
assumption of great catastrophes and repeated destructions
of the organic world, as well as of corresponding repeated
creations—an assumption which, by completing anthropomorphism, at the same time reduced it to an absurdity.
The extinct forms appeared as so many unsatisfactory and
abandoned attempts. At the same time, geology cut the
very ground from under the old theory. Under Lyell's
leadership it went over to the conception that the earth
owes its form, not so much to single violent catastrophes
as to the summation, in long geological periods, of the
uniform effects of the same forces which are still operative
now.

Thus the times were prepared for the great revolution in biological views which is connected with Charles Darwin's name. The work in which he first presented the new theory, *On the Origin of Species by Natural Selection* (1859), marks the beginning of a new epoch, not only in biology. Together with the work on *The Descent of Man* (1871), it exercised a significant influence upon our entire conception of the world, above all, upon the historical sciences, including politics and morals. I shall attempt to specify the main points of the theory.

Darwin's merit does not consist in his having been the first to conceive the idea of evolution, nor, more properly, in the discovery of the causes of transmutation—in an introductory historical sketch, he has himself shown with that frank and joyful recognition of the merit of others which makes him such an amiable scientific character, how all his thoughts had been expressed before him, at least in outline—but in the application and verification of these ideas in the world of facts. Darwin possesses the gift of ingenious combination, critical judgment, and astonishing perseverance, and these powers enable him to form, from scattered thoughts and facts, a theory, or rather a principle of investigation, the fruitfulness of which in the hands of others is the best proof of its value.

The principle of transmutation which Darwin regards as the real motive force in the evolution of living forms is the struggle for existence and the natural selection depending upon it.

The essential question at stake here (if for the moment we ignore the first origin of organic life) is this: Can new species arise from the species existing now? Old biology negates the question; experience shows that the offspring invariably resemble their parents. To be sure, slight variations in shape, size, color, etc., take place, but they are deviations from a constant mean that constitutes the specific type. The specific types are constant: that is the fundamental law of old biology.

Darwin's attention was early drawn to a field in which these slight variations play an important part—the field of domesticated animals and plants. In the case of domestic animals and cultivated plants, the deviations are not only numerous and important, but they have become fixed into permanent types, the varieties or breeds. Horses, cattle, sheep, pigs, dogs, chickens, pigeons, and likewise garden plants, fruit-trees, flowers, grains, appear in exceedingly diverse and varying forms, all of which, however, point to an original wild form as their common ancestor. And every day the gardener or breeder produces new forms, new varieties of flowers, pigeons, dogs, etc. How does it happen? Well, through natural selection. From the individuals at hand such animals are selected for reproduction as possess certain desired qualities in a marked degree—peculiar plumage, fine wool, flesh, swiftness or strength, etc. From the offspring which inherit the parental qualities, selections are again made according to the same principle. In this way we produce, in a comparatively short time, by the summation of slight differences, such considerable changes in form as, for example, English cattle, sheep, and hogs display in comparison with the original form.

Well, says Darwin, nature acts in the same way on a large scale; she is the great breeder. She too selects the individuals for the propagation of the species. It is true, the selection is not an act of deliberation, and the guiding principle is not, as in the former case, external utility for man, but immanent utility, that is, utility for the preservation of the individual and the species.

Natural selection occurs as follows : Life is for the living being a constant strife for vital conditions. The number of creatures that live and desire to preserve themselves is always greater than the number of seats at the table of nature—a consequence of her lavish production of living germs. The fertility of species differs very much; but there is no species a single pair of which would not, under favorable circumstances, be able to fill the earth with their offspring in the course of a few centuries. That this does not happen is due to the parsimony of life-conditions. In the battle ensuing for the possession of these, the great majority prematurely perish. It is, however, a further fact that the individuals of a species do not enter the struggle with exactly equal powers; many minute deviations occur. The result is that the individuals whose variations are advantageous have the greatest prospect of surviving the struggle; superiority means preservation of life. The qualities which constitute superiority may be very different in kind: unusual strength, swiftness, sagacity, and intelligence, or advantages in the possession of weapons of defence or attack; the power to avoid detection, or a greater ability to resist injuries of all kinds. Each of these advantages may make its possessor superior in a struggle, successful in flight, able to endure frost and famine, while other less-favored animals will perish. Accordingly, also, the same individuals will have the best prospects of leaving numerous offspring; and by transmitting to them their endowments, it happens that advantages which were at first individual gradually become properties of the species. The individuals best adapted to the conditions of life determine the type of the species. A one-sided excess in the evolution of certain qualities, for example in that of size or defensive organs or swiftness, could not be the result, because such qualities would disturb the general equilibrium and thus diminish the capability of life. An animal economy must, like an economic or political system, distribute its tasks among the different functions according to the measure of their importance: among the functions of defence, locomotion, nervous activity, etc.

In such a way, then, development or progressive evolution, in the sense of immanent teleology, can take place without the need of an intelligence, interfering from without, as a principle of explanation. And with the enhancement of the species, a differentiation of types also occurs. The maximum of life possible at any given moment is increased by a division into different types having different needs and different organizations. More individuals of different species can exist together than individuals of one species, because they fit into the vacant places and fill out all possible space. Darwin shows the validity of the law for plants. Deviation from the average in vital conditions is an advantage that tends to preservation and hence to the formation of new species. On it depends the disappearance of the mean forms; the extremes do not come into such strong competition with each other.   Here, too, a state of equilibrium is gradually reached that represents the maximum of life possible under such conditions.

Alongside of and together with the principle of natural selection which Darwin places in the foreground, he furthermore recognizes other principles as co-operative; thus the principle which Lamarck regarded as the essential cause of variation: changes in the conditions of the earth's surface.   By producing alterations in vital conditions, they necessitate modifications in function, and changes in the use of organs finally lead to alterations in structure. Migrations, which are occasioned by the struggle for existence, since it forces animals to wander, produce the same effect.   And as a second co-operative principle Darwin mentions the principle of correlative changes.   An organism is a unitary being that cannot be modified at any point without necessitating compensatory changes in other parts.   As no side or angle of a triangle can be altered without at the same time altering other sides or angles, no part of the organism can be altered by itself.   The strengthening of one part of the skeleton, *e.g.*, necessitates corresponding changes in the other parts, were it only for the purpose of maintaining the external equilibrium.   It is true, many changes take place here, the necessity of which is by no means clear to us; thus, for instance, there is a connection between the development of the sexual organs and simultaneous changes in habits and appearance.

Such are the principles of transmutation of the new theory.   Do they solve the problem of the origin of species?

First of all we must mention a fact that is not always sufficiently considered.   The presupposition of all development, without which the above-mentioned principles would have no support for their activity, is, of course, the will to live, the will to struggle for existence, common to all beings taking part in the evolution.   They do not suffer the development passively, they are not, like the pebbles in the brook, pushed into a new form by mechanical causes acting from without.   Their own inner activity is the absolute condition of the efficacy of natural selection.   The struggle for existence is not imposed upon individuals from without; it is their own will to fight the battle; and without this will, the will to preserve and. exercise individual life and produce and preserve offspring, there could be no such struggle for existence at all.   And moreover, the will to live is the absolute original precondition; it cannot in turn be derived from natural selection.   Otherwise we should have to assume that organic formations first arose in which it did not yet exist and which were indifferent to the preservation of individual and generic life; that, then, individuals possessing the first traces of such impulses happened to arise through accidental variation, and were thereby enabled to supplant others not possessing the impulses for food and reproduction.

Many Darwinians are inclined to overlook this fact. The most popular scheme of natural selection is that of a purely mechanical selection; as, for instance, the phenomenon of the adaptation of some insects to the soil on which they live, according to color, form, and marks (the so-called mimicry).   The specific type of the insects is here transformed in a purely mechanical way: those differing most from their surroundings are continually eliminated until at last only such remain as are the same in color.   In a similar manner the Madeira beetles are said to have lost their wings.   "For during many successive generations each individual beetle which flew least, either from its wings having been ever so little less perfectly developed or from indolent habit, will have had the best chances of surviving from not being blown out to sea; and, on the other hand, those beetles which most readily took to flight would oftenest have been blown to sea, and thus destroyed." (*Origin of Species*, chap. v. pp. 101 f.)

Since, in this case, we can hardly speak of an impulse to avoid danger by inactivity, the transformation of the specific types took place by a purely passive extermination. This, however, is apparently but one of the occuring forms of natural selection; here the struggle for existence is a pure metaphor.   It is not always metaphorical, however. As a rule, the impulse to preservation is the precondition of preservation, be it in competition with rivals or without such competition. Those who ignore the fact should be reminded of Goethe's lines, which were not, of course, originally intended for them:

> " Kein tolleres Versehen kann sein,
> Giebst einem ein Fest und lädst ihn nicht ein."

Certainly, we do not mean by this will something supranatural, which occasionally projects its spectral activity into the corporeal world. On the physical side we are to interpret it according to the scheme devised in our ontological discussion: the will to live is the same thing, looked at from within, that meets the physicist externally as a body organized in a given way. The physical fact which is designated by the expression, will to live, impulse to eat and propagate, is the tendency of an organic body to react upon certain stimuli with movements and inner activities that make for the preservation of the system, that is, of any particular body and any particular species. The concrete representation of the nature of such a system is left to the physiologist. Its existence is not at all doubtful: we perceive it plainly in every seed of grain, in every impregnated egg; it is nothing but a concrete tendency to development, i.e., a system of forces, which will act in the predetermined manner as soon as certain external circumstances like heat, moisture, etc., arise. Whether we shall ever succeed in explaining the peculiar combination of molecular forces existing in a grain of wheat or in the shell of a hen's egg, does not concern us. That the problem has already been solved, that the " Newton of the blade of grass ", whose possibility Kant once denied, has appeared in Darwin, as Haeckel says, Darwin himself would have denied most emphatically.

And now a further question arises at this point: Is the immanent tendency by itself able to develop and to enhance the species, or does it invariably presuppose the struggle for existence and natural selection? It seems to me, nothing stands in the way of the first supposition. Such a process does undoubtedly occur in the individual. The inner disposition spontaneously determines the development in the pre-established direction. The individual having the form of the genus incompletely developed at the beginning of life realizes the complete form essentially by an exercise of its powers and dispositions, that is the result of spontaneous impulse. This is true of vegetative as well as of animal functions; through exercise the rudimentary organs in the young plant or animal reach their perfect development. Nor need the activity be universally conditioned by necessity : it breaks out from within, sometimes at first as an accidental variation, in which case the circumstances act merely as a stimulus and potentiality. Is the immanent tendency not merely the primary condition of evolution in the development of the individual as well as of the genus, but also sufficient in itself to initiate a progressive growth? Could there be a transition to newer, more perfect, more advanced forms even in cases where the struggle for existence and natural selection are not active? I believe there could.

Fechner somewhere suggests the following thoughts : The cock has spurs, plume, and comb, while the hen does not have them. Darwin, he says, explains the fact as follows : The rudiments of such characteristics due to accidental variation gave their possessors an advantage in the struggle for existence. For many generations the cocks best equipped in this respect invariably defeated their opponents. In such a way the complete extermination of the defenceless type took place and the present type became fixed. Fechner believes that if all the teleological equipments of animals, even the internal ones, were to be explained by such an accumulation of accidental variations, our brain would reel. "I am rather inclined to believe, that at a time when the organization was easily alterable, the psychical impulse to injure the opponent in battle as much as possible, the anger, which still impels the spur to action, was able to bring out the parts by modifying the processes of development. Though the impulse may not have been able to develop such parts in grown-up cocks, it was nevertheless able to predispose the germs and hence the offspring. These psychical desires, I, of course, regard simply as the inner side of the physical-organic phenomena." *

* Fechner, *Einige Ideen zur Schöpfungs- und Entwickelungsgeschichte der Organismen* (1873), p. 72.

Indeed, I see no objection to this view. The impulse to exercise the predisposition universally acts also as an impulse to develop form ; the individual receives its characteristic and perfect form by exercise. If the acquired characteristics are transmitted—and they cannot be altogether exterminated, even though the part played by them in heredity is very modest in comparison with inherited characteristics—if, therefore, the acquired parental habits act upon the germ, and hence upon the development of the offspring, helping to determine it, then we may say that the impulses and activities of all individuals will finally, in the course of generations, determine the specific type. Natural selection would then simply be a factor supporting and accelerating the process.

Darwin is not unfamiliar with the thought. He does not enter upon the question, Whence arise the individual variations which furnish the material for natural selection? Nothing hinders him from assuming that such variations are not altogether haphazard, but have a certain purpose, that is, they tend to the adaptation and advancement of the generic type. Cocks doubtless never showed a tendency to vary in the direction of forming fins or hoofs, which in turn had to be exterminated in the struggle for existence as unfavorable variations. It is more likely that the variations tended to be useful. "The purposive impulse," which is so pronounced in all the activities of an individual, extends also to the specific types. The egg or the young individual is predetermined in its development along certain lines, and has its will directed towards them. Similarly we may say of the specific types *in statu nascendi :* they are predisposed to develop in a definite direction, and their wills are bent upon that direction. The will, not a prescient will governed by purposes, but a will manifesting itself in impulsive feelings and acting in all individuals of the species, would then, in the last analysis, be the creator of the form. As the physiognomy and habits of an adult human being, his habitual mien, bearing, and actions, are, in a measure, his own work, so too the organic form would, in a certain sense, invariably be the product of the will.

Wundt has elaborated this thought (in the *System der*

Philosophie, pp. 325 ff.). All organic activities are originally acts of will. In the primitive forms, even the vegetative functions depend on impulsive acts; "the protozoon appears as a being acting in all its parts according to will-impulses. As almost each of its parts is homogeneous with the rest, so too its entire corporeal mass is one single organism determined by unitary volitional acts." But since the activity leaves a disposition behind and becomes fixed in the organism as a habit, it produces permanent structural changes transmissible by heredity. The activity is thereby made mechanical, and the will left free for new and higher functions. We see the same process in a higher stage of development. Action that was originally voluntary is transformed into habitual and finally into automatic action. Hence the organism is, as it were, congealed voluntary action. Of course, the result did not pre-exist in a mind as a purpose; the will was at every given moment directed only towards some particular activity. But the effects transcended the immediate aim,—a relation which we still find on the highest stage of development, in mental life, where the effects also regularly go beyond the immediately desired aims. Thus customs, legal norms, fixed rules of all kinds, arise; the will's immediate object is some immediate present aim, but by exercise it simultaneously produces unintended results — custom, predisposition, and habit, and finally a fixed transmissible form. Wundt has created for this peculiar circumstance the notion of the *heterogony of ends.*

In this sense, too, we may characterize the forms of living beings as the result of purposive activity—the purposive activity, namely, of all the individuals concerned in the evolution. At no point of the development was there present an idea of the future form; nevertheless the form is the result of the will and impulse, and, in so far as the goal momentarily aimed at by the will lay in the direction of the goal attained by the total development, we can say that the aim is also subjectively willed.

What we vaguely surmise and outline in the lower world is found more distinctly and explicitly in higher mental life. In the human world it is doubtless the will

which determines the form of the being. The form hovers
before the mind as a goal, at least in its most general outlines: as such we call it an ideal. Individuals as well as
nations have a more or less definite ideal of perfect culture, and the ideal has a formative influence upon their
development, and through education also upon the mode
of life of succeeding generations. In this way the will
objectifies itself by realizing the idea of its being.

Nor is Darwin unfamiliar with this thought. It is implied in the principle which plays so great a part in his
second main work, *The Descent of Man*, that is, in the principle of *sexual* selection. A large mass of facts is given
there, which lead us to the view that peculiarities of structure and appearance in the male are the effects of the
female's selection among her suitors. Hence the generic
ideal would, as it were, be unconsciously present in the
female and itself manifest in her preference for the males
who most nearly approximate it. And the same idea
may also have an influence upon the form of the fœtus.
Here, too, we must leave it to the physiologists to explain
physiologically the " idea " as a definite arrangement of the
nervous system which acts and reacts upon suitors in
certain ways and exerts certain influences upon the processes of fœtal life.

Let the above suffice as a characterization of the new
conception of the origin of the organic world. Numerous problems and difficulties are still contained in it.
How are we to explain the origin of the first living beings?
How does the principle of heredity operate? How are we
to explain the absence from palæontological remains of the
countless extinct links which must be presupposed? Must
we not also assume, in addition to infinitely small variations,
variations *per saltum*, in order to explain the great morpho-
logical differences in the various types? Such abrupt
deviations from the type might, perhaps, be explained most
satisfactorily as follows: Under unusual conditions of life
a germinal form arises that varies from the parental type
(so-called heterogeneous generation). I am not competent
to enter upon a further discussion of the subject. Time
will solve many a riddle, many another will in all proba-

bility remain unsolved. Only, we should not regard unsolved problems as refutations of the theory. The evolutionistic theory is not and will most likely never be a theory which can give a perfectly satisfactory answer to all questions that might be raised in reference to the formation of organic beings. We shall probably never have an uninterrupted history of the evolution of organic beings upon our planet; we have too few examples of the development. All that we can expect is a knowledge of the general principles and a schematic outline of the history of development, in which we are guided by the empirical proposition, that the evolution of the individual is an abbreviated repetition of the evolution of the genus. The same may be said of other fields of learning. Geology cannot explain every elevation and depression of the earth's crust, nor can meteorology explain every vibration in the atmosphere. In the last analysis, the problem of every science is an endless one. Darwin did not write the final chapter of biology. On the contrary, he has proposed new and grave problems to it. So much, however, we can say: The theory of evolution is really a theory in the sense of having established a principle of investigation that leads to real natural-scientific knowledge. That cannot by any means be claimed for the old hypothesis, which explains things by the influence of an intelligence operating from without according to design. This theory was never more than an attempt to escape a perplexity that was occasioned by the awkward dilemma mentioned above—either organisms owe their origin to the accidental congregation of atoms or they are the work of intelligence. It really accomplished what words generally accomplish—it repressed the immediate feeling of wonder and the spirit of inquiry; which is certainly not a creditable achievement for a scientific hypothesis. The new hypothesis proves its worth by suggesting new questions and stimulating us to answer them. Darwin, too, may say with old Xenophanes: "The gods have not shown forth all things to men from the beginning, but by seeking they gradually find out what is better."

5. Mental Evolution.

It has often been observed that the products of the historico-mental sphere greatly resemble those of the organic world. From the times of Plato it has been usual to regard the state as a human being on the large scale. A. Schäffle makes a detailed comparison between society and natural organism in his great and ingenious work, *Bau und Leben des sozialen Körpers* (Structure and Life of the Social Body). It is likewise usual to characterize language as an organism—perhaps it would be better to call it an organic system that belongs to the organism of a people. Indeed, the homology is obvious. We have here, as in the organic body, a great variety of heterogeneous parts which regularly co-operate to produce a rational total effect.

Take language. A great variety of heterogeneous parts co-operate to produce a total result, the living speech, which is obviously an effect valuable and suitable to the possessor of the organ, that is, to the people. Without it there could be no unity of mental life, no national life at all. Thousands of words, which may be compared to the cells that make up the bodily organism, are united in language for a common function. The stock of words perform the task of representing a people's entire wealth of thoughts and feelings in sensible sounds ; each word has its definite, limited function and significance within the whole. The organic character of the language manifests itself also in the peculiar elements of form. The different parts of speech (substantive, adjective, verb, etc.) correspond to large classes of ideas ; by their form they express that the thing designated belongs to the objects, qualities, or events. Each word is again endowed with a highly ingenious mechanism (by means of which it is able to express its relations to the elements with which it is connected), namely, with that system of minute changes in form which we call declension and conjugation. Thus language is a highly complicated and at the same time wonderfully accurate apparatus, whose object it is to represent all possible thoughts and feelings with the slightest shades of difference, an organon possessing such nicety and perfection that the most skilful machine is a simple instrument alongside of it.

How did this organism arise? At present it is transmitted by parental generation. The children learn the language from their parents; but what is the primitive origin of language? Was it accidental? Did one individual and then another emit an articulate sound on a particular occasion, a sound that was understood and retained, and thus became the name of an object or occurrence? That is apparently absurd. Consequently, language must be the work of intention and invention. So the rationalism of the last century, following the rationalism of antiquity, explained the matter. Human beings, thus the Marburg Professor Tiedemann philosophizes in his *Versuch über den Ursprung der Sprache* (1772), at first lived in an animal state. This was inconvenient and burdensome. They desired a better mode of life; which impelled them to unite; and thus there arose the need of a means of communication. "Perhaps they first hit upon gestures. But it could not have been long before they saw the inadequacy of such a language. Then they observed that emotions expressed themselves in sounds. They also became aware that animals employed sounds with good results. What was more natural than that they should attempt to utilize the discovery and use sounds as the signs of their thoughts?"*

Such reflections strike us as somewhat comical: they seem almost like a parody on the *Aufklärung* by the Romanticists. And yet the explanation has an advantage over the attempt to explain the organic world by means of the activity of a cosmical intelligence: it reckons with a known and given cause. It is true, this very advantage

---

* Quoted by Steinthal, *Der Ursprung der Sprache in Zusammenhang mit den letzten Fragen alles Wissens* (4th ed., 1888, pp. 6 ff.). This instructive little treatise gives a survey of the history of the theories of the origin of language up to the present time, together with hints at the author's own theory. Steinthal presents an elaborate exposition of the psychological foundation of the latter in his *Einleitung in die Psychologie* (2d ed. 1881), the first part of an outline of the science of language. *Umrisse der konkret-historischen Ausführung in der Klassification der hauptsächlichsten Typen des Sprachbaus* (1860).

results in a disadvantage; the cause is too well known to permit us to expect such effects from it. What were the details of this invention? we ask further. Did some clever fellow among those speechless men sit down one day and devise a language, as Volapük was invented in our day? Did he secretly invent the thousand names of objects, qualities, occurrences, relations, declension and conjugation, and then surprise his companions with the complete system? Did he show them the utility of his invention and its application, and so persuade them to learn and adopt the language?—It would hardly surprise us if the statement were added that the same man had previously also invented the intellect and had persuaded others to adopt it.—Did many co-operate to achieve the task? Was a commission appointed for the invention of language—an idea upon which we should at once hit in our day? Or did the many co-workers act separately: did this one, then that one, contribute his share—say a dozen names or a couple of prepositions? And then did another invent declensions —perhaps only the first declension; and then did still another invent the second, etc., until at last the four or five declensions, or as many as there may have been, were made? And then did a new inventor, encouraged by the happy successes of his fellows, hit upon conjugations and finish the active voice, and did still another add the passive voice, leaving it to a third to puzzle out the subjunctive mode? And did a particularly clever genius invent Greek, and did some thick-headed fellow sprinkle in the irregular verbs? That is the line of Tiedemann's thought—only, he always disclaims the principle of invention, leaving all to chance and necessity.

The same dilemma evidently confronts us here as above. Does language, do animals, owe their origin to chance or to methodical invention? There seems to be no middle course, and yet both of these views are equally inconceivable.

The science of language was the first to master the difficulty, and it did it in exactly the same way which biology afterwards followed. What caused the unfortunate dilemma was the notion that languages like species of plants and animals are immutable, fixed forms. So the grammarians had hitherto looked upon the matter : a language is a finished tool which the grammar describes and teaches us to use. The historical view, which arose on the eve of the nineteenth century in all fields of learning, under the influence of the great and universal reaction against the obstinate rationalism of the age of enlightenment, and for which the way was paved in the philological world by men like W. v. Humboldt, Bopp, the two Grimms, entirely destroyed the old conception of the nature of language. It came to the conclusion that language is not a finished tool transmitted from generation to generation, but a function that is always new, or, to use Humboldt's expression, not an ἔργον, but an ἐνέργεια. Thus modern linguistics regards a language as a function that continually changes its form with the life of a people, and whose present form is the result of the development of thousands and thousands of years and at the same time the starting-point for new formations. Evidently this is the same idea which modern biology holds of plant and animal forms.

The science of language, however, possesses a great advantage. The process of evolution, or at least a part of it, occurs before its very eyes. The modification of historical organisms takes place more rapidly than that of physical organisms. We know the form which the German language had five hundred or a thousand years ago; we have in the Gothic a form that is five hundred years older. In the written monuments we possess petrifactions, as it were, of the old forms of language, and that too, petrifactions far more perfect than those at the disposal of the biologist in palæontological remains. Here we have a few isolated fragments, in part only traces, of the past forms of life. In the former case we have not the fulness of life either, it is true,—sound and accent we can only guess at; but still we possess, relatively speaking, a wonderfully complete exhibition of the structure and the function of the language. We can also trace the development of the Latin language through a space of more than two thousand years. Here we can see the process of the development of new languages taking place before our very eyes. French, Italian, and Spanish are daughters of a common mother, the Latin language, which continued to flourish alongside of these as the language of the church and of learning. Comparative philology goes still farther: it undertakes to explain almost all languages that are and were spoken in Europe, as well as those of the Persians and Hindoos, as historical modifications of an original language common to the Aryan peoples.

We have in this case, therefore, what the critics of Darwinism miss in the biological sphere—the formation of new species between which no fertile crosses occur. Latin, French, and Spanish, not to speak of Greek, Polish, and German, are not variations or dialects of one language, but different languages which do not cross and which are no longer intelligible to one another. How did such new species originate? They are obviously formed by the gradual accumulation of slight changes; intentional invention or transformation plays as good as no part in the process. On the other hand, we can detect the working of the same principles which are regarded in biology as the causes of transformation. The desire to express thoughts and feelings by means of articulate sounds, or rather to communicate them to others, here represents the universal will to live. The conditions favorable to change are, on the one hand, contact and mixture with other foreign languages; on the other, the constant change in the inner world, in the world of thoughts and feelings, which is connected with the generative changes; it brings with it the tendency to vary words and forms. The most suitable variations are selected just as in a struggle for existence, and incorporated into the general vocabulary. The essential standards of fitness are: brevity and ease of enunciation, distinctness and definiteness of expression, finally, power and emphasis of speech, which, above all, consists also in the ability to express and arouse emotions.

In this way a language develops according to the principle of formal teleology, without any real designed invention. Certainly not by means of a purely mechanical selection; at every point the fitness of the new form will be decided by a more or less conscious judgment of taste or intellect. But the total development is not governed by a foreseen purpose. It is the province of the history of each particular language to point out the gradual changes of its forms and words in detail, and to explain them from these points of view. Physiological arrangements most likely play an important part in the development of articulate sounds and forms. In the development of the syntactical forms, a striving after distinctness shows itself; in the development of the vocabulary and the phraseology, plastic and emotional force is of great importance next to ease and preciseness of expression. From these points of view we may in a certain degree form a comparative estimate of the value of different languages. Thus, for example, we may say in general that the languages derived from the Latin are superior to the mother language in logical excellence. The substitution of prepositions for declensional endings, the regular employment of the pronoun and auxiliary verbs in the conjugations, as well as the order of words in the sentence, render the diction more definite and transparent. It is true, the language thereby loses its elasticity.*

With the same means, and by the same forces and tendencies that still determine the transformation of language, philology explains the origin of inflection, which bears such resemblance to an artificial and designed product. Thus, for example, we may see how the conjugation of the Indo-Germanic languages arose through the gradual fusion of sound-groups that were formerly independent. The flectional language was preceded by a stage in the development of language which possessed only immutable and independent words, the so-called roots. Comparative grammar teaches us to recognize in the personal endings the abbreviated and mutilated personal pronouns which have become dependent suffixes. In the Greek conjugation in *mi* the orginal form is still recognizable: the termination *mi* comes from the first personal pronoun as it appears

---

* Interesting statements concerning the forces at work are made in v. d. Gabelentz, *Die Sprachwissenschaft, ihre Aufgabe, Methoden und bisherigen Ergebnisse* (1891). The importance of the emotional phase in the development of language is traced in an attractive work by K. Bruchmann, *Psychologische Studien zur Sprachgeschichte* (1888).

in the oblique cases; similarly, the original *si* is the second and the *ti* the third person. The subject becomes clearer in Sanscrit. In the connected speech the pronominal root and the verbal root were joined together into a single sound by the accent, and then the unaccented suffix was more and more abbreviated. In this way inflections arose.

Finally, philology also attacks the last problem which the organic world proposes, the problem of the *generatio æquivoca*, the origin of the organic from the inorganic. In this field the problem reads as follows: How were these roots, these first articulate sounds, in which the uninflected primitive language expressed the names of things and occurrences, originally produced? History deserts us here, it is true; it nowhere reaches the beginnings. Yet we may attempt, with the aid of biology, physiology, and psychology, to make the process clear to ourselves. Biological reflection considers the sound-reflex as the starting-point of sound-symbolism, which attains to its highest development in language. All intense inner emotions are involuntarily accompanied by diverse sounds. We find this even in the animal world; sounds occasioned by the influence of the emotions on respiration as well as movements accompany inner processes: pain, pleasure, desire, fear, lead to the utterance of variously-articulated sounds. The sound-reflex unintentionally becomes a means of communication, by arousing sympathetic emotions in the fellows of the species. However, sounds are also used in the animal world as an intentional means of communication. The dog makes a great number of sounds: he whines, growls, howls, and barks; and each of these sounds in turn runs through the entire scale; the dog employs them with a certain deliberation to express his inner states, particularly in his intercourse with men.

If we assume that such a form of sound-symbolism also existed among the ancestors of man, the problem would be to explain the development of the organized language from this, as it were, inorganic sound-material. What differentiates human language from the presupposed primitive form is essentially this: the articulation of the sounds and the employment of sound-groups as symbols of objects. These alone would distinctly differentiate the assumed original form of language, which consisted merely in the arrangement of immutable sound-groups in successive order, from all animal language. Animal language, if we can call it such, has no articulation, and its sounds have no objective meaning; that is, they are concomitants and symbols of subjective volitions and emotions, but not names of things and processes. We have human language wherever an articulate sound-group is employed as the name of a thing or occurrence. Sighs and cries are not language. Language has not lost the element of subjective excitation; it shows itself in the timbre and in the accent of the voice, but the word as such—and even the root is a word—is the sign for a definite idea. We might, therefore, characterize the problem of linguistics as follows: It must derive the origin and growth of an ideational language containing articulate sound-groups from an inarticulate volitional language.

The general conditions for the solution of this problem, which will most likely never be entirely accomplished, must be supplied by physiology and psychology. The former will point out the fact that by his upright position man's chest became free, which made it possible for him to produce finer distinctions and articulations in sound; furthermore, that, as the hands became more developed, the mouth, which often has to serve animals as a prehensile organ, became free for other purposes. Psychology will point out that the social life of man, which was especially conditioned by an unusually long period of infancy, had to become particularly intimate, and that the strong impulse to communicate which characterizes man finds its cause in this fact. It will also point to the development of intellectual life, which was favored by the diverse activities made possible by the hand, as well as by the multiplicity of social relations. The increased stock of distinct ideas and the intensified need of communication may thus be regarded as the constantly-efficient motives for a nicer and richer development of the symbolism of sounds.

How the development took place in detail, how in the language of the Aryans the root *da* became the word for to give, *sta* to stand, *reg* to erect, to make straight, how *plu* came to be connected with water, and *luk* with light,—these questions will never receive a certain answer. Most likely we shall always find ourselves reduced to the old view which derives the first characteristic sounds from the sounds which the occurrences and objects themselves produce. Even now, particularly in the first year of life, the sound excites the tongue to imitation, in answer, as it were, to the call. Perhaps, as has been recently pointed out, the human activities and the sounds which they occasion or by which they are accompanied by those performing them, particularly by individuals working together, gave rise at first to the origin of radical words. If the act of reaching was originally accompanied by a reflex-like sound *da*, as we still notice in children, it is conceivable how this sound came to be used and understood as the regular sound-symbol, whenever the impulse made itself felt to arouse in another the idea of reaching and giving. Of course, demeanor and gesture largely helped to make possible a more exact interpretation of the meaning of sounds. And so we believe that we can detect in the root *plu*, which underlies our word *to flow*, the sound which the water makes when a stone is thrown into it or when it moves quickly. With such primitive formations as the starting-point, roots may then have been formed to express processes not audible as such. In this case a certain similarity between the impression and a sound may have been perceived and may have produced the sound combination. A word like *to flash* still has onomatopoetic value for us; it could not be replaced by the word *to crack*. Nor could we substitute *darkness* for *light*, nor *cark* and *care* for *love* and *lust*, without hurting our onomatopoetic feeling. And from such original roots, secondary roots perhaps arose in consequence of the differentiation in pronunciation that accompanied the differentiation of meaning, which was originally very indefinite. From a root like *mar* or *mr*, which, perhaps imitating the sound of bodies rubbed together, meant to rub, to grind, the word *mal* (from which the word *mill* takes its name in European languages), and *marj* = to rub off, clean, may have arisen, and in this way an endless number of derivations may have sprung from a primitive root.*

Be that as it may, there will always be plenty of room here for conjectures and guesses; which is not such a great calamity after all. For who would care to be a philologist if we knew everything exactly? At all events, we may be permitted to say this: We see how even the first beginnings of language could have arisen without methodical invention and construction, by a kind of *generatio æquivoca.* Intentional invention most likely played but an insignificant part in the process. In the same way the farther development took place. In proportion as the world of ideas developed and became relatively free from the will, its phonetic expression, language, developed, not, however, in consequence of conscious or intentional activity. It is only on a high plane of mental progress that we reflect on language, and with reflection begins the tendency arbitrarily to interfere with the development, more for the sake of preserving than for the purpose of developing the language. Grammar is conservative; it opposes the natural inclination to variation.

The same law of development which we meet in the evolution of language governs all mental life; all its products arise through a kind of spontaneous growth, not through methodical invention.

Take the practical field, the development of *morals, law,* and *the State.* The moral laws were not invented by the moralists, no more than the logical laws were thought out and prescribed by the logicians, or the grammatical laws by the grammarians. Morals are general forms of action, whose primitive form consists in the stereotyped reactions called animal instincts. In so far as man becomes conscious of these, conscience arises, and this keeps on developing with mental life. Moral philosophy develops, explains, and proves the moral laws, but does not invent them. The case is not different with law; it is not an invention of the jurists or legislators; it grows with the social life of the people as the external form of their union. Originally it is custom, then at a certain stage of develop-

---

* M. Müller, *Lectures on the Science of Language,* pp. 408 ff.

ment it is separated from the collection of universally obli-
gatory forms of life and action and forms a separate field
of social compulsion. From that stage on it becomes, it is
true, an object of conscious consideration; by the side of
the unwritten law written law arises; so that at last, in the
great collections or codifications, law looks like an artificial
product. Whoever considers the subject historically will
easily observe that the body of the law, the legal system
as a whole, is not made. All that is done in such cases
is essentially this. What is current and traditional is systematically incorporated. Occasional slight adaptations
to the changing life-conditions of a people are made. We
may say of the legal codes what we say of the state con-
stitutions, which indeed are but a part of the general code
of laws : they are not made ; they grow. And the same is true
of the entire State. It is not, as the rationalists of the last
century conceived the matter, an institution invented for
definite purposes, which was one day established by vote
and resolution ; it is the form of life into which a people
naturally grew. The human society which is analogous to
the animal herd is to be regarded as its original form.
Here, too, we get a good view at least of the last part of
the process of development, sufficient to recognize how little the existing form of our state is as a whole the result of
methodical invention. Intellect and deliberation were always operative in the transformation, but only in the sense
of seeking at all times to adapt the existing institutions
to new needs and conceptions. And ultimately, even here
blind instincts often played a larger part than deliberate
reason.

Nay, the case is not much different in the theoretical
sphere, which is the particular domain of the intelligence
and in which one would expect design and invention to
play the largest part. Sciences were not invented and
developed according to plan; they grew. Mythological
cosmology is their original germinal form, the first rough
outline of a unitary world-view. From it philosophy developed, and from philosophy the separate sciences gradually grew like so many different branches of a common
stock. The entire unitary evolution was not thought out

by a human intellect and designed, as a builder designs
the work which is executed by a thousand hands, in the
course of so many decades. The germ of knowledge unfolded itself by a kind of inner necessity ; not without the
aid of individual reason, it is true, but yet in such a way
that no one commanded a view of the whole and the entire
course of the development. The individual investigator
and thinker works in the dark, as it were. He does not
know the place which his work occupies in the chain of development, at least not the relation it bears to future
events. It may give rise to new problems and new
notions in other minds, but he cannot foretell their nature.
It is a matter of the most common experience in the history
of human thinking that an idea provokes thoughts in the
minds of others that are entirely different from those intended by their originator. All that the individual can do
is to appropriate existing ideas as well as he can, and
to make them serviceable to his conception of reality.
Whether his successors will utilize his work and how they
will do it, is concealed from him. And perhaps we may say
in this connection, that the less he thinks of others, of his
contemporaries, and of the future, the more he attends to
the subject-matter itself, the more fruitful will his labor be.
And we may say in addition : The greater and more fertile
the thoughts are, the less did they owe their origin to
methodical invention. Newton did not make up his mind
to discover the law of gravitation, nor Darwin the theory of
evolution, nor Schopenhauer the voluntaristic psychology
and metaphysics. Great thoughts arise through a kind of
mental conception and not through workmanlike planning.
They come as if of their own accord when their time has
arrived. After that they are verified and applied according
to method. The process here is similar to that which takes
place in a work of art or fiction. This too is not constructed
according to plan, but grows from within outwardly, by
the unfolding of a germ. The cheap productions are
manufactured according to plan. At first there is present a
general desire to make something, then a search is begun
for a subject and a form. In this way the imitations arise
which invariably shoot up like mushrooms whenever a great

work arouses popular attention and comes into fashion. They are manufactured articles, not works of art. In the same way factory-wares are made in science, the exhibits of the dissertation-factories, the collections of the commentators, the comprehensive and final systems of the registrars of science,—here, too, the primary purpose is to do something that may gain for the author favorable and profitable recognition ; then a search is begun for some original subject, and if the seekers are lucky in their find, they at once " work it up " according to some methodical plan. Great thoughts, on the other hand, such as open up new paths to knowledge, are not made and invented, they come as if by inspiration.

And as the highest intellectual activity has not the form of plan and design, so also intelligence itself is not, in its origin, the result of plan. The intellect is not made; it grows. We cannot make ourselves believe that a particular individual among a lot of irrational men first recognized the utility of the thing and then invented the process of deduction and the syllogism, concepts and judgments. These processes gradually evolved like natural products of mind. As the original form of the intellect we may regard instinct, that wonderful faculty of anticipating as existing what does not yet exist, and of giving it the force of a motive. Intellect gradually developed out of instinct ; the stereotyped reactions were broken up, and active deliberation began to intervene between the different members of the series. The ultimate effect is presented as the end, the activity as the means. Thus we have the knowledge of cause and effect in its most primitive form.

We may say, then, of all phases of mental and historical life : The necessary and teleological is not formed by anticipating reason, according to design and plan, but arises gradually like the forms of organic life, through spontaneous growth. And what is true of the separate organs and products is true also of the historical organisms themselves. A people live a unitary life. Every historical account intentionally or unintentionally represents this life as a unity. By dividing the course of history into periods, it introduces the idea of organic unity. It has always been customary and natural to compare national life with individual life: the great stages, childhood, youth, manhood, old age, recur here, or to convert the proposition: The fundamental law of the development of national life is repeated in the life of the individual. Well, a nation does not design its life and then complete it according to a plan; its life is gradually unfolded, unknown to the people themselves. The retrospective historian is the first to see unity and harmony in it. The same is true of the life of the individual. A man does not plan the course of his life. In the years of youth we are apt to think that we first fix our goal, then make a plan, and fashion our lives and influence the world according to this plan. Youth is rationalistic in its views; it believes in thoughts and in their power of transfiguring reality: all revolutions have been inaugurated by young men. Old age becomes historical even in its thinking; it sees how little it had to do with fashioning its own life, how it was formed by environment and fate and by many originally unimportant accidents. Great historical traditions gain more and more prominence in the eyes of old age. The youth has an idea that the world really dates from him, that he must bring it forth anew in his own head. The longer we live, the more we understand how short a distance we have traversed, how near we are to the starting-point upon which youth, full of hopes and plans, once turned its back.

And now let us sum up. Plan and design do not play a very important part in the history of mind. The same law of development prevails in the mental world that prevails in the organic world. Organic creations are produced in nature as well as in history, not by forethought, but by the spontaneous unfolding of germinal beginnings. Things are not made, they grow; that is the fundamental law of reality. Even the works of the human mind are on the whole the results of unintentional growth. The planned product is but a slight collateral form of growth.

6. Insufficiency of Atomistic Metaphysics. The Notion of Interaction.

Let us return to the starting-point of our discussion. Three forms of the view of the world, three cosmological hypotheses, seemed conceivable to us: Anthropomorphic Theism, Atomism, and Pantheism.

In the preceding sections we tried to show that the first hypothesis, far from being a proved theory, does not even possess the form of a scientific theory. The conception of natural and historical reality which assumed an architectonic intelligence and held that this intelligence constructed the universe according to plan and with a purpose intelligible to us, has been altogether superseded by a later theory, the evolutionistic hypothesis. And it would be sheer self-deception to assume that we can adhere to the former theory after its presuppositions have been overthrown. It is hardly credible that the evolutionistic view will disappear like a passing fashion, as some believe. It may have to undergo many changes, but anthropomorphic theism will never regain a single inch of its territory as long as scientific interests cast the deciding vote.

The question now arises: Which of the two remaining cosmological theories deserves the preference? Is atomism or is a pantheistic monism more in accord with the facts?

The opinion widely prevails that materialistic atomism is the view of the world forced upon us by science. Darwin, it is said, removed the only difficulty hitherto involved in it. Now there is no essential obstacle in the way of an explanation of the world by atoms. The following thought is common to both adherents and opponents of Darwin: The presupposition or the final consequence of his view is that we can dispense with God or a principle of unity; reality can be explained by the principle of the uniform interaction of the parts.

I regard that as an error. An atomistic metaphysics is neither presupposed nor favored by the doctrine of evolution. Indeed, the theory by no means bears such an intimate relation to metaphysics as is usually assumed. Like every explanation of particular facts, it is as compatible with an idealistic-pantheistic metaphysics as with a materialistic-atomistic one. Which of the two views to choose depends upon more general considerations. And these do not seem to me to indicate that the solution of the world-riddle is to be sought in atoms: on the contrary, I find myself driven to the other view from every side. Let me point out the thoughts which influence me, without claiming for them the weight of cogent proofs. The time has probably gone by when men believed in their ability to demonstrate the logical necessity of a given view of the world. The arguments for a final conception of things will essentially consist in showing that the facts point to such or such a conclusion, or, as it were, converge to such a conception. We shall have to presuppose here the results of our ontological discussion. It convinced us that the materialistic explanation of reality is insufficient, and that we must assume a universal correspondence or concomitance between physical and psychical elements. First, however, let us take the standpoint of the physical view.

First of all, I call to mind that atoms are not actual facts or objects; they are not objects of real or even of possible observation. Bodies, or rather, the unified corporeal world exists. Thought analyzes this into separate objects or bodies which appear as being in uniform motion or at rest. Bodies in turn split up into parts: a piece of chalk may be broken into pieces or ground into dust and yet it is still further divisible; the quality of the parts remains identical with that of the whole. Furthermore, the same chalk can be separated into heterogeneous parts, into the chemical elements calcium and carbonic acid, the latter in turn into carbon and oxygen. But not even in this way do we reach the atom as an empirically given object. The concept of the atom is merely a subsidiary notion formed for the explanation of physical and chemical facts; it is the ultimate point in the analytic reflection of the chemist.

Metaphysical atomism, however, reverses the process. It asserts: The ultimate reached by analysis is the ultimate of things, or rather the first and absolute beginning of reality. The world is composed of atoms, of absolutely indestructible and absolutely independent little particles.

This view has no more justification than the thought •
that letters are the first, absolutely independent, original
constituents of speech. A boy beginning to study Latin
is very apt to reason thus : The Latin language, like every
other language, consists of words, words consist of syllables, syllables of letters, and the latter are consequently
the real ultimate constituents, the atoms, as it were, of
speech. A little reflection will suffice to show the error of
this view. The living speech is the only reality ; words,
syllables, and letters are abstractions, which do not exist
as such. The grammarian analyzes speech into separate
words and sounds. He cannot describe his whole subject-
matter at once, hence he analyzes, and then evolves the
whole out of the parts. In reality, however, the whole is
not produced in that way. Language did not begin with
the utterance of single sounds or letters, a, b, c, which were
then combined into syllables and words, the latter being joined together to form the sentence. Language exists
only as connected living speech. Letters and words as such •
exist only in the grammarian's mind. Most letters cannot
even be pronounced by themselves. A similar relation
obtains in soul-life. In reference to this, too, the notion
prevails that it is composed of ideas, sensations, and emotions, as independent elements. Such a conception is
absurd. The unitary whole alone has reality, and this
psychology analyzes into separate parts and elements for
purposes of investigation. Indeed, we may go further and
say : Not even the individual soul exists as an independ-⎰
ent element. The total life exists, and of it the individual ⎱
life forms a part or member. We may isolate it in thought,
but we cannot find it in the world as an originally independent element, and then make a whole by the combination of many parts. The old rationalism regarded a people ⸝
as an aggregation of individuals. Here again Aristotle is
right : the whole is before the parts; the parts exist only ⎰
through the whole.

The same thoughts are applicable to the physical world :
the atom is an abstraction, like the letter ; it does not exist
alone and isolated any more than the letter does. It is an
object no more existing or capable of existing independently

than a mute consonant. Try to picture it to yourself as an
independent reality. What does it look like? Is it extended
like a body? If with ancient atomism we affirm the question,
it immediately follows that the atom is divisible. Whatever
is extended has parts that exist by the side of each other; it
will therefore depend upon the definition whether we can
divide the atom or not. If we can, it is not a metaphysical
ultimate, a unitary being, but composite like the body.—
If we deprive the atom of extension, if we identify it with
a point, as mathematical physics does and may do for its
purposes, the troublesome question confronts the materialistic metaphysician who would make of the atom the
absolute principle of the universe: In what does its
essence consist? What is a real point? If we reply: a
system of forces, we deprive it of its independence, not to
mention other difficulties. A force is real only in so far as
it acts. Activity, however, presupposes something acted
upon. Without this the atom of force can neither exist
nor be conceived. And in what does the empty space between the atoms consist? When we try to answer such
questions, we may perhaps find that Kant's hypothesis
of continuity which regards space as continuously filled,
though with different degrees of intensity, is, to say the least,
likely to remove a number of very troublesome problems.
At any rate, we cannot but be convinced that, however
simple the matter may seem at first sight, atoms do not
solve the problem. They have their legitimate value as
working-hypotheses in physics and chemistry, and these
sciences may conceive them as it suits their purposes. But
no one can speak of atoms as existent, ultimate, independent
elements of reality, except the man who has never given
the subject any thought, and permits himself to be deceived
by a seductive analogy. As a wall is composed of bricks, so
a brick in turn is composed of smaller bricks, until we finally
reach ultimate bricks, which are so small that it is no
longer worth our while to trouble ourselves about their
nature.

Let me suggest a thought that is common to Lotze's
metaphysics: The separate object has reality only as a
part of the whole upon which it acts and by which it is

acted upon. Popular opinion imagines that the individual object may be posited by itself without reference to its effects. That is a delusion. An object that does not act does not exist. It has reality only as a member of the whole. Reality means, in this case, to stand in active and passive relations with other things.

A second reflection, which leads to the same result, proceeds from the concepts of activity and passivity themselves. Common-sense employs these concepts day after day without finding any special difficulties in them. It reasons about as follows : For things to act and to be acted upon two objects are needed, each of which is a reality in itself. But now it so happens that the object, regardless of its independence, suffers a change of condition, that is not caused by itself ; we say, it suffers an influence which proceeds from without, from the other thing. And in the same way it in turn exerts an influence on the other object.

It has always been the lot of philosophy to take umbrage at what everybody regards as wholly unobjectionable and self-evident, *nodum in scirpo quærere.* Here, too, she asks : What does it really mean—to exert an influence? We say, the moon exerts an influence upon the earth ; for example, it attracts the water-masses of the ocean, thereby occasioning the phenomenon of the tides. What happens in this case? Does something separate itself from the moon, then float through empty space over to the earth, attach itself to the water-particles of the ocean and carry them back to the moon? Does an effluence proceed from the moon, which, diffusing itself equally in all directions, fills and, as it were, scours space ; and whenever this effluence meets a body, be it large or small, does it forthwith attach itself to this and draw or push it towards the moon? Or, how else shall we picture to ourselves the behavior of this influence? Is the moon connected with the earth, is every mass-particle connected with every other particle, by an invisible rope or band, by means of which the former draws the latter to itself? Physics knows absolutely nothing about these things. What it really tells us when it calls the tidal wave an effect of the moon's power of attraction is this : The movement of the water-masses which we call ebb and flow regularly follows upon certain changes in the moon's position to the earth ; in form and magnitude it corresponds to the motions of falling bodies on the earth. And likewise the proposition : All mass-particles gravitate towards each other, simply means : Whenever and wherever two masses stand in a definite spatial relation to one another, both tend to move towards the common centre of gravity, depending on the size of the mass and the distance. And, finally, the proposition : A and B act and react upon each other, signifies : When A enters upon the state *a*, B enters upon the state *b*, and conversely. *A uniform and spontaneous concurrence of changes at different points of the world* is all that reciprocal action means for us. Nothing whatever is known of effluences and influences, of bonds and connections, of compulsion and force.

A physicist may answer : Perhaps that ·is the case in the given example. At present we can do nothing but describe and mathematically formulate the phenomena of gravitation ; we cannot explain them. But the time may come when it will be possible to give a causal explanation of such phenomena.

Very well. Let us assume that the time has come, that we have succeeded in reducing the apparently immediate *actio ad distans* of gravitation to a known form of molecular action, say to pressure and impact, to which natural-scientific explanation ultimately leads. Would we then know what happens between the bodies in question, beyond the fact that the movements coincide ? Would we even get rid of the notion of *actio ad distans*, which is so obnoxious to many physicists ? A billiard-ball in motion strikes one at rest and transfers its own motion to it. Do we see an influence passing over, do we see the motion jumping over upon it ? Does every atom of the ball in motion, perhaps, touch every atom of the other and transmit to it its motion ? Impossible ; for only small portions of the surfaces of the balls touch. Is the motion of every atom detached from it, and does this motion travel, continually passing to its nearest neighbor, in the direction of the point of contact of the two balls through the body of the first ; and is this motion then diffused over the second ball until each element of motion has again found an atom which it now carries off in its own direction and with the velocity belonging to it? I believe it will not be necessary to enlarge upon the strange perplexities to which such a conception gives rise.

Let us further simplify the case. Let us put in the place of the two balls two atoms; let us say that an atom in motion sets an atom at rest in motion by impact and then comes to a stop itself. Do we see, in this case, an influence passing over from A to B? Did the motion detach itself from the first atom as though it were a skin, and attach itself to the second, dragging this after it? But motion is nothing corporeal, nothing substantial, that can detach itself and exist by itself. Hence, what has taken place between the atoms? I believe that the best we can do is to confess: We do not know. All that we do know is the fact that at a certain period of time A moved, that the movement ceased at a certain point of time—when the atoms came in contact, and that simultaneously with its cessation B began to move in a like manner, and finally, that the same thing invariably occurs in identical cases. But how the process takes place we know no more in this case than we know of the transference of motion between colliding billiard-balls or of the heavenly bodies that attract each other and mutually determine their orbits. Reciprocal action is a term that has no other meaning than : *uniformly corresponding change.* The only advantage which the notion of the mechanical transference of motion has over other forms of reciprocal action is that it is the form of action with which we are most familiar and which is most common. We ourselves move and fashion bodies by pressure and impact. In itself it is not more intelligible, nor is its inner possibility and necessity or the *how* of its process any more transparent than any other form of reciprocal action.*

---

* That the force of attraction acting at a distance is just as intelligible or as unintelligible as action by pressure and impact is shown by Zöllner in a discussion on *actio ad distans* in the first volume of his scientific treatises. He appeals to Kant's *Metaph. Anfangsgründe der Naturwiss.*, in which matter is explained by the forces of attraction and repulsion, and in which the statement is made "that the original force of attraction is not in the least more inconceivable than original repulsion. Only, it is not such an immediate object of the senses as impenetrability." (2 Hptst., Lehrsatz 7, Anm.)

The inadequacy of this false notion of the causal relation, according to which the cause pushes the effect forward
and uses force on it, as it were, is still more apparent in
the psychical world. We also apply the causal notion to the
processes of inner life. I look at a picture that comes from
my home ; it calls up the memories of my youth; feelings of
sadness and longing awake ; the desire to behold the old
scenes again arises in me, and is soon transformed into a
decision. Everybody agrees that there is a causal connection here, whether we can analyze it into its ultimate
and unanalyzable elementary connections or not. It is
certain that we see nothing of the force and compulsion
by which each element is supposed to drive the succeeding
element before it, and to push it into existence or consciousness, as it were. Each element follows upon the
other spontaneously. It is also certain that we are not
able to recognize the relation as logically necessary. We
simply observe : When such and such a percept arises in
this particular consciousness, certain groups of ideas and
emotions follow. But *how* the percept manages to produce an idea, or *how* a feeling is aroused by an idea, is
absolutely unknown to us ; and the physiologists may
torture the brain of the dog as much as they please—they
will never find out anything about it. The fact that when
the one element appears, the other appears or tends to
appear, is all that we know.

David Hume was the first to carry out this thought
concerning the nature of causality, and that is what gives his
Inquiry Concerning the Human Understanding the important
place which it occupies in the history of philosophy. The
most penetrative analysis, he shows, finds nothing whatever
of necessity in the relation between cause and effect:
neither a necessity of thought,—one, for example, that
would enable us logically to deduce the effect from the
notion of the cause,—nor a coercion by means of which
the active element forces a change upon the passive element.
There is no tie at all, no inner connection assignable between cause and effect, which could make the connection
between them a necessity of thought. All that we know is
that there is *regular coexistence of phenomena in time.* Kant

agrees with Hume in this respect: The statement that a causal relation obtains between two phenomena means that they are regularly coexistent in time. He denies no less emphatically than Hume that thought can deduce the effect from the notion of the cause, or that it can reduce the law of causality to the principle of contradiction.

Nor are these reflections unfamiliar to the older, to the metaphysical school of modern philosophy. Leibniz, in particular, entertains the same notion when he substitutes the principle of *pre-established harmony* for that of the recip-rocal action between the elements of reality. The passage of influences from one object into the essence of another seems to him also to be an absurd conception. Monads are not extended beings, with windows and doors through which the "influences" could enter. What really happens is *concomitance;* accompanying, corresponding changes; when a change occurs at one point of reality, corresponding changes take place at other points. Occasionalism had prepared the way for this conception. In one case it had not been able to discover the "inner bond" which joins together cause and effect—in the relation, namely, between the body and the soul. Leibniz, following Spinoza, gener-alizes the thought. He rejects the *influxus physicus*, not only here but everywhere: all things spontaneously har-monize with their changes. Or, the bond which exists between cause and effect is not an accidental and particular bond: it is the universal and essential bond which binds to-gether all the elements of existence. The latter are not foreign and external to each other; they are members of one being: God is the bond which unites all things in essence; he is the being in whom all are one.

Among contemporaries it is Lotze who again adopts this notion and makes it the cardinal point of his system.* Though not seeking any alliance with Hume's empiricism, he insists with him that all causal relations are accidental concepts, that it is impossible to show a tie between cause and effect. With Leibniz, whom he esteems and likes to ac-knowledge as his guide, he deduces the same far-reaching

---

* *Microcosmus,* I. 412 ff., III. 481; *System der Metaphysik,* 134 ff.

consequences from this view. The presuppositions of atomism, he finds, make the fact of reciprocal action inconceivable and inexplicable. If, as that theory maintains, existence really consisted of a plurality of absolutely independent substances, the fact that they coincide in their changes would be absolutely unintelligible. If every atom, if every element of reality, is a thing for itself, wholly independent in its existence and nature, how comes it to regulate its behavior according to that of other elements? In that case we should expect each element to follow a course of its own, regardless of all the rest.

Or, is it, perhaps coerced by the laws of nature? But these are not outside of or above the things; they are in them, they are merely the expression of their actual behavior. In reality, nothing in any way compels them to be and to act otherwise than according to their own nature. It is not the earth's power of attraction nor the law of gravitation which keeps the moon in its course around the earth, but its own sweet will, so to speak. If it should ever leave its orbit and fly off at a tangent, the earth and the law of gravitation would not hinder it. The moon solely obeys its own nature or inclination in pursuing a curvilinear direction constantly deviating from the straight line towards the earth. This is universally true: the laws of nature do not compel things to act in a certain way; these laws are the expression of the spontaneous activity of the things. They do not explain *why* things behave as they do, but simply state in a general formula *how* they behave. They do not solve the riddle; they are riddles themselves.

Indeed, atomism should ponder over the question which Lotze asks: How does it happen that so many substances act with such uniformity as to enable us to reduce their behavior to general laws? Why does not each one act differently if each is wholly independent in its nature and existence from all the rest? The uniformity of nature might suggest a different view. If we should find a great lot of rocky fragments scattered over a mountain valley, all of them shaped alike, we should surmise that they are the fragments of a former whole. Is a similar conjecture perhaps possible in our case? Is it not possible that the apparently independent parts of the world are also, if not ruins of a former whole, yet living members of an existing unitary being?

Lotze draws this conclusion. Reciprocal action and the reign of natural law indicate that the elements of the world are not as unrelated to each other as atomism supposes. The universal connection between all things can be understood by us only on the assumption that they are all parts of a unitary being, of a single substance. No isolated changes occur in the organic body. Whatever change takes place at a given point necessitates a corresponding change at all the other points. So, too, the world is a unitary system which invariably excludes isolated processes. Each process is related to all the rest; it is the partial alteration made necessary at any given point by the changes occurring in the whole system. If we call the whole, the All-One, God, as Spinoza calls it, then all reciprocal action takes place in God, since the motion at every point of his being coincides with that occurring at all other points and so forms a system of universal motion.

Thus, if we pursue the thought of universal reciprocal action and carry it out consistently, we are forced to regard reality as a unity: there is but one unitary being acting in a uniform and harmonious manner; the individual objects are but parts of its being; its actions, determined by reciprocal action, are in reality sections of the uniform spontaneous movement of the substance. Or in Kantian phraseology: The universal reciprocal action in the *mundus sensibilis* is *unitas phœnomenon*, to which corresponds a *unitas noumenon* of the substance in the *mundus intelligibilis*.

May we now connect this view with the results of our ontological discussion, according to which all processes in the corporeal world indicate so many corresponding inner processes? And may we see in the unification of all cosmical movements by interaction the reflection of an inner harmony, the manifestation of the unified inner life of a spiritual All-One? This would give us the view called *Pantheism*. We can also designate it as *monotheism* in the strict sense of the term : *God alone exists; everything that is, is through God and in God.*

Why c call this man 'all-one' - God?

Before I attempt to answer the question, let me first consider briefly the relation between causality and finality.

7. Causality and Finality.

It was remarked above (p. 160) that the rejection of anthropomorphic theism and its explanation of nature by design is not equivalent to the rejection of a teleological conception of the world. In resuming these reflections at this point we first ask the question: What characterizes a combination of elements as teleological? The word itself gives the answer: the fact that their arrangement or activity appears to be directed towards an end (τέλος). We regard the result of the arrangement or movement as an end, however, only in case it was willed, and in case the appearance of the result is felt with satisfaction. To this statement we must add, first, that the causal connection of the elements is not excluded but presupposed—every teleological combination is at the same time causal; secondly, that design is not included in the notion of finality. It is not necessary that the aim pre-exist in consciousness and that the movement occur according to a finished plan. The term *Zielstrebigkeit*, purposive impulse, has been created by an ingenious natural scientist to characterize the notion of teleology without design.*

The nature of teleological combinations clearly manifests itself in the processes of inner life where teleology is at home. Psychical states are also causally related to one another. A percept or an idea calls up another idea; its appearance is the cause of the appearance of the second. An emotion, a desire, determines the attention and changes the course of presentation. But the same process of association produces a result desired by the will; groups are formed which the will welcomes as rational and valuable. Still this end or aim did not pre-exist in idea, at least not as a prearranged plan that was subsequently realized. An architect designs the plan of a house. After it is com-

---

* K. E. von Baer, *Studien aus dem Gebiet der Naturwissenschaften* (1876). In several thoughtful essays the author attacks the "teleophobia" of modern natural science and shows the inevitableness of a teleological view of the organic world.

pleted, the masons and carpenters execute it in wood and stone. The plan itself, however, was not made according to a prearranged plan; nevertheless the intellectual labor of the architect is teleologically conditioned no less than that of the workmen. An orator delivers a speech; he has been attacked, he wishes to defend himself and to annihilate his opponent. Now the thoughts, the arguments come into his mind; the illustrations and periods, the catchwords and quotations, the spiteful remarks against his opponent and the pleasantries to his hearers, fall from his lips, spontaneously as it were. His thoughts obey the laws of association. Each preceding element arouses its successor; but of a thousand possible asociations that one is invariably effective which leads to the desired end. And so the entire speech is both causally and teleologically conditioned. The will ultimately determines the direction of the thoughts and experiences a keen satisfaction at their successful realization. Not everywhere is the process of presentation as teleological as here; there are vague, indefinite associations which in dream-life and in mental aberration gain the ascendency. But in a healthy mind the course of ideas is universally determined by what is teleologically necessary.

In every mental system, the elements are in like manner both causally and teleologically connected. In every argumentative discourse, in every poetical work, each part is essential to the whole, essential to the realization of the idea; it is in its proper place an ἐξ ὑποθέσεως ἀναγκαῖον. At the same time, it has been caused by associative connection. Causal dependence and inner, æsthetical or logical necessity go together. If we run through the series from the beginning, we see how each element produces each subsequent element. If we reverse the process, beginning at the end, we see how the result determines everything that precedes, from the very start. The thing to be proved governs the course of the whole argument; the issue of the drama influences the exposition. Hence, the last is at the same time the first cause from which the movement proceeds; the τέλος is, as Aristotle says, also the ὅθεν ἡ κίνησις. Everything is attracted by it, and everything tends towards it. In the mental world, action takes place, not by an impact from behind, but by the spontaneous striving for the goal. The goal, however, is not the external end, but the *realized whole*, the completed unity of the poem or of the argument or speech; it is the *entelechy* of Aristotle.

What is true of the separate mental products is also true of soul-life as a whole. A healthy human life forms a complete whole, a rational unity. It is not a series of accidents, a mechanical displacement of elements of consciousness, but a unity held together by an inner necessity and having many parts, similar to a symphony with many parts and arranged for many voices. We cannot, it is true, interpret every element as a teleological necessity, as in a work of fiction. An element of what we call chance enters here. But we cannot refrain from viewing the whole as a unity combined by inner necessity. Every biographer contemplates the life of his hero as a whole bound together by an inner, intelligible necessity. Every man pictures his past to himself in the same way. And at every moment of life the living being feels life as a tendency forward. Movement does not take place by a pushing and pulling from behind, but, as it were, by being drawn to the goal. The goal, however, is the realization of the idea. The image of the man is, in the soul of the boy, the hidden motive-force which governs his development. The idea of a life-work which is itself unfolded in the course of life directs the activity of man and gives it force. Purposive impulse characterizes all healthy life. And the same is true of the life of a people. This too moves, not pushed by pressure and impact, but attracted by an idea, as it were, of its complete development. Not as if a nation were determined by a simple and clear idea present alike in all! The nature of the people is developed by the living interaction of the most diverse tendencies, but that which moves all by its attractive force is an idea; the future development of the people is somehow present in all. All groups, all parties, behold in the gray dawn of the future the vague outlines and the glamour of perfection, and are irresistibly attracted by these.

Hence causality and finality go together in mental evolution. Mental action is characterized by the spontaneous concurrence of a plurality of elements in a series, every member of which is determined by an inner logical, æsthetical, or ethical necessity.

Herein, let us remark in passing, lies whatever of justification there may be for the opposition to *deterministic* theories. If the nature of causality consisted of an external necessity which excludes inner necessity, they would be right who rebel against its application to the mental world. Only, in that case they ought to go a step farther and maintain that the causal law is invalid not only for the will, but for the entire soul-life. But if we define the notion of causality correctly, if we mean by it what Hume and Leibniz meant by it, that is, the regular harmony between the changes of many elements, then it is plain that it prevails in the mental world no less than in nature. It may be more difficult to detect uniformity in the former case or to reduce it to elementary laws than in the latter. Still it is evident that such uniformity exists. Isolated or lawless elements exist in neither sphere ; each element is definitely related to antecedent, simultaneous, and succeeding elements. We can hardly reduce these relations to mathematical formulæ anywhere ; but their existence is perfectly plain everywhere. Everybody tacitly assumes : Under wholly identical inner and outer circumstances the same would invariably ensue ; the same idea, the same emotion, and the same volition would follow the same stimulus. Freedom by no means conflicts with causality properly understood ; freedom is not exemption from law. Surely ethics has no interest in a freedom of inner life that is equivalent to lawlessness and incoherency. On the contrary, the occurrence of absolutely disconnected elements, isolated volitions standing in no causal connection with the past and the future, would mean derangement of the will, nay, the complete destruction of psychical existence. If there were no determination whatever of the consequent by the antecedent, then, of course, there could be no such thing as exercise and experience, there could be no efficacy in principles and resolutions, in education and public institutions. Without causality, no finality.

What then is the relation between causality and finality in the *physical world?* Do they go together here also, or is there no finality, no inner necessity in nature?

The latter is the prevailing opinion ; it perceives external necessity in nature, but not inner necessity. It regards the mechanical transference of motion as the original form of natural efficiency. With a teleological necessity, on the other hand, it will have nothing whatever to do. v. Baer is evidently right : the current view is afflicted with *teleophobia.* It seems to me that he is also right in finding the reason for it, not in nature, but in the natural scientist's fear of a false teleology. Teleophobia is the reaction against the old teleology of design, which repudiated and wished to replace a causal explanation.

First, let us remember what we discovered in the preceding chapter as the real nature of the causal relation in the physical world : Reciprocal action is nothing but corresponding change. Influences and compulsion are out of the question. The universal reciprocal action of all the parts of the universe means that the world forms a unified system with unified motion, in which each movement of each part is inserted into its proper place as a member harmonizing with the movements of all the other parts. We cannot emphasize this strongly enough : necessity exists in logical thought but not in nature ; all uniformity in nature is spontaneous coincidence of all the parts.

Here also the coincidence is reciprocal. The antecedent determines the consequent ; but we can say equally well : The consequent determines the antecedent. The warmth of the room is an effect of the heated stove ; but we can say with equal right : The absorption of heat by the surroundings is the cause of the cooling of the stove. The impact of one body upon another is the cause of the movement of the second ; but it is just as correct to say : The movement of the impelled body is the cause of the impelling body's loss of motion or coming to rest. We conceive the matter in this way wherever we have to do, not with the instigation but with the cessation of a movement. Hence, generally speaking, without the cause the effect could not be, but just as little could the cause be without the effect.

The question now is: Is the causal connection in the external world at the same time a final connection just as it is in the inner world? Does an inner teleological relation exist between the members of the series in the former case? In one field everybody regards the subject in this light, that is, in the matter of life. Vital processes form a connection of causes and effects; they are everywhere conditioned by the uniform reciprocal action of all the parts, but at the same time they are "purposive impulses" in the sense that they combine themselves into a unity, that is, life, which we cannot help regarding as the aim which all functions serve as means. Pursuit, the seizure of prey, the devouring and digestion of it, are causes of the preservation of life; but at the same time life is the end, and these functions are means to that end. And if the functions are means, the organs surely are. If seeing exists for the sake of life, the eyes exist for the sake of sight. They are formed for this purpose in the fœtus.

Not at all, the teleophobic natural philosopher answers; only the first half of the proposition is valid: the animal sees because it has eyes, but the eyes do not exist in order that it may see; it butts because it has horns, it has not horns in order to defend itself and to butt. That is illegitimate anthropomorphism. Teleology perverts and destroys the causal, that is, the true conception of nature; it turns things upside down. Such is the view of our modern materialistic, mechanistic, natural philosophers, who in this respect agree with old Lucretius.*

They ought to continue and say: The steer butts, not in order to overcome his opponent, but his opponent falls because he butts. The spider does not spin her web in order to catch flies, but because the web exists, flies are caught in it, and because the spider has feeding-organs, the fly gets into them, and because matters have now gone

---

* Lucretius, *De rerum natura*, IV. 830:

    Omnia perversa præpostera sunt ratione,
    Nil ideo quoniam natumst in corpore, ut uti
    Possemus, sed quod natumst id procreat usum.

so far, the fly is transported to the inside and digested. Ends are wholly out of question; we have here only causal connections. And if what our materialistic philosophers say is true of the spider, they ought to continue the thought and say: The case is not different with man; he does not weave the net in order to catch fish, but because his hands move as they do, the threads are twisted together into a net, and because the net is dragged through the water in such a way, the fishes are brought out by it.

Perhaps this will be too much even for the teleophobic physicist. He will say: No; in man teleological activity is really present; here we have *volition* and *presentation of the end* as the beginning of the series, and hence the causal series is also a final series.

Very well. Let us assume this. But ought we not to claim the same for the spider? For is not the materialistic philosopher wont to insist emphatically that man is a member of the animal series? What does the spider lack that its vital activity should be treated differently? Volition and presentation of the end? Surely not volition, unless we deny all inner life to it. Shall we say then that it is without presentation, that it does not anticipate the result? And would that deprive its action of its teleological character? Would you ascribe such action to the spider, only in case it deliberated and said to itself: Life consists in metabolic change, hence the materials consumed must be restored by food; flies are food, and nets a means of catching flies? It is plain, however, that on that condition only a small portion of human activity can be regarded as purposive. Perhaps our fisherman knows no more than the spiders of metabolic change and the necessary restoration or of the fitness of such and such substances for such and such purposes. Shall we therefore say that only some of the acts are purposive? Shall we say that making nets and catching fish are purposive acts, but that there is no purposiveness in chewing, swallowing, and digesting? Are we concerned here solely with causal, not with teleological, series? Does the process of mastication and digestion become purposive only for the physiologist who has a clear conception of it? I believe this separation of human vital processes into purposive and purposeless ones, into such as are both causal and final and such as are causal only, is utterly absurd.

Well, if it is true that the *entire* life of man must be conceived as a teleological process, because and in so far as it corresponds to a will, even though the ends and means are not wholly in consciousness, the same must be true of the animal world. And if the activities which tend to the preservation of individual life are purposive impulses, those will be no less so that have as their objective aim the preservation of the genus : nest-building, ovulation, hatching and brooding, and what not. And if this is the case, we cannot help but look at the development and formation of organs in the same way.

Indeed, it is in every way impossible to contradict the one statement without denying the other. It is impossible to regard human actions as purposive impulses without acknowledging the acts of animals to be the same. And it is equally impossible to concede the point in the case of the so-called animal or voluntary activities without assuming it also for the vegetative processes, which are not merely the essential preconditions of the former, but could never be wholly separated from them. Indeed, both forms of vital processes everywhere merge into one another. And again, if we grant that the teleological view is valid for the vegetative processes in the animal world, we cannot reject it in the plant world ; for the processes are certainly the same.

But after having gone so far, it will be difficult to stop. Living beings did not suddenly drop down from the skies : they are the legitimate products of the world ; they are fashioned of the elements which constitute the body of the earth ; they arose under the influence of the entire cosmic-telluric system. These particular fish could arise only in this particular ocean, and our animal world only upon our earth and beneath this sun. The co-operation of all things was necessary to produce this particular animate world. "This animal kingdom," v. Baer declares, " cannot exist without the vegetable kingdom ; this again cannot arise before the stony crust of the earth has been disintegrated into loose soil by physical and chemical influences. We must further presuppose that this soil is watered by rains from time to time. The rain can fall only on condition that the water has previously been absorbed by the air, that it has been carried to a higher stratum and then condensed by a change of temperature. The water, again, cannot rise unless the earth is heated by the sun's rays. Hence the smallest blade of grass really calls into play the entire planetary system with all its arrangements and movements, and all the laws of nature." The poet Goethe, who is inspired as no other with the thought of the unity of the world, expresses this truth in the lines:

> Das Stäubchen, selbst der unfruchtbare Stein,
> Indem er sein Gesetz hat, muss er wirken
> Und thätig für das grosse Ganze sein.

And so it happens that this "purposive impulse," when once admitted at a single point, extends over the whole of nature. It is mere caprice to insist, on the one hand, that man is but a piece of universal nature, that the territory he occupies is not exempt, not an *imperium in imperio*, and then, on the other hand, to protest against the theory of finality, on the ground that it is an altogether inadmissible anthropomorphic conception of nature. If nature acts anthropomorphically at one point, and that cannot be denied, it is hard to see why a similar procedure should be so absolutely out of the question at other points.

But, says the teleophobic natural philosopher, outside of organic life the principle is lacking without which there can be no purpose at all, that is, inner life and will.

This brings us to the very root of the opposition to the teleological view of nature. It springs from the materialistic conception of nature as an aggregation of inert atoms mechanically moved according to laws. And here the old teleology of design wholly agrees with the mechanical theory. It, too, regards nature as a mass of lifeless, inert matter, but adds : Hence nature could not have arranged itself as we find it arranged ; it is therefore necessary to assume that an intellect outside of nature has joined things together according to design. But the theoretical conscience of the natural scientist rebels against this conclusion. We know nothing whatever of such external interference by a spirit, nor would it explain anything; it is a mere *asylum ignorantiæ*. So far, so good. But the scientist does not stop here; he goes on to deny final causes altogether, even in the organic world. This brings him face to face with the above-mentioned absurd consequences against which the theory of design again directs its attacks. So we are driven around in an endless circle.

As far as I can see, there is but one way of escape from this labyrinth. We must abandon the assumption that nature consists of dead matter and accept the ontological theory of parallelism established above (pp. 80 ff.). The inner world, the world of will, is coextensive with the physical world. Then we may say: Strictly speaking, only physical causality prevails in the physical world, while finality universally coexists with it in the concomitant inner world. The mechanical philosophy of nature is right: All natural processes, even vital processes, may be explained purely physically; there is no interference by an intelligent cause. But Spinoza is also right: All physical processes point to concomitant inner processes and are teleologically related. And so we may assign a teleological character to physical processes in relation to the inner life of which they are the manifestations. Take an example. The physicist explains the working of a pipe-organ in a purely mechanical way. Here you have pipes arranged in such and such a way, there you have compressed air. When this particular valve is opened, the air rushes into the pipe and causes the column of air in it to vibrate in a particular manner. And then the physiologist comes along and gives a similar explanation of the organist. Here we have a peculiarly-arranged brain and nervous system into which certain stimuli passing from the sheet of music and the keyboard enter through the eye. These act as purely physical causes and discharge reactionary movements so that the fingers press the keys in a particular order. That is the physical side of the process. There is, however, another aspect to it: visual and auditory sensations exist, and the notes and the melody arouse feelings of pleasure. The members of the latter series have an inner, teleological connection. And this inner side is really the essential element, of which the process in the nervous system of the organist is but an external manifestation. We simplify our language and call these physical states, which express inner states, purposive actions, such as playing on the organ and writing music, making nets and catching fish. So we come to assign teleological activity to organic life in general, not in the sense that the organism is jointed together by a thinking being external to it, but because it is the manifestation of an inner life unfolding itself with inner necessity. The phenomenal purposive impulse of the body is the reflection of the real purposive impulse of an inner life.*

Assuming the validity of our ontological argument, we shall go on and say : This is not an accidental and isolated fact, but absolutely universal. Not merely a few movements in nature, the so-called voluntary movements of animals, but all movements are accompanied by inner processes which are like those experienced in ourselves. Will, we felt ourselves impelled to say with Schopenhauer, is that which appears in all physical processes, in the vital processes of animals and plants, as well as in the movements of inorganic bodies; not a will, like our will, enlightened by ideas, but none the less will in the broadest acceptation of the term, embracing under it blind impulse and striving devoid of ideas. If this view is tenable, then all natural processes, in so far as they are manifestations of will, will have to possess the characteristic of the will, purposive impulse. And in so far as the will-units of a lower order are comprehended into a higher and finally into a highest and ultimate will-unity, universal nature will have to be regarded as the phenomenon of a unified system of ends. Then all ends will meet in the life of God; in him each element of reality will be a necessity of

---

* Spinoza has not the heart to deduce this consequence from parallelism; he is too much absorbed in his opposition to the teleology of design. But Leibniz, who looks at things more impartially, consistently draws the conclusion : " Les âmes agissent selon les loix des causes finales par appétitions, fins et moyens. Les corps agissent selon les causes efficientes ou des mouvements. Et les deux règnes, celui des causes efficientes et celui des causes finales, sont harmoniques entre eux."—*Monadology*, § 79.

thought; his self-realization or entelechy will be the
ground and the end of all things.

Of course, we must immediately add : We cannot complete the thought, we cannot conceive the inner side of
the whole of reality. Its external side is the immediate
object of our knowledge. For that reason the causal conception predominates in our science. The teleological interpretation is hardly more than a postulate or uncertain
possibility. We can calculate the motions of the planets,
but the ear cannot apprehend the harmony of the spheres.
The attempt to understand the order of nature from its
meaning simply makes us conscious of our inability to
penetrate through phenomena to their meaning. Hence
natural science is right for confining itself to the purely
causal view. But it is in the wrong for charging the failure
of a teleological explanation of nature, not to the subject,
but to the objects; and for not saying: The purpose of
nature transcends our knowledge; instead of : There is no
purpose or meaning in nature.

In one of the essays mentioned above, K. v. Baer declares that the natural scientist invariably has three questions to answer: What or how? By what means? Wherefore or to what end? I for my part do not blame the
scientist as such for ignoring the last question and for believing that his task is limited to the description of the
facts and the explanation of their causal connection. But
as a human being he will inevitably raise the last question :
To what end? We find the idea of the *wherefore* or *to what
end* expressed in our own lives and we cannot avoid pro-
jecting it into the nature surrounding us. Everybody actually reads a teleological connection into the vital processes. No one merely regards all processes in animal
life as equally real and equally important links of a causal
chain, but emphasizes certain parts around which as the
purposive impulse the others are grouped. An insect
passes through a series of stages of development; it exists
as an ovum, as a caterpillar, as a chrysalis, and as a butterfly, and then the cycle begins anew in the ovum. We say
the life of the butterfly is the climax of this development;
the other forms of existence are its preliminary stages or

necessary preconditions. We should likewise distinguish a climax or goal in the evolution of a planetary or solar system if we had a comprehensive view of the whole. But, of course, we cannot *prove* it. The different phases of in-sect-life are all equally real, and the butterfly is as much the condition of the origin of the egg, as the egg, of the butterfly. Whoever regards the ovum or the caterpillar as more beautiful and important than the butterfly cannot be contradicted. And even if some one were to assert that the little heap of dung which an animal produces in the course of its life and finally augments with its decomposing corpse is the real aim of life, he could not be refuted. Perhaps a man who has grown rich on the guano-trade would not find such a view so very absurd. For the notion is indeed very common that the trees of the primeval world have grown in order to supply us with fuel. The case is not different with an individual or natural life. Whoever regards the stimulation of the palate or other sensuous pleasures as the highest content of life cannot be refuted. And if a man should happen to have no feeling whatever for the distinctions of value between the differ-ent modes of life, if they all struck him as equally impor-tant or equally unimportant, no line of reasoning could create such a feeling in him. Here we are not dealing with *objective* knowledge; *influenced by our subjective feelings we accentuate certain elements.* A man entirely devoid of voli-tion and feeling, having no appreciation of these things, a man consisting of pure intellect, would never reach a teleo-logical view, or be able to appreciate one. For him, one thing would be as important or as unimportant as the next, or rather not important or unimportant at all, but simply an existing fact. All predicates expressing rela-tions of value would be wholly unintelligible to him.

In a certain sense, the natural scientist transforms him-self into such an abstract, pure intellect; and he must do it in order to fulfil his mission, which is to explain the ob-jective causal relations of things. Only, he must not think that what constitutes the perfection of the natural scien-tist as such—that is, freedom from inclinations and aver-sions—also constitutes the perfection of man as such. It is absolutely characteristic of man to feel and appreciate distinctions of value, to distinguish and feel the good and the bad, the beautiful and the ugly, the sublime and the insignificant. The loss of this faculty would be equivalent to the loss of personality itself. A human being is not mere abstract understanding.

This æsthetico-teleological conception of reality finds its true expression in *art* and *poetry.* Its real function consists in showing and making intelligible the *meaning* of a natural being or a mental evolution, by pointing out and emphasizing certain features. *Religion* is also concerned with the interpretation of the value of reality, and is therefore most intimately connected with art and poetry ; as is universally proved by anthropology. Artistic-religious interpretation and scientific explanation consequently form an antithesis, but do not exclude each other. The latter appeals to the understanding; it strives to reduce the world to general concepts and formulæ, without regard to subjective distinctions of value. The former, on the other hand, appeals to the will, to the feelings; it aims to evaluate not only the facts of human life but of universal existence; it strives to reveal the aims and ideals which, as standards, guide our judgments of worth, and, as motives, govern the will and fill the heart with joy. This difference of function does not render the two conceptions hostile to each other, but invites them peacefully to supplement each other. On this point we agree with the remarks of A. Lange in the last chapter of his *History of Materialism,* concerning what is allowable and inevitable in the *idealization* of reality. He does not mean that it is advisable or permissible to delude one's self and to falsify reality, as it were. The faculty of not seeing what exists and of seeing what does not exist, though it may be common, especially among politicians and lawgivers both of State and Church, can certainly not be reckoned among human .perfections. But yet it is inevitable that a man who has a heart as well as a head should select certain elements of reality and evaluate them, and furthermore that he should regard what he chooses as the essential and truly real element. This happens when we try to understand a person; the heart tells us what he is in reality and in his true nature. We do the same in the case of a nation; in fact we do it all the time. We idealize things in so far as our love selects the features by which we determine their essence. And then this essence or the inner form, to use Aristotle's words, appears to us both as the end and the moving cause of their origin and activity; it moves, however, by exciting desire (κινεῖ ὡς ἐρώμενον).

8. Pantheism and World-soul.

We now return to the question raised above: Is all striving and willing, as it confronts us in the thousand diverse forms of existence, finally combined into the unity of one being and will? Does a unity of inner life, in whose self-movement and self-realization all individual life and striving is included, correspond to the unity of the physical world in universal reciprocal action? The affirmation of this question gives us the conception of the universe called *Idealistic Pantheism.* Let me state its fundamental features in a few formulæ.

1. Reality is a *unity.* The individual objects do not possess absolute independence; their reality and essence is contained in the All-One, in the *ens realissimum et perfectissimum,* of which they are the more or less independent members. Or, in Spinoza's proposition: Reality is *one* substance, objects are modifications of its essence posited in it.

2. The essence of the All-One reveals itself to us, in so far as it reveals itself at all, in the two aspects of existence, in *nature* and *history.* In Spinoza's proposition: The substance is developed and conceived under two attributes, *extension* and *consciousness.* This proposition is then modified by epistemological reflections to mean that the mental world is the true reality, the corporeal world, however, its phenomenon and representation in our sensibility.

3. The universal reciprocal action in the corporeal world is the manifestation of the *inner, æsthetico-teleological* necessity, with which the All-One unfolds its essence in a variety of harmonious modifications, in a cosmos of con-

crete ideas (monads, entelechies).   This inner necessity is
at the same time absolute freedom or self-realization.   As
Spinoza says : Substance is *causa sui* or *causa libera ;* it unfolds its essence with inner (logico-mathematical) necessity.
    Is there any foundation for this view ?   After what has
gone before, I cannot be expected to establish it by proofs
that bind the understanding.   All that can be done is to
show that whoever attentively and candidly inquires into
the meaning of things and impartially observes reality,
finally accepts such thoughts.
    I call to mind the starting-points of the reflections in-
dicated in the preceding sections.   I remind the reader of
the unity of the physical world with its universal interaction and universal uniformity ; of the spontaneous harmony
of all the parts ; there is no necessity in nature.   Furthermore, let him remember that reality as a whole is free from
external compulsion ; its motion can be explained only as
spontaneous movement proceeding from within ; there is
no force outside of reality by means of which this motion
could be imparted by impact.   I again mention the dual
form in which reality confronts us at the point at which it
is most clearly revealed to us, in our own nature, as body
and soul ; a fact which leads us to presume that corporeality universally points to a concomitant inner life.   Finally,
I call to mind the "purposive impulse" which meets us in
the little fragments of existence of which we have something more than a mere astronomical knowledge.   We are
not doing violence to the facts when we interpret them
after the manner of speculative philosophy, which in this
respect simply follows in the footsteps of popular opinion.
The evolution of the earth strives after the realization of
life, life after consciousness, consciousness after mind : the
evolution of mind is the central purpose of earthly existence.   Hence, if the conclusion from the part to the whole
is valid, the highest mental life is the central purpose of
all reality.   Should any one, however, object to the proposition and say : As far as we can see, mental life is the
highest aim and the permanent good not even upon our
earth ; nay, it can be regarded only as a slight incident
which will soon vanish, for the disappearance of life and

mind is the inevitable result of the earth's cosmical position,—that would not disconcert us. If it is so, we should
say: Plants, too, wither and die, while the elements of
which they consist remain; yet that does not hinder us
from regarding life and bloom as the purpose of the plant.
So, too, the earth may at some time wither away and die,
but none the less life, mental life, was the goal of its development. And even if it does come to an end, it is not
lost. Reality is not annihilated by becoming a thing of
the past. The past remains an eternal constituent of reality, and the present moment does not comprise the whole
of reality. Besides, what do we know of the fate of the
earth and the solar system? They may be drawn into
larger spheres and destined for a greater future than our
cosmical physicists dream of now. If there is no original
state of existence, but only an ultimate point for our inquiries, the same most likely holds of the final state. The
limit of our wits is not the limit of existence. The day-fly
may think when the sun sets and its life ends with the
coming of night: Now it is all over; the light is extin-
guished forever and the whole world is sinking into darkness and death. Man, who has seen so many suns rise
and set, ought to have learned enough to believe that the
infinite contains possibilities and issues that are hidden
from him.

May we now gather all these reflections into a single
thought and say: What we see in our own lives on the
small scale, what we seem to recognize also in the life of
the earth, is true of the world at large? Are its aim and
being contained in a universal life, in an eternal spiritual
life, the fulness of which far surpasses our notions of it,
but of whose essence we get a glimpse in our own spiritual
natures?

I believe that we may make such statements and that
we may add: There is no view which explains existence
more simply and clearly. Moreover, this view is the only
one which explains the fact for which every philosopher
has been trying to find a place in reality, the fact of life;
it is the only one which harmonizes soul-life with the rest
of the world, and for the first time makes its origin and

existence conceivable. In atomistic materialism mental
life appears as a strange anomaly; we cannot brush it
aside, its existence is an indisputable fact, and yet it is a
stumbling-block to the theory; if it were not for it, what
an easy matter the explanation of the universe would be!
As it is, an unwelcome remainder is left over, and many
are frank enough to confess with Du Bois-Reymond that
soul, consciousness, and mind are in their conception of
the universe an "absolute world-riddle." In our view,
however, mind may feel at home in the world; it may regard itself as flesh of its flesh and bone of its bone. I do
not believe that a stronger argument can be offered against
the truth of a conception of the world than the fact that it
is compelled to give up the explanation of mind as an absolute riddle. And, on the other hand, I hardly know
what argument could convince the human mind of the
truth of a theory more than one in which it can, as it were,
feel at home in the world.

That this view is indeed more plausible than any other
is shown by the fact that all thinkers, with the exception
of a few philosophizing physicists, are remarkably unanimous in regarding it as the final explanation of the universe. In the East as in the West, in ancient as well as in
modern times, the thoughts of the freest and profoundest
have converged towards this point. The meditations of
the great civilized nations of the East came to rest in an
idealistic pantheism. The Greek mind also found its
world-formula in a similar line of thought, in the Platonic-
Aristotelian philosophy: Reality is a unity, an absolute
unity of everything spiritual and good. The thought of
the middle ages also gravitates towards our conception;
we might almost say, against their will. Wherever modern philosophy finds its freest and boldest expression, it
invariably returns to this view. Bruno and Spinoza are
driven to it by modern cosmological and scientific reflections, speculative philosophy by its new mode of conceiving historical life: Existence is a unified spiritual life, the
visible part of which is the evolution of psychical life, and
particularly of earthly human life.

During the ascendency of speculative philosophy, this

theory, in which the world was supposed to have become conscious of itself and to have conceived itself as spirit, was regarded as absolute truth. There was no doubt in the minds of its adherents that it was destined to be accepted as universal truth. It was called the secret religion of the cultured classes, and its followers were convinced that it would gradually penetrate into such circles as were as yet unable to grasp truth except in concrete images. But it happened otherwise. As far as there can be any question of a philosophical world-view among the cultured (most of them get along without any), it is more apt to be found along the lines of natural-scientific materialism or of an epistemological scepticism. The physical view of things has dislodged the poetical-speculative reflection. The notion of an inner universal life is, for the most part, wholly foreign to our natural scientists. The idea of a world-soul, of a spiritual universe, a *mundus intelligibilis*, seems to them to be as childish a dream as that of anthropomorphic gods. They do not need the hypothesis, they can explain the world by means of atoms and physical forces, excepting, perhaps, that small remainder, the states of consciousness in the brain of living beings. Science, it is said, has entered upon its period of manhood; it no longer allows itself to indulge in the childish play of such fantastical speculations. Let him who has a craving for them apply to the philosophical stragglers. And the educated classes, intimidated by the self-assurance of natural science, are ashamed to profess views that do not bear its stamp.

I am far from wishing to force my notions upon the reluctant by means of arguments. I look upon such an enterprise as hopeless, or rather, as absolutely impossible. If any one desires to stop at the astronomical-physical view of the world, we cannot dislodge him. He can say: This is what we know; beyond it we know nothing. States of consciousness are isolated phenomena incidental to living beings. Whether any further cosmic importance is to be attributed to them, we cannot know. With metaphysical hypotheses, however, I shall have nothing to do. The person speaking thus cannot be assailed. He lays himself

open to attack, however, as soon as he goes further and
declares : That of which we have no knowledge does not
exist ; all that can be said of the universe is what astronomy and physics teach of it.

The best way, perhaps, of meeting such a negative dogmatism is to ask questions. As Hume remarked and Socrates perceived before him, the questioner invariably has
an advantage over those making positive assertions concerning such subjects. So you know all about the world,
do you? we shall ask. It is a great collection of atoms ;
there is no such thing as soul and spirit, except in the few
brains which the earth and perhaps some other planet occasionally produces? On what is this knowledge of yours
based? Upon the fact that you have never seen a world-
soul or anything like it? But have you ever seen the soul
of an animal or of a man? And yet you believe in its
existence. Why? Because you happen to see brain and
nerves? Very well. And would you, then, believe in a
world-soul if we were to show you the brain and the nerves
of the world? But if the world had a brain, it would presumably have to have eyes too, and ears and legs and
wings or fins, and a spinal column and a heart and a stomach? Hence, if all these things were shown to you, if the
world had the form of an immense bird or whale or elephant, if it masticated and digested food like other animals,
then you too would believe there must be a soul in that?*

What a wonderful being that would be! Perhaps it
would be easy to convince a biologist that if there is a
world-soul, it did well not to assume such a form. To be
sure, an animal needs all these things; it needs legs for
support and motion, and a stomach and teeth for the digestion of its food, and eyes for the detection of prey, and
a central nervous system for the adaptation of its move-

---

* "Before the natural scientist can concede the existence of a world-
soul," says Du Bois-Reymond, " he must demand that there be shown to
him somewhere in the world a collection of ganglionic cells and nerve-fibres
corresponding to the mental capacity of such a soul, imbedded in neu-
roglia, nourished by warm arterial blood under the proper pressure, and
equipped with suitable sensory nerves and organs." (*Grenzen des Naturerkennens*, p. 50.)

238 <i>THE COSMOLOGIGAL-THEOLOGICAL PROBLEM.</i> [BOOK I.

ments to the external world. But the universe has no use
for them. It needs nothing to support and move it, nor
does it need an apparatus for metabolic change, nor eyes,
nor ears—for outside of it there is nothing to see and hear
—and hence, what could it do with a brain and nerves? Or
ought it, nevertheless, to have equipped itself in such a
manner, simply in order to assure a thorough-going, scep-
tical nineteenth-century scientist that the limitations of the
universe are not identical with those of a Laplacian mind?

Or would our Pyrrhonic scientist allow us to presuppose such a unified inner life, if, instead of being an immense animal, the universe had assumed the shape of a
large united body, say of a sphere? Would our view appear less objectionable to him if the universe formed a
continuous whole, instead of a system of bodies scattered
through immeasurable space? Is this evident lack of unity
an obstacle? Well, what gives an animal body its unity?
The contiguity of all its parts? Evidently not that, but
the functional unity of all its parts. Do the molecules
which make up the brain of an animal come in contact
with each other? Perhaps they are separated by spaces
which are larger than their diameters. If the atoms are
conceived as unextended centres of force, then the spaces
between them are infinitely great when compared with
their diameters. The absence of contiguity, therefore, is
no obstacle to unity. Whether the parts are separated by
millionths of millimeters or by millions of miles is immaterial, as long as they constitute a unity of motion. And
as far as we can see, that is absolutely true of planets. Or
is the motion too simple and uniform? Can only such
complicated systems of motion as animal bodies be regarded as having life and soul? Fechner answers (<i>Ideen zu
einer Schöpfungsgeschichte</i>, p. 106): "However complicated
our brains may be, and however much we may feel inclined
to attach to such a complexity the highest mental properties, the world is unspeakably more complex, since it is a
complication of all the complications contained in it, the
brain among them. Why not, therefore, attach still higher
mental properties to this greater complexity? The form
and structure of the heavens seem simple only when we

consider the large masses and not their details and concatenation. The heavenly bodies are not crude homogeneous lumps; and the most diverse and complicated relations of light and gravity obtain between them. That, however, the plurality in the world is also grouped, comprehended, and organized into unity does not contradict the thought that it is also comprehended into a corresponding mental unity, but is in harmony with the same."

Indeed, what hinders us from viewing a planet as a ganglionic cell in the world-brain? Is it too big? But why should not the world-brain form larger cells than an animal brain? Or is it not composed of the right materials? The same substances are found in it, carbon, oxygen, nitrogen, iron, phosphorus, and many others besides. And these act and react on each other in a thousand different ways, just as they do in the ganglion, no doubt. Nay, who knows how great and evident the similarity would appear to us if only we were able to magnify the ganglion sufficiently to recognize its structure and to observe the thousand forms of movement in its interior? Nägeli suggests such a thought in the treatise on the limits of natural-scientific knowledge, mentioned before, in which he constantly and strongly emphasizes the empirical limitation of our knowledge in regard to the infinite, the infinitely great as well as the infinitely small. "There is no limit to divisibility. We must also infer from the analogy of our entire experience that the combination of separate individual parts continues down to the infinitely smallest parts. Similarly, we are obliged to presuppose an endless combination of matter into ever larger individual groups. The heavenly bodies are the molecules which combine into groups of lower and higher orders, and our entire system of fixed stars is but a molecular group in an infinitely larger whole, which we must conceive not only as a systematic organism, but also as a small part of a still greater whole."*

The physicist will exclaim: What idle fancies these are! Well, they do not profess to be much more. But

---

* *Mechanisch-physiologische Theorie der Abstammungslehre* (1884), p. 576.

fancy, too, has its rights and its mission, if it were only to remind the understanding of its limitations. That would not be a superfluous task in an age in which science is so inclined to rest satisfied with the finite. Let scientific investigation quietly pursue its journey, regardless of such fancies. But let it not claim that there is nothing in the world except what our physiologists and cosmologists know of it. There may be a thousand things in heaven and earth, as little dreamt of in our philosophy as in the days of Hamlet; nay, perhaps less dreamt of now than then. Indeed, our age believes that it has almost entirely done away with dreaming. With the exception of a little superstition here and there, the whole world is enlightened. Everybody believes in physics and atoms and a few world-riddles, but beyond that no one troubles himself about things.

Natural science might learn a lesson from its own history. What wonders have been discovered during the last few centuries, on earth by the microscope, in the heavens by the telescope! Had the mediæval physicist been told what every school-book nowadays contains about the systems of the milky way and cosmic evolution, about the structure of the eye and the motion of light, he would have seen nothing in this but the dreams of an exalted fancy. Suppose we should come into the possession of similar aids for acquiring a knowledge of the inner world, or suppose we were endowed with the gift of reading the soul, who knows but that wonderful discoveries would be made in this sphere also? Is it the corporeal alone that has new and newer wonders to unfold? Or if our eye were opened to see the inner world, would it not reveal to us a still richer content, a greater nicety of articulation, and still more comprehensive organization?

To be sure, we do not possess such gifts. Aided by analogy we attempt to guess at the psychical meaning of bodies and corporeal forms by laboriously spelling it out, as it were. Only in the human world do we acquire some skill in this art; of the subhuman world we get a faint glimpse at least; of the suprahuman world, however, we know nothing whatever. Our knowledge does not transcend our experience : to understand God would mean to be God. But it does not seem wise to say, because our eye does not reach that point, there is nothing there. Dogmatic negation is no less presumptuous than positive dogmatism. It is meet for man to bow in reverence before the infinite and unfathomable, the source and end of all life and being.

Rückert, the thoughtful and profound interpreter of nature and of life, expresses this feeling of devout reverence for the great mystery of being in the following lines :

> Ein Vorhang hängt vorm Heiligtume,
> Gestickt mit bunten Bildern
> Von Tier und Pflanze, Stern und Blume,
> Die Gottes Grösse schildern.

> Die Andacht knieet anzubeten
> Vor diesen reichen Falten.
> Ein Lichtstrahl hinter den Tapeten
> Verkläret die Gestalten.

> Ich neige mich zum tiefsten Saume
> Und küss ihn nur mit Beben,
> Mir fällt nicht ein im kühnsten Traume,
> Den Vorhang wegzuheben.*

The relation, however, of the individual mind to the universal mind must be conceived as somewhat similar to the relation between the different factors of an individual mind and that mind itself. The separate feelings, strivings, and thoughts are inserted into a greater combination. In the same way we are to regard the entire soul-life as inserted into the all-embracing combination of God's life, inserted perhaps into a long chain of intermediate links. This would not deprive it of its relative independence. The particular impulse or feeling, the particular thought-series or presentation-groups, have a certain independence in our soul-life, and yet belong to the whole and act for the whole. Similarly, an entire soul-life would be inserted into a wider whole having a greater independence corresponding to its richer content. The organization of the corporeal world would be the expression of this relation in the phenomenal world. The organic cell is a relatively-independent member of a body that is itself a dependent and at the same time independent part of the earth-body, with which it is inserted into still larger combinations.

That we have no immediate consciousness of this articulation of our psychical life with a larger combination proves nothing against its truth. The whole surveys the part, but the part does not survey the whole. If a brain-cell had a unified inner life and consciousness, it would not be immediately aware of the psychical life of man and its own relation to the same. Similarly, our intuitive knowledge cannot grasp our relation to the higher forms of life above us. Our abstract knowledge, however, enables us to see that our psychical life is not absolutely independent, but is contained in a larger system. We are in a measure able to comprehend its most immediate environment, that is, the historical life of a people. We can also comprehend the connection between our corporeal life and surrounding nature which fosters and supports it. But we cannot transform this nature into mind, and then conceive our soul-life as contained in the psychical system, or, in Kant's phraseology, we cannot articulate ourselves as *noumena* with the inner system of noumena, or insert ourselves into the *mundus intelligibilis*. Here our knowledge has to content itself with schematic outlines.

Now as regards the objection that our view introduces the false, the perverse, and the evil into the system of divine life, let me simply state that no attempt at interpreting reality has yet mastered this difficulty. I shall come back to the question; meanwhile let me point out the fact that here too we might pattern our conception after our own inner life. Error and false ideals are apt to possess us for a long time, until the soul succeeds in overcoming and eradicating them, not, however, without our having grown in power and experience in consequence thereof. What would a thinker amount to if he had not suffered from the errors of his time? Nay, it also happens that a personal conflict arises in an inner life between opposite tendencies and impulses, a conflict between contrary thoughts and feelings, without our being able to reconcile the discord. Is not the opposition between the flesh and the spirit one of the most universal and deepest experiences of the human race? And so we may believe that God's life is not without inner conflicts, only that in his case all the contradictions and discords of reality are finally resolved into a great harmony, a harmony, to be sure, that no mortal ear has ever heard. Finally, let me also say, the fact that we retain the past in memory gives us an idea of the permanent relation existing between the individual soul and the universal spirit. *Immortality* in the sense of eternity is doubtless a necessary conception. It is not conceivable that a psychical life should absolutely perish. An event cannot become unreal by becoming a thing of the past. If it were so, if the past were absolutely and in every sense unreal, as unreal as that which never was, there would evidently be no reality at all; for it cannot exist in the present, which is an unextended point of time. Now, what is my psychical life which belongs to the past? We say that it exists in memory and, as it were, continues to participate in the further development, and thus it remains related to the present. If a similar relation obtained between the individual life and the universal mind, it would mean that the individual life has permanent existence and activity even after death. It would continue as a permanent element in the divine life and consciousness. And nothing would hinder us from thinking that it also retains its relative independence and the unity of its consciousness within the whole. Fechner develops such thoughts at length in the second volume of his *Zend-Avesta* as well as in his *Büchlein vom Leben nach dem Tode* (3d ed. 1887). I simply refer to them here.

9. The Relation of the Pantheistic Notion of God to Religion.

The attempt has been made in the preceding section to determine the relation of the pantheistic view of the world to the natural-scientific conception. I shall now consider its relation to religion. Is pantheism compatible with religion; I mean with the possession of an inner religious disposition, not with any particular system of dogmatics or church doctrine?

Before we can answer the question we must come to some agreement concerning the nature of religion. Hence, a word in reference to this point. Religion is not knowledge; we have a knowledge of religion, history of religion, and philosophy of religion, but that is not religion. Nor is religion action; there are acts in which religion expresses itself, acts of worship, but they are not religion. The essence of religion consists in a peculiar disposition of the heart. Two phases, two habitual emotions, are distinguished in it. I call them *humility* and *trust, fear of God* and *trust in God.*

Humility is the feeling of insignificance in the presence of the sublime, the feeling of finitude in the presence of the infinite. Man is placed in the midst of infinity, surrounded by it on all sides and upheld by it. The infinity of space and of objects spreads out around him, he but a vanishing point in it. Similarly, endless time extends before him and behind him into an eternity. What is man but an existent nothing in the immeasurable All? And he has religion because he becomes conscious of his insignificance. Animals have no religion because they do not rise to a consciousness of themselves and their relation to reality; they live without becoming wholly conscious of themselves. In man the feeling of his own insignificance, nothingness, and transitoriness arises with his self-consciousness and his consciousness of the world. Emerging from darkness into the light of the sun, he lives a moment, subject to the thousand accidents of nature, and then death hurls him back again into the night of forgetfulness. Such reflections occur again and again in every religious fancy. Nowhere is the thought expressed with so many variations or with such deep feeling as in the poetry of the Old Testament. Nor is it wanting among the Greeks. We find it often in Homer and the tragic poets : Like the leaves of the forest, so are the generations of man.

This is one phase of the religious temperament. Schleiermacher calls it the feeling of absolute dependence.

Its other side is *trust*, the assurance that the infinite is **not** merely the immense and the omnipotent, but also the all-good, that I may acknowledge it and safely entrust to it

myself and all that is near and dear to me. Herein consists the real essence of religious faith. Faith in religion
does not mean knowledge that is less certain or merely
conjectural, a sense in which we often use the term. Religious faith is the immediate certainty of the heart that the
real is derived from the good, that everything that happens·
is meant for the best, for my best. This faith does not
rest upon theoretical investigations and proofs, it does not
spring from the understanding, but from the will. So the
Apostle expresses it : " Now faith is the substance of things
hoped for, the evidence of things not seen ;" hence a practical trust that depends, not upon sight and knowledge, but
upon hope and will.

We use the word in the same sense in other connections.
A mother has faith in her child. Her son pursues many
a path and many a false path ; others lose confidence in
him ; he will amount to nothing, they say. His mother,
however, clings to the belief : he will not be lost in the end.
She can give no reasons for her trust, she cannot prove it
to the doubter, perchance because she has a deeper
psychological insight into his nature ; she believes not
with the understanding, but with the heart ; her life hangs
on her faith, and so she cannot give it up. So, too, a man
has faith in his nation. He sees much of which he does
not approve, injustice and falsehood and hypocrisy, wanton arrogance and coarse vulgarity even among such as
imagine themselves to be superior to the rabble. Yet he
does not lose his faith ; that is not the true essence of my
people, he says, but an excrescence really foreign to them.
At bottom they are really honest and sound, truthful and
true ; they will cast off what is mean and offensive. He
can prove it neither by statistics nor by history ; he, too,
believes, not with the understanding, but with the heart,
with his whole being and will. Without this faith he would
despair of himself, of his work, of his life ; he could not
endure a life, himself the only honest soul among such repulsive hypocrites ! and so he believes in his country.

Religious faith belongs to the same class. It, too, has
its root, not in the understanding, but in man's innermost
essence and will. Generally speaking, it consists in the

trust that the reality of which I am a part is good and has a rational meaning, which I may unravel; that the world and destiny are not a lot of blind and aimless accidents, but that they are determined by an idea of the good, by God, the all-real and all-good being. This trust first appears in a crude form in the most primitive idol-worship ; it is the trust that there are powers of good in or beyond reality that are able to ward off the evil and to promote what is favorable and wholesome. It assumes a more perfect form in the theistic belief held by great historical peoples ; it is the gods, spiritual and good beings, who hold the course of the world and the fate of man in their hands and protect the right and good with an irresistible power. This trust reaches its final form in the belief that there is an all-governing Providence without whose will nothing happens, by whose will everything that happens makes for the good. First of all, I have faith in my own life and its immediate surroundings; I believe that nothing can befall me that is not meant for the best; that misfortune and sorrow are not intended to destroy me, but are destined to carry me safely through the school of chastisement and probation. This faith necessarily comes to embrace wider circles. My country, too, experiences both good and bad fortune ; but here, also, says faith, want and defeat are not intended as evils, but as blessings. It is only by misfortune that all the virtues and powers of a nation are unfolded, while defeat makes it aware of its own real nature. The same is true of humanity; ultimately all its fortunes make for the great goal, the realization of its divine destiny. In the words of Christian faith, the kingdom of God is the goal ; its realization forms the essential content of the history of the world. Hence, expressed in the most general way, the belief in God amounts to this: Not only is it possible for humanity to realize its highest purposes in the world, but, more than that, the world is so predisposed as to realize them ; not a blind and external, but an inner teleological, necessity prevails in it ; the *natural* order of the world is at bottom a *moral* order. *Atheism*, however, would be the denial, not of the demonstrability, but of the legitimacy, of such a faith ; it would be the dogmatic assertion: There is no *moral*, but *only a natural*, order of the world.

This faith is not a theoretical truth; it is not the result of teleological arguments drawn from history or the life of the individual; it is not based on reasons at all, but on practical needs; it makes life, and particularly suffering, endurable. The beast suffers whatever befalls it dumbly and without reflection; man, who reflects on objects and life, emancipates himself from the pressure of pain and the greater pressure of fear, by reading a meaning into his lot. He would not be able to endure life if he were obliged to regard the world as an enormous machine, and himself as the shuttlecock of blind forces.

That this faith cannot be proved but only believed, Christianity does not doubt. The Holy Scriptures tell us in a hundred places: God's ways are not our ways, his counsels are past finding out. That is, if we had had the making of fate and the world, were we ever so clear-sighted and well disposed, we should have made a hundred things otherwise than they are. How often a blind occurrence in nature seems to us to bring ruin into our lives, and to cross our highest purposes in the most indifferent manner! Quite frequently the course of history seems to favor the wrong.. In many cases we ourselves judge differently afterwards; we discover that what originally seemed an evil proves in the end to be a blessing. Our faith is strengthened by such experiences; it loves to remember them in order to overcome the impressions made by our present misery. But we do not believe that a satisfactory theoretical proof can be constructed out of them. The contrary experience, that want and wretchedness also embitter and devastate our inner life, and that apparent blessings bring nations as well as individuals to irreparable ruin, would be cited as the eternal counter-proof against all attempts at a theodicy aspiring to the dignity of an established theory.

Faith, however, will not be shaken. Before such statements as these it falls back upon the limitations of human knowledge: God's thoughts are higher than our thoughts. The believer is, at all events, certain of one fact: Everything is meant for the best of those who love God. Nor does this trust fail him in the wreck of all human hopes. The understanding looks on, a helpless spectator, unable to comprehend it all. It offers no contradictions, it recognizes the uncertainty of every judgment concerning what is good or bad for a human being or a nation. It forbears to judge, doubts, and is silent. Faith, however, confidently pursues its journey. It needs no proof, it is impervious to doubt, it is grounded in the deepest conviction of the believer: Surely the world is so constituted as to enable me and everything that is nearest and dearest to me to exist in it.

Such in general is the content of religious faith. It is never realized in this abstract form, but only in concrete embodiments. Faith is comprehensible and transmissible only when expressed in the intuitive ideas and symbols of historical religions, in the sensuous-suprasensuous pictures of a supramundane world painted by fancy. Nay, it is only then that it becomes wholly believable. And, above all, it is in this way rendered accessible to art and poetry, the real exponents of the inexpressible and transcendent.

Indeed, faith is thereby also opened to reflective thought. The attempt to comprehend the nature of the supramundane world and its relation to us gives rise to a *doctrine* of faith. Dogmas and creeds arise as soon as a community having a common belief formulates its articles of faith in rules that are binding. This is what happened to the religion of Jesus. It was taken up by the philosophizing Hellenistic world, and assumed a form which naturally led to the error that Christianity is essentially a doctrine possessing theoretical worth, like a system of philosophy, that it can and must be apprehended by the intellect.

This, however, is not the real import of Christianity. The church creed does not in its most general formulæ, the three articles, express an intellectual judgment, but a practical certainty that unites the entire community of Christ. In the first article they confess their faith in God the Father, Creator of heaven and earth; which does not really mean that they have theoretical knowledge based on scientific investigation, but an immediate cer-

tainty that the world is not the work of chance or, as some
believe, of the devil, but that it comes from God and returns to God, the all-good One. And by confessing, in the
second article, its faith in Jesus Christ the Son of God,
born of the Virgin Mary, Christianity does not mean to
imply that it possesses reliable information concerning a
historical fact or, what is more, concerning a physical
anomaly, but expresses its immediate certainty that, in
Jesus, God has revealed himself in the flesh, that in him
the almighty and all-good being has manifested his essence in so far as this can be manifested in a son of
man. A man who asks nothing for himself, who does all
the good he can to everybody, without expecting thanks,
who suffers the bitterest and most ignominious fate without
hating and cursing his persecutors—such a man is God,
God in human form. "To be good," says Savonarola,
" means to do good and to suffer evil and to persevere in
this to the very end." The third article likewise expresses
a practical certainty, the certainty that humanity is called
to the kingdom of God, to the eternal communion of the
saints, and to life everlasting, and that the spirit of God
will live and act in all true disciples united in Christ, as
long as human hearts beat on earth.

Hence the faith of Christianity is not a philosophical
system, not a theological dogma or a last relic of ancient
superstition, but an immediate and living certainty, the
heart's belief in the good and its significance for reality.
Such a faith is as possible to-day as in the times of
Luther and Augustine, as when the disciples saw Jesus
in the flesh. Did the Christian faith consist in all kinds of
opinions and dogmas, those would be in the right who long
ago pronounced it dead. Dogmas and opinions are not of
such long life. If Christianity consisted in the literal acceptance of the assertion that the world was created out of
nothing five thousand years or so ago, that the first human
beings were called Adam and Eve, that the former was
made of a lump of clay, the latter out of Adam's rib, that
they lived in a beautiful garden in which God himself took
an occasional evening stroll, until one fine day they were
persuaded by a serpent to eat of the fruit of a particular

apple-tree, and that for this act they were driven out of paradise by an angry God, and that they and all their descendants were visited with suffering and death;—if Christianity consisted in regarding these and similar things as true—the stories, for example, which are told of Christ's fatherless birth, or the miraculous change of water into wine, or the feeding of five thousand men with a few loaves of bread—or if it consisted in the acceptance of the dogmas of the two natures or the three persons in one, or of the dogma that God the Father had to cause the death of God the Son in order to obtain satisfaction for Adam's sin, or in the assertion that a certain collection of writings is not the work of believing and pious human minds, but that God himself composed them by some unknown process called inspiration, and that each line of these writings must therefore be taken as literal and holy truth;—if the Christian belief consisted in accepting all this, then of course it would be impossible for a liberal-minded and thinking man of to-day to accept it. But that is neither the faith of Christianity nor the religion of Jesus. And even if the guardians of all the creeds in existence should assert that this is the Christian faith, and that whoever does not hold it has no share in Christ and in salvation, that does not make the statement true. No one has ever been saved by believing such things. On the contrary, by demanding a belief in the opinions of men the church has driven many an honest man from its fold, and is continuing to do so day after day. If I am not allowed to take the dogma, Jesus is the Son of God, as an expression of religious fancy, if I must mean by it that I have been convinced by historical evidence that his birth occurred otherwise than that of ordinary human beings, then, instead of my frank and joyful avowal of the unique greatness of this man, I am forced to burden my conscience and to subscribe to a negative proposition of whose meaning no one can form a positive idea. Then the creed becomes a formula that really signifies nothing but a willingness on the part of the confessor to subject himself and his intellect to the absolute control of the church.

But if I am allowed to say what I mean and to believe

what I can understand and conceive, then, unmindful of
the ridicule of the scoffer and the hatred of the guardian
of literalism, I may, even in our days, confess to a belief in
God who has revealed himself in Jesus. The life and
death of Jesus make plain to me the meaning of life, the
meaning of all things in general; but that which enables
me to live and shows me the import of life I call God and
the manifestation of God. The most upright, truthful, and
liberal-minded man may subscribe to all that to-day as
openly as ever before. But if we crowd him and demand
that he believe in all the things mentioned above—in the
fatherless birth of Jesus and the immaculate conception of
his mother, or in the resurrection and ascension of his dead
and buried body, in the "with, under, and by" of his
" real " body and blood in the bread and wine,—then he will
turn away, saying: Spare me ; we do not understand each
other. But, if you must argue the matter, go to Byzan-
tians and Alexandrians.*

We now return to our question: Is such a faith compatible with the above-mentioned monistic notion concerning the constitution of reality? It seems to me, by all
means. Perhaps a practical belief in the good is incompatible with no cosmology. At any rate, it is an undeni-
able fact that even men who reckon themselves among the
materialists in metaphysics profess an absolute faith in the
future of the human race and its progress towards justice
and truth. In order to reconcile this faith with their
metaphysics, they would be obliged to say : Atoms were
accidentally formed and arranged in such a way as to real-

---

* I should like to call the reader's attention to the excellent work of a
Dutch theologian : Rauwenhoff, *Religionsphilosophie* (tr. into German by
Hanne, 1889). The view concerning the nature of religion, which I have
hinted at in the above, essentially agrees with Rauwenhoff's more elaborate
exposition of the subject. As the chief constituent of faith, he designates
the trust that the world is so arranged as to enable the moral law to govern
it. Such a belief presupposes a teleological conception of the world.
Faith, however, becomes religion only when poetic fancy embodies it in
images and symbols. W. Bender's work, *Das Wesen der Religion und die
Grundgesetze der Kirchenbildung* (1886), contains similar thoughts : Religion is faith in the realization of the ideal of life ; the impulse to self-preservation universally and necessarily produces faith as an ideal remedy
against the evils and obstacles of the world.

ize the highest good with mechanical necessity; which would indeed be a somewhat remarkable effect. We may say, however, that such a faith is more compatible with a philosophy that views reality as the manifestation of a universal life unfolding itself with inner teleological necessity. Pantheism is not a religion, but a cosmological hypothesis which aims to reflect the total impression produced in the thinking man by reality. But we may declare, not without justice, that the faith which sees the All-Good in the All-Real finds in the hypothesis a notion that meets it half way.

It is true, theological critics of philosophy are usually of a different opinion. They incline to the view that only one notion of the universe is compatible with religion—the theistic conception, namely, which conceives God as a being separate from the world. For them pantheism is not less irreligious than atomism. What pantheism calls God, they hold, is not God, but nature or the All; and Spinoza's formula, *Deus sive natura,* is simply a misuse of the term God. God is endowed with *personality;* not so nature or the All. This difference, it is held, gives us a fixed line of demarcation : Every philosophy that does not assume God to be a *personal* being is irreligious.

Here, too, it will be well to begin our discussion with the Socratic preliminary question : What does personality mean? We assign it first of all to human beings, do we not? Animals and lifeless objects are without personality; it is the *form peculiar to human life.* We may define it as self-conscious and rational thought and volition.

The question would then be : Has the inner life of the universal being the same form? Our answer is : We cannot presume to give an exhaustive definition of the inner life of the all-real God. The undertaking would be about as hopeless as the attempt of a worm to give definitions of the form and content of the human mind. But not without reason shall we say : The difference between human and divine inner life must indeed be great and thorough-going, so great that there can be no homogeneity at any point. Neither the volition nor the thought of the All-One, if we are at all permitted to speak of his volition and thought, can be grasped by us.

First, as regards willing we may say that in man it owes its origin to such impulses and desires as are suited to the state of a being that has limitations and needs. The rational will is nothing but a species of self-regulation of impulses by reason. We cannot ascribe such functions to God. He has no needs, hence no desires and no will, in the human sense. Besides, there are no objects outside of him for him to act on. Theologians express this idea by attributing *all-sufficiency* to God. Nor can action like human action be attributed to him. Theologians ascribe *omnipotence* to him as an acting being. Well, the action of an almighty being differs from ours not merely in extent, but in kind also. The distinction between design and execution, ends and means, is peculiar to our activity. We first form an idea of something that does not yet exist, then we prevail upon the objects, which exist independently of us, to yield to our purposes, outwitting them, as it were. In God, volition and execution must coincide; he thinks, and the act takes place: reality is his volitional and actual thought, or, in Spinoza's words, the explication of his *actuosa essentia.* The same is true of the *moral* qualities of man: they cannot be applied to God. We cannot speak of duties and virtues in his case. Self-control, temperance, courage, presuppose desire and fear; justice and benevolence presuppose self-abnegation and sacrifice of individual desires. God must become a man in order to be merciful and benevolent like a man.

The same remark may be made of the *intellectual* side. Our knowledge proceeds from our senses. We construct concepts out of our percepts; their significance consists in the fact that they conceive intuitions. We have no other kind of knowledge, even of our own essence. And another feature is essential to our thinking: the opposition between ego and non-ego. Our self-consciousness is determined by the opposition between the ego and the external world. None of these peculiarities belongs to the All-One. The theologians attribute *omniscience* to God. It has not escaped them that omniscience differs from our knowledge not merely in extent, but also in kind: God's thinking, says scholastic philosophy, is not discursive and conceptual,

254 THE COSMOLOGICAL-THEOLOGICAL PROBLEM.

but intuitive ; yet not intuitive like our intuitive knowledge, which is determined by space and time; God contemplates all things at a glance, the past and the future as well as the present. It is evident, we can form no conception of such knowledge or consciousness ; when the limitations are removed from human knowledge it loses its definiteness. An intuitive understanding is an empty form which we are not able to fill in.

If, then, it is impossible to attribute to God the form of human psychical life, it will not be possible to ascribe personality to him in the sense in which we use the term. Only when we rob the concept of all human limitations, does it become somewhat less objectionable; but by doing that we at the same time deprive it of all content and definiteness.

This would be generally conceded were it not for the apprehension that God might lose somewhat in dignity if personality were denied to him. In that case he would have to be called an impersonal being, which would place him among sub-human beings.

But such fears are groundless. Pantheism, as we understand it, has no intention of depriving God of anything or of denying him anything but human limitations. It will not permit us to define God by the concept of personality, simply because the notion is too narrow for the infinite fulness and depth of his being. Still, in order to remove the apprehension, we might call God a *suprapersonal* being, not intending thereby to define his essence, but to indicate that God's nature is above the human mind, not below it. And pantheism might add that it finds no fault with any one for calling God a personal being in this sense. Insomuch as the human mind is the highest and most important thing that we know, we can form an idea of God only by intensifying human attributes. When art undertakes to represent God, it pictures him with the body of a man, not in the belief that God really possesses the corporeal form of a man, but because the noble human countenance is for us the highest and most important bodily form. In the same sense we may also attribute to God the mental form which we revere in the best and greatest men. When we speak of his holiness, wisdom, goodness, and blessedness, we use symbolical expressions that do not define his essence as they define the essence of a man; we simply indicate the direction which we must take in order to approach his nature.

That is *the possible and inevitable anthropomorphism of all religions.* We know no other mind than the earthly and human mind ; hence we represent God as having it, not because he is really like our picture of him, but because our ideas do not transcend our experience. And for that reason this anthropomorphism necessarily goes a step farther. Each nation endows God with the attributes which agree with its notions of goodness and beauty, dignity and holiness. It is as Goethe says :

> Im Innern ist ein Universum auch,
> Daher der Völker löblicher Gebrauch,
> Dass jeglicher das Beste, was er kennt,
> Er Gott, ja seinen Gott benennt,
> Ihm Himmel und Erden übergiebt,
> Ihn fürchtet und womöglich liebt.

In such a *symbolical anthropomorphism* philosophical reflection and religious faith approach each other. Knowledge makes no protest. Its own presuppositions carry it to the notion of the All-One, but it cannot determine its content. Hence it is left to the poetical spirit of the race or to the religious genius to embody this concept in intelligible ideas and images. On the other hand, religious faith is far from regarding its symbols as scientific definitions. They are something infinitely higher and more significant than scientific concepts and formulæ, so much higher as God is higher than human thought and understanding. Discord arises between philosophy and religion, only when philosophy seeks to exclude faith, maintaining that the definitions of science comprehend and exhaust reality, and that such symbols are childish dreams which either have no value whatever or have value simply for the masses who cannot think in concepts. Or the clash occurs when a religion, or rather a church community, palms off its symbols as definitions, and its articles of faith as scientifically-demonstrable truths, and then demands that all thinkers fall into the same con-

fusion under penalty of being branded as heretics or atheists. In both cases a deadly enmity ensues. The understanding rebels against a faith that pretends to be the
only valid science. The heart and fancy rebel against a
philosophy that leaves no room for faith and poetry. A
faith, however, that desires to be nothing but a faith, and
a philosophy that is conscious of the limitations of human
knowledge, can exist side by side. It is natural that the
individual should, according to his individual disposition
and education, incline to the one or to the other of these;
just as he may have greater talents and a greater interest
for research and science than for art and poetry, or *vice
versa.* But he can and should appreciate and respect both
phases of mental life. That is the view for which Kant
paved the way during the last great epoch in history.
Schleiermacher introduced it into theology. I shall return
to the subject later on, but I cannot deny myself the
pleasure of quoting in this place a passage from the *Reden
über die Religion.* Schleiermacher discusses the possibility
of reconciling religious faith with a philosophical pantheism. He says: If the pantheist refuses to conceive the
godhead as a person, this may be due "to the humble
consciousness on his part of the limitations of all personal
consciousness, and in particular of the consciousness dependent on personality." Whether any one will conceive
the godhead as a personality or not depends essentially on
the direction of his fancy. And finally, he holds, the two
conceptions are not so far apart after all, " only we should
not read death (the inert dead being) into the one, but
should do all we can to remove the limitations from the
other." But whoever, he adds, insists on regarding piety
as dependent on one's acceptance of the notion of God's
personality does not know very much about piety. Indeed, such a one must be unacquainted with the profoundest works of the most zealous defenders of his own faith.
Schleiermacher is evidently thinking of the mystics.

The notion common to controversies on theism and pantheism are *transcendency* and *immanency.* Theism, it is said,
teaches the transcendency, pantheism the immanency, of
God in the world. Let me apply these terms to the view

set forth above and say: Immanency and transcendency do not exclude each other. Theism cannot exclude the immanency of God in the world. If God is the creator and preserver of all things, it is his power in the things which gives them their reality at every moment of time. On the other hand, philosophical pantheism does not exclude transcendency; God and nature do not absolutely coincide. This is true as far as their quantity is concerned. The nature which we see is finite, God is infinite; it is merged in him, but he is not merged in nature. The world known to our cosmology is but a drop in the ocean of reality. The same statements may be made of his quality. The essence of things as it is known to us is not absolutely different from God's, but God's essence itself is infinite; it is not exhausted by the qualities of reality which we behold: by mind and body, extension and thought, or however we may designate the most general qualities of existence. Hence God is transcendent in so far as his infinite nature infinitely transcends the reality known to us. It is idolatry to identify God's essence with the nature known to us and with the essence of creatures. As a rule, however, such idolatry is less common to pantheism than to theism, which in defining God's essence by human attributes not seldom shows a decided tendency to a false immanency.

I hear an adherent of the old orthodoxy exclaim: All that sounds very well and looks simple, and it seems a plausible thing to say; but there is something wrong somewhere. What the religious disposition desires is a God with whom it can come into a *personal relation*. Such a union is possible if God exists outside of and above the world as a personal individuality; it is not possible if he is such an all-one or all-real being. And what the religious soul demands besides is a God who sympathizes with his creatures and hears their prayers, a God who takes pity on their misery and is ready to help them in the hour of need. A God who stands above the course of nature as a ruler of the universe can do such things. Spinoza's substance can answer no prayers and perform no miracles.

In answer to the first point, we must repeat what has

just been said in our discussion of the question whether
God is a personal being or not. A personal relation is,
first of all, a relation such as exists between man and man,
a relation making possible a mutual exchange of thoughts,
feelings, and actions. Even the boldest anthropomorphism
will pause before assuming that the same relation obtains
between man and God. Or has any one the courage to
maintain that the same relation exists here as between
parents and children, friends and neighbors?

We may, however, without doing violence to the usage
of language employ the term in a wider sense. We should
call the relation between a man and his nation a personal
rather than an impersonal one. At any rate, it is a relation
that is of the utmost importance to his way of feeling and
thinking, to his actions and life. He receives from it the
strongest impulses. Like a hero he labors and battles for
his country. In the belief that his conduct will redound
to the glory and advancement of his country, the political
martyr is ever willing to suffer disgrace and persecution.
The poet expects appreciation and sympathy from his people, and he knows and feels it when his words have touched
their hearts. Now in a similar though much vaguer sense
we may characterize the relation of the pious man to God
as a personal one. He orders his life for the glory of God;
undoubtedly, for does not every good deed and every pure
and beautiful life redound to the glory of God? The cru-
sader regarded himself as God's warrior, the missionary as
a fellow-craft in the temple of his kingdom. He is certain
of God's approval; why should he not be, and why should
he not find strength and consolation in the belief?

But the God of pantheism has no feelings; how can we
attribute feelings of satisfaction to the feelingless All-
One? Well, is the All-One, or—since there may be some
who object to pantheism on account of its indifference to
the gender of the deity—is he, the All-One, is God necessarily an unfeeling being according to this conception? I
do not believe that a pantheistic philosophy is bound to
concede it. If God is reality in the form of a unified self-
existent inner life, then whatever occurs at any point of
reality will be of importance to him as an element of his

being. To be sure, the theory will guard against ascribing human feeling to God, but it will be equally careful not to deny him any qualities. Spinoza speaks of the love and blessedness of God, not in the belief that the pathological states peculiar to man are found in God also, but meaning that whatever is found in the individual being must pre-exist in germ in the being of the infinite, from which it springs. "He that planted the ear, shall he not hear; he that formed the eye, shall he not see?" We might like-wise say in this connection: He that made feeling, shall he not feel? But as seeing and hearing are not used in their real sense in the former case, so feeling is not used in the real sense of the term in the latter. Hence the ex-pressions are not meaningless, they are designations that have value in so far as they symbolize the inconceivable and unspeakable. That is what Scripture means: God dwelleth in light which no one can approach unto. Natural theology trusted in its ability to conceive God with its thought. It spoke of God almost as one speaks of a col-league whose thoughts one perfectly understands and exam-ines. The relation of the pious man to God does not rest on concepts, but on faith.

But, some one asks, how about the *efficacy of prayer* and the *performance of miracles?* This brings us to the very root of religion. In the hour of need, the heavy-laden heart craves a savior who may ward off the ills with which nature threatens us; that can be done only by a God who stands *above* the natural course of events, not by one who manifests himself *in* them.

I believe, Spinoza would have answered such objections about as follows. It is true, he might say, there are yearn-ings, the satisfaction of which by God my philosophy does not encourage you to expect. I do not dare to think, he might go on, that changes can be produced in the natural course of events by the expression of a wish. Prayer as an inner state of the soul may have effects on the soul-life, but I do not believe that it can deflect a streak of lightning or a bullet from its path, or that it can draw fire from heaven as was done by the prayer of Elijah.

Indeed, the question here is not concerning the evalua-

tion and interpretation of facts, but concerning the existence of facts : Are prayers invariably or even occasionally
efficacious in producing changes in the natural course of
events ? No decision can be rendered for or against the
efficacy of prayer on *a priori* grounds. Consequently the
question must be decided by experience, say by experiment, something like the one forced upon the priest of
Baal by the prophet Elijah, or perhaps by a statistical procedure. We might, let us say, consider questions like the
following: Does a constant relation obtain between the
amount of damage done by thunder-storms and the tendency to ward it off by the transcendental method, which
certainly differs for different localities? Are large cities
afflicted oftener than the lowlands? Or can we detect any
differences in the frequency of other occurrences, say of
hail-storms, animal epidemics, and the like, according as
the owners of such fields and stock pray or do not pray?
Or has the average term of life decreased since public and
private prayer for protection against sickness and death,
pestilence and famine, has become less frequent? I do not
believe that the demand for such a mode of proof would
meet with favor anywhere. Indeed, the mere mention of
such a possibility may be regarded by many as sacrilegious,
a sign that faith in prayer is not based on investigation
and observation, but precedes them, and that faith is resolved to avoid all attempts at empirical verification.

Besides, there can be hardly a doubt that this belief is
rapidly declining. Originally it prevailed universally; it
is perhaps one of the oldest and most universal dogmas of
the human race that the utterance of certain formulæ and
the performance of certain acts are means of warding off
evils and of conciliating the gods. It has waned pro-
portionately to the increase of our knowledge of things.
That it is losing ground is noticeable in the European
world since the beginning of modern natural-scientific research. In the measure in which meteorology explained
atmospheric occurrences and physiology and pathology
laid bare the processes of bodily life, natural preservatives
or remedies took the place of supranatural ones. We cannot prove absolutely that the natural causal nexus is with-

out exceptions and breaks, but we are getting more and more accustomed to presuppose it.

And, let us say in conclusion, we surely have no reason to be dissatisfied with this state of affairs. Though the inexorableness of nature may be a hardship in particular cases, yet we could not, on the whole, desire uniformity to give way to caprice. If the wish of a man expressed in prayer could move mountains and cause the sun to stand still or make rain and sunshine, life and death, we should not gain anything by that. The world invites us to seek after knowledge and to work, and these functions suit our nature. We could fearlessly entrust so great a power over things only to a will that is in full accord with God's. Such a will, however, desires nothing except what God desires, and that certainly happens as it is.

It is obvious that Christianity does not encourage the tendency of the natural man to bring about by supranatural means results in the sensible world which he cannot attain by natural means. Christianity consists essentially in withdrawing the heart from the worldly goods which the natural man craves, and in turning it to the heavenly and eternal possessions. Jesus promises his disciples, not wordly happiness and welfare, but peace with God and peace in God. And this is what they pray for. The desire for inner spiritual goods marks the death of the old magic prayer which originally sprang from the covetousness and helplessness of the sensuous man. The presupposition of the prayer is: Your heavenly father knows what you need; and its concluding sentence is: Not my will, but thy will be done. Its aim is not to conquer nature by supranatural means, but to conquer the human heart, which, wavering between defiance and despondency, is not able to yield and adapt itself to its fate.*

But, another objection is heard: By identifying God and

* With impassioned eloquence Fichte attacks the attempt to degrade the Christian religion into a necromantic idol-worship in his *Appellation an das Publikum*, written during the atheism-controversy. "The system which expects happiness from an all-powerful being is a system of idolatry and idol-worship, and as old as human corruption." The Christian religion, he says, is strenuously opposed to this view; it absolutely refuses to promise the sensuous man worldly happiness.

reality, pantheism destroys the quality of God which alone makes him God: absolute goodness and holiness. I cannot and ought not to worship and believe in the empirical existence before me. The world as it exists is by no means adorable. The base and the evil have as much reality in them as has the good. Pantheism effaces the distinction between the good and the bad; it regards all existence as divine, as a manifestation of the All-One, and thereby destroys the notion of God.

Let me reply that this is a mistake. Pantheism by no means expects us to regard everything that is and happens as perfect and divine, and to revere it. It is true, it does assume that nothing that has existence is wholly foreign to God. But God's nature itself remains transcendent. All things transitory, we may say with Goethe, are but symbols. But not every symbol is intelligible to you. Hence you select what you can understand, and behold in it a revelation of the divine essence; everything else you simply ignore.

Take an example. You think of your country with feelings of piety. You sang in your youth and you go on singing: I sacrifice my heart and my hand, to live and to die for my German fatherland. What is this fatherland, this German people, to which you consecrate yourself, your strength and your life? Is it the collection of individuals whom you know and whom you meet? Is it the persons with whom you are thrown daily, with whom you do business or whom you meet in your official capacity? Certainly not. Most of them are indifferent to you, while some of them even annoy you. Is it the narrower circle with which you are more closely connected; is it your acquaintances and good friends, your colleagues and superiors? It is to be hoped that there is many a man among them whom you honor and esteem, but you probably know, when you speak of him, how far he is from being perfect. And you surely do not intend to live and die for these men. And yet you sing the song with real emotion. Where, then, is this German people? It is in the heart of your mother; it is in the language which she has taught you; it is in the song which goes to your heart; it is in the face of your

child ; it is in the faithfulness of a friend, in the love of a
wife ; it looks at you even out of the blue eyes of a strange
child that plays by the wayside ; it is in every word of
instruction and wisdom that a faithful teacher has imparted
to you ; it is in the memory of your dead ; it is in the pictures
of the great men who have inspired you, whose thoughts
have enriched you. It is a picture which you have made
for yourself, an ideal form whose features you have
gathered together from the dearest, best, and most remarkable things you have met. And now you say, leaving out
of account everything else : These are my people, such is
their real essence, these qualities reveal but do not exhaust
their true being, for countless stores of riches are hidden
from me.

Well, you treat reality in the same way. You gather
the features in nature and history which impress you most
profoundly and please you most, you form an image out of
them and say : Behold here the real essence, the profoundest meaning and content of reality ! You contemplate
the setting sun and drink in its light ; you breathe the air
of spring and feel the throb of nature ; you see the sprout-
ing leaves, and the infinite wealth of beings that act in
harmony with each other ; you gaze upon the mountains and
the sea, upon heaven and the eternal stars, and say : That is
the work of God ! You read the works of the great poets
and seers of all peoples ; you try to follow their thoughts
and to grasp the eternal images, and feel therein the breath
of the spirit of God. You hear the Gospel ; you lose yourself in the words and life of Christ ; you experience the
history of his passion and death, and you say with the
centurion : Certainly this was a righteous man and the
Son of God. Here you grasp the meaning of life, the
meaning of things ; this it is through and for which reality
exists.

It is true, we have besides, the trivial, the vulgar, and
the evil. Besides Jesus, the pride and hatred of the
scribes, the self-satisfied righteousness of the Pharisees, the
contemptible complaisance of the procurator of justice who
makes himself popular with the masses, the bloodthirsti-
ness of a blind mob, the baseness of a traitor, and the weak-

ness of a denier. All these blemishes are there, and just
as real as the other items. Nevertheless you say : These
are not the essential elements of the historical event which
interests us, the life and death of the innocent and just man
constitute the essential factor; this is the great world-
stirring fact; all else is but a secondary means to an end,
essential to the outcome and exposition, but not part and
parcel thereof.

Of course this is arbitrary. You cannot convince any
one by argument who does not feel as you do. Should
any one maintain that the servant Malchus or the crowing
cock is just as much of a reality ; that there is no difference
that would justify you in showing any preference, you
cannot force him to a different view. It is not the understanding but the heart that makes distinctions. The intellect views each part of reality as equally real. The distinction between the important and the unimportant, the
essential and the accidental, is made by the intellect, not by
the will. The heart tells you what is truly essential in the
infinite wealth of real things. If a man had no heart, if he
were mere, pure understanding, everything would be
equally important, or, rather, equally indifferent, to him.
This is what happens to the blasé individual whose heart
is dead, whose feelings are blunted.

Hence it makes no difference here what cosmological
notion you happen to have concerning the origin and substance of the world. The pantheist as well as the theist
selects what he regards as the true import or the real essence of things, and his choice depends, not on his cosmological speculations, but on the immediate interest which
the objects arouse in him. Nor is the theist determined
in his decision by other principles. When he grounds
his judgment on the Bible, it is simply because the book
itself and its contents have a meaning for him. And when
he accepts the authority of a church in interpreting things,
it is because he regards the same as a historical institution
having absolute importance.

But many believe that theism has an advantage in
handling such facts. Pantheism must assume that evil too
proceeds from the universal being ; hence the relation of

God to good and evil becomes a doubtful one. Theism separates God from the world so far that he is freed from the imperfections of empirical reality.

True; but theism can free God of these imperfections only at the price of dualism. If we assume two original principles, we can indeed foist the responsibility for everything that displeases us upon the evil principle, upon matter or the devil, and then reserve the other principle as the ground of everything good and pleasing. But, as is well known, the church doctrine was not willing to make the sacrifice. Hence its theism has no advantage over pantheism even in this regard. If God has created all things out of nothing, they are and remain his products, and all attempts to shift the responsibility for the imperfections of the given world from him to something else are labor lost. They never have satisfied and never will satisfy the intellect. Whether we seek the first cause of evil and wickedness in the free will of man or in that of a fallen angel, the understanding will always go a step farther and inquire into the cause of the first cause. And if there is a cause for the existence of man or angel, he will regard this as the cause of his nature, and will, perhaps, with Jacob Böhme, attribute it to some obscure original cause, to God, or, with Leibniz, to some metaphysical limitation of his creative power.

We may say with greater justice that pantheism can explain these facts more satisfactorily. It may, like Spinoza, either identify reality and perfection and attribute their apparent discrepancy to our arbitrary notions of good and evil, perfection and imperfection; or it may with evolutionistic pantheism explain the process of the development of reality as the progressive, increasing self-realization of the idea, so that perfection is the end, not the beginning. Whatever the value of such theories may be in other respects, they lack the extreme onesidedness which characterizes the notion that an almighty will, anticipating all things, by an act of absolute will created our world as an absolutely good one. But this same world was so corrupted by the fall of a creature that acted from absolute caprice that it must be regarded as belonging to the devil. Lucilio Vanini once suggested the thought which J. Stuart Mill repeats in his posthumous essays on religion: God desires the salvation, the devil the ruin, of all human beings. But, since all infidels and heretics are lost *eo ipso*, and since the members of the church who die in cardinal sin or in hostility to the church are also lost, the result is that the will of the devil is realized to an infinitely greater extent than God's. For these views Vanini was burnt at the stake, a mode of argument that neither convinces the intellect nor satisfies the heart. I do not claim that the above-mentioned reflections of the pantheistic theodicy accomplish this; but there is certainly something consoling about them. Besides, the theistical attempts at a theodicy ultimately reach the same conclusion. The statements about the unreality of evil, and the faith of men in the final restoration of all things, show that this is so.

10. Historical Evolution of Theism and Cosmology.

To the critical and dogmatical treatment of the cosmologico-theological problem let me append the outlines of a historical exposition. I have already said that, in my opinion, the development of human thought tends to *idealistic monism*. Scientific and philosophical reflections lead to it on the one hand, while the development of the religious view of the world leads to a monotheism that, if consistently carried out, deprives God of all finiteness and limitation, and therefore of all finite determinations, leaving no place for an independent world alongside of him. If monotheism is logically carried out, its most universal world-formula coincides with pantheism : μόνος ὁ θεός, God alone exists.

Historical investigations cannot, of course, determine the truth of a cosmical theory. Nevertheless, the historical proof, if we wish to designate these reflections as such, is not without its value. All philosophers acknowledge this by the desire which they manifest to represent their own views of the world as the climax of the preceding philosophical evolution. Feuerbach and Büchner are just as intent upon proclaiming their systems as the necessary end of the series as Hegel and Comte; and rightly so. Wherever we have to deal with the knowledge of particular historical or physical facts, the investigator will trust only the methodical investigation, and demand that the decision be left to it exclusively. But wherever the question is concerning ultimates, wherever we have to reflect the total impression which the world makes on the human mind, the individual needs the support of collective thinking: it is important that he obtain the *consensus gentium* or, if that is not possible, the *consensus historiæ ;* he must convince himself that his views are really the sought-for goal to which the preceding development necessarily leads.

It is customary in the natural history of religion to distinguish three fundamental forms or stages in the development of the belief in God: *Fetishism* or *Spiritism* (also called animism, naturism), *Polytheism,* and *Monotheism.* The faith in a suprasensuous being that acts upon the sensible world is common to all. The forms, however, differ which they ascribe to the suprasensuous and its activity. *Fetishism* or *Spiritism* prevails among the savage tribes in all parts of the world. Its concomitant is *Shamanism* or necromancy. A fetish (from the Portuguese *feitico,* amulet, idol) is any given object in which dwells a magic power or a spirit. A stone, a sherd, a bone, a bunch of herbs or hair, a roughly-carved image, is worn on the body or hung up in the hut of the negro. The object receives some marks of attention from him ; food and drink are placed before it. In return the worshipper expects the fulfilment of his wishes: protection against disease, evil magic, and all kinds of misfortune. If these expectations are not realized, the fetish is regarded as having no power and is thrown away, and an attempt is made to get possession of a more efficient one. The manufacture and treatment of fetishes is the great science of the magic priests who have control over 'the spirits. Even animals, trees, groves, mountains, streams, lakes, the ocean, the moon and the sun are looked upon by many as the abodes of spirits, and propitiated with acts of worship. It is also very common to worship the departed souls of ancestors. Finally, gods of a mythological and cosmological character are spoken of, spoken of more often than worshipped. We hear of gods or a God who originally created the world and man. The religious ideas of negroes and Indians, of northern Asiatic tribes and the inhabitants of Polynesia are essentially alike. Fetishism and shamanism are their most prominent elements; in addition to these we find the rudiments of cosmogonic mythology; and here and there mention is made of a great spirit, of God, who has created all things, from whom man in particular is descended. Occasionally, too, we find the statement that the old and great gods gave way to new and lesser gods.*

What is the nature of the "divine" which is worshipped? It is hard to determine it. This stage is characterized by the vagueness of its notions of God's essence and by the uncertainty of his activity. It is an error to suppose that the particular accidental thing is the object of worship. A suprasensuous element, a "spirit," is everywhere assumed, upon which and through which effects are produced. The negro believes that "a spirit dwells, or may dwell, in every sensible object; and that too, a great and mighty spirit in wholly insignificant objects. He does not conceive this spirit as bound to the corporeal object; it simply makes it its customary abode." (Waitz, II. 174.) That the negro has a bent for metaphysics is shown by a story narrated in the same work (page 188). "A negro was worshipping a tree, supposed to be his fetish, with an offering of food, when a certain European asked whether he thought the tree could eat. The negro replied : 'Oh, the tree is not the fetish; the fetish is a spirit and invisible, but he has descended into this tree. Certainly he cannot devour our bodily food, but he enjoys its spiritual part, and leaves behind the bodily part, which we see.'"

Polytheism is the second fundamental form. It differs from the first in this, that in it the suprasensuous element assumes the form of *personal* beings. Instead of idols, the vague, perishable, nameless, and shapeless incorporations of magic power, we have gods: permanent, fixed, personal, and

---

* References in Th. Waitz, *Anthropologie der Naturvölker* : II. 167 ff. for the negroes ; III. 177 ff. for the Indians ; V. 184 for Micronesians ; VI. 229 ff. for the Polynesians.

historical beings. The Greek gods are the most perfect examples of this type of religion. Each member of the kingdom of the gods is a well-defined historical personage ; his corporeal as well as spiritual nature exhibits the general characteristics of human nature. They are, however, exalted human beings, without the limitations of mortals. They are not subject to the laws of nature, which govern our existence ; space, time, and causality are not applicable to the gods. They are not absolutely incorporeal beings, but can assume any shape ; they are not omnipresent, but are where they desire to be, without using our slow means of locomotion ; they are not outside of time, but do not grow old and die ; their life is eternal youth; they are not omnipotent, but their wishes determine reality without employing the roundabout means peculiar to human action.

Polytheism is peculiar to the earlier periods of historical nations. We find deities similar in their fundamental characteristics to the Greek gods among all historical peoples : among Egyptians and Semites, among Hindoos and Persians, among Teutons and Slavs. In the New World the nations among whom we find the beginnings of historical life, the inhabitants of Mexico and Peru, are likewise remarkable for the fact that they have created a world of gods.

This coincidence is not accidental : historical gods are the transcendent reflections of a nation's own historical life. The restless fear and covetousness of the savage are reflected in fetishism. He is without lasting thoughts and recollections, without aims and ideals that go beyond his sensuous individual life ; and so he lives in the present, subject to the needs of his sensuous nature. His gods are like himself ; they are transitory, ephemeral creatures like the fear and the desires which produce them. Similarly, the gods of historical peoples resemble their originators. The permanent union of the tribe organized into families gives the individual a share in the historical life of the whole and thus raises him above the transitoriness of animal existence. So, too, the gods become historical personages, whose relations to each other and to mankind are

lasting. As the people become settled, their gods too become settled ; the temple rises by the side of the town-hall
as the permanent dwelling-place of the god.

A closer examination into the nature of the gods leads
us to distinguish three elements, which, of course, form an
undivided unity of personal life in the consciousness of the
believer. They are : (1) *personified magic powers ;* (2) *personified natural forces ;* and (3) *personified ideals.* The first
class betrays a similarity with fetishism. By influencing
the gods we may indirectly influence the course of nature.
Acts of worship are means of procuring in a supranatural
way what the natural powers of man do not secure. In
true religion this is always the first and most important
factor. True religion does not consist in mythology, but in
worship. Health and wealth, harvests and children, victory
and good fortune, and the great science of the future are
what all believers constantly strive to obtain from the gods
through prayer and sacrifices. Everywhere we find a professional priesthood that performs the acts of worship and
divination, everywhere also all kinds of superstitions and
charms which in no wise differ from fetishism.

Secondly, the gods are personified natural forces or natural beings. This is the phase with which the mythologists
mainly occupy themselves. Zeus is the bright sky or the
celestial force which manifests itself in the weather, above
all in the lightning ; Demeter is the fruitful soil, which bears
in its lap grain and fruit ; Poseidon, the sea or the force of
the sea encircling and agitating the earth ; Apollo and
Artemis, the two great luminaries of day and night. The
inexhaustible fertility of the Greek fancy has brought the
thousand forms into thousandfold relations with each other
and with man. Natural and human elements are woven
together, forming a variegated web of myths. The analytical investigator distinguishes therein anthropomorphic
and symbolic interpretations of natural phenomena, transformed historical reminiscences, tribal legends and legends
pertaining to places of worship, etymological and geographical fictions, and undertakes the arduous and hopeless
task of explaining the historical development of this world

or the more hopeless one of reducing it to a systematic unity.

Finally, the gods exhibit still another phase : they are personified ideals; they are the concrete representations of a people's ideas of human perfection. Zeus is the ideal of the ruler ; dignity and might, based on power and right, are the elements of his being. In the person of Apollo the Greek idea of the free and exalted spirit is represented ; spiritual freedom and prudence are perfectly harmonized in him ; the Muses are his attendants. And so, Hera, Athene, and Aphrodite are types of female perfection.

> Und wir verehren
> Die Unsterblichen,
> Als wären sie Menschen,
> Thäten im Grossen,
> Was der Beste im Kleinen
> Thut oder möchte.

Before I turn to monotheism, I shall briefly enter upon the question whether fetishism, polytheism, and monotheism are to be regarded not merely as three fundamentally different ground-forms, but also as successive stages of development ; in particular, whether fetishism was the primitive form of religion, preceding all others. For it does not seem doubtful that monotheism is the historical outgrowth of the preliminary stage of polytheism. The former view has, as Max Müller * shows, become prevalent since the middle of the last century. The theological conception that polytheism and fetishism are corruptions of the original, pure, monotheistic religion of Adam used to be the prevailing one prior to this time. M. Müller rejects the latter opinion as unscientific, but also denies the truth of the former. Fetishism, he declares, is never a primary form, but a corrupt survival of an originally more exalted conception of the Deity ; with the decline of civilization, the higher intellectual significance of the acts of worship was lost and degenerated into "the worship of stocks and stones."

---

*M. Müller, *Lectures on the Origin and Growth of Religion* (1891), pp. 54 ff. Cf. also O. Pfleiderer, *Religionsphilosophie auf geschichtlicher Grundlage* (1884), II. pp. 3 ff.

Indeed, if we mean by fetishism the worship of material, "inanimate" objects—and such worship may exist among individuals and degraded tribes—then M. Müller is undoubtedly right in his statement. Such an irrational fetishism presupposes "antecedents" which made it possible, and as whose "inanimate" survival it remained after the real import of fetishism had been lost. But the case is different if we mean by fetishism what was suggested above and what Waitz, to whom M. Müller himself appeals, regards as alone according with the facts, namely, that fetishism is the worship of "spirits" temporarily residing in a given object. If the *historical* life of civilized nations was preceded by an *unhistorical* or *prehistorical* stage, we cannot but regard the historical gods as the outgrowth of prehistoric gods. For surely, nothing can be more certain here than the universal proposition that the nature of a people is reflected in the nature of the gods whom they worship. The vague, perishable, formless "spirits" of fetishism are such prehistoric gods.

Nor does the history of the Hindoo religion contradict this view, as far as I can see. M. Müller calls the oldest stratum that can be reached in the literature of the Hindoos "henotheism": the divine exists in many and in changeable spectral natural forces, among which now the one, now the other appears as the first and highest. According to his description, we may regard this form as a transition from the primitive belief in spirits to the later polytheism of the Hindoos with its personal and historical gods. It may have been preceded by a stage of development that cannot be historically accounted for and that wholly agrees with the current conception of fetishistic spiritism. By the very nature of the case, fetishism can leave no historical monuments. Survivals only are preserved, and with such the anthropologist is confronted everywhere.*

---

* Nowhere in the Homeric world is there any mention of soul-worship and of the influence of departed souls upon our earth. The world of the dead is absolutely separated from the world of the living. E. Rohde (*Psyche, Seelenkult und Unsterblichkeitsglaube bei den Griechen*, 1890), however, shows from numerous traces and survivals that this stage was preceded by another, during which the Greeks believed in and feared "spirits" and developed a soul-worship. Rohde connects the disappearance of the belief

Every attempt to solve the problem concerning the primitive *origin of the belief in gods* or supranatural beings seems to reach the same conclusion.

Three different ways of explaining the origin of religion have been suggested. One hypothesis starts out from the theoretical impulse, from the causal instinct in man. O. Peschel prefaces the section on religion in his *Völkerkunde* with the following proposition : "On all stages of culture and among all human tribes, religious emotions are invariably aroused by the same inward impulse—the need, namely, of detecting a cause or an originator of every phenomenon and event." And he repeats this statement at the conclusion, adding that the causal need of inferior minds is satisfied even by a fetish. The first form of causality and the one best known to man is his own activity. He contemplates the world according to this category and regards all events in the heavens and on earth as the acts of volitional beings. In this way, mythology arises as a product of anthropomorphic apperception.

Another explanation takes as its starting-point, not the intelligence, but the will ; not theoretical, but practical needs. So Ludwig Feuerbach in his work, *Das Wesen der Religion.* It must be said, however, that Hume, Spinoza, and Hobbes preceded him in this, and that nowadays many agree with the general current of his thought. According to Feuerbach, magic constituted the essence of all primitive religions. The gods are wish-granters whose business it is to fulfil the wishes which man himself cannot realize. As necessity is the mother of all arts, so, too, she is the mother of the art of sorcery. The part which intelligence plays in the matter is secondary ; it furnishes the will with the means, with the idea of a " spirit " or " God," that is,

---

in spirits with transmigration and the transition from the older mode of burial to cremation. The psyche's double is destroyed by cremation, and in this way the soul itself is completely and definitely separated from the material element, so that it belongs exclusively to the dark realm of the shades in Hades and can no longer haunt the bright and sunny earth. Thus the Greeks of the Homeric age freed themselves from the phantom-world of spirits. At a later, more religiously inclined age the survivals of primitive faith were revived in Greece in hero- and soul-worship.

274 THE COSMOLOGICAL-THEOLOGICAL PROBLEM. [Book I.

with the idea of a supranatural power on which the will can act and thus indirectly assert itself in nature.

The third starting-point is the belief in the continued existence of departed spirits. Herbert Spencer emphasizes this factor. His natural doctrine of religion (in the first volume of the *Principles of Sociology*) concludes with the assertion "that ancestor-worship is the root of every religion."

As far as I can see, these explanations do not exclude but supplement each other. First as regards Peschel's theory, the intellectualistic theory, which for the most part also underlies the explanations of the mythologists, we may say that taken by itself it is evidently insufficient. It expects too much of the intelligence or the causal need of primitive man. If, as Genesis tells us, man had suddenly appeared in the world, one fine day, with the entire mental equipment of the present, or even with superior powers, only as yet without knowledge, then indeed his first feeling might have been one of wonder, and his first concern the question regarding the creator of these things. If, however, he was evolved from lower forms of life, then we are hardly permitted to regard surprise and wonder as playing an important part at the beginning of his career. Animals show us daily how little purely sensuous beings are impressed by celestial phenomena, which according to the mythologists first arouse the causal impulse : sunrise and the dawn of day, eclipses and storms. Only a highly-developed mental being feels astonishment at the processes which it has long ago been accustomed to perceive. I believe that the notion of spirit had to be present before the mythological interpretation of sun and moon, of storms and clouds, of earth and sea was at all possible. And hence I do not doubt that Herbert Spencer is right when he derives the original notion of a spirit from the belief that the departed continue to exist as spectres. The unusual amount of anthropological material collected and so well arranged by him shows how universal the belief is, and at the same time makes clear its origin. It also explains how the belief came to form the basis of an animism that endows everything with souls, of an anthropomorphic apperception of natural events, and finally of a mythical conception of nature.

Then again, it is plain how the belief in spirits might in a *volitional* being form the beginning of the practical series, of magic and worship. The original type of worship universally seems to consist in invoking the spirits of the departed and offering them a share in the meal. But since the spirits themselves are not real beings in the common acceptation, the intercourse with them has a peculiar, one might say a spectral, character. They do not really eat the food, like living beings, nor do they give an audible answer. They appear now at this place, then at that; now in this form, then in that; they are not bound by the laws of corporeality, of space and time, and hence they exert spectral, supranatural influences. If one only knew the art of gaining their favor, one might certainly produce many an effect otherwise impossible. If one only knew how to question them properly, one might receive many a revelation from them that no one else can know, especially of the future, since they themselves do not exist in time, at least not in the proper sense of the term.

This explains the origin of the art of magic. Feuerbach is right: It is the will which makes it universal and makes shamanism and sacrificial worship, augury and oracles, an essential part of human life. The desire exists to assert one's will, while there are a thousand hindrances and obstacles that cannot be overcome by natural efficiency; the ardent desire also exists to foresee the future, which lies concealed from mortals in impenetrable darkness. The idea of a spirit offers itself with its supranatural power and knowledge. Seizing upon this, the will, made inventive by necessity, hits upon an endless variety of suprasensuous or transcendent acts and interpretations, which confront anthropological and historical research at every step. If the necessity were not so urgent and the will to live not so strong, the belief in spirits would not have gained such immense importance in the history of thought. Spinoza appreciates this fact. "If human beings," so he begins the preface to his *Tractatus theologico-politicus*, "were able to govern their affairs by firm decisions, or if fortune always

favored them, there would be no superstition. Since, however, necessity renders them absolutely helpless, and since
they are tossed between fear and hope in their eager desire
for the uncertain gifts of fortune, their minds are ever ready
to accept any belief and superstition."

Finally, however, the intellectualistic conception of the
mythologists is not without an element of truth. The
mythologist will find no difficulty in showing that Herbert
Spencer is wrong in deriving the entire world of gods, with
its euhemerism, directly from deified ancestors and kings.
Zeus and Demeter, Apollo and Artemis, Indra and Rudra,
Nitra and Varuna are certainly not deified kings and
queens. We might, with greater justice, call them personified or deified natural forces. It is true, their origin
was first made possible by the belief in the continued
existence of the dead. But after the idea of a spirit has
once been formed, it separates itself from its origin and becomes the starting-point for new and independent creations :
natural events are interpreted spiritistically or anthropomorphically. The details of this process, how the spirits
became personified natural forces or the natural forces incorporated spirits, cannot, of course, be concretely shown.
We cannot trace the history of the particular gods to their
origin in the popular soul. What we can attempt to do is
to point out the general psychological possibilities. And
hence we may with Max Müller consider the influence
exerted on thought by primitive speech, which personified
everything. It constantly provoked fancy, as it were, to
think of an active subject behind the natural processes,
thunder, rain, and storm. But what could this being be
other than a spirit, like the one that dwells in the surrounding tangible, material objects? Inward relations are then
established between the spirit and the manifestations of
the object in which it resides, and the spirit becomes a
natural spirit, a personified natural force ; Apollo or Mitra
becomes the all-seeing sun- and light-god, who scatters
darkness and sends his arrows broadcast. Zeus or Indra
becomes the celestial god, who holds the forces of the upper regions in his hand, gathers the clouds, causes rain
and snow, and above all hurls the mighty thunderbolt. At

the same time, the poetical and religious fancy performs its share by anthropomorphically interpreting external phenomena as expressions of inner moral states or experiences, and so the gods arise, those wonderful beings in whom physico-cosmical and historico-mental elements are combined into a unity that is so strange and full of contradictions.

We now turn to the third and last fundamental form of religion, to *monotheism.* It is peculiar to the more advanced mental culture of historical peoples. It is characteristic of the great monotheistic religions, first, that they originated in *historical* times and through *historical* personages; secondly, that *they spiritualize the divine element.* The gods are sensuous and suprasensuous beings. Monotheism entirely removes the sensuous part. God is spirit, incorporeal, formless, inconceivable by the sensuous imagination. This view completely divests the transcendent world of its anthropomorphic garb, at least so far as the principle is concerned, for the masses will never give up sensualizing spirit. With the disappearance of human limitations, the deity ceases to exist as a particular being. The individual is a being limited by time and space. A being that is absolutely free from these limitations ceases to be an individual being. God is *the* being, the *one universal being,* whose power and essence penetrates and fills all spaces and times. And hence, still another limitation disappears: the *national* limitation. The gods of polytheism are the gods of a particular people; other nations have other gods. The one God, the world-god, is the only true God, besides whom there are no other gods. All the monotheistic religions have a predilection for international propaganda, which is foreign to the polytheistic religions. True, the Greeks and Romans also carried their gods into foreign lands, but it never occurred to them to make the souls of foreign nations subject to them. The desire to convert, which manifests itself in diverse ways, in missions and crusades, is peculiar to monotheistic religions.

Monotheism appears in history as an advance over polytheism. We may, to a certain extent, trace the course of evolution in the Greek world. The progress of mental

culture exerts a destructive influence upon anthropomorphic polytheism. The old gods are no longer able to satisfy the demands either of the advanced moral or theoretical consciousness.

At first we notice a tendency on the part of the Greeks
to remove from the *moral* nature of their gods such features
as the more sensitive consciousness is unable to tolerate.
If the gods are really what the reverent believer takes them
to be, the establishers of order, the bestowers of blessings,
the protectors of right and custom, we cannot and must not
attribute to them everything that legend and myth refer
to them. Priests and philosophers, poets and artists assisted in the work of purification, by means of which the
mythico-anthropomorphical and magico-fetishistic features
were subjected to a process of elimination since the sixth
century.* The development likewise tends towards unity.
Homer does not take exception to the fact that the gods
are hostile to and at war with each other, that they are on
opposite sides in their interference with the affairs of men.
A later age, however, cannot bear the thought of such discord. Goodness and justice are one, and there can be no
conflict between them. Hence the gods are of one mind
and desire the same ends. It is not at first the metaphysical unity of the divine being which is an ethical postulate,
but the unanimity of the divine will. The demand for unity
found its literal expression in the term "the divine" (τὸ
θεῖον), which has been current since the days of Herodotus.
The term does not preclude the idea of a plurality of beings or, we may even say, of names or persons (characters
or manifestations). For the religious feeling of the Greek
people would not have been willing to dispense with these.
"For the Greek, the entire beauty, the entire warmth, the
entire sublimity of his religion is essentially based on the
idea of a *world* of gods. Nor can we appreciate the complete grandeur of that religion even now, unless we conceive it in the same way. These beings spend their happy
lives in heaven and on earth, either alone or in each other's
society, being everywhere present and taking part in every-

---

* L. Schmidt, *Die Ethik der alten Griechen,* I. 133 ff.

thing, sympathizing with their human favorites and their fates, loving them, watching over them, punishing them, and governing them. A rigorous monotheism, with its chilling solitude, would have seemed to the ancient Greeks like atheism." *

Thus polytheism remains morally possible. Its existence is, however, threatened by the development of theoretical speculation. The *unity* of nature was the feature in reality which attracted Greek philosophy from the very outset. All the endeavors of the most ancient philosophers are devoted to the discovery of the unitary principle of reality. If this principle is spiritual and personal, it cannot but be a unified one. The cosmos does not look like a work in which many participated, but like the product of an all-ruling reason. The first decided hostile conflict between philosophy and popular polytheism seems to have occurred in Eleatic speculation. The position of the ancient gods became even more precarious with the rapid development of the positive sciences after the fourth century. An age that busies itself with zoology and botany, anatomy and physiology, cannot regard the Olympic gods otherwise than as fictions. The initiated may avoid the conflict with the traditional popular religion and treat the gods sparingly; he may transform them and find æsthetical pleasure in their contemplation, or give them a dwelling-place on earth where they can no longer disturb the course of nature, but he can no longer believe in them.

The philosophical conception of the world which supplants the mythological view and in a certain sense supplies the loss of the old world of gods is an *idealistic pantheism.* I shall briefly trace the historical development of this view, which is to this day one of the fundamental forms of thought, if not the fundamental form of philosophical thought, in the West.†

---

* K. Lehrs, *Populäre Aufsätze aus dem Altertum*, pp. 148 ff.

† I call the reader's attention to the brief but full and clear exposition of the *History of Ancient Philosophy* by W. Windelband, which together with a valuable supplement, S. Günther's *Umriss der Geschichte der Mathematik, Naturwissenschaft und Kosmologie*, shows the growth of Greek thought. It forms a part (V, 1) of the *Handbuch der classischen Philologie*, ed. by J. Müller.

In the philosophy of Plato this conception is for the first time consistently carried out. It is true, there is, besides, another view of the world which is the antithesis of Plato's idealism: the *materialistic atomism* of Democritus. But the train of thought initiated by Plato became the prevailing one even in antiquity, and gained still greater prominence during the middle ages and in modern times. Indeed, it was received, though with considerable modifications, into the scholastic systems of the church, and thus became an element of popular thought, against which it had originally taken so hostile a stand. The facts from which it proceeds are familiar to Greek thought: A rational order governs nature and in particular the heavenly bodies; justice rules the human world, the life of individuals as well as of nations. These facts, which Democritus and Epicurus do not deny, but attempt to explain after their own fashion, Plato interprets in his *theory of ideas*, utilizing and developing many thoughts of his predecessors: Reality is in truth nothing but a *unified system of actual, harmonious thoughts.*

By this great paradox the philosophical thought of the West definitely severs its connection with popular opinion. "Opinion," which contemplates reality only with the senses, adheres to the notion that the world consists of an aggregation of objects which move in space and originate and perish in time. The philosopher who does not contemplate reality with the senses but with the intellect recognizes its true essence; he comprehends it by means of dialectical speculation, by thoughtful reflection, as that which it is in itself: as an actual, timeless and spaceless, eternal and immutable system of thoughts. As a poem, a philosophy, or a geometrical system exists as an actual system of thoughts, so reality in itself, the κόσμος νοητός, the *mundus intelligibilis*, exists as such a system. In the former case, a plurality of elements is combined into a unity by inner logical or æsthetical necessity, and exists as such outside of time, whereas subjective consciousness can comprehend it only in time-relations. Similarly, the actual world exists as a plurality of thoughts or ideas connected inwardly by logical and æsthetical necessity. To be sure, the existence of a thought consists in being thought, and hence the existence of reality as such consists in the unitary system of thought being eternally thought, or in the self-consciousness of the idea, which constitutes reality, or, as we may say, in the living self-existence of God, who is the All-Real and the All-Good.

Thus the philosopher conceives reality; he attempts to repeat the actual thoughts, the thoughts which constitute the essence of God or reality. Of course, he sees reality in another form also; like others he, too, beholds it with the senses, and it appears to him as to them: as an aggregation of objects scattered through space, changing, originating, and perishing in time. But the illusion does not deceive him; he knows that the actual cannot originate and perish. Besides, the true reality everywhere shines through the phenomenal world. The eye of the philosopher everywhere detects the idea, even in the spatial-time world. There is a rational mental factor in all things; it exists as mathematical uniformity in the order of the celestial system, as a teleological, rational correlation between the organs and functions of living beings. It is true, this factor is, as it were, concealed or obstructed by " another," an irrational factor. In all corporeal things we find besides a rational, definable, and hence conceivable element, besides form and law, something that is formless and undefinable, something that is absolutely impervious to thought; and it is owing to this that things are spatially extended. Since this "other" does not belong to the world of thought, it is not real at all, it is, so to say, a μὴ ὄν, a mere illusion. Nevertheless it is again endowed with a kind of reality in Plato's natural philosophical expositions, especially in his *Timæus*. It is there used as a " co-operative cause" existing alongside of the real cause or the actual thoughts which now become formative ideas of purpose, in order to explain the world of sense ; above all, in order to saddle the disturbances and malformations upon it. But in the philosophical writings proper, the imperfections do not attach to reality itself, but simply to our sensuous perception of reality. Reality and perfection are already what *realitas* and *perfectio* came to be later on, identical concepts; God, the living, self-existent world-thought, who harbors in himself an infinite wealth of inner qualities, is at the same time the All-Real and the All-Good. The Aristotelian conception of the universe is closely akin to the foregoing view. It is true that Aristotle himself feels and accentuates the opposition which exists between himself and Plato. He discovers it especially in the fact that he is not willing, like Plato, to separate the actual thoughts from reality. The "ideas" are not outside and alongside of objects. They are in the objects as the actual realized ideas of purpose. Or expressed differently (for Plato would reject this exposition as not representing him fairly: ideas are not something alongside of an "other"; they themselves constitute reality): According to Aristotle, the world of particular sensuous objects is the real world; the κόσμος αἰσθητός, the world of plurality, of origin and decay, which Plato explained as a mere reflection of the actual ideal world upon our sense-perception, is, for him, the real world; it is the object of his theoretical interest and tireless investigation. But in his real explanation of things, in his metaphysics and natural philosophy, he altogether follows in the footsteps of his teacher. He, too, finds a dualism in all objects: a rational factor, the "form," the idea, the purpose, and an irrational factor, the "other," matter, which, as such, is formless, nonconceptual, and inconceivable, not reducible to thought. In the relation between the body and the soul we have the most significant pattern of the dual nature of all things: the soul, the rational and ideal element of the living being; matter, out of which it fashions the body, the irrational part. And he, too, regards the rational factor, which is the real, knowable element in the object, as the true reality. Matter as such is an unreal or merely potential factor, which becomes a definite, concrete reality only through the idea or the ideal purpose. It is true, the idea of the purpose is not in itself real either; it becomes so only when it is realized in matter. But ultimately, in his theology, which is the final completion of his philosophy, the ideal element is raised to the rank of the only and self-existent reality: all ideas are finally included in the one, all-embracing idea, in the world-thought or world-form, that is in

God. God, however, is pure form without matter, *actus purus*, and his reality consists in pure thinking. His existence is the thinking of the absolute content of thought (νόησις νοήσεως), the self-realization in self-consciousness of the idea which is reality.—That is exactly what Plato says: The unified, self-existent system of ideas which realizes itself in thought constitutes the absolute reality. God is the unity of thought and being. The only difference would be that Aristotle has ideas of individual things, whereas in Plato only the general, and not particulars, occur in the real world of thought. Still Plato does not always adhere to this view; for him souls are "individual ideas." And he would likewise recognize his own thoughts in Aristotle's conception of the relation between God and nature : the whole of nature has a purposive impulse and makes for the good ; the good, however, is nothing outside of nature, but its own perfect form. At least so far as man is concerned: for Plato regards the good as nothing but the perfect realization of the idea of man in an individual form. Moreover, both accept the same fundamental conceptions in ethics.

The *Stoa* follows the same line of thought. A universal reason that pervades the whole of reality with its own inner necessity and everywhere produces form and order, the rational and good element, is the ultimate world-principle or the true essence of reality. Besides this ideal or rational factor of reality, the Stoics also recognize the "other," a material factor by the side of reason. But they make a somewhat violent attempt to overcome this dualism again by assuring us that the rational element is likewise the material element, or, conversely, that the material principle, or the primitive fire from which everything comes and into which everything is resolved, is, at the same time, the ideal principle, the universal reason. If we disregard the somewhat extreme formulation of their view, we shall evidently find a rational meaning therein. It is at bottom the same conception which later philosophers desired to reach in their doctrine of the parallelism between thought and extension, or of the identity of the ideal and the real, or the view which Plato established by conceiving the corporeal world as an illusion—namely, a monistic ontology.

In the theosophical speculations in which Greek philosophy finally culminates, the features of idealistic pantheism are everywhere recognizable. The transcendency of God is emphasized; his essence transcends all existing attributes, even the attribute of mind. Nevertheless the category of mind expresses his essence most adequately; thought is his first revelation, and the old attributes of unity and goodness are his formal qualities. And to conclude, I shall let the Peripatetic Simplicius, one of the last thinkers of the old Hellenic world, express the fundamental conception common to the times. His commentary on the little handbook of Epictetus begins as follows : " The good is the source and origin of all things. For it is the origin and the goal of things, that towards which everything strives and tends. And the good produces all things out of itself —the first, the middle, and the last. But the first and the nearest it makes like itself; the one good creates many other goods; the one simplicity and unity which is higher than all unities, many unities ; the one origin, many origins. For it is unity and origin and goodness and God."

Let me mention in brief that the development of the theological and cosmological conceptions of the great eastern branch of the Aryan race, the Hindoos, culminated in a similar goal. After the creative fancy of the Hindoos had produced in the Devas a world of bright and eternal gods, it came in its philosophical reflections to a radical denial of the existence of many persons and names of the Deity, and recognized in *Brahman* a unitary absolute world-soul. The Brahman is no longer an individual ego. It is of neuter gender, rising above distinctions of sex. It is the supra-individual, suprasensuous, suprareal, universal spirit, which reveals itself in the individual soul as a fettered, divided, and sensualized being. " The Atman or Self within thee is the true Brahman, from whom thou wast estranged for a time through birth and death, but who receives thee back again as soon as thou returnest to Him, or to It." It is true, polytheism and sacrificial rites remained undisturbed alongside of this view. The different phases in the evolution of the collective mind are preserved in a very remarkable degree as stages of individual life, and assist us in understanding our own historical world. " Every religious thought that had once found expression in India, that had once been handed down as a sacred heir-loom, was preserved, and the thoughts of the three historical periods, the childhood, the manhood, and the old age of the Indian nation" (represented in literature : childhood, by most of the Vedic hymns ; manhood, by the Brahmanas ; old age, by the Upanishads), " were made to do permanent service in the three stages of the life of every individual." " There are still Brahmanic families in which the son learns by heart the ancient hymns, and the father performs day by day his sacred duties and sacrifices, while the grand-father, even though remaining in the village, looks upon all ceremonies and sacrifices as vanity, sees even in the Vedic gods nothing but names of what he knows to be beyond all names, and seeks rest in the highest knowledge only, which has become to him the highest religion, viz., the so-called Vedânta, the end and fulfilment of the whole Veda." *

Before we trace the further course of thought in the West, it will be necessary to cast a glance at the second great factor which influences its intellectual life : we mean the growth of the monotheistic conception of the universe in a Semitic tribe, the people of Israel. The goal is reached in the latter case, not in a speculative, but in a practical religious way. This is in accord with the entire disposi-tion of the race, which is diametrically opposed to the temperament of the Hellenic people. While the Greeks are pre-eminently endowed with intelligence, with highly sus-ceptible sensibility, and a surprisingly facile understand-ing, the special gift of the Israelites lies in the earnestness and depth with which they grasp moral and religious facts. The prophets of Israel correspond to the philosophers of the Greeks ; they are characters of austere force and grandeur, the like of whom no other people can produce. From Elijah, who begins the series, down to John the

---

* M. Müller, *Lectures on the Origin and Growth of Religion*, pp. 349, 350.

Baptist, who ends it, the fundamental characteristic common to the prophets is that they obey the voice of God in their hearts and rebuke the world and the people, the rich and the great, those who are powerful at court and with the populace, tradition and custom in conduct and worship ; that they measure the nation by its own standard, which is to be the chosen people of God, and find it wanting : instead of walking in justice, love, and humility before your God, you despise the lowly, devour the substance of widows and orphans, and follow other gods who give scope to the lusts of your hearts. And from the same point of view the prophet interprets history; he shows that the hand of God governs the fate of nations. The philosophy of religion, we might say, is the creation of Israel, as cosmology and mathematics is that of the Greeks. Of course, it is not a popular science; its sermons find no well-disposed audience; hence solitude and exile is the lot of the prophet, and the desert his retreat.

At their appearance in history, we do not find the people of Israel occupying the standpoint of a theoretical monotheism. Their religion is a practical monotheism of worship, one that may perhaps be best characterized as the worship of one god. The first commandment, "Thou shalt have no other gods before me," does not prohibit the belief in other gods, which it rather presupposes, but the worship of them. Israel shall serve Jahwe alone, and he will aid his people against their oppressors. We have scarcely any historical knowledge as to how the Israelites arrived at the exclusive worship of one god from the former polytheism of all Semitic tribes, traces of which are everywhere apparent in their traditions. On the other hand, we can follow the development of the worship of one god to monotheism in the literature which we possess. It is the combined work of priests and prophets. It is, moreover, a consequence of the first step : the nation has an interest, as it were, in making its God the only true God ; in making a world-god of the national God. In the Psalms, in the Prophets, and in Genesis, Jahwe is no longer merely the God of Israel, but absolutely the only true God, the God who created heaven and earth. The gods of other peoples are mere images made of wood and stone, powerless and unreal idols. We may mention as special phases of this development, first, the centralization of the worship by the monarchy and priesthood, then the moralization, denaturization, and finally denationalization of the notion of God by the prophets. Impressed by the great historical experiences of their country, the prophets become convinced that Jahwe is not a God who is blindly devoted to the people of Israel and prejudiced in their favor, or that he can be bribed by an external worship. Not the descendants of Abraham, not those who sacrifice at Jerusalem, but the righteous are his people. " Will the Lord be pleased with thousands of rams or with ten thousands of rivers of oil ? And what doth the Lord require of thee but to do justly and to love mercy and to walk humbly with thy God ? " (*Micah* VI. 7, 8.) If Israel fails to do his will, they are no longer his chosen people; he will repudiate them. " The prophets were able to see that Jahwe was destroying the nation and the kingdom founded by him. They conceived him above everything else as the God of justice. He was the God of Israel only in so far as Israel complied with his demands of justice. They therefore reverse the traditional order of the two fundamental articles of faith. In this manner Jahwe escaped the danger of coming into collision with the world and of being vanquished in the conflict. The dominion of justice extended beyond the jurisdiction of the Assyrians. This is the ethical monotheism of the prophets ; they believe in the moral order of the world, in the unconditional validity of justice as the highest law for the whole world." *

The process of denaturization and denationalization of Jewish monotheism was completed in *Christianity*. Jesus draws the final conclusion : The kingdom of God is not of this world at all. Judaism, even the prophets, clung to the belief that the righteous must succeed in *this* world; that the people of Israel would, by serving Jahwe faith-

---

* J. Wellhausen, *Abriss der Geschichte Israels und Judas*, in his *Skizzen und Vorarbeiten*, I. 50. For the investigation of the sources and a clear exposition of the development of ceremonies and traditions, see the same author's *Geschichte Israels*.

fully, be re-established, that the kingdom of David would be restored. Jesus abandons this Messianic hope ; he also abandons the presupposition of Jewish piety that the just man will ultimately thrive in the world, and the unjust be confounded. "My kingdom is not of this world," nor is the kingdom of God ; it is not at all like the old kingdom of David, nor like anything that impresses the natural man as glorious and grand and desirable. The kingdom of God is in you, a store of blessedness and peace hidden from the world and unappreciated by it ; it has nothing to do with the gifts which the world can give and take away ; earthly poverty and shame are easily compatible with it. The kingdom of God consists in the communion of the believers and the saints, in the community of the disciples of Jesus, who live as strangers scattered over all the kingdoms of the earth, without taking or seeking part therein. And, finally, the kingdom of God is the eternal glory of God in the hereafter, not bounded by time and space : the world which his children will behold long after nature and the universe have passed away.

Under the influence of these two forms of monotheism, the Jewish-Christian and the Greek, the theological and cosmological conceptions were formed which came to prevail in the church, and through it among the European nations. The practical-religious attributes in the notion of God are derived from Israel : God is holy and just, and also gracious and merciful in Christ. From the Greeks come the speculative or metaphysical elements : infinity, omniscience, omnipotence, all-sufficiency, in short the qualities which make him the All-One, through whom and in whom everything is that has existence and essence. The theology and philosophy of the Christian church grew out of the constantly-repeated attempt to combine Greek philosophy and cosmology and the Christian religion into a complete system. The fundamental conception of its philosophy is a *monistic theism*. The church as a practical institution emphasizes theism. God is a personal, supranatural, extramundane being who comes into personal communion with man ; to the popular mind he appears as a wholly anthropomorphic being with feelings and aspirations like a human being. In speculation, however, the monistic element is accentuated. As soon as we endeavor to define a being who originally created all the rest out of nothing, and whose will alone preserves them, it follows that he is the only independent being, and that there is no room for other independent beings alongside of him. Monotheism comes to mean that God alone exists ; it becomes pantheism : God is the All-One.

The entire history of the church shows how these two tendencies, the religous and the speculative, oppose and interpenetrate each other in many ways. Visibly, for instance, in Augustine, in whose powerful soul both impulses are strongly developed. Neoplatonism led him out of the labyrinths of Manichæism, and from Neoplatonism he gets his idea of the universal reality of God : there is no being except in God; outside of him there is only non-being. This acosmistic pantheism merely serves him, however, to use Harnack's words, as a foundation on which to rear the Christian view, which is the result of his own innermost experiences : The highest being is holy goodness acting on the will as almighty love.*

These thoughts exert a permanent influence upon the entire theology of the West. Wherever the speculative interest grows more intense, the pantheistic notion is straightway accentuated. This fact is already noticeable in the middle ages ; the church again and again finds occasion to take measures against the pantheistic turns which are given to its teachings both on the rationalistic and on the mystical side.† This pantheism became still more

---

* A. Harnack, *Lehrbuch der Dogmengeschichte*, iii. 101 ff.

† As an illustration of the mystical-pantheistic mode of thought I append the beginning of *Die deutsche Theologie* (ed. F. Pfeiffer, 1851), a work belonging to the fourteenth century. "The perfect is a being that contains and completes within itself and its being all beings, and without which and outside of which no true being exists, and in which all things have their being. For it is the being of all things, and is in itself unchangeable and immovable, and yet changes and moves all other things. But the divided or the imperfect is that which originates in or grows from this perfect being, like a ray or a beam that emanates from the sun. And that is called a creature. And of all these divided things none is perfect. Nor is the perfect one of the divided things. The things are conceivable, knowable, and expressible ; but the perfect is inconceivable, inexpressible, and unknowable by all

290 THE COSMOLOGICAL-THEOLOGICAL PROBLEM. [Book I.

pronounced when, at the beginning of modern times, the power which the church exercised over education gradually weakened, and the theoretical interest grew in strength. Above all, the great revolution produced in cosmical conceptions exerted an influence in the same direction. By destroying the firmament, it deprived the anthropomorphic idea of God of the support of sense-perception. We may say: Wherever philosophy is free to follow its own inclinations and is not subjected to the external or internal pressure of ecclesiastical systems or, on the other hand, is not under the ban of natural-scientific thought, it is pantheistic or monotheistic in the sense of the formula: God alone exists, μόνος ὁ θεός.

I shall touch upon the main points in the historical development.*

During the seventeenth century, after the great century of revolution had cleared the way for it, modern thought constructed the first great systems. Descartes and Hobbes may be regarded as the leaders, the former of the theoretical, the latter of the practical philosophy of modern times. The metaphysics of Descartes, however, is visibly affected by his desire to reach a system that may not give offence to the church. Hobbes, on the other hand, is above everything else a political and then a natural-scientific thinker, while his metaphysics does not attain to an independent development. But in Spinoza we have the first great metaphysician of modern times. Regardless of his age and its claims, in the solitude of his attic, he carries out the logical consequences of his thought to the bitter end. In clear and exact definitions, his *Ethics* formulates the doctrine of a consistent pantheism: God is the actual, the *one independent* being or

creatures in so far as they are creatures. Hence the perfect has no name, for it is none of these. If the perfect is to be revealed to a creature, the latter's creatureship, egoity, selfhood, and all the like must be lost and annihilated."

* Let me refer the reader to the excellent account of the history of the philosophy of religion in the first volume of O. Pfleiderer's *Religionsphilosophie* (1884). I also mention J. E. Erdmann, *Grundriss der Geschichte der Philosophie* (3d ed., 1878; tr. under the editorship of W. S. Hough, 1890); R. Falckenberg, *Geschichte der neueren Philosophie* (2d ed., 1892; tr. by Armstrong, 1893); R. Eucken, *Die Lebensanschauung der grossen Denker* (1890).

substance; the world is the immanent evolution of his essence. The objects which popular thought fettered by sense-perception regards as independent beings are not really independent; the intellect conceives them as dependent determinations of the All-One, modifications of the substance, which have their essence and their existence in it alone. Or if, following the popular usage of language, we prefer to call God the cause of things, we must add: He is not a cause in the sense in which a particular object is the cause of another that exists independently of it; he is the immanent cause of all things, and hence remains in them, or, rather, they are in him; he is the cause not only of their form and movement, but also of their essence and existence. But as regards God's own essence, we may say that the two fundamental forms of reality which present themselves to the intellect, the corporeal and the mental worlds, suggest two phases of his being which we may ascribe to him as attributes—extension and consciousness; and we may, therefore, call God an extended and thinking being (*res extensa, res cogitans*). But here, too, it must be stated, we are not permitted to use these terms of God in the same sense in which we apply them to objects. God is body, but not like the particular corporeal object, limited, figured, and movable; he is the unitary principle of the corporeal world. God is a spirit, but not like a particular spirit; we cannot ascribe thinking, feeling, and willing to him. He is the unitary principle of the conscious world, but the finite qualities which it manifests do not belong to him.

These definitions are more accurately determined and restricted by their contraries, by anthropomorphic theism on the one hand and materialistic atomism on the other. Spinoza frequently and strongly emphasizes the former antithesis. Popular anthropomorphic theism makes God act according to design, like a man. It is plain that this conception of God is not compatible with monotheism consistently carried out. An almighty creator is not at first possessed of empty designs which he afterwards realizes by such and such means; that is the manner in which finite beings act who make a world that is independent of them conform to their thoughts. Creation is specifically distinct from making things according to design. The latter category is peculiar to polytheism: gods are, like men, beings who act upon objects that are not dependent on them for their existence, *ab extra* and according to design. The notion of creation out of nothing, on the other hand, belongs to monotheism. If God is the only original being and *causa sui*, his activity can have the form of creation only, which posits the existence and essence of reality, not, however, in the sense of making it independent of him. That is the only thing that God cannot do: he cannot make objects that are independent of himself. Creation is evolution in God. With the formula *Deus sive natura* Spinoza opposes the philosophical notion of God to popular thought.

Less frequently and less strongly does he emphasize the other antithesis, the opposition to atomistic atheism. The reason is most likely that such an antithesis hardly existed in the philosophy of his age. Had Spinoza foreseen that atheism and naturalism were, for an entire century, destined to become the catchwords of his philosophy, or had he lived to see our age in which atomistic atheism is so loudly and emphatically proclaimed as the only scientifically-possible world-view, he might perhaps have laid more stress on the convertibility of his formula: *Natura sive Deus*. To be sure, he might have said, I know nothing of a God who has I know not what reality outside of the world. Nor, conversely, do I know anything of the world which the materialists construct out of innumerable small, absolutely independent substances called atoms. The very first and most certain fact which my intellect affirms of the world is that it is not a mere accidental conglomeration of many substances, but a unity, in which every particular thing is absolutely determined by the whole, hence *one* substance, which by its existence and by its essence first makes plurality possible. If that is monotheism, and I hardly know what else we could mean by the term unless we are willing to relapse into the conceptions of polytheism, which regards the gods as individuals among others, then my system is complete monotheism: God, the One and the All.

Of course, he would not have succeeded in convincing his contemporaries. They would have gone on accusing him of confounding God with nature, of atheism and naturalism. Words, Hobbes once said, serve not merely to define concepts, but also to express judgments. Though the term atheism is unsuited to characterize Spinoza's view of the world, it was well fitted to express and arouse repugnance. For a whole century the *Ethics* was the most notorious philosophical work in existence, a *liber horrendus*, and its author a man with the mark of reprobation on his brow.

The two philosophers whom the eighteenth century follows are Locke and Leibniz. Both repudiate Spinoza, Leibniz explicitly, Locke tacitly. Both seek a philosophy —and have according to the conviction of their age found it—that better reconciles the modern scientific truths with the old faith.

Leibniz's system is absolutely determined by his relation to Spinoza. In his younger years he had been considerably and positively influenced by that bold and vigorous thinker, and had, in particular, clearly recognized the metaphysical consequences of the Cartesian philosophy of nature. But after his youthful *impetus philosophandi* had been moderated by the prudence and discretion of the politician, his chief concern became to free his thought from the " profane " Spinoza and his unacceptable views.* That is the mission of the *monads*—they are to overcome pantheism ; Spinoza would be right, *s'il n'y avait point de monades*. The monads step between God and nature and keep them from merging into each other. The monads are the ultimate, independent elements of reality, metaphysical points, unextended, spiritual atoms. In themselves or for the understanding they are characterized by inner life (sensation and desire) ; looked at from without, in the confused presentation of sensibility, a combination of monads

---

* A detailed account of the relation between these philosophers, based on original sources, has recently been set forth in the work of L. Stein, *Leibniz und Spinoza* (1890).

is represented as an extended body. The monads, there-fore, possess the two attributes of the Spinozistic substance, *cogitatio* and *extensio*, spirituality and materiality, so, how-ever, that spirituality constitutes their essence, while ma-teriality is merely their phenomenon. Spinoza, on the other hand, regarded both aspects as of equal importance ; in-deed, in so far as *corpus* and *res* are universally assumed to be equivalent, extension, as it were, receives more reality than the other factor.* The monads further resemble Spinoza's substance in that each evolves its essence from within outwardly, without being affected from without ; hence it is, in a certain measure, *causa sui.* True, this evolution takes place in pre-established harmony with the development of all the other monads.

There can be no doubt, this view absolutely overcomes pantheism. The one macrocosmic substance of Spinoza is broken up into countless microcosmic substances, each of which can exist and be considered by itself ; indeed, each would have to look upon itself as the absolute substance. But, one feels inclined to say, the work is done too thoroughly. From the Scylla of pantheism we are drawn into the Charybdis of atomism and atheism. And now Leibniz tries to ward off the danger by adding to the many substances of which reality consists, a " necessary sub-stance " whose " essence involves existence," and then goes on to assert: This substance, called God, is "the original unity or the original substance ; all created or derivative monads are its products and are produced, from moment to moment, by constant radiations, as it were." †

Well, Spinoza would declare, if you really mean what you say, we can easily agree. Then your original sub-stance is simply what I call absolute substance, and its fulgurations, the common monads, are somewhat similar to my *modi*, and I shall willingly concede relative indepen-

---

* Spinoza explains *mens* by *corpus:* it is nothing but the idea of a definite individual body which is its object (*Eth.*, II. 11, 13). Leibniz conversely ex-plains *corpus* by *mens;* if *mens* is, in the former case, *nihil aliud quam idea cor-poris, corpus* is, in the latter, *nihil aliud quam idea mentis*, or, he might also say, *mens phenomenon sive objective existens.*

† *Monadology*, §§ 38 ff. *Opera philosophica*, ed. Erdmann, p. 708.

dence and unity to them. And I likewise find no essential difference in our determinism. There is no mention in my system of mechanical necessity (*necessité brute*); it is a conceptual-mathematical, hence ideal, necessity—a concept from which, as far as I can see, you have not rid yourself either. Indeed, the maximum of compossible reality or perfection is ascertained and produced in your case also by a kind of conceptual calculus in the *intellectus infinitus*, by a "metaphysical mechanics." I do not care to dispute over names, much less to sail under the colors of orthodoxy.

Locke sought and found a new way of reconciling modern science with the church doctrine. Not metaphysics but the epistemological critique of metaphysics appeared to him as the right path to the goal. It shows that our knowledge is necessarily confined to experience. Experience, however, does not comprehend and exhaust reality, hence there is room for faith alongside of science. This is the view which was universally accepted in England even in the nineteenth century. Not seldom it assumed a somewhat pitiful form: strict abstinence in thought, joined with ecclesiastical and political orthodoxy, became the basis of social respectability. The dogma of such abstemious and respectable persons is : On the one hand we have the sciences, mathematics and physics, psychology and "Essays Concerning the Human Understanding"; on the other, we have the Thirty-nine Articles. But we have no metaphysics, nor do we need or care for metaphysics; the Thirty-nine Articles will serve us in their stead. Upon them rests the church, and the church is a part of "the best constitution." Whoever fails to see that, is past help; he is suspected of not belonging to the respectable members of society. Hence nothing further is to be said on this point. The most one may do is to prove, on every hand, the necessity and impregnability of the church doctrine by adducing philosophical, natural-scientific, and historical *evidences*. Locke's empiricism and positivism paved the way for such intellectual abstemiousness. He has, at the same time, shown us how a man may, on occasion, produce an orthodox metaphysics in spite of his principient continence: he tries to prove the existence of an "eternal, most powerful and most knowing being" with "mathematical certainty" (*Essay*, IV. 10), an undertaking for which he drew upon himself Kant's severe but not undeserved censure.

This initiates the philosophy of conciliation which prevailed during the eighteenth century. Leibniz's name is famous in Germany, Locke's in England, and soon after also in France. Both endeavor to reconcile the modern sciences with the old system of dogmatics. Both turn away from the scholasticism still dominating the universities, both are adherents and lovers of the modern sciences, but both also prove the reasonableness of faith. Leibniz writes *de la conformité de la foi avec la raison*, Locke proves the *reasonableness of Christianity*. The chief articles of the creed, the existence of God and the immortality of the soul, philosophy can prove with the means at its disposal; in addition to these there are, of course, also articles of faith which it cannot prove, and which are derived from revelation. But even here philosophy may accomplish something; if it cannot certify their truth, it may at least prove that they are possible: *fides non contra, sed supra rationem*. Leibniz frequently mentions as one of the many advantages of his philosophy the fact that it leaves room for the possibility of transubstantiation, in the interest of harmony with Catholicism.

The science which deals with the articles of faith that are demonstrable by reason only is the so-called *natural* or *rational theology*, which is distinguished from the *theologia revelata*. The former constitutes the principal part of the philosophy of the last century. It demonstrates, first, the *existence of God*, on theoretical and practical grounds. The theoretical reasons are comprehended in the two arguments which Kant distinguishes as the *cosmological* and *physico-theological* arguments. From the dependence and contingency of the natural world, the cosmological proof infers the existence of an unconditioned and necessary being; and with the aid of the physico-theological reflection, the nature of this being is then more accurately defined by the predicates, wisdom and goodness. By setting forth the reign of law in the universe, on the one hand, and gaining a deeper insight into the teleology of organic forms, on the other, the modern sciences themselves subserve the interests of a "rational" theology.

In the second place, philosophy proves the *immortality of the soul.* The simplicity of the soul is inferred from the unity of self-consciousness ; then its indissolubility and indestructibility are deduced from the nature of a simple, immaterial substance and identified with immortality. Practical reasons are added. The desire for ·a further development of the capacities preformed in man, and the demand for retributive justice, presuppose a future life and a judge after death. Nay, even ordinary honesty and the existence of civil society could not be secured without such a faith. The audacious statement, "If there were no God, we should have to invent one," expresses this thought, which, by the way, has not become extinct in our own age.

That is the cosmology of the age of enlightenment. It is a compromise between theology and the modern sciences. Modern thought, the product of the modern sciences, makes this concession to theism : God is a supramundane being, who made the world and human beings according to plan and design, and prescribed to them his law. Theology, in turn, concedes the uniformity of nature. Although philosophy, should occasion demand, has a place for miracles (*supra non contra rationem*), which formerly constituted the chief proof of religion, they are gradually abandoned as a part of the old faith that is no longer compatible with the spirit of the times. A miraculous providence, as old Samuel Reimarus points out in the same chapter in which he shows "the flimsiness of the doubts against divine providence," would be both against the perfection of God and his works and not advantageous to man himself, nor conducive to his perfection or his virtue." * And theology itself gradually learns, first,

* S. Reimarus, *Die vornehmsten Wahrheiten der natürlichen Religion,* ch. IX. §§ 14 ff. Reimarus is also, as is known, the author of the Wolfenbüttel fragments. The two phases of the philosophy of the last century, the one facing "natural" religion and the one averted from "revealed" religion, are very distinctly exemplified in him.

to do without miracles, and finally, in pronounced rationalism, to grow ashamed of them and to discard them altogether.

This compromise was again dissolved towards the end of the eighteenth century. It had been introduced both by a German and an English thinker. It was dissolved by a similar combination; Hume and Kant mark its end. Kant's *Critique of Pure Reason* (1781) and Hume's posthumous *Dialogues on Natural Religion* (1780) appeared almost simultaneously. Both works subject natural religion, or rather philosophical theology, to a scorching criticism : the so-called rational theology is a pseudo-science ; it is in no wise possible to prove the existence of an extramundane creator of the world and the immortality of the soul, on rational grounds.

Hume starts out from an empirical epistemology ; hence he does not dwell on *a priori* proofs. The only attempt at a proof is the teleological argument; but it too lacks all the requirements of a real proof. The origin of a universe is an event absolutely beyond our experience ; there is no similarity whatever between human art and creation out of nothing. The purpose of the world is by no means patent to us. Whatever conception of the design of the creator we may form,—happiness, civilization, or the perfection of living beings,—reality offers an infinite number of objections to it. If we were informed of the existence of an all-wise and all-good creator in some other way, we should attribute such riddles to the limitations of our knowledge. But rational theology has no right to appeal to that; its very aim is to derive the nature of the creator from the given world itself. We can, however, draw conclusions only from what we know, not from what we do not know.

Kant proceeds from a different starting-point, but he comes to the same conclusion : all attempts to prove the existence of God and the immortality of the soul on rational grounds are futile. He takes up the reasons in their order and shows their absolute insufficiency. To infer from the unity of consciousness the simplicity of a soul-substance and then from this to infer its indestructibility and the continuance of personal life and consciousness is simply begging the question. Nor does the ontological argument for the existence of God amount to more. From the notion of God it tries to prove his existence ; the definition of the *ens realissimum* includes all positive predicates, hence also existence. But existence is not a conceptual characteristic like weight, magnitude, wisdom, and goodness; it consequently cannot be deduced from the concept of the subject by means of an analytical judgment. All the propositions concerning existence are synthetic and can be verified only by experience. The cosmological proof passes from a conditioned to an unconditioned, and seeks the latter in a being whose existence is not determined by another being, but necessary in itself. But the causal *regressus* invariably carries us only to a conditioning cause ; the problem then becomes to inquire into its conditions. It is pure caprice to stop raising the question at some point or other and to assert that we have arrived at the unconditioned. Experience, at least, can never reveal the same. Hence it would have to be known through its concept as a being necessary in itself. The cosmological proof consequently resolves itself into the ontological proof. Moreover, however far the physico-theological argument may take us, it surely does not go beyond the notion of a world-architect governing our limited sphere of experience. It does not carry us to the church dogma that God created all things out of nothing. It is, furthermore, doubtful whether the entire teleology of nature is more than a subjective reflection, conforming to the nature of our understanding. Hence scientific knowledge acquired by speculative reason is out of the question here.

Hume stops at the negative result ; he merely intimates incidentally that if he had to decide in favor of any cosmological view, he would esteem none more plausible than that of the ancient philosophers, "which ascribes an eternal inherent principle of order to the world" (Sixth Dialogue). Now Kant, in whose system, let it be added, the old idealistic-pantheistic metaphysics everywhere shines through the epistemological conception—he never wholly abandoned the thought elaborated in the treatise on *The Only Possible Foundation for a Demonstration of the Existence of God* (1763),

that God is the total unity of all that is possible and hence
of all that is real, which can be conceived merely as a
limitation of his being—Kant joined to the negative conclusion reached in the *Critique of Pure Reason* the positive
results of his practical philosophy. The ideas of God,
freedom, and immortality, whose reality cannot be demonstrated to the understanding, are nevertheless the most
certain elements of a cosmology that bases itself on the
facts of practical reason. They are not concepts that have
theoretical value, concepts by means of which we can conceive and understand nature. Nothing can be accomplished with the notion of God in physics, nor with that of
freedom in history. But nature is not reality in itself; it
is nothing but the sum-total of possible phenomena. In
the notion of duty we are confronted with an order of the
universe which we are inwardly constrained to accept as
absolutely valid. Thus arises the idea of an absolute
world-order, which is higher and, as it were, more real
than the natural order; the practical reason in us makes
us a part of this world-order.

We may say: This thought of Kant's is the revival and
complete realization of the original tendency of the Luth-
eran Reformation, *the separation of religious faith from
theoretical knowledge.* What repelled Luther in scholasticism, that is, in the theology taught in all the universities
and sanctioned by the church, was the amalgamation of the
word of God (the Bible) with the philosophy of the "godless
heathen" Aristotle. To banish reason from theology and
to make faith independent was his first concern. But the
undertaking was premature; soon Protestant theology also
began to construct dogmatic systems in which metaphysics and revelation were cemented into a harmonious whole.
And that can be easily understood. The entire science
and philosophy of the middle ages, their geocentric cosmology and the anthropomorphic conception of the universe
consequent thereon, their ecclesiocentric interpretation of
history,—all these facts urgently demanded that faith be
based on the scientific knowledge of the world. First, the
foundations of the mediæval conception of the universe had
to be demolished. As long as they continued to stand,

their philosophy and "natural" theology could not be shaken. This happened gradually in the course of the centuries following Luther. The Copernican cosmology slowly came to the front during the seventeenth century; modern physical, physiological, and biological conceptions began to spread; the historical horizon was widened by a closer contact with the Eastern and Western worlds, the world of the past and the world of the future. Everywhere the discovery of new facts was bursting asunder the framework of the mediæval system. From this altered state of affairs Kant skilfully deduced the consequence: the scientific knowledge of the universe, in the form which it has assumed, cannot be employed as the substructure of faith. If religious faith is to remain, it must be established on a new basis, and this can be furnished by the facts of the moral world alone. Luther's aim had been to base faith on the written letter and on authenticated historical facts. Kant bases it on a fact that is eternally alive and present, on the moral consciousness. This and this alone carries us beyond the order of nature, not, however, by means of knowledge and proofs, but by practical faith. Here the demand of the Reformation is actually carried out. Faith is not grounded on philological and historical arguments adduced from canonical books, nor on physical and metaphysical speculation, nor even on external authority; it rests on itself. The will to do good is the ground of our faith in the good, that is, in God.

It is not easy for our age to form an adequate idea of the extent of the revolution which the critical philosophy created in the minds of men. Natural theology was the basis of the entire thought of the eighteenth century; indeed, it seemed to be the basis of its whole life; to tamper with it meant to turn all divine and human order upside down. Listen to so liberal-minded a man as Wieland *: " The belief in God, not only as the first original cause of all things, but also as the absolute and highest law-giver, regent and judge of mankind, together with the belief in a future state after death, constitutes the fundamental article

---

* *Über den Gebrauch der Vernunft in Glaubenssachen* in the *Deutscher Merkur* of 1788 (Works, Hempel's ed., XXXII. 336 f.).

of religion. To strengthen and support this belief in all possible ways is one of the worthiest and most useful occupations of philosophy, nay, in view of the indispensableness of faith, a duty. To assail it and weaken its hold on the hearts of men, by all kinds of doubts and sophistical reasons, or, what is worse, to overthrow it, not only does no good, but virtually amounts to a public attack on the fundamental constitution of the state, of which religion forms an essential part, and on public peace and security, of which it is the support. Hence I have no scruples against giving the following humble advice to the king or prince who might ask my advice concerning such matters, say in about fifty years from now (a thing hardly to be expected): The foolish and offensive controversies against the existence of God or *against its accepted proofs*, when no better ones can be adduced, as well as the public denial of the immortality of the soul, ought to be declared an outrage against humanity and against civil society, and should be prohibited by a special penal enactment."*

The remonstrances of the older generation were in vain. Kant had understood his age and its deepest need. The younger generation felt that the word of deliverance had been spoken, that the fetters imposed by the compromise between science and faith were burst asunder, that science might, from now on, fearlessly finish its journey, and that religion held a permanent place in the human heart. Rejoicing in her newly-acquired freedom, philosophy at once began with zealous rivalry to construct idealistic-pantheistic systems. The philosophy of the nineteenth century, and in particular German philosophy as the boldest and freest, is thoroughly pantheistic or monotheistic in the sense of the formula: God alone is; everything that exists is and must be conceived in God.

---

* From Feder's autobiography (*J. G. H. Feders Leben, Natur und Grundsätze*, 1825) we may glean how deeply the revolution penetrated into all personal and university affairs. Feder had for a long time been a popular and illustrious teacher of philosophy at the University of Göttingen. But the rise of Kantian philosophy in the eighties brought him into such discredit among his colleagues and students that he voluntarily resigned his position and left the town. His experience helps us to understand why it was that the Prussian rulers succeeding the great Frederick became so apprehensive and prohibited Kant's religio-philosophical lectures.

It is, moreover, worthy of note that the poets were in advance of the philosophers. Lessing, Herder, and Goethe advocated the philosophy of Spinoza, while the philosophers (see, for example, the outline of the history of natural theology in Feder's *Logik und Metaphysik*) were still speaking of him " as of a dead dog." In a conversation held a year before his death, Lessing made the following confession to Jacobi: "I can no longer accept the orthodox notions of the deity, I can't swallow them. Ἐν καὶ πᾶν. I know nothing else!" And when his perplexed friend replied that he had come to him for help against Spinoza, Lessing answered: "You had better become his friend altogether. There is no other philosophy outside of Spinoza's." * Herder follows with his treatise, *Gott, einige Gedanken über Spinoza's System* (1787). And Goethe's early poems are thoroughly saturated with a pantheistic adoration and conception of nature.

> Was wär ein Gott, der nur von aussen stiesse,
> Im Kreis das All am Finger laufen liesse.
> Ihm ziemt's die Welt im Innern zu bewegen,
> Natur in sich, sich in Natur zu hegen.
> So dass was in ihm lebt und webt und ist,
> Nie seine Kraft und seinen Geist vergisst.

The storm and stress in literature is followed by storm and stress in philosophy. New states and dynasties were springing up each year and disappearing again during the political revolution of the age. So in Germany each spring gave birth to a new speculative philosopher and to a new system claiming absolute and universal dominion. They all show their contempt for the old theological and philosophical orthodoxy, and agree as to the direction along which to seek the new truth. The old philosophy is *deistical*, the new, *pantheistical* monotheism. Deism conceives God as a supramundane being; he made the world and everything in it according to a plan, and separated it from himself; now it works in obedience to natural laws, not unlike a machine set up by a skilful machinist for a definite purpose. This idea of God and the world strikes modern

---

* F. H. Jacobi, *Über die Lehre des Spinoza in Briefen an Herrn Moses Mendelssohn*, 1785.

philosophers as exceedingly shallow and vulgar; it is of a piece with the same shallow rationalism that derives everything in the historico-mental realm from individual plan and design : Language and religion, laws and states, were all of them devised and realized by inventive men because of their great usefulness, and it was likewise the utility or convenience of the thing which, according to the notions of rational æsthetics, induced poets to make poems, artists to paint, musicians to compose music. And even now these enlightened creatures are on the point of inventing the perfect education and devising the perfect constitution wherewith to make the perfect man. They resemble Wagner, who produced the *homunculus* in the retort, without the aid of the vulgar forces of nature, simply as the result of intelligence and art. This one picture of theirs serves them as a pattern for their conception of God: he is the great mechanician who devised and constructed this great puppet-show of a world.

Contempt for the preceding view is the chief characteristic of the new epoch. It opposes its *organic* conception of the universe to the *mechanical* system of the *Aufklärung*. The notion of making things according to design is discarded and replaced by the idea of organic development. The change is first brought about in the field of æsthetics. Art and poetry are not manufactured according to plan, that is, genuine and original art and poetry, for the verses composed by the *professores poeseos* and their pupils to commemorate the birthdays of high personages and other events, may, perhaps, be made with the help of Gottsched's *Dichtkunst* or some other rational guide. But real poetry grows from within, like an organic form, unfolding with inner necessity. That is true of all folk-poetry; it is true of the grandest poetry of the popular soul, its religion. It is especially Herder who teaches the new conception of historico-mental things, and Goethe is the living manifestation of the poet by the grace of God or by the grace of nature. The new way of looking at everything culminates in the new notion of God, in Spinoza's notion : God, the All-One, who reveals himself in nature and history. Like an organism or like a poetical idea, God's essence is unfolded with inward æsthetico-teleological necessity into the manifold forms of reality. The business of philosophy is to set forth this process of self-evolution of the absolute by means of the dialectical self-development of the notion.

It was Fichte who first marshalled the new thoughts against the old ideas. While Kant had treated the deistic conceptions of God and immortality sparingly, and had readmitted them into his system without any real modification, by simply changing the key, as it were—they are not theoretically valid notions, but practically necessary ideas—Fichte attempts to get rid of them altogether, regarding them, as he does, as useless, nay, as worthless. According to him.they are derived from eudæmonism, and that seals their doom : God is according to natural theology an individual by the side of other beings, and his real mission is to procure happiness for the sensuous man in this life or at least in the life to come. Fichte's rigorous, not to say fanatical, moralism revolts against this notion. Such a God is not a God, but an idol; God is in the moral world only ; in the voice of duty speaking in thy heart the suprasensuous reveals itself, and that is God. But again to make of the suprasensuous being a separate substance, that is, as critical philosophy would put it, a being existing and acting in space and time, whose object is to procure happiness, is an utterly contradictory and impossible undertaking. In his *Appeal to the Public,* in which he defends himself against the charge of atheism, he sharply accentuates the opposition between the new philosophy and the old philosophical orthodoxy, and hurls the most violent accusations against the latter. Eudæmonistic dogmatism, whose cosmology is a natural theology, those philosophers who "conceive the infinite one under a finite notion and admire the wisdom of God for having arranged everything exactly as they themselves would have done," or make of him a judge of the world who punishes vice and rewards virtue with happiness, thereby achieving the distinction "of obviating the imperfections of the police system,"—those are the real atheists. "A God who is to satisfy covetousness is a despicable, wicked being, for he encourages and perpetuates human corruption and the degradation of reason. Such a God is a prince of the world in the real sense." This is the God whom *they* serve; "hence they are the real atheists, they are absolutely without God, and have made for themselves a vicious idol. And because I refuse to acknowledge their idol instead of the true God, they call me an atheist."

The great crisis brought about in Fichte's life by his attitude towards the prevailing views, his dismission from the Jena professorship and his removal to Berlin, also marks a turning-point in his thought. True, his fundamental conception remains the same. The starting-point and fulcrum of every cosmology that rises beyond the physical view is determined by the experiences of moral life; they lead to a belief in a suprasensuous being that cannot, however, be conceived as an individual being or as a separate substance. But he executes a change of front. Hitherto his attacks had been directed against the philosophical and theological orthodoxy of the state-church, now they are turned against the negative enlightenment. Thus his expositions receive a more positive character. In his *Speeches* he explains the true nature of God and of divine life to " an educated public" who seem to him to have not too many, but too few, articles of faith.

In the year of the atheism-conflict (1799) there appeared also Schleiermacher's *Reden über die Religion an die Gebildeten unter ihren Verächtern* (Discourses on Religion addressed to the Educated among those who despise it). They no less emphatically renounce the traditional notions of the philosophical church-orthodoxy. Religion does not originate in dogma or in action, but in feeling; in feeling the finite becomes immediately aware of the infinite and the eternal. Every true feeling that springs from the fulness of the heart and turns toward the whole of things is religious. The emotions of awe, admiration, joy, love, gratitude, humility, and reverence, which are aroused by a contact with nature and humanity, excite piety, in so far as, in and with these particular feelings, " we are affected by the whole, which is the revelation of God, and hence take up, not particular and finite elements, but God himself, in whom alone the particular is One and All, and in so far as not this or that particular function, but our entire being, with which we approach the world and live in it, the immediate divine element in us, is aroused and revealed by the feeling." On the other hand, "the common conception of God as a particular being outside of the world and in back of the world is not the alpha and omega of religion ; it is simply a mode of expression that is seldom absolutely pure and always unsatisfactory. Whoever constructs such a notion with impure intent, say because he needs a being like that to console and help him, may believe in such a god without being devout. Nor is the goal and character of a religious life determined by the immortality which many desire and believe in, the immortality outside of time and behind time, or rather only coming after the present time, but none the less in time ; they are determined by the immortality which we may immediately possess even in our temporal life and which is a problem in whose solution we are constantly engaged. The immortality of religion means : to be united with the infinite in the midst of the finite and to be eternal at every moment of time."

In Schelling, *moralistic* pantheism is followed by a *naturalistic* pantheism. Nature is for him not a mere reflection of the ego, but, as with Spinoza, one side of reality ; the other side is spirit, the evolution of which constitutes history. The system of identity, as set forth, say in the lectures on the system of philosophy delivered in 1804, is so dependent on Spinoza's conceptions that almost every sentence of the *Ethics* recurs in it. Schelling regards it as his immediate task to raise the science of nature from the deplorable condition into which it seems to the young philosopher to have fallen, to transform the heap of accidental and scattered truths into a system of rational knowledge. The object is to demonstrate the whole of nature as a unified system governed by inner logical and æsthetical necessity, or to reveal the reason inherent in nature.

Hegel's philosophy, finally, has not inappropiately been termed *logical* pantheism. In an all-embracing system it aims to conceive nature and history as the self-development of the idea, which takes place, with inner logical or dialectical necessity, as the self-development of the ideal content of reality. In the mind of the poet a plurality of incidents, actions, and persons are evolved from the idea of a poem, of Hamlet or of Faust, and finally constitute a complete whole in which each particular element has its fixed place. Similarly, the world or reality, which is unfolded before us in nature and history, is a unified whole, in which the position of each particular element is determined with logical and æsthetical necessity. We think we understand a poem when we see how each scene or each event is essential to the exposition of the one idea, and that something would be wanting if it were left out. So, too, we would have a perfect knowledge of the great divine poem which we call the world, if we could, in the same manner, set forth each natural form and force, each historical product, as an inner element essential to the exposition of the whole. The natural sciences do not accomplish this, indeed they do not even attempt it. The natural sciences collect facts and seek to reduce them to formulæ which simply express external connections, the causal laws; but they let the facts and laws stand as blind, brutal facts. Nor do historical investigations act otherwise; they, too, gather together endless masses of facts; they also attempt a kind of causal explanation, but the question concerning the meaning of the facts they do not answer, nay, they do not even put it. Now that is the function of philosophy. What is the meaning of nature? In what does the inner necessity of all those processes and their laws, the mechanical, chemical, and organic occurrences, consist? What is the meaning of history as a whole; what is the reason expressed in it? Wherefore did all these nations, the Chinese and the Hindoos, the Persians and the Egyptians, the Greeks and the Romans, have to pass over the earth and develop such states and laws, such religions and arts? These are the questions which Hegel's philosophy attempts to answer. It desires to tell what each particular object really is, by revealing its *raison d'être* in the whole of things. And by thus unfolding the reason pervading the entire universe, the idea of reality, it sets forth God's very essence and life: God is nothing but the one, actual, living thought of the universe evolving into self-consciousness. Nor is reality anything else, that is, reality as it is in itself : it is the active idea unfolding itself, comprehending itself in self-consciousness. There is no such thing in reality as a dead, inert, merely existent being outside of the idea; this occurs only in the barren notions of a philosophy dealing with abstractions. And therefore the world is exhausted by the thoughts of the true philosophy, because it is itself a thought. Thus, in Hegel, modern philosophy returns to its starting-point in Platonic-Aristotelian philosophy : Reality is a system of thoughts expanding into self-consciousness, νόησις νοήσεως; philosophy is the reflection of the objective movement of thought.

The time has long passed since these conceptions dominated the intellectual world of Germany, since the youth, always eager for novelty, were gathered together to experience the moment of the awakening of the absolute spirit into complete self-consciousness. The dialectical reproduction of the self-movement of the idea is a thing of the past. We can hardly understand the belief that Schelling's or Hegel's philosophy explains the inner necessity of history and nature as a good interpreter elucidates a drama of Shakespeare or Goethe. We cannot see much more in it than an arbitrary schematic arrangement of the general forms of reality. And we wonder at the arrogance with which such vague reflections on the world at large, which, like passing mists, assume all kinds of shapes, attack scientific inquiry, as though they had achieved a task infinitely more important and dignified.

One thing, however, German philosophy retained : the view of the whole of reality from which speculation set out. We look for the completion of the thoughts which the contemplation of reality suggests to us along the same lines: an idealistic monotheism or pantheism is the goal towards which the thoughts of the most vigorous and careful thinkers converge even to this day. Fechner and Lotze may be mentioned as leaders. Lotze endeavors to approach the goal by means of abstract-metaphysical reasoning; he appeals to historico-philosophical and religio-philosophical reflections for assistance. Fechner remains a philoso-

pher of nature ; in the visible world he seeks and universally finds symbols of the invisible.

More timidly and standing aloof, as it were, the positivistic school points to the same goal. Let H. Spencer speak
as their representative. In a noteworthy reflection with
which he concludes the exposition of the religio-ecclesi-
astical development in his *Sociology* (§ 659 f.) he shows that
the results of the scientific investigation of reality by no
means mark the end of all religious conceptions : " Amid
the mysteries which become the more mysterious the more
they are thought about, there will remain the one absolute
certainty, that he (the investigator) is ever in presence of an
infinite and eternal energy, from which all things proceed."
What is this energy ? " Consequently the final outcome of
that speculation commenced by the primitive man is that the
Power manifested throughout the universe distinguished as
material, is the same Power which in ourselves wells up
under the form of consciousness." " When the explorer of
nature sees that, quiescent as they appear, surrounding
solid bodies are thus sensitive to forces which are infinitesimal in their amounts ; when the spectroscope proves to
him that molecules on the earth pulsate in harmony with
molecules in the stars ; when there is forced on him the
inference that every point in space thrills with an infinity
of vibrations passing through it in all directions, the
conception to which he tends is much less that of a
universe of dead matter than that of a universe everywhere
alive ; alive if not in the restricted sense, still in a general
sense."

Here too, then, a way is opened for symbolical anthropomorphism and the idealizing metaphysical conception
which A. Lange, the representative of positivism in Germany, regarded as indispensable. Different paths meet at
the same goal.

In conclusion, let us survey the entire course of the long
intellectual development and describe it as follows : Religion has gradually eliminated the elements which originally
occupied the foreground—theurgic practices and mytho-
logico-cosmogonic fictions. In the measure in which civilization advances and the scientific knowledge and the

resulting technical control of nature increase, the old forms of sorcery and legendary tales disappear. The ethical element, however, which is in the beginning simply a secondary issue, comes to the front; the nature of the divine is determined by moral goodness. On the other side, science withdraws more and more from the domain of religion. Dogmatic orthodoxy, which strove to determine the nature of the suprasensuous by means of concepts that seemed at least theoretically demonstrable, has been abandoned like the natural theology of the eighteenth century, which occupied the same ground, only that it still further restricted the sphere of the provable. The philosophical speculation which believed that its absolute definitions exhausted reality is also given up. Philosophy has grown more modest, but the facts seem to her to suggest the assumption of an ultimate, all-embracing, essential unity of reality, a unity that cannot be external and accidental to a mechanical system, but must be conceived as similar to the inner unity of a spiritual being. But it relinquishes the task of elaborating these thoughts, leaving that to the creative fancy of the religious genius. Like the creative artist, he gives the idea of perfection an intelligible form ; he interprets the meaning of the great mystery which we call reality by words and by deeds, by teaching and by example.

I am well aware that the course and goal of history are differently conceived by others. Many agree with L. Feuerbach that the great truth reached by our century is: *God has not created man, but man created God.* To these, my notions will seem old-fashioned and antiquated.

I have no desire to make any one dissatisfied with his views. Yet I cannot refrain from remarking that the truth of the first statement does not seem to me to exclude the truth of the second. I am quite willing to grant the proposition: Man has created God, in idea namely, and that too in his own image. But the other proposition is not incompatible with this: God created man in his own image, not merely, however, in idea, but also in reality. Man, says the philosophy in question, is a product of nature. Of course he is ; but what is nature ? A great heap of infinitely small grains of sand? And feeling and thinking beings are to be evolved from these by mere juxtaposition? Surely, in Goethe's words, some anonymous element must have had a hand in all this. And our philosophers, who think that the days of the belief in God are numbered, will, perhaps, be a little puzzled by the fact that, according to their theory, the growth, transformation, and ultimate rejection of a fantastic conceit constituted the essential element of the entire history of mankind. For it is certainly an indisputable fact that all great historical movements were of a religious nature; Buddhism, Christianity, Mohammedanism, the Reformation, these are the greatest themes of the history of the past. Can it be that the world and the human mind are really so strangely constituted that when they come in contact this great illusion must ensue?

But the future, they say, the whole endless future belongs to reason purged of prejudice and superstition, belongs to pure knowledge not blinded by fancy and fiction. I do not know what the mental content of the future is going to be. Still, should any one declare, The notion that the world is really nothing but a conglomeration of very minute grains of sand will be regarded by future generations as the strangest aberration of the human mind, I should not contradict him. He might say : The remarkable progress of mathematical and physical knowledge, accompanying, as it did, religious intolerance and the political corruption of religion, for a moment—if we measure time by centuries—so dazzled many minds that they were deluded into the belief that spirit is something absolutely foreign to reality, and that it is an absolute mystery how it ever got into the world. And the judgment of the future will be : Compared with such deluded mortals, who are at the same time possessed of the proud consciousness that they have reached the pinnacle of human culture, the poorest idol-worshipper, who throws himself upon his knees before a spirit which he believes exists in objects, seems like a being who has at least an inkling of the great meaning and value of things.

I once read a passage from Jean Paul : "How arrogant

the clouds are in presuming to belong to the heavens and
to the stars, whereas they are not much farther removed
from us than our cold breath !" We may apply these same
words to the opinions of those who do not see the infinite
heavens for the mists of their narrow thoughts, and therefore claim : There is no such thing as heaven ; it is simply
an ancient superstition ; no one has ever seen it.

The negative dogmatism of materialism is, in my
opinion, the mere counterpart of the positive dogmatism
of the old theological orthodoxy. Both conceive religion as
a collection of dogmas which are to be taken literally and
to be accepted by the understanding, only that the former
says No wherever the latter says Yes. They are at one in
their narrow intellectualism, which fails to appreciate
poetry and art. They also often accept the same rigorous
moralism that has no appreciation for the individuality and
the freedom of the spirit ; they also betray the same im-
perious fanaticism that would absolutely subject everybody to its own creeds, be they negative or positive.

11. The Relation between Knowledge and Faith.

In conclusion I should like to offer a comprehensive
exposition of my idea of the relation between philosophy
and religion, knowledge and faith, a subject upon which I
have repeatedly touched in the foregoing.

Philosophy is not religion and cannot take its place.
It does not aim to be faith, but knowledge. Nevertheless
every philosophy that strives to be a philosophy in the old
sense, a conception of the world and of life, also contains
an element of faith, which science as such does not contain.
The ultimate object of all philosophy is to bring a meaning
into things, or rather to reveal the meaning which underlies
all things. In the last analysis, however, this meaning is
not a matter of knowledge, but of volition and faith. What
the philosopher himself accepts as the highest good and
final goal he projects into the world as its good and goal,
and then believes that subsequent reflections also reveal
it to him in the world. In this sense the words of Augustine,
fides præcedit rationem, express a universal human truth,
nay, the real key to an understanding of all philosophy.

This is obviously true of all *idealistic* philosophy. It is the fundamental conviction common to all objective idealism, that the goal towards which reality tends is the evolution of self-consciousness : reality, being thought as such, aims to comprehend itself as what it actually is, as thought or reason. The Hegelian formulæ characterize the fundamental notions of all idealistic philosophy. The eternal self-consciousness of the ideas, the thinking of the absolute content of thought, to use the Aristotelian expression, is the beginning and end of reality, is reality itself.

It is evident that the ultimate origin of such a conviction is to be sought in one's own experiences. For Aristotle as well as Plato, philosophy was the most important business of life. Hence it is, so their ethical systems declare, the chief constituent and the highest good of human life, and hence, so metaphysics goes on inferring, it is the highest goal of all life and existence in general. The universal reality, the godhead, is conceived as the great thinker after the pattern of the little thinker. For Fichte and Hegel, too, philosophy is the most important and most valuable among all the facts which the world offers ; consequently, thought is the ground and goal, nay, the real essence of the world. Had Fichte been asked what event he regarded as the most important fact of the eighteenth century or even of modern times, he would most likely have answered without a moment's hesitation : The appearance of the *Wissenschaftslehre* which begins with Kant. In his *Reden über die Grundzüge des gegenwärtigen Zeitalters* (Discourses on the Features of the Present Age), he gives an interpretation of the entire course of history ; it revolves around modern philosophy as its axis ; the great turning-point of the times, the transition from the descending to the ascending movement, is marked by the entrance of transcendental philosophy ; in it, reason, which had been enslaved by nature, again became conscious of itself. Hegel, too, regards the world-process as directly converging in his philosophy. In it reality reaches the goal of its self-movement, absolute self-consciousness. Thus the philosopher interprets the universe according to his own nature and highest aspirations. The world-process invariably passes right through the head of the philosopher.

The same may be said of Schopenhauer, the antithesis of Hegel. He, too, reads his own nature into the world. His own life's goal gives him an inkling of that of the universe. He calls his chief work, *The World as Will and Idea ;* he himself is the model of the world ; its two sides are the sides of his own nature, intelligence and will. And he believes that in the world at large the same relation exists between these two phases as in himself : the intelligence is the bright and joyful being, the will, the dark, blind, desiring, fearing, envious, hating, miserable, and unhappy being. His intelligence procured for him the great and pure joys of life, his will brought the daily big and little sorrows./ Hence to be delivered from the will and to become pure intelligence, that is a consummation devoutly to be wished. Then he reads this goal into the world. If it is in its origin blind, impulsive, impetuous, unhappy will, it will evolve intelligence out of itself, and intelligence is the principle of deliverance. Through the knowledge of its own nature, will succeeds in negating itself and hence in obtaining peace. History proves it. In the great religions of redemption, Christianity and Buddhism, mankind reaches its life-goal, deliverance from the will. Here, too, the philosopher's own experiences give him a clue to the meaning of the world.

We may say the same of the positivistic and materialistic philosophy. Comte's *Positivism* professes to be, first of all, pure knowledge, a mere synthesis of all scientific knowledge. But it, too, is mixed with elements of faith, especially in its philosophy of history. Like all philosophies of history it represents history as striving for a goal. The philosopher knows what the goal is and that really constitutes his great science ; in it he holds the key to the secret of the world. And this knowledge of his gains disciples for him. Of old, the faithful multitudes crowded around the oracles and prophets ; now they gather around the philosophers, to hear from them whither the road leads, what the future holds. Comte's philosophy aims wholly at a philosophy of history ; it is an attempt to survey the past experiences of mankind as a whole, in order to determine the future course of history. The position and the problem of the present are determined by the law of the three stages. The problem is, of course, the very problem which the philosopher is about to take up or which he has just been fortunate enough to solve in outline ; hence, in this case, it is the proof of positivistic philosophy as the final form of human knowledge, and the foundation of positivistic politics, which also reaches its systematic completion. Henceforth the problem will be to apply these thoughts to reality. So here, too, the world-process runs right through the brain of the philosopher, not without unbalancing it a little : during his later years Comte felt and acted like the high-priest of humanity, who, holding the past in his left hand and the future in his right, weighs and guides their destinies. Perhaps we expect too much of the human brain when we make it the pivot of the world-process.*

Materialism in principle rejects the attempt to interpret the meaning of the world ; it has no meaning ; rational products are merely accidental and occasional results. Accidentally and occasionally molecules form such combinations in a brain as produce a poem or a philosophy. Nevertheless this theory, too, possesses elements of faith. The philosophers of materialism also appear as prophets ; they, too, own the great science of the past and future. L. Feuerbach† unravels the meaning of history to the believers as follows : " The so-called modern times preceding our own constitute the Protestant middle ages, during which we retained the Roman Church, Roman law, the penal code, the old-fashioned universities, etc., only half negating them and using them as mere makeshifts. But now that the

---

* In his *Geschichte der Ethik*, Jodl places A. Comte by the side of his German contemporary Krause (ii. 102 ff.). In the title of his later writings Comte proclaims himself as the founder of the religion of humanity, for which he invented a form of worship as well as a calendar and saints. Similarly, Krause, in the solitude of his little chamber, founded a " union of mankind" (*Menschheitsbund*) in 1808, from which he dates a new epoch in the history of our race and a new chronology.

† In an essay, *Grundsätze der Philosophie*, 1842–43, in Grün, *L. Feuerbach, Briefwechsel und Nachlass*, pp. 411 ff.

Christianity of Protestantism has lost its force as a religious truth and power determining the mind, we have entered upon a new era. Realism is the spirit of the times or of the future. Unbelief has taken the place of belief, reason the place of the Bible, politics the place of religion and the church, the earth the place of heaven, work the place of prayer, material want the place of hell, man the place of the Christian." Hence a new philosophy is necessary, for every age needs its own philosophy. " Hitherto, Christianity was unconsciously denied ; it is now, for the first time, consciously and voluntarily repudiated, the more so since Christianity has become implicated in the attempts to obstruct the essential impulse of modern humanity, the desire for political freedom. This conscious negation begins a new era and makes necessary a new, open-hearted philosophy—one that is no longer Christian, but decidedly unchristian." Now this new philosophy demanded by the times is offered by Feuerbach. It is realistic, atheistic, and democratic, and will doubtless, so he believes, triumphantly conquer the world and point out the road to salvation. Thus unbelief itself is turned into a new belief.

Here, too, it is evident that philosophy is not a product of the understanding merely, but of a man's entire personality. The will, the revolt against a miserable present, determines the direction it will take and arouses its passions.

It would not be hard to prove that the above remark is applicable to more recent philosophers of this stamp, to Dühring and the Socialists. As anger and indignation once inspired Juvenal to write verses, so they inspire men with thoughts to-day. What influences the votaries of materialism is not so much reasons, not so much the arguments of science and metaphysics, as the conviction that materialism makes the most resolute onslaught against the conception of the universe on which our present conditions seem to them to be founded ; it is, so they believe, the basis of all injustice, falsehood, and tyranny. The philosophy of history and the interpretation of the future also constitute the heart of this philosophy, and the heart of this heart consists of ideas of justice, freedom, and welfare, the realization of which, in a new order of human things, forms the problem of the present and the content of the future. Thus the founder of the "materialistic conception of history," Karl Marx, explains the development of economic phenomena as moving towards a socialistic order of society : the expropriation of the laborer, with which society began, is now followed by the expropriation of the expropriator, by the transformation of private into collective property, and here the goal is reached : the thoroughgoing organization of economic activity. First the system of production will be organized, then distribution. Friedrich Engels fortifies the old ideas with the most modern theories of anthropology and likewise explains history as a unified process. It starts out from a natural order of society, in which maternal law and collectivism prevail, passes through a period of coercion and statehood, characterized by paternal law and private property, and finally returns to a condition of freedom with collective property and the free community of families.*

So everywhere a man's ideal of the future is the fixed point from which his interpretation of history proceeds. It determines the most significant points of the past, and through these points the curve is plotted which describes the course of history. Hence every reform-movement straightway sets out to change historical values ; such changes are essential to its philosophy of history. Think of the Renaissance, the Reformation, the French Revolution, the *Nationalverein,* and the German empire on a Prussian basis ! By changing historical values each reform became convinced of its own inner necessity. Socialism now does the same. When looked at from the new point of view, events which mankind formerly regarded as great and important, the theses of Luther, the battles of Leipsic and Sedan, dwindle into ordinary incidents of the day. On the other hand, an occurrence hardly noticed by others assumes importance and makes an epoch in history ; e.g., Karl Marx's Communistic Manifesto, the foundation of the national German labor-union by Lassalle. Here again we

---

* Fr. Engels, *Der Ursprung der Familie, des Privateigentums und des Staates,* 3d. ed. 1890.

find what we saw before : every new party has an impulse to make its own chronology, its own calendar and new saints.

To believers the new evaluations seem as credible as they seem absurd to believers of the old school. Only, they will not believe that it is *faith* and *not knowledge* on which their view of things depends. Why, they protest, do we not plainly see that history moves towards the goal ? "Science" is the second word of the social-democracy. Of course ; you put yourself at the goal, and it is quite natural that history should appear to be moving towards you. But science did not put you there ; your own loves and hates, your desires and aversions, put you there : not your understanding, but your will. You cannot prove the truth of your view to one who does not share your loves and your hates, your hopes and your ideals. All you can do is to appeal to the future ; but the peculiarity about the future is that it is open to faith, not to knowledge. Perhaps five hundred years from now, when the new order of things will have arrived, everybody will recognize the true importance of the beginnings of the great revolution. We all appreciate the historical significance of the beginnings of Christianity now, and even the reluctant are forced to confess the importance of our Christian era. But if some one had told a Greek philosopher or a Roman historian, eighteen hundred years ago, that all the European nations would date their era from the birth of a poor little boy, occurring several decades ago in the land of the Jews, he would most likely have questioned the prophet's sanity. At any rate, he would have refused to discuss the possibility of such a view. For the present the most recent changes of chronology seem to me to be in the same predicament.

That does not diminish the importance of the matter. Not knowledge, but faith works miracles ; not every faith, of course, but only the true faith which divines what is to come. Ideas, says Hegel, are the efficient forces of history. Very true ; for ideas of what is to come are motive forces in the aspirations and minds of men. That will be the case as long as men live, not on the joys of the present but on the hopes of the future. And so long will faith play its part in the life of humanity.

In this sense, then, faith is an element, nay the real formal principle of every philosophy. This belief in the future fashions a man's notion of historical life, and the philosophy of history fashions his conception of the world. Astronomy does not make a *Weltanschauung*, it simply presents us with a general outline of reality. Physics does not determine one's conception of the nature of the real; it supplies the necessary aids for the technical treatment of things. Biology does not determine one's conception of life; in a few broad outlines it indicates man's general position in the world. An answer to the question concerning the meaning of life, the essence of reality, the ground and goal of the world, is ultimately sought in historical phenomena which form the real and most immediate environment of the mind. Our interpretation of mental life, however, is not based on the science of the past, but on the idea of perfection which every man carries along with him. It tells him the direction of the movement; and when he knows that, he soon discovers whence it comes. And when he knows the import of history, he soon finds out the import of nature and the world at large. What seems important to me is the essential element in the world : this is the universal pattern according to which the human mind draws its inferences, and it will hardly abandon the scheme, unless, of course, the head and the heart, the intelligence and the will, should each carry on its affairs separately. So long as they remain united, there will be no change. Whatever fails to arouse the will, whatever bears no relation to its purposes and problems, and to its ideals, cannot excite the attention; it will be ignored and consequently have no influence on a man's idea of reality. Hence, *what is important* necessarily becomes essential, and *what is essential* becomes the sole reality. As the snail builds its house to suit its body, so the will constructs its cosmology, from which it views things and acts upon them.*

---

* The idea that cosmologies have their root in the *historical* consciousness of mankind, is finely carried out in the half-forgotten work of Bunsen, *Gott in der Geschichte* (God in History), 1857. I cannot deny myself the pleasure of inserting a passage from his splendid preface : "The feeling

As was shown above, the thought just expressed forms the real cardinal point of *Kantian philosophy*. One's view of the world receives its most powerful and decided impetus, not from the understanding, but from the volitional side, from the practical reason. The belief in the possibility of our ultimate purposes, in the realization of the highest good in the world, really forms the starting-point of one's cosmology. Kant has formulated this thought in the doctrine of the postulates and the primacy of practical reason. We should say : We are here concerned, not with a demand that imposes faith upon the conscience, but with a fact. No one believes and no one can believe that reality is wholly indifferent or even hostile to that which seems to him to be the highest goal and good. And though a man might, in principle, deny the validity of the belief that reality has regard for human values, yet, as a matter of fact, he presupposes such an agreement. The materialist, too, believes in the victory of the good cause, in the ascendency of reason, truth, and right ; he believes, therefore, in a *moral* world-order. The pessimist, too, ultimately believes in the triumph of the better principle in so far as he believes in the deliverance from evil ; for is not the non-existence that is to be better than existence ? Thus we find faith even among those who in principle repudiate faith and grant only the claims of knowledge. They themselves fail to deduce from their principle its logical consequence, or, on the other hand, they deny the legitimacy of what they do themselves, *i.e.*, of transcending knowledge by believing in the future.

Kant undertook to vindicate this procedure, which is,

---

that the course of history is divinely ordered and the revelation of a divinity is an original, divine endowment of human nature. From the very outset man knows himself not merely as one among many, but as a member in a series of developments of his own being. It is the original consciousness of man that all life, individual as well as social, evolves into humanity according to a law that is inherent in him, but has its temporal centre in mankind, its eternal one in God. The consciousness of the world, *i.e.*, this historical consciousness of God, the consciousness that God acts in history, is at the same time the innate feeling of the individual's relation as a microcosm, as the divine world in miniature, to the macrocosm, to the great world of God, and to the All."

as a matter of fact, universally followed, against those who reject the same in theory. His aim is to procure for the belief in the " teleological realm " (*Reich der Zwecke*) its just rights against the radical negation of dogmatic atheism. But not by means of theoretical arguments. That was the old method ; the attempt was made to prove by metaphysics, by teleologies and theodicies, that goodness is the ruling principle of reality. Kant abandons this argument ; an objective proof compelling the understanding is, in the very nature of things, impossible. Every argument may be opposed by a counter-proof of equal cogency. Here, too, we have a dialectic with antinomies. And the solution of this dialectical antinomy is effected in the same way in which Kant resolves the cosmological antinomies : the conflict is decided by a change of venue, as it were. Space and time, causality and necessity, exist only in the subject ; consequently the dialectical antinomies, which rest on the premise that they are predicates of things-in-themselves, disappear. So, too, values exist only for the subject ; however—and that is the decisive fact—not for the understanding, but for the will, for " practical " reason. And then the analogy carries him farther : nature is, according to the *Critique of Pure Reason*, nothing but a system of phenomena arranged by the necessary functions of our intelligence. For that very reason the forms of our intelligence have the value and validity of universal and necessary determinations of our knowledge of nature, and hence of nature itself. In the same way, the *Critique of Practical Reason* adds, the categories of the volitional side of our nature possess the value and validity of universal and necessary determinations of our views of the world. As the intellectual law of causality is the basis of our belief in the natural order, so the moral law is the basis of our faith in a moral order. Wherever the moral law is accepted and has validity as an identical expression of the legislative reason, the belief in the " realm of ends," whose law is the moral law, is valid.

We may object to the way in which Kant introduces and carries out this thought. The fundamental idea is thoroughly justified. It would be utterly impossible for a being that has no will, but is pure intellect, to explain the value or even the meaning of a realm of ends and a moral world-order as the internal law of the same. But for a human being with a will determined by the highest ends of humanity, the belief in a moral world-order is natural and necessary; and such a belief necessarily becomes the keystone of his entire view of the world. Our philosophy will inevitably bear the impress of the will as well as that of the intelligence. And we have no more reason to say that our concept of the universe is falsified here than in the space-time-causal form of our knowledge. Our philosophy is a human philosophy; as human beings we can neither have nor endure any other.*

Negative dogmatism will raise the objection : That would be making a principle of a natural error of thought. Of course we are inclined to believe what we wish. But it is the business of philosophy and science to free knowledge from the influence of the will. Originally the will rules absolutely, and completely determines our conception of things ; which explains the many superstitions related by anthropology and history. The intellect has gradually asserted itself in science, and the conscientious observation and impartial recognition of facts has taken the place of a biassed interpretation. Now science universally proves that the course of nature is by no means subject to our will or changeable as' the naïve fancy imagines ; nay, it runs along absolutely indifferent to human designs, obeying only the eternal great laws. Hence why delude one's self ? Why imagine things that do not exist ? It is both wise and

---

* This is the point in Kantian philosophy which modern Protestant theology makes the starting-point of its religious reflections. I have already referred to the works of Rauwenhoff and Bender. Let me add another important book : J. Kaftan, *Die Wahrheit der christlichen Religion* (1888). His arguments are based on Kant : A theoretical proof of the truth of the Christian faith is impossible. The intellect cannot be convinced of the truth of this belief either by means of the old orthodoxy's philologico-historical method of Scriptural proofs or by philosophical speculation. The only possible argument is the one that appeals to the *entire* man ; it must show that the idea of man's historical destiny or the necessary idea of a highest good is realized either in Christianity's mundane or supramundane kingdom of God. I do not wish to deny that I do not agree with the author's rejection of all metaphysics, nor with his way of introducing the supranatural.

courageous to take things as they are. What is the use of
pursuing error ?

None whatever, to be sure. It happens daily, without
doubt, that the course of nature crosses our plans and even
destroys what is near and dear to us. But does that mean
that reality is indifferent not only as to particulars, but
also as a whole ; regardless not merely of occasional particular plans, but also of our ultimate and highest ends ? And
does it therefore mean that the belief in a " moral world-
order" is a wanton illusion ?

I do not propose to enter here into a discussion of the
old problems concerning the nature and meaning of evil
and the possibility of a theodicy. Let me simply ask the
question : How would the world have to be constructed so
as to render such a faith at least possible ? Would the natural course of events have to yield to every wish, or even
anticipate it ? In that case should we have reason to believe that the natural course of events is ordered by Providence for our good ?   L. Büchner holds (*Kraft und Stoff*,
p. 236) : " It would indeed be *foolish* for any one to assert,
in all seriousness, that the earth was constructed by an all-
wise and all-good Providence as a suitable dwelling-place !
Only through the most strenuous exercise of his bodily
and mental powers is man enabled to escape the thousand
dangers that constantly threaten him, and to exist upon it."
Accordingly, would a belief in a Providence be justifiable,
only in case nature enabled us to live without exerting our
powers ?   If there were neither work nor failure, neither
sickness nor death, if the world were a Utopia, would we
then and only then be permitted to believe that it is the
creation of a benevolent God ?

Of course, at some time or other, we all dream of a land
in which there will be no work and no unrest, no evil and
no wrong,—the fond dream of paradise. But in our waking moments we see enough to know that, as long as we are
what we are, such a paradise is not for us. We belong on
the earth and not in paradise. A world in which there
are neither conflicts nor obstacles, neither failures nor evils,
would be no world for us. What opportunity would there
be for healthy volition and brave action, for earnest battle

and glorious victory? An environment is good for me that offers tasks suited to my powers. That world is good for a people and for mankind which brings out and develops predispositions and powers. Without conflicts, natural and moral, there would be no problems and no work, no life and no history whatever. Whoever desires life and history, human life, desires the conflicts too, desires also evil and wrong, not for their own sake, but as the conditions of human volition and work, as a means of exercising powers and virtues. The world is destined for the exercise of powers, not for passive enjoyment.*

Hence whoever wishes to prove that the world is bad must prove that it does not realize this aim, that it does not supply individuals and society with appropriate tasks, that man needs another world for the development of his natural capacities. Or he would at least have to show that a differently constructed universe would have been more in accord with our ultimate aims than that which, unfortunately, happens to be the real one. Until then, until we get a clear description of the better world,—better, not because of the absence of certain inconveniences and conflicts, but better fitted for the perfection of human capacities in general,—why should we not persevere in the belief that for us the existing world is a suitable world, nay, the best world? We do not claim to know this or to be able to prove it; we have no other possible worlds and no other possible human natures with which to compare our own; but we do claim that there is nothing to contradict the belief that our world is suitable and good for us, that the ways through which mankind, and each one of us, has been led are good ways, the ways of God. A scientific theodicy is impossible, but a scientific anti-theodicy is equally impossible. The intellect is indifferent to the problem whether the world is good or bad.

Or, we might add, if it takes sides at all, it cannot favor the view that reality is bad and unsuited to man. To the advocates of the modern biological theory the opposite conception would seem more in accord with the facts. If

---

* The reader will find an elaboration of these suggestions in my *System der Ethik* (8d ed., 1894, vol. I. pp. 92 ff.).

man was not set upon the earth from without, but originated and grew with it, then the harmony between his nature and his environment appears to be *a priori* necessary ; then his whole nature is adapted to this environment, and he would seem out of place in any other world. All his powers and capacities, nay, his essence and his will, his senses and his intellect itself, are fashioned for the earth and the conditions of life which it provides; hence why should it not be fit and good for such a being? Has she not been a kind mother to him? Well, you say, she has inflicted many a severe trial upon him. But perhaps that was exactly what he needed. Or do you know better? Thus we are forced to repeat the demand: Out of all the infinite possibilities construct a world that would have been better fitted than ours to educate man and would have accomplished more.

Let me also remind the reader that, according to the combined experience of nations, whatever morality declares to be good and just is found to preserve and advance individual as well as social life, while the evil impedes and destroys. Sometimes it may seem otherwise; injustice and falsehood are often triumphant. But the right rules in the end, so the wisdom of nations declares in a thousand proverbs. And they find the truth confirmed in their historical reminiscences. True, the great and the good was often misunderstood and oppressed during its life, while littleness and sham and wickedness flourished and was honored. But history changes the rôles ; it makes it clear to all the world that the worthless, specious though it seemed at first, is worthless, and that the good, simple and insignificant though it was, is real and valuable. Wickedness may rule the day, but to truth and goodness belongs eternity. That is above all the grand teaching of Christianity; through suffering and death we pass to resurrection and glory. Its faith triumphantly exclaims : "O death, where is thy sting? O grave, where is thy victory?" Evil and wickedness have no power over those who rest in God's hand. It may strike them from without, it cannot overcome them from within, and thus it simply serves to glorify the name of God in them.

In conclusion, I again protest against the misconception

that such discussions are adequate theoretical proofs that bind the understanding, or that faith and religion can or must be produced by them. Their sole significance consists in this : they free the judgment and enable it to oppose the negative dogmatism of a purely physical view of the world. Religion does not originate in thought, but in what we experience. This is true of the religion of individuals as well as of nations. Life and death are the great preachers of religion ; and while they continue to preach, religion will not disappear from the world.

There are, in particular, three feelings in which religion has its eternal, living roots ; they are continually aroused in the heart of man by the phenomenon of life and death : *fear, joyful admiration,* and *disappointment.* Not until these emotions die out will religion die ; not until then will pure knowledge rule the day.

Fear and *distress* are the primary roots of religion ; it was they that taught men the art of magic. Magic was found above to be the primitive form in which man's relation to a suprasensuous being is conceived. Even now the fear of death and the anticipation of the pain of death are the powerful motives which cause us to fall on our knees and impel us to seek refuge from nature with something that is beyond nature. The fear of death is the strongest, be it fear of one's own death or of that of some one dear to us. The horror of annihilation moves the heart to throw itself upon an eternal and suprareal being that is not subject to destruction.

In *rapture* and *admiration* we have another root of religion. Youthful vigor and health, hopeful action and happy success produce joyful emotions which tend to break forth into gratitude. The pure contemplation of nature arouses a reverential mood that looks upon nature as pointing to something higher, of which it is the product and revelation. When you lose yourself in meditating upon the works of the mind, upon the creations of art and poetry, upon the lives of great and good, brave and holy men, the heart is filled with feelings of the beautiful and the sublime, feelings of admiration and veneration, and these emotions, too, naturally turn the soul heavenward, towards an all-good and perfect One, of whom everything that is beautiful and good on earth is the reflection. That is Goethe's religion :

> In unsres Busens Reine wogt ein Streben,
> Sich einem Höhern, Reinern, Unbekannten
> Aus Dankbarkeit freiwillig hinzugeben,
> Enträtzelnd sich den ewig Ungenannten ;
> Wir heissen's : fromm sein !

Then, again, religious feeling springs from *disappointment* and *world-weariness*. This phase appears in a pronounced form in the religions of salvation. Life and the world have not fulfilled what they promised the hopes of youth ; bitter disappointment and grim remorse gnaw at his heart, and it saves itself from despair and disgust by abandoning this world for a better world ; it flies from the hardness and self-righteousness, the baseness and deceit of men to the heart of God. There is a trace of this feeling in all idealistic philosophy ; we find it in Plato and in Fichte. The indignation at the world and men as they are provokes the remark : This world is not the real world at all, nay, it cannot be, it is too low for that ; there is, there must be a purer, higher world beyond the hazy atmosphere of sense.—Who is utterly devoid of such a feeling? Something of the *contemtus mundi*, which is so marked in Christianity, is surely experienced by every fine-grained soul. Men are not what our childlike trust imagined them to be ; behind the beautiful masks with which they know how to disguise themselves lurk the base impulses of a vulgar soul. They care not for the beautiful and the good, they pursue trivial aims and mean designs and presuppose them in others ; grandeur and excellence fill them with envy, serious and great endeavors arouse in them distrust and hatred, and a merciless judgment is pronounced upon him who will not agree with them in calling the trivial great, the false genuine, mere semblance truth. And then the heart sorrowfully and indignantly turns away and appeals from the court of men to a higher and juster judge. It becomes the law of its life to seek consolation in God and not to rely on vain and venal men, not to build on the *creatura fallax*. No great work has been done on this earth without the presence of some such feeling. And there is another disappointment which no man is spared. You yearned for the things of the world, for money and wealth, for honor and position, for enjoyment and good living, and you discover what has been experienced a thousand times before—that they cannot satisfy the heart. You were full of grand purposes, you imagined you would win beauty and truth, and now after many wanderings and meanderings you are lost in error and darkness. Once upon a time you set out to do battle for freedom and right, but you grew weary and pliable and have now made your peace with the world. Such a disappointment, too, becomes a motive for looking heavenward; it becomes a yearning for deliverance from your entire sensuous and temporal existence. Everything worldly seems flat and dreary to the world-weary soul, and with the poet to whom nothing human was foreign, it exclaims:

> Ach ich bin des Treibens müde!
> Was soll all der Schmerz und Lust?
> Süsser Friede,
> Komm, ach komm in meine Brust!

Such are the emotions that arouse a longing for religion in the human heart. So long as they are not wholly stifled by well-fed security and pride of culture, by self-admiration and Byzantianism, this longing will constantly well up in the breast of man.

It is satisfied, however, only by an existing, *historical* religion, not by ideas or images invented by the individual. The invention of one's own thoughts is an arbitrary product that one may hold or set aside at will. But man demands that his religion raise him beyond himself and his caprice, and place him upon firm and solid ground. A historical religion, the faith in which his fathers lived and died, can alone accomplish that. The great symbols from which he gleaned the meaning of the world even as a child are rekindled in his bosom when the religious need makes itself felt. The heart now contemplates them as something that is fixed and eternal, as the only stable element in the ever-changing maze of opinions. The doctrines of the philosophers, the theories of the savants, the systems of the theologians, pass away like the clouds that come and go from night to morn, but the great symbols remain like the stars in heaven, even though the passing mists momentarily hide them from view.

As the traveller returns from the mountains to the plains, the neighboring foot-hills obscure his outlook on the summits. The farther and farther he wanders away, the smaller the foot-hills grow, until at last the solitary caps of snow loom up above the outstretched plain. The child of man makes the same experiences with his religion. In the beginning the first great impressions of childhood are displaced and even totally submerged by a wealth of new impressions which the world and life make upon the youth as he enters the world. But when the time comes for looking backward, when our parents are dead and gone, and new young life plays at our feet, then the memories of home and the days of youth grow strong, and with them arises the recollection of our spiritual home, the realm of symbols and images, in which the consciousness of the child once dwelt. And now the great meaning of these things dawns upon the soul which has been enriched by the varied experiences of life, and the impulse arises to perpetuate them and to unite the future generations with their ancestors by the transmission of the great truths that were so mysteriously revealed. So the germ of religion is transmitted from generation to generation. Our experiences develop it, not always in the same way, it is true, and many a seed fails to sprout altogether, but there is no more *generatio æquivoca* here than anywhere else in the organic and historical realms.

Religion exists and can exist only in the form of concrete popular religions that have grown historically and express themselves in symbols and sacred ceremonies. An abstract religion like the systems that went under the title of rational or natural religion is an impossibility. All attempts made in this direction by particular thinkers are the dying embers of a living, concrete, real religion.

Renan happily expresses this thought in his suggestive essay on metaphysics and its future (*Fragments philosophiques*, p. 327): " Its simplicity will always hinder deism from becoming a religion. A religion that is as clear as geometry would excite neither love nor hatred. That alone forms a bond of union among men which leaves room for free and personal choice. The more evident a truth is, the less we care for it. Only what is obscure arouses passion, for evidence excludes individual choice." Hence the critical philosopher will not attempt " to divest religion of its particular articles of faith ; he does not believe that he would find the truth at the bottom of the crucible by analyzing the different religions. Such an attempt would result in nothing. Each thing has a value for us only in the peculiar form which characterizes it. He takes every symbol for what it is, for the peculiar expression of a feeling that does not deceive us. The truth of a symbol does not therefore bear any relation to its simplicity. In the eyes of the deist Islamism would of necessity be the best religion. In the eyes of the critical philosopher Islamism is a very inferior religion that has done the human race more harm than good. Let us allow the religions to speak of God, and let us not, in our desire to simplify them, destroy them. Let us not boast of our superiority. Their formulæ are only a trifle more mythical than ours, and they have great advantages which we never attain. A formula is a boundary and open to objection. A hymn, a harmony are not open to objection, for they are not logical propositions. We cannot dispute about them. The dogmas of the Catholics repel us ; their old churches enchant us. The Protestant confessions of faith do not satisfy us, while the austere poetry of their worship fills us with rapture. Ancient Judaism does not please us, but its psalms still remain a source of consolation to us."

Those who endeavor to construct new religions by means of philosophy should not forget this fact. A religion does not consist of definitions, but of concrete symbols. Symbols, however, cannot be made, they are historical products. A religion may assimilate new elements, the old trunk may throw out new shoots, but it is not the result of a *generatio æquivoca.* See how Christianity retains the elements of the religion of Israel in all points, in its faith as well as in its worship ! It seems to me, the man who has the least appreciation for the poetry of history must be overcome with an awful weariness and be chilled to the bone when he compares a real historical religion with such attempts at an artificial reform as Comte's religion of humanity and its concepts and formulæ, its symbols and its worship.*

Nor should the founders of new religions forget that there can be no religion without the *transcendent element.* To do away with the transcendent means to destroy religion. We may love and admire a historical personage or any man, but we feel religious awe only in the presence of a metempiric, suprareal being. Every real being has its limitations, the ideal alone is without negations. A historical being can become the object of religious reverence only by being raised above the empirical world into the realm of poetry, ideals, and symbols. If instead of the four gospels we had a biography of Jesus in four volumes, telling us the smallest details of his daily acts and sayings, the impression on the heart would be infinitely less than it is. A biography of him would reveal the man with all his limitations; the gospels give us a few grand and sublime features; the trivial characteristics of his daily routine are lacking or only faintly suggested. So it is that we behold in Jesus the image of the suprareal, infinite God. For that reason the faith of the church is justified in deifying Jesus, and is compelled to do so : the object of our religious adoration is not the empirical man, but God, who appeared to us in this man and indicated the path that leads to life and happiness.

Positivism believes that man is about to give up his longing for the infinite and transcendent, which has characterized religion in the past. I regard that as a delusion. The vague yearning for an infinite and all-good being is an innate and permanent craving of the human soul.

---

* In connection with the above see the statements made by the Jesuit H. Gruber in his book, *Comte und der Positivismus* (1890), a work that is full of interesting facts, and then read another work by the same author, *Der Positivismus vom Tode A. Comte's bis auf unsere Tage* (1891). We find therein detailed accounts of the ceremonies of the orthodox positivists in France and England. They have their liturgy, prayers, sacraments, pilgrimages, everything but God; humanity takes his place in their prayers as well as in the text of the *Imitatio Christi.*

Man is not completely satisfied by earthly gifts and forms, by the world of experience. There are, at least, times when all that is earthly and ephemeral seems mean and insignificant, when he is seized with a longing for the eternal and imperishable. And the reality before him becomes too narrow for his intellect as well as for his heart. What if you knew all sciences, what if you could answer all the questions which historians and naturalists are struggling to solve; would that be such a wonderful achievement? Reality and perfection lie beyond the knowable, beyond the realm of the conceivable and expressible. Such moods do not lay hold of the modern man as often as in the days of Faust, speculative philosophy, and romanticism. It is characteristic of the spirit of the present that it rests satisfied with the finite and the trivial. The same is true of the *Aufklärung :* Clearness and utility were its chief delight. But after the illumination, the oscillating pendulum of history brought storm and stress, romanticism and mysticism. Has the pendulum possibly reached its extreme point to-day, and is it swinging back again? Be that as it may, the climax of the movement has been passed that overrated scientific research and its results, and our admiration for realistic politics also appears to be on the wane. If we may judge from certain symptoms, there again seems to be a desire for a new, richer, freer, more spiritual life among the nations of the West : there is a yearning for principles, a yearning for religion.* Even though the mind may momentarily seem to abandon itself to the temporal and perishable, the time will come when all those things which it eagerly pursued will weary it, when, sated by national wealth and gorgeous pleasures, by fame and universal education, it will again reflect on itself and the eternal.

> Doch ist es Jedem eingeboren,
> Dass sein Gefühl hinauf und vorwärts dringt,
> Wenn über uns, im blauen Raum verloren,
> Ihr schmetternd Lied die Lerche singt,

---

* The fact that P. de Lagarde's *Deutsche Schriften* (3d ed., 1891) are gaining in popularity is such a symptom; the breath of the future is in them. His harsh criticism of the present for sating itself with what is coarse and trivial affects one as the chill breeze which precedes the rise of the sun.

Wenn über schroffen Fichtenhöhen
Der Adler ausgebreitet schwebt,
Und über Flächen, über Seen
Der Kranich nach der Heimat strebt.

Religion in this sense is compatible with philosophy, faith with the freest kind of thought. Religion does not demand that we think what cannot be thought, but that we believe what satisfies the heart and the will, and does not contradict reason.

If all that is true, how shall we explain the violent opposition between faith and science, between real convictions and creeds, which is the great disease of our age ? It is evidently due to the fact that religion has been converted into a pseudo-scientific system for whose formulæ an unqualified recognition is demanded. The spirit of freedom and the more sensitive theoretical conscience of modern times rebels against the attempt to subject it to such dogmas constructed by human hands. It has been customary to lay infidelity on the wickedness of the will which refuses to be subjected to a wholesome discipline. Perhaps there is some truth in the saying. But it would be wilful self-delusion to attribute all estrangement from the church and all opposition to faith to this cause. Outside of the narrow circle within which this notion prevails, no one any longer believes that wicked men are the only unbelievers in the church sense. The whole world knows that almost all the men whom our people honor as their intellectual leaders and as good, true, and brave men, that, Goethe and Schiller, Kant and Fichte—and what name shall we omit here ?—belong to the unbelievers, as the church understands the term.

Hence the reason for the wide-spread dislike for religion and the church must be sought elsewhere. It is found in the demand that is made in the name of religion, that men subject themselves, not to the command of God, but to human dogmas. The creed becomes a yoke by which to test a person's obedience, a means to *præmium servitutis*, to office and promotion. That arouses hatred. Whoever appreciates simplicity and truth, grandeur and sublimity, must surely find pleasure and consolation in the Sacred

Scriptures. The reason why many a man does not care for them, or even hates them, is that he is not allowed freely to appropriate from them what suits him, but is expected to regard them as inspired and literally true propositions concerning natural and historical facts. Think of the state of the many thousand teachers who daily suffer the torture of being compelled to teach what they do not believe, and of not being allowed to say what they think! The old symbolical ceremonies, hallowed by the veneration of thousands of years, must surely seem venerable and sacred to every man who has the slighest appreciation for history. Police compulsion and impertinent prescriptions concerning what we ought or ought not to think and feel have made them unbearable. The creed as an unconstrained confession that we desire to belong to the great moral community that has existed for thousands of years and regards Jesus as the Savior, that we wish to live and to die in it, would break from a thousand hearts, who now look upon it with distrust and aversion. They learned to hate the creed because, as children they were compelled to commit the three articles to memory, as boys to explain them, and during their youth to make a public declaration of the faith.

Faith is by nature the tenderest, freest, and innermost function of life. It perishes as soon as constraint, the fear of man, and politics come into play. That is the most evident of all the truths which the history of Western nations teaches—a truth, to be sure, that politicians will not learn. What can we do to preserve the religion of the people? I am sure I do not know, unless it be that when you consider the question of preserving religion you first think of yourselves.

BOOK II.

THE EPISTEMOLOGICAL PROBLEMS.

INTRODUCTORY REMARKS.

THE problems of epistemology are at present the central objects of interest in philosophy. Or perhaps we had better say, they were so until recently, for a noticeable change has taken place of late. In many instances they wholly diverted the attention from metaphysical questions; many identified philosophy with epistemology altogether. At any rate, the opinion prevailed that the epistemological inquiry into the functions and limits of knowledge must precede all further discussions.

History did not pursue this path. Philosophy universally began with metaphysics. Inquiries into the form and origin of the universe, the nature and origin of reality, the nature of the soul and its relation to the body, constituted the primary objects of philosophical reflection. Only after such questions have been discussed for a long time will the question concerning the nature of knowledge and its possibility arise. It is provoked by the conflicting views to which reflection on physical and metaphysical problems leads. The presence of so many contradictory opinions suggests the question : Is the human intellect at all able to solve such problems ? Epistemology is a critical reflection on metaphysics. So it was in ancient times and so it is to-day.

Greek philosophy begins with cosmological speculations of a natural-philosophical character. The Ionic, Eleatic, and Atomistic philosophies are, above everything else, metaphysical systems. They also speculate on the nature and the origin of knowledge, but their views are based on their metaphysics. The case is the same in the great conceptual and speculative systems of Plato and Aristotle.

A theory of knowledge is not wanting, but it is treated from the standpoint of metaphysics : Knowledge too is an existing fact, and hence the problem is to determine its position. Only in the later Academic and Skeptical schools did the question concerning the possibility and certainty of knowledge, which the Sophists had been the first to ask in a general way, come into prominence.

Modern philosophy likewise begins with the construction of metaphysical systems. In this respect the seventeenth century with its great systematizers, Descartes, Hobbes, Spinoza, and Leibniz, resembles the fifth century B.C. Epistemology is not wanting, but it depends on metaphysics. With the appearance of Locke's *Essay Concerning the Human Understanding* the theory of knowledge becomes independent. As the preface of this work shows, epistemology is the result of a critical reflection on metaphysics, first on the prevailing metaphysics of scholasticism, which with its barren notions beclouds the intellect and hinders the progress of knowledge, then also on the metaphysics of the modern systems, especially that of Descartes. Its aim is to ascertain the objects of possible knowledge and to stake out the limits of knowledge. Four sciences are possible : mathematics and morals are demonstrative sciences, physics and psychology empirical. There is really no place for metaphysics unless we mean by it the reflection on knowledge. Hume leans on Locke. Comte is the chief representative of this view in France; he called it *Positivism.* It is introduced into German philosophy by Kant, not, however, without considerable changes. He calls it *Criticism.* The new metaphysical systems which speculative philosophy constructed on an epistemological basis, and the successor of the same, dogmatic materialism, were followed in *Neokantianism* by the critical reflection, that is, epistemology.

An introduction to philosophy is obliged to follow the course of history and to begin with metaphysics. Besides, metaphysics will always be the central object of general interest. Moreover, I am of the opinion that the metaphysical problems demand wholly independent treatment and cannot be replaced by epistemological discussions. Wherever such a thing is attempted, they will come back to us in a different guise and in a less convenient form. Kant did not set German philosophy a good example by depriving metaphysics of its independence and relegating it to epistemology. The problems of psychology, cosmology, and theology are cast aside and repudiated rather than discussed and solved in his *Dialectic*.

I shall simply give a few outlines of epistemological speculation in the following, as much as I deem necessary and sufficient to acquaint the reader with the general character of such investigations, and to supplement the preceding metaphysical treatment of philosophical subjects. Let us first consider the main problems of epistemology and their possible solutions.

As was shown above (p. 49), epistemological inquiries culminate in two questions : What is the *essence*, and What is the *origin* of knowledge ? *What is knowledge*, and *How is knowledge acquired ?* Each of these questions gives rise to views that are diametrically opposed : *Realism* and *Idealism* or *Phenomenalism* are the two opposite fundamental theories that answer the first ; *Sensationalism* or *Empiricism* and *Rationalism*, the second.

Realism answers the question concerning the essence of knowledge as follows : Knowledge is a copy of reality. The idea is an absolute representation of the object. It is an *alterum idem* of the thing ; only, it is without corporeality or reality. *Idealism* or *Phenomenalism*, on the contrary, asserts that ideas and things, thought and being, are absolutely different and not to be compared.

The question concerning the origin of knowledge is answered by *Sensationalism* or *Empiricism* as follows : All knowledge springs from perception, that is, from outer or inner perception ; experience arises by combining percepts, science by collecting and arranging experiences. *Rationalism*, on the other hand, asserts : All real or scientific knowledge is derived from reason ; it is the result of the immanent evolution of consequences from *a priori* certain principles which do not arise from experience.

Inasmuch as every theory of knowledge must answer both questions and hence come to some conclusion concerning these antitheses, we get four possible fundamental forms of epistemology. They are :

1. *Realistic Empiricism.* It asserts : We know things as they are in themselves by perception. This view comes nearest to the *popular conception.*

2. *Realistic Rationalism.* It asserts : We know things as they are, not by the senses, but by reason. This view is common to the great metaphysical systems. Plato, Spinoza, and Hegel all claim that an adequate knowledge of reality is reached by reason.

3. *Idealistic Empiricism.* It asserts : We know of things only by perception, which, of course, gives no adequate knowledge. This is the view of the epistemological critics of rationalistic-metaphysical systems. Hume is its most consistent representative.

4. *Idealistic Rationalism.* It asserts : We can know reality *a priori* by pure reason ; however, not as it is in itself, but only as it appears to us, and only as to its form. This is Kant's view.

Historians of philosophy also mention another form of epistemology : *Skepticism,* which asserts that we can know nothing at all. Every once in a while some one takes the trouble to refute this view. It seems to me to be a superfluous endeavor. Whether real skepticism ever existed or not, one thing is certain : it has become extinct in modern times. No great philosopher now doubts the existence of real knowledge, that differs from ignorance. Hume is commonly mentioned as the representative of skepticism. It is true, Hume juggled with the term, and he has been sufficiently punished for it by having his views misinterpreted. But he never dreamed of saying that science does not exist. He simply maintained, on the one hand, that natural theology with its arguments for the existence of God and the immortality of the soul is no science ; on the other, that it is impossible to know facts except by experience, and hence that there can be no universal and necessary knowledge of facts.—It was Kant who stamped Hume as a skeptic, against whom the sciences or the possibility of metaphysics, physics, and even mathematics, must be vindicated. As far as pure mathematics is concerned, Kant's criticism of Hume's skepticism rests on an absolute misunderstanding. As far as metaphysics is concerned, he repudiates rational theology, cosmology, and psychology no less than Hume. Physics remains; both grant that there is such a science. Only, they differ in their notions concerning the form and the nature of its certainty. Kant thinks it contains absolutely universal and necessary propositions (synthetical judgments *a priori*), while, according to Hume, even the principles are merely experiential propositions that are probably universal; a difference of opinion which is not properly characterized by the statement that Hume denies the possibility of physics altogether.

As far as I can see, the same may be said of all other so-called skeptics. They do not deny the possibility or the existence of science, but simply emphasize the limitations and uncertainty of human science, when compared with a possible ideal of knowledge, such, for example, as might exist in a divine mind. In reality the skepticism of modern philosophy invariably combats the presumptuous claims of transcendent speculation; it is Janus-faced in so far as it either defends religious faith or empirical research against the encroachments of speculation.

CHAPTER I.

1. The Idealistic Train of Thought.

HERE too we start out from the popular conception,
whose standpoint is *naïve Realism*. It is convinced that
our ideas resemble the things as copies resemble their
originals ; that is, the true ideas, for the false ones are false
simply because they are not true copies of reality. Hence
outside in space there are bodies in motion; they are extended, impenetrable, have form, color, taste, smell, etc.;
all these are absolute qualities that are impressed upon our
presentation by the senses, as it were.

Upon reflection all kinds of doubts arise. The senses
deceive us, at least at times. A stick in the water appears
to the eye as broken. Here the sense of touch corrects
the illusion. But what controls the sense of touch? The
fever-patient sees and hears things that do not exist; he
mistakes hallucinations for percepts. The dreamer believes
in the reality of what his dreams picture to him. What
criterion have we for distinguishing hallucinations and
dreams from real percepts? The fever-patient does not
think he is sick, and the dreamer knows nothing of his
dreaming. Indeed, it sometimes happens that we dream :
This time it is no dream that I am flying or that I am finding a treasure, but absolute reality.—Or conceptual thinking, seeking to justify its better right, rebels against sense-
perception. Motion is not conceivable, Zeno argues, hence
it cannot exist, unless we are willing to say that a body
can be and not be in the same place at the same time.
Hence the senses, which give us the idea of motion, delude
us. And Plato takes up the argument : Perception pictures

344

reality as in a state of growth and decay, *i.e.*, as both being and not being. Since that is inconceivable, it cannot be real; consequently the entire sensuous conception of things is a great illusion. Truth can be found only in conceptual thought, which deals with unchangeable objects, like mathematics.

In modern times we have, instead of such puzzles and dialectical arguments, reflections on the nature of normal perception, that are based on the *physiology of sensation.* They have completely destroyed naïve realism. We may outline such reasonings about as follows : We call a food wholesome, a fruit palatable. What does that mean ? Is the wholesomeness in the food, or the relish in the apple ? Apparently not ; even common-sense sees that; it is in the person eating the food. In the apple there is nothing but the power to affect the sense of taste in a certain way. We call sugar sweet. Is the case different? Perhaps common-sense will hesitate : Why, sugar is really sweet in itself. Of course it is, but what does that mean ? Upon closer examination you will find it to mean simply that sugar placed on the tongue tastes sweet. If it did not taste sweet, you would not say that it is sweet. The taste, however, is surely not in the sugar, but in you. There may be a power in it, a property that gives you such a taste. If there were no tongue, nothing would taste either sweet or bitter, and there would be neither sweetness nor bitterness in the world. And the same will be true of the qualities perceived by the eye and ear. If there were no ear, there would be no sounds ; if there were no eye, light and colors would not exist. All we can assign to things is a property or the power of affecting the sense-organs in such a manner as to produce certain sensations in consciousness. Modern natural science has discovered this force ; we know that the movement of air-waves or some other elastic medium is what produces the sensation of sound ; that the oscillatory motion of the ether arouses the sensation of light.

Here epistemological reflection usually makes its first stop. We should then have the following conception : Bodies exist outside in space ; they are extended, impenetrable, movable, and endowed with all kinds of powers. The qualities yielded by sense-perception do not, however, belong to them as properties; these are in the subject only, the things merely possess the power of arousing them. Moreover, there is absolutely no similarity between such powers and their effects. The sound does not resemble the air-vibrations which excite the auditory nerve; nor does light resemble ether-waves; nor is green a copy of the nature of the body which reflects green light. The sensible qualities are mere symbols of reality, just as letters are symbols of sounds, words symbols of ideas; they are not similar copies.

The epistemological reflection of the seventeenth century did not go beyond this view. Descartes, Hobbes, Spinoza, and Locke agree that sensible qualities exist only in the consciousness of the subject; outside of us, however, there are bodies in motion by which such sensations are aroused. Locke formulated this view in his classification of primary and secondary qualities. The primary qualities are extension, impenetrability, divisibility, and motion; they belong to the body as such, which is proved by the fact that they belong to all bodies, even to their smallest parts, and that they belong to them under all circumstances. The secondary qualities, color, taste, smell, and the like, do not belong to bodies as such, but only in relation to our sensibility. Even in our day, many physiologists and philosophers do not go beyond this view.

I do not believe that we can stop here. The distinction between primary and secondary qualities cannot be adhered to. Extension, solidity, and motion are no more absolute qualities of things than colors and sounds. The same arguments that lead us to refer the secondary qualities to the subject compel us to assume the subjectivity of the so-called primary qualities.

In the first place, we get our ideas of them from the same source, from perception, or at least not without perception. Without the sense of sight and the sense of touch, we could no more talk of extension and solidity than of sounds without hearing. Let us imagine a man born not only without the sense of sight but also without the senses of touch and motion, a man who has never experienced the movement of his own limbs or the resistance opposed to them by his surroundings. It would be just as impossible to make clear to him what a body is as it would be to make clear to a blind man what red or blue is. Hence corporeality is a constituent of perception.

Moreover, what is true of secondary qualities is true here also : Perception does not passively derive its content from the external world ; it produces the same spontaneously. Common-sense will be inclined to reason as follows : Extension is immediately perceived, the eye receives surface-images of extended bodies, the general intuition of space, however, is an abstraction from the spatial perceptual images. A little reflection on the facts of physiology will show the error of this notion. It is true, a spatial image of the object is traced on the retina, but this picture is not the percept. A percept is produced only when the impressions which the light-rays make upon the terminations of the optic nerve in the retina are conducted to the brain by the fibres of this nerve. But the actual image is, of course, not transmitted to the brain : the image is not detachable nor can the nerve-fibres transport such images. And even if the image could be detached and carried piece-meal over the separate fibres of the optic nerve to the brain, as through pneumatic tubes, and even if it could be joined together again in the brain, that would do us no good, for the brain is dark. And even if light were brought into it, that would not help us either, for we should need another eye to apprehend the image, and another brain to receive it. Hence whether there is extension in the external world or not, the space-picture is under no circumstances carried in from the external world, but produced anew on occasion of some excitation, just like sound or color. And the same is true of the impressions of the tactile sense. Finished spatial copies of bodies cannot be transported into consciousness by the touch-nerves. Lotze sets forth these arguments in a very convincing manner in his *Medizinische Psychologie :* Not extended images, but qualitatively different excitations are conducted to the brain by the separate fibres of the sense-nerves, and these cause the soul itself to construct the perceptual image. Consequently we have no more ground for regarding extension as an absolute determination or property of the things themselves than color or taste.

This conception destroys the objective existence of the body. A body, we should accordingly say, is a subjective creation that is produced by our intelligence on occasion of certain excitations. At any rate, we have no reason for asserting that something similar to our idea of a body exists outside of our world of ideas. Extension, solidity, and motion, like smells and tastes, colors and sounds, must be regarded as mere symbols of a transcendent reality.

Berkeley was the first to see the logical consequence of the epistemological reflection on the nature of perception, and to draw it without hesitation. Bodies are ideas, their existence consists in being perceived (*esse est percipi*). Besides, the older metaphysical school proceeding from different starting-points had again and again approached this conception; thus, for example, Spinoza and, in a greater degree, Leibniz. So Plato in Greek philosophy. All of them came to the conclusion that the spatial world cannot be the absolute reality; extension and divisibility are not compatible with absolute reality. The historical importance of Berkeley rests on the fact that he made epistemological idealism the basis for metaphysical idealism.

Kant introduced this conception into German philosophy: The corporeal world or the whole of nature is a phenomenal world that is subjectively conditioned. And subsequently epistemological idealism forms the starting-point for metaphysical idealism. This happens in a measure in Kant's own philosophy, although here metaphysics is squeezed in between the theory of knowledge and morals, and does not attain to an independent existence; but it is decidedly the case with speculative philosophy as well as with Schopenhauer and Herbart and their successors.

It is furthermore worthy of note that Kant leads his readers and, as it seems, was himself led to phenomenalism from a different starting-point, namely, from the critical reflection on the *nature of space and time*. What is *space* in and for itself? Common-sense, which regards it as an independent reality, imagines it to be somewhat like an empty vessel in which things exist and move. Even if the things were absent, empty space would still remain a reality existing in and for itself. But as soon as we attempt to take this view seriously, countless difficulties arise. What is this empty space anyhow? What is it that makes empty space more than nothing? Or, of what do the walls of the vessel consist? Or has it no walls at all, is it unbounded? It surely must be, for to imagine space as limited is utterly impossible; every boundary irresistibly points to something beyond. Well, a vessel that has no walls, and of which we cannot say anything at all and cannot tell in what it differs from nothing, is indeed a very strange reality, and Kant is not to be blamed for calling it "an existent nothing" (*ein seindes Unding*). The same remarks apply to *time*, the empty vessel containing all occurrences. Nay, the matter becomes even more wonderful here. Time consists of the past and of the future, which are separated by the movable present. Since, however, the past no longer exists and the future does not yet exist, time would be a reality consisting of two halves neither of which is real.

Kant believes that you can escape from all these difficulties if you make up your mind to say: Space and time are not existing realities; as such they would indeed be "existent nothings," but they are the subject's forms of intuition. Space is the form of external intuition, that is, the subjective arrangement of the visual and tactile sensations, to which also all other sensations are reduced. Similarly, time is the form of the inner sense. Of course, these forms of perception are not to be considered as ready-made empty drawers; they are merely functions that bring all elements into an ordered relation with each other. They are not innate either; though based on inherited tendencies, they are acquired or developed in the course of a lifetime. Empty space and empty time would then be our notion of the general possibility of bringing bodies and movements and inner processes into such particular relations with each other. This conception also removes the strange perplexity involved in the question : Are space and time finite or infinite ? Our answer will be : Neither the one nor the other. We cannot say of a numerical series : It is finite or it is infinite; but only : We can develop it from any given point. The same holds of space and time. It is possible to proceed from any given point in any direction whatever. There are no more obstacles in the way of our synthesis of space and time than in addition. Nor does analysis hit upon ultimate parts any more than division.

Kant embodies his meditations in the formula : Space and time have *empirical reality,* but *transcendental ideality.* For our perception of reality, space and time are universal and necessary conditions, and hence whatever is true of space and time in general is also true of nature, which is nothing but space and time filled with phenomena. But it is not true of things-in-themselves. We have no reason to believe that the order of our sensations is an absolute order of reality as such. Or to express the thought more concretely : We may imagine beings whose sense-organs and percepts are different from ours, and who therefore have different forms of arranging the elements. We can imagine an intellect for which neither the " before " and " after " nor " the outside " and " by the side of " have value or meaning. The parts of the mathematical demonstration or calculation are not outside of each other in space ; their symbols, the signs, are ; the factors themselves, however, are not, nor do they come before or after each other. It is true, in the consciousness of the man who works out the problem they occur in succession, but that is an accident; in themselves they are simultaneous, or rather, they have no relation to time at all. For a perfect consciousness only the inner conceptual relations of the elements would be present, without any intermixture of spatiality and time. Now if we imagine that the things themselves are like numbers, and that the same inner relations exist between them as between numbers, then the most perfect conception of reality would be that of the mathematician who can comprehend all these elements and their relations at a single glance or thought. And if we

are now further assured that the reality of existence consists in its being thought, we shall have the notion which
Kant introduces for the sake of clearness—the notion of
an *intellectus archetypus*, of a creative and non-sensuous
thinking. *Our* knowledge of reality, however, is external
and contingent; our intelligence does not create reality,
but by coming in contact with the existing world it is stimulated to produce sensations, and these do not express the
nature of objects as much as our own nature. Nor does
our intelligence grasp the real relations of things, the
inner mathematico-logical or æsthetico-teleological arrangement of the elements of reality, but, instead, orders our
sensations externally, in space and time.

To these reflections Kant adds another: Our intellectual forms, like our forms of intuition, have only empirical, not transcendent, validity. Causality and substantiality, the two highest categories, are subjectively necessary
forms of ordering our perceptions, and not existent forms
of absolute reality.

Such premises seem to necessitate an absolutely universal phenomenalism. The world of ideas nowhere coincides with reality ; we have no adequate knowledge either
of the outer or of the inner world.

One more step is possible : the abandonment of things-
in-themselves. Fichte is usually credited with having consistently completed the Kantian thought by repudiating
things-in-themselves. For things-in-themselves, it is held,
are really at variance with Kant's presuppositions. We
cannot enter the system without things-in-themselves, and
we cannot remain in it if we retain them. We have ideas ;
how can we pass from them to things-in-themselves? Kant
says : The latter affect us. Hence, according to the law of
causality he argues from sensations as effects to the
existence of things-in-themselves as causes. But he himself,
it is claimed, has made such an inference impossible by
conceding to the law of causality only empirical-immanent
and not transcendent validity.

Absolute phenomenalism would then be the ultimate
outcome of our reasonings : My world of ideas constitutes
the only reality ; beyond that there is nothing.

2. Reconstruction of the Realistic Conception for the Inner World.

I shall preface my examination of the phenomenalistic train of thought with a remark concerning the point just mentioned. Many an elaborate treatise in the epistemological literature of the present might make it appear as though there were really danger of our being forced to think : The world is the sum of my percepts and ideas, and outside of these there is nothing real whatever. I do not believe that the danger is very great. No normal mind, and perhaps no abnormal one either, ever, even for a moment, doubted the existence of a world independent of its own ideas. Nor did it ever enter Fichte's head to believe that he, Johann Gottlieb, and his thoughts made up the whole of reality. Hence we may for the present regard the refutation of so-called solipsism as a superfluous undertaking. The question is not: Do things exist outside of my world of ideas ? but, What does the claim mean, and how do we come to believe that a reality exists independently of our ideas, of which I and my ideas form an infinitely small part ? If the ego knows of the world only through its own ideas, how does it happen to pass from them to an absolutely existing reality ?

It seems proper that I should consider the other problem first: Is there any ground for the assertion of phenomenalism that our knowledge nowhere coincides with reality, that we have as little adequate knowledge of our own inner life as of the world outside of us ?

First, a word concerning the meaning and import of the question. It has been said that phenomenalism as it is taught by Kant is really a hopeless skepticism ; what room is there for knowledge if I cannot even know the real essence of my own self ? Kant's *Critique*, it is held, really destroys knowledge. The attempt has even been made to connect Faust's complaint,

> Ich sehe dass wir nichts wissen können!
> Das will mir schier das Herz verbrennen,

with Kant's *Critique*.

Such complaints and accusations are utterly groundless.

Above all, it must be said : No theory of knowledge causes the slightest change in the stock and the value of our knowledge. The sciences remain what they were before ; knowledge is not going to be abolished or destroyed by a theoretical reflection on knowledge. And the sciences will have the same value for us as before ; neither their practical nor their theoretical value is diminished by criticism. Our astronomy, physics, psychology, and history remain what they are, and they accomplish the same results, regardless of the outcome of subsequent epistemological reflections. Indeed, their historical development seems to be absolutely independent of epistemology.

Perhaps the misunderstanding is due to an improper use of terms. Kant's view is often stated in the formula: We know the phenomenon only ; we cannot penetrate into the inner essence of things. This seems to indicate a certain defect in our knowledge that could be ascertained and removed if only our intellect were enlarged and enlightened. When we say, the nature of the aurora borealis or of electricity is as yet unknown ; or, I do not clearly understand that man, we point out a defect in our knowledge ; for the present we know only the external phenomenon and not its ultimate causes; or, I know what the man looks like, what position he occupies in society, but I am unacquainted with his character, his principles, and his views, hence I do not know what to expect of him. When I know all that, when my knowledge of him is based on my long and friendly association with him, when I am certain how he is going to act and judge in a given case, then I say : I know the essence of the man.

The distinction, however, between a phenomenon and a thing-in-itself in epistemology means something quite different. If I had the most perfect knowledge of the disposition, the character, and the previous life of a man, so that I could predict his behavior with as much certainty as I can foretell an eclipse of the moon, still, according to Kant, I should not have anything but a knowledge of phenomena : I should know nothing whatever of the soul itself, nothing whatever of what it is in itself or in its essence.

What shall we say of the statement that we know things only as they appear, not as they are in themselves? Has it any foundation? Let us first investigate the knowledge *of our own inner life.* Here, too, the assertion is made: we must distinguish between the phenomenon and the thing-in-itself. Even the ego does not know itself as it is in itself, but only as it appears to itself. The essence of the soul, which manifests itself in states of consciousness, is as impervious to knowledge as the essence of the things, which occur in consciousness as a corporeal world in motion. Is there any truth in the claim?

I do not believe that we have any ground for saying so. Two assertions are included in the proposition: first, outside of or behind conscious states, the phenomena of soul-life, we have an additional element, the soul itself as a thing-in-itself; secondly, we do not know this thing-in-itself. The second item is undoubtedly true: all that we know of our self is in fact such states of sensation, presentation, feeling, and striving; a thing called soul or ego never occurs in our self-consciousness. But, we must immediately add, the first statement is without foundation: a separate thing called " soul " does not exist in reality. The notion of a soul having I know not what kind of reality as a thing-in-itself, apart from soul-life, is a barren abstraction. The soul itself is nothing but the unity of psychical life; its existence is identical with its "phenomena"; there is no such thing as a dark residuum of reality which knowledge fails to penetrate.

Although this conception has already been established above (pp. 129 ff.), the subject is of such importance for epistemology and metaphysics as to demand fuller consideration here. Whoever desires to reach a sound philosophy must sooner or later grapple with the question of a "soul-in-itself."

According to the notions of common-sense, reality is constructed about as follows. There are *three kinds* or *stages of reality:* (1) reality of the first order—*the things* or *substances;* (2) reality of the second order—*properties* or *powers;* (3) reality of the third order—*activities, events, and relations.*

The reality of the third order has the least independence. To become real, activities or events need some other thing by which they are temporarily introduced into existence; they need powers. But the powers or properties cannot exist by themselves either; they, too, require something else in which to inhere, that is, substances. The latter alone are self-dependent and need nothing else in order to exist, hence they constitute reality in the true sense of the word. The substances, again, popular metaphysics, following Descartes, divides into two classes, into corporeal or extended, and spiritual or thinking substances without extension. They have different powers, corresponding to their different natures. The general powers or qualities belonging to bodies are : impenetrability, weight, chemical affinities, in short, powers of attraction and repulsion. As psychical powers, however, we are to regard the faculty of sensation, memory, imagination, appetition, feeling, and will.

Is this a tenable hypothesis of the inner constitution of reality? Let us first direct our attention to the *properties* or *powers.* Do they really constitute a self-existent element of reality in addition to the phenomena or manifestations? Let us take any body whatever, a piece of chalk for example. It has a number of powers or properties. First, it has the quality of impenetrability, or the power to prevent other bodies from penetrating the space which it occupies; then it has the quality of whiteness or the power to reflect light falling upon it, in a particular manner; further, the quality of weight or the power to exert a pressure upon its support, or, if the support be removed, to execute a certain movement; it has, moreover, the property of a writing material, or the power to make white lines on a slate. What does all this mean? Do all these qualities or forces dwell in the chalk as separate realities, can we see them in it or otherwise discern them? Does the power to draw lines, or, to be more exact, to draw white lines on a black slate, inhere in the chalk as a characteristic, constantly-present, persistent element of reality? And of course a corresponding power or faculty of having lines drawn upon it dwells in the slate. And is there in the hand, besides the thousand other powers which it has, a writing-power, and does this exist in many forms as a chalk-, pencil-, or pen-power, as a German-, Latin-, Greek-letter-writing power? Surely no one believes that. To say that chalk has the power to draw lines means nothing but this: when it is passed over a rough surface, particles are detached from it which adhere to the slate and show traces of the movement. The lines are not in the chalk, nor does a line-power dwell in it; we simply anticipate what will happen under certain circumstances. Such fore-seen events—we call them possible—we combine, hypos-tasize, and then assign to the chalk as a permanent posses-sion. The same may be said of the other powers: we foresee that the chalk will, under certain circumstances, act in a particular manner, that it will, in a certain meas-ure, move, exert pressure, and accelerate another body. We hypostasize such anticipated processes, and ascribe them to the body as weight. And the same remarks apply to the active energy of a body in motion; the work which we expect of it we project into it as a force. Energy is therefore not a separate, existing reality, but a form of thought, by which we represent the connection of phenom-ena. A power is defined by its possible effects or by the work it performs. The explanation finds its complete ex-pression in a law of nature which states the amount of acceleration possible in a given mass.*

The same is true of the powers of the mental sub-stances. Here the matter is still more evident. We speak of moral powers, of a power of self-control, of courage. We simply mean that we expect a certain kind of behavior of a man when danger or temptation threatens him. We do not mean to say that self-control is situated in the soul as a peculiar substantial something. The same remarks apply to the memory, the intellect, the will, and to other powers of the soul. Psychology has long ago seen into that. Among the Germans it was especially Herbart who emphasized this point: the psychical faculties are not separate elements of reality and explanatory causes; ideas,

---

* See the discussion of the concept of force in Fechner, *Physik und philos. Atomenlehre*, 117 ff., and in Wundt, *System der Philos.*, 297 ff. Cf. also Helmholtz, *Populäre wissenschaftliche Vorträge*, 2. Heft, p. 190.

desires, and feelings are the realities, and the problem of science consists in discovering the uniform relations existing between such processes. Should any one find it impossible to part with powers as separate elements of reality inhering in substances, let him try his hand at answering such puzzling questions as the following : Is the power always active ? What is it doing when it is not acting? Are these powers scattered through the entire space which the body occupies? And how are they housed in unextended substances or connected with them?

If we abandon the notion of such intermediary powers, substances and events remain as explanations of reality. How about the *substances?* Are they separate realities alongside of the accidents?

Let us first consider the soul-substance. The opinion is that, in addition to the sensations, ideas, feelings, and desires, the soul itself exists as a separate reality or, to use Herbart's expression, as a real; that states of consciousness are merely activities of the soul, not, however, the soul itself. They may come and go, they may also, at least temporarily, disappear entirely, but the soul-substance remains as an unchanged and undiminished reality.

It seems to me to be utterly impossible to adhere to this conception. Soul-substances are exactly what soul-powers are, hypostatizations of processes; they are, one might say, hypostatizations raised to the second power. The soul-substance is the faculty of the faculties, the general faculty of such special faculties. As a power can be defined only by its effects, so a substance can be defined only by its powers; it is nothing but the sum-total of powers, hence, in the last analysis, a totality of possible events. The life of the soul consists in its activities, in the unity of correlated psychical states. If we take away the latter, no remainder is left over. States of consciousness constitute the real reality ; they do not need anything else, a soul-substantiality, to make them real or to hold and support them in reality. There is no such thing as that.

Common-sense will at first consider it hard, if not absolutely impossible, to abandon the notion of a bearer or support. Surely, a sensation or a feeling cannot exist absolutely; there must be a sensible or feeling being present that has it. Can there be an idea without some one to have it? Why, language itself repudiates the unreasonable claim. And how are we going to explain facts like the unity of consciousness, attention, self-observation, or self-control, without a soul?

Well, of course a soul exists, and it is not our purpose to get rid of it, but simply to come to some agreement as to what it is. Our contention is that it is not an unchangeable, rigid, absolutely persistent little point of reality, which, existing in and for itself, acts as a support for powers and processes, but the unity of psychical activity, the sum of the correlated conscious and subconscious inner states themselves. Each particular state in this totality is and is felt as a part belonging to the whole. The little bits of universal "reality-stuff," however, which some assume, have no real existence at all; they are nothing but the hypostasized shadows of false metaphysical notions.

The self-existent soul-substance is not so priceless and indispensable a possession of thought as popular metaphysics imagines. We may, perhaps, most easily convince ourselves of this truth by trying, at some time or other, to answer such questions as these: In what does the essence of the soul-substance consist? It must surely have an independent existence of its own, apart from its accidents, for it is supposed to be the precondition of the latter. Then what is it? Can you tell me? Or are you in the same predicament that confronted Locke when he examined the notion of substance? He finds that it is something or other, the essence of which cannot be ascertained.*

---

* *Essay*, II. ch. 23: "So that if any one will examine himself concerning his notion of pure substance in general, he will find he has no other ideas of it at all, but only a supposition of he knows not what support of such qualities which are capable of producing simple ideas in us." If any one should be asked, What is the support wherein these qualities inhere? " he would not be in a much better case than the Indian before mentioned, who, saying that the world was supported by a great elephant, was asked what the elephant rested on; to which the answer was, a great tortoise. But being again pressed to know what gave support to the broad-backed tortoise, replied, something, he knew not what."

Well, in that event you will certainly be able to tell us what it does or accomplishes. To be sure, it is the support to which the accidents adhere or in which they inhere. But what do these terms mean? I know very well what you mean when you say: The horse supports the rider. Does the soul support its thoughts in the same way? Or does a passion adhere to it as color adheres to the canvass? You answer: Such expressions are inappropriate figures of speech. Well, then make clear to us the meaning of your words. Perhaps you will say: I mean that the substance evolves the accidents out of its essence or is realized in them? But let us be sure whether that will mend matters. I know very well what you mean when you declare: A tree produces buds and fruit; a seed is realized in the shoots, cotyledons, etc., which it produces. But I really do not know what you mean by saying that an immaterial something or other brings forth ideas and feelings. It seems to me these are mere empty words—drafts, as it were, on a meaning which the imagination refuses to accept.

But you reply: Surely the unity of self-consciousness can be explained only by a unified and persistent soul-substance. I confess, I cannot understand what good such a substantiality is going to do us. It is a fact that our inner states are not isolated occurrences, and that each state is conscious of belonging to the unified whole of a particular individual life. I am no more able to explain how such a thing can happen than I can tell how consciousness itself is possible. One thing, however, I think I can clearly see: Such a hypothetical "support," the something or other which is dubbed soul-substance, does not by any means make the subject more intelligible; it is itself a riddle, but not the solution of a riddle. Can the mere fact that the states a, b, c, "inhere" in the same A produce the consciousness of their unity? In that case, every combination of accidents in a substance would be self-consciousness. Hence the soul-substance needs another special quality in order that its accidents may become parts of a unified consciousness. And the problem would consequently be to ascertain what this quality is, if the notion of substantiality is to do us any good. But, as far as I can see, we really lose nothing at all by abandoning this "something, I know not what."

To be sure, we should not therefore conclude that there is no soul, but simply: The soul is the plurality of inner experiences combined into a unity, in a manner not further definable. And we shall in no wise alter the popular mode of expression; we shall go right on speaking of the soul and the processes occurring in it, of the thoughts which it produces, and the inner feelings which it cherishes or rejects. Nor shall we have any scruples against applying the word substance to the soul or against speaking of its qualities and states. We shall not even discard the tabooed expression, faculty of the soul. All that we wish to do is to make clear to ourselves, once for all, what these words mean. It will be found that such traditional designations have their *raison d'être.* Only, they do not mean what a metaphysical system, misled by physical atomism, thinks they mean. If we designate that as substance which has independent being (in Spinoza's definition: *id quod in se est et per se concipitur*), then, indeed, the soul is substantial and the particular processes contingent (*in alio esse et per aliud concipi*). They exist and are conceived only in relation to the entire soul-life. It is a fact that sensations, ideas, thoughts, and strivings never, so far as we know, exist as isolated states, but always only as parts of a totality of inner processes called a soul-life. And the latter is not like a compound, the product of ready-made, particular elements, but, to repeat the words of Aristotle, the whole exists before the parts: the particular elements are, we might say, produced by the whole or posited with inner necessity as belonging to it and as essential to realize the whole.

An illustration will make the subject clear. A language consists of words; moreover, it consists solely of the sum-total of the words and forms. Take away all the words, and the language no longer exists. It does not remain behind as a separate reality, as a language-substance, in addition to the words. Yet, on the other hand, it is not an aggregate of previously-existing, separate words, as a wall is a combination of finished stones. But language constantly produces new words and modifies them as occasion demands. Each word is a contingent, perishable accident, which language creates, transforms, and finally abandons. Similarly, a poem is not a combination of separate verses, nor does it exist apart from the different verses as a self-existent substance; the idea of the whole posits the particular or unfolds itself in particulars. So, too, the soul does not exist apart from or under the states of consciousness as a hard, rigid, unchangeable real; it is merely in them, not, of course, in the sense of being compounded of previously-existing and independent elements; it produces the separate elements and is realized in them. Here, too, the idea of the whole posits the parts: this particular thought, or feeling, or desire can occur and be conceived only in this particular soul, and is therefore related to the latter as an accident to the substance.

Compared with the particular, inherent, dependent, and transitory element of consciousness, the soul-life as a whole is an independent and permanent being, a substance. If that is true, we cannot, of course, stop here. This whole must in turn be explained as the dependent member of a larger whole. The individual life, again, is related to the life of the people as an accident to its substance. The people or the national soul exists only in the individual souls, but here, too, not in the sense of being a combination of them; it produces them out of itself and realizes itself in them. And the life of a people is in turn inserted into a larger life, into the life of humanity, and is with the latter included in the unified total life of the earth, the external manifestation of which the physical history of the earth delineates. Ultimately, however, all life emanates from an all-embracing life, the unified life of God. From this direction too, then, we are carried to the thought: God is the substance, the only truly independent, self-existent being, to whom every particular reality is related as a dependent accident.

The idea which we have just developed is not new. Indeed, it may be said to run through the entire history of philosophy. I do not wish to write a history of it here, but simply to suggest a few points.

Epistemological reflections led Hume to it. We saw
before how he scattered the mists which surrounded the
notion of causality in the metaphysics of the school. He
likewise banished the phantom of a soul-substance lurking
behind the activity of the soul. In the concluding sections
of the first book of his first work, *The Treatise on Human
Nature*, he criticises the traditional metaphysical notion of
a soul-substance. He regards it as having no foundation
whatever. It is utterly impossible for him even to comprehend the meaning of the question as to whether ideas
inhere in a material or an immaterial substance, much less
to convince himself of the necessity of assuming an immaterial substance as the bearer of ideas. He consequently
prefers to stop at what exists: a totality of conscious states
comprehended into a unity by memory and causal relations.
"There are some philosophers," he declares in an oft-
quoted passage, "who imagine we are every moment intimately conscious of what we call our *self;* that we feel its
existence and its continuance in existence; and are certain,
beyond the evidence of a demonstration, both of its perfect identity and simplicity." He goes on to state that un-
luckily his experience does not agree with these assertions.
"For my part, when I enter most intimately into what I
call *myself*, I always stumble on some particular perception or other, heat or cold, light or shade, love or hatred,
pain or pleasure. I never can catch *myself* at any time
without a perception, and never can observe anything but
the perception."

Starting out from metaphysical speculations, Spinoza,
whose theory, it must be confessed, Hume introduced into
the discussion just mentioned, transformed the concept of
substance or rejected the popular interpretation of it.
Particular things are not substances, but accidents (*modi*);
this is true of bodies as well as of souls. Only God, the
sum-total of reality, is substance and independent; every
particular reality is posited in the All-One as dependent
and limited, with logico-mathematical necessity. To be
sure, God's substantiality is not to be conceived after the
pattern of an extended corporeal atom or of an unextended
psychical atom. His unity is not a contiguous or punctual

unity, but an ideal unity which realizes itself in a plurality of elements. Leibniz, too, who regards forces as constituting the essence of substance and finally comprehends the many finite substances into the unity of the one substance, really accepts the same view.

Proceeding from Hume, Kant comes to the conclusion that substantiality and inherence are to be conceived as forms of thought, not as forms of existence. That is, of course, equivalent to rejecting the notion that substance is a reality existing in and for itself. Substance is the persistent element in the *phenomenon*. It is true, this thought is afterwards somewhat obscured by the introduction of the thing-in-itself, which is alleged to be behind the phenomena. Every now and then it seems as though the thing-in-itself were identical with the hidden substance, the " something or other I know not what" of Locke. Fichte takes up the problem at this point, and that is the real significance of his oft-mentioned destruction of the thing-in-itself : His fundamental conception is that being is life, inner life. There is no such thing as a dead, rigid, absolutely persistent being, a soul-atom behind soul-life. A substance, having nothing but being, no more exists in the mental world than in the corporeal world, which, in truth, has no absolute existence at all, but is simply a reflection of the inner world. This thought remains the fundamental presupposition of all *speculative philosophy*, within which we cannot take a single step without having made it our own. Lotze gets it from this source. He emphatically rejects the notion of a universal reality-stuff, a little piece of which is supposed to be concealed in every real object as its innermost kernel. The soul is for him nothing but an existent idea, posited, in an inconceivable manner, in the form of independent activity. He does not consider it as needing an additional point of support in order to exist. Fechner adopts the same view, and Wundt now embodies it in his concept of the actual soul.* The expression suggests the *actus purus* of the schoolmen, the pure entelechy of Aristotle : God is *actus purus*, not

---

* Lotze, *Microcosmos,* II. 143, III. 531; *Metaphysik,* 100, 480; Fechner, *Atomenlehre,* 114; Wundt, *System der Philosophie,* 289, 585.

dead being; his essence is the eternal thinking of the absolute thought which constitutes reality. And that brings us back to the original source of this entire stream of thought, to Plato, the great founder of Western philosophy: The real world is an ideal world, an existing system of thoughts, and these thoughts constitute the true reality itself, and need nothing else in which and through which to be. The ideas are certainly not rigid images which stare at the world like lubbers, but a living content, such as we find realized in the soul.

Why is it that common-sense so vehemently protests against this conception? Our first feeling upon meeting it for the first time is undoubtedly that it is inconceivable; a thought must be in a soul-substance, otherwise it has nothing to hold it. And it will do no good to point out the weakness of the support. Popular metaphysics, which, let it be said, is not restricted to charcoal-burners and tile-makers, will still insist that without something to bear it, without a little block of reality to which to attach it, we cannot conceive how a thought can be real. Perhaps the ground for this inconceivability may be found in the following.

We may distinguish between real or *logical* and false or *psychological* necessity. The former belongs to every deduction that is formally correct. If you accept the premises, you cannot escape the conclusion. The unreal or psychological necessity, however, is the result of habit. Whatever we often or always see, hear, or think, at last seems necessary to us, and its opposite impossible. When the King of Siam was informed by the Dutch Ambassador that water sometimes becomes so hard and firm in his country that one can walk upon it, the King regarded the thing as utterly inconceivable and impossible. Had he studied scholastic philosophy in his youth, he would most likely have insisted on proving the impossibily: To be liquid, belongs to the essence of water; hence it is impossible for it to become rigid.

We meet such necessity everywhere. What I have never seen is impossible; that is the great principle which governs the judgment of the average intellect. The educated man who has no religion himself and who has never seen any really religious people does not believe that it is at all possible for any one to be religious; those who profess to be so are simply hypocrites or deceivers; at best they deceive themselves. A physiologist who has never observed hypnotic phenomena confidently declares such occurrences to be impossible. The same necessity of thought determines our ideas of the future: what does not exist to-day can and will never exist. No great change has ever occurred in historical life, the impossibility of which was not clearly demonstrated beforehand. Without slavery, intellectual culture is impossible; without flogging, discipline cannot be maintained in the army; without the Latin composition, the gymnasium is inconceivable.

The same necessity of thought controls popular physics. A heavy body that is not supported must fall; it cannot be conceived as retaining its position by floating freely in space. Inasmuch as the earth is a heavy body and does not fall, as our senses tell us, it must be supported; that is the cardinal teaching in all primitive cosmology. Hence, it either floats on water or, as the Hindoo philosopher already mentioned assumes, it is supported by a huge elephant, which in turn rests on a tortoise, and so forth, until the questioner grows tired of asking.

Well, the necessity of the soul-substance belongs to the same category. Sense-perception invariably teaches us that all properties and occurrences are attached to some substance: color, weight, heat, and motion are always in a body, in a tangible substratum. Consequently ideas and thoughts must also be attached to some substance. Popular thought, of course, first regards the body as such a substance. But now a strange difficulty arises. Psychical states cannot be attached to an extended substance; how are we to imagine a feeling of love or hatred in or upon a brain or ganglionic cell? Is the feeling itself distributed over the extended mass? Does the notion of a circle, do the propositions relating to parallels, occupy a space in the brain? Perhaps when the thought is thought: It is impossible to square the circle, a series of movements or chemical changes or some other processes take place in more or less extended areas of the gray matter, but all that *is* not the thought itself. It is evident, the thought cannot be imagined as a process distributed in space. It is this difficulty which gave rise to the notion of a special soul-substance. We cannot employ the common notion of an extended substance ; we cannot abandon the substance altogether ; consequently there must an unextended or *immaterial substance.*

Of course, the immaterial substance is a marvellous thing. What it gives with one hand it takes back with the other. Hence a tendency arises again to trade off this unreal shadow of a substance for the real tangible thing which we know how to handle. Everywhere we observe how the natural tendency of thought invariably endeavors again to materialize the spiritual substratum, to imagine it as a fine, wholly ethereal substance. Only in this way is the term rendered acceptable to the intuition ; we cannot imagine the unextended, immaterial soul-atom. Hence the spiritualism which needs a soul-substantiality always relapses into materialism. The fact is, if you are unable to conceive that a thought exists as an independent reality, without being attached to a substance, you are necessarily a materialist, however much you may protest against the accusation. Spiritualism consistently carried out is possible only on condition that we discard such a shadowy corporeal substance and regard psychical states as floating freely in reality, just as we have accustomed ourselves to conceive the heavenly bodies as floating in space unsupported.

We now return to the original question : Do we know the real essence of our own inner life? The answer is : Certainly ; in consciousness it occurs as it is in itself. Feelings, strivings, ideas, and thoughts are felt, presented, thought, as they are in themselves ; indeed, their being is nothing but their being felt and being thought. If now the soul consists in nothing but the content of soul-life, if no dark, impenetrable soul-atom is left over as a residuum, we shall say : The distinction made between a phenomenon and a thing-in-itself has absolutely no meaning here. Being and being known coincide at this point. Of course, empirically considered, even the knowledge of one's own ego is limited and deficient. Of our past life nothing but fragments are retained in memory, and these are joined together into a total view, and interpreted now in one way, now in another, according to what for the time being occupies the foreground of consciousness. Beneath the threshold of consciousness a thousand processes are constantly taking place, which only occasionally cast their shadows into consciousness or disturb the course of our ideas and emotions. Besides, the future is dark. Only gradually, as life advances, is our own ego revealed to us, not unfrequently disappointing our own ideas and expectations of ourselves. Hence a much more extensive and profound knowledge of my ego than I possess is undoubtedly conceivable. In a measure and under certain circumstances such a knowledge may be acquired even by others. The biographer who possesses the advantage of surveying a finished life as a whole, together with its preconditions and its effects upon others, often judges more clearly and soundly than the hero himself. But all this simply means that our knowledge of self is limited by experience. But there is no such thing as transcendental limitation here ; no distinction can be made between a thing-in-itself and a phenomenon. And so we regain the first and fixed point for a *realistic* view of knowledge : *I know reality as it is in itself in so far as I am that reality myself.*

Let me briefly consider an objection that might be raised against this assertion on the strength of a previous discussion. We agreed with Kant that time is not an absolutely existent order of the absolute reality, but a subjective form of intuition, and I do not believe that we can retract our statement. Time can be construed only as an order of arrangement for the elements of consciousness. It is conceivable that for a different intelligence the order of the before and after does not hold, or at least not in the same way ; it may perceive reality as timeless, *sub specie æternitatis,* to use Spinoza's expression. But inasmuch as we necessarily present our inner life as taking place in time, our knowledge of self also seems to become phenomenal.

I reply : Here too we have to deal with an empirical rather than with a transcendental limitation. We cannot say that this falsifies the knowledge of our own inner life. Such an absolute intelligence, which would regard reality as timeless, could not really see anything in my life different from what I see. If it did, I should say : I am not what you see ; the phenomenality or inadequacy is all in you. Such a hypothetical absolute intellect does not perceive a different content from my own, it simply sees it differently ; it has a more comprehensive, an all-embracing view of the same content. A thousand years would be but a single moment for a being that would survey the yearly revolution of the sun around the earth at a glance, as our eye sees the oscillation of a second-pendulum, or that would survey the evolution of a planetary system as we see the growth and the withering of a blossom. In the sight of the Eternal One, time vanishes altogether. He sees the past and the future as one ; at every moment he sees all causes and all effects, that is, he sees reality as a unified whole, as an ideal system in which each element is conditioned by the whole and is essential to the whole. The boy who is learning to read, first sees letters only, gradually he notices words, then he learns how to construct sentences and to understand their meaning, and finally the man is able to comprehend a book as one single great thought which unfolds its content in a plurality of elements. The connection between these elements is, then, not temporal but eternal. A logical or æsthetical necessity unites all the parts and assigns a place to each. God perceives all things in this manner ; the time-succession is lost in the inner relation, in the inner conditional order, to use Lotze's terms (*Microcosmos*, III. 599), according to which the most remote and most immediate are combined in his consciousness. Our poor consciousness strives to combine words and sentences ; it can grasp even its own content, only by running over it successively in memory. And of the thousand relations which it bears to the world, only a few are occasionally noted ; of its causes and still more of its effects it has but the most general knowlege. Our life is like groping in a labyrinth. God's knowledge of our life is like the view of the man who looks down from above and surveys all the tortuous passages at a glance.

3. The Knowledge of the External World.

The existent world is presented to our consciousness as a world of bodies in motion. Bodies, however,—such was the result of the epistemological reflection from which we started out,—are phenomena, subjective creations that are composed of elements of perception and presentation. Whatever we may predicate of a body—that it is sweet, white, heavy, extended, impenetrable, soluble in water, decomposable into such and such chemical elements—may ultimately and invariably be reduced to sense-qualities and percepts. Corporeal objects are permanent sensations ; their essence consists in the different forms of their sensibility. Or, to speak with J. S. Mill : Bodies are permanent possibilities of sensation.* When I say, This corporeal thing exists, it means when reduced to its simplest terms : I am convinced that such and such percepts are possible in such and such combinations. When I say, Here lies a piece of paper, it means : I have certain visual percepts, and I would have certain tactile sensations if I were to execute certain movements. On leaving the room I say : A piece of paper is lying in there on the table. This means : I am convinced that if I or any one else should go in, we should be able to see and feel such and such things. Unless I believed that, I would not make these assertions. If on going into the room I should not find what I expected, I should declare : The paper has disappeared. In case I do not believe in the possibility of having such percepts in some place or other, I shall say : The paper no longer exists, at least not in its old form ; and if I do not believe in the possibility of perceiving its remnants somewhere or other, in the shape of ashes or mould, I shall say : It has ceased to exist altogether. Hence the relation to perception universally obtains. When we speak of the reality of corporeal objects, we mean possibility of perception.

---

* J. S. Mill, *An Examination of Sir W. Hamilton's Philosophy* (1865), ch. XI.

But common-sense will reply : The paper surely remains, even when I cease to perceive it. The elements of which it consists will still be present long after life itself has become extinct on our earth, just as they existed before there was such a thing as life and feeling. Certainly ; only, the meaning of the proposition is simply this : Had a feeling and presenting being been present, he would have been able to have such and such perceptions, he would have seen the earth, say as a liquid mass of fire, and in it he would have perceived the carbon, which after a thousand transformations was finally converted into paper. But we can never get rid of such a point of relation, a particular consciousness. We may ignore it in each particular case because it is a regular and universal precondition, but we cannot brush it aside altogether. To assign existence and qualities to a corporeal object always means to posit it as the sum of possible percepts for a possible consciousness ; without perception and consciousness, no body. Consequently, bodies have only relative, not absolute, existence ; or they are, to use Kant's words, phenomena for a " consciousness in general."

Does an absolute existence, an existence in and for itself, correspond to such relative existence, to the existence for a consciousness ? Are the phenomena which we call bodies manifestations of a reality that exists regardless of my consciousness?

Everybody is convinced that they are. We all believe that the world is more than a phantasmagoria in our consciousness, that the phenomenal corporeal world suggests a thing-in-itself that appears in it. What is that thing-in-itself ? Kant says : We do not know and cannot know ; it is the necessary correlate of consciousness, the transcendent. Is the case really so hopeless ? I do not believe it. I think we may say with Schopenhauer and with all idealistic philosophy : We do indeed know something about what reality is in itself. Everybody believes he knows at least what living creatures are in themselves. They are presented to us as bodies having a peculiar structure and manifold external and internal processes of movement. Even the most penetrating physiological analysis reveals nothing else. Nevertheless everybody believes that there is still another reality present here, and that is an *inner life*, comparable with that which he experiences in himself.

What is the ground for such a view ? Schopenhauer is evidently right when he discovers the reason for it in the fact that we look at ourselves from two aspects. I have immediate knowledge of myself as a willing, feeling, perceiving, presentative being. On the other hand, I also know myself as a corporeal being. I perceive my body and present it as a corporeal object among others. Now a regular correspondence occurs between processes of inner life and corporeal life. Feelings are accompanied by changes in the circulation and in the demeanor of the body, impulses and strivings by movements in the entire organic system or in parts of it. Effects on the body appear as inner states, as feelings or sensations. Hence the life of my body is the mirror of my soul-life ; the bodily organism is the externally-perceivable expression of the will and its system of impulses, the body is the visible manifestation or the phenomenon of the soul.

The ego, which is thus known to itself as a dual being, furnishes the key for our interpretation of the external world. Schopenhauer calls to mind the bilingual inscription of Rosette, by means of which it first became possible to decipher the Egyptian hieroglyphics. Here the same content was expressed in known and in unknown characters, which led to the interpretation of the unknown signs. In a like manner the coexistence of the inner and outer sides of reality in our own life furnishes the key for the interpretation of the external side in general. We come to regard the corporeal forms and processes as symbols of inner processes. We acquire remarkable skill in interpreting human beings. Every movement, every gesture, every twitch of the facial muscles becomes an intelligible symbol of an inner state. In speech we wholly forget that we are dealing with symbols; we have an idea that we immediately hear or read thoughts. It requires some reflection on our part to discover that we get nothing from without except vibrations of the atmosphere which are caused by a body through a peculiar mechanism. Similarly, everything that a book presents to our perception consists solely in little accumulations of printer's ink on white paper. Thoughts no more lie within the leaves of a book than they float to our ears through the air. The reader or hearer creates thoughts by interpreting symbols which, taken by themselves, contain no thought whatever. If the book contained ready-made thoughts simply waiting for us to take them out, there would be no need of an art of interpretation, nor would there be any difference of opinion as to their meaning.

How far may we go in this process of interpretation? No hard-and-fast line can be drawn. In general we may say: Our ability to interpret the corporeal world diminishes in proportion as the bodily occurrences grow unlike our own bodily states. The greater the similarity and the closer our relations to such bodies are, the more correctly will we interpret them. We understand our most immediate surroundings best; the certainty of our knowledge diminishes as we pass to the people of our own tribe and country. It is much harder to understand the citizens of a foreign nation, especially the subtler, more spiritual phases of their inner life. Only by the most painstaking study of their language do we gain possession of the most important system of thought-symbols, and as a rule this too is a more or less imperfect instrument. The art of interpretation fails to distinguish the finer shades of difference between ideas and feelings. Only when we have become assimilated with a foreign nation in consequence of long association with its people and have become a part of it, as it were, do we acquire that nice understanding of them which we have for the soul-life of our own people. Moreover, even within a particular nation there are social barriers that make it more or less difficult for the different classes to understand each other. It is still harder to appreciate different races and different circles of civilization. All that we can do here is to observe the general characteristics of their mode of thinking and feeling. When we descend to the animal kingdom we no longer have language to guide us, the most delicate system of symbols, in which the presentative side of the soul objectifies itself. Hence we can form only very vague notions of this phase of the inner life of animals. The volitional side is more intelligible to us ; from analogous organic systems and their functions we infer analogous impulses and feelings. In the measure in which the similarity between the organic systems grows fainter and fainter, our knowledge of this factor also diminishes. In the lower animal world the analogy simply suffices to acquaint us with the most general characteristics of an inner life ; in the vegetable kingdom we are still less able to comprehend the psychical aspect; while in the inorganic world even the last faint trace vanishes : the corporeal world then wholly ceases to be a decipherable symbol of an inner life. Epistemological considerations, however, point to the existence of an inner side in the latter case also, just as our previous metaphysical speculation, which insisted on the uniform connection between the inorganic and the organic worlds, suggested it. To say that inorganic bodies are merely bodies is equivalent to saying that they have relative existence only and are nothing in themselves at all. Whoever refuses to accept this proposition will have to grant that the elements of inorganic matter are also symbols of something in itself, the nature of which we can determine only by following the direction indicated by the development of this thing-in-itself in the animal world.

The result of our discussion would therefore be : I know reality as it is in itself, in so far as I am real myself, or in so far as it is, or is like, that which I am, namely, spirit. This is the truth contained in the old saying of Greek philosophy : The like is known only by the like.

In this connection it is worthy of note that a peculiar relation exists between our external or phenomenal knowledge and our understanding of phenomena which rests on interpretation. We may express it in the form of a paradox : *The better we conceive things, the less we understand them,* and conversely. We conceive the inorganic processes best, that is, we can define them so accurately as to make them calculable. The vital processes are not so easily reduced to conceptual mathematical formulæ and calculation. Biology works with empirical laws altogether, the complete reduction of which to ultimate elementary laws of nature has so far proved to be impossible. Man is the most incalculable being in existence. Hence it is that his acts are still regarded as absolutely indeterminate, or as the effects of an indeterminate agent, the so-called free will, which is simply equivalent to denying the possibility of conceiving or defining him. The reverse is true when it comes to understanding him. Human life is the only thing that we understand perfectly. We reach the maximum of understanding in history; it is less complete in zoology and botany, and vanishes altogether in physics and astronomy, where we have the most perfect mathematical conception of things.

Let us sum up our thoughts in an illustration. The universe is written in a cipher that has many signs. Each symbol, each more or less independent corporeal system, stands for a divine thought, for a concrete idea that is an element of the one, great, all-embracing idea of reality. The human mind knows how to decipher but a few of these ingenious signs with any degree of certainty, that is, the symbols of human life, with which it is most familiar. Other signs, as, for example, the different species of organic life on the earth, are somewhat analogous to these: and even here the translation of the cipher is very imperfect—think of the instincts of animals. Finally, we are encompassed by innumerable signs, the existence of which we do indeed observe, while their meaning eludes every attempt at interpretation. I refer to the domain of physico-chemical and astronomical facts.

I shall now briefly consider the question: How does the belief arise that there is a reality independent of my presentation? Only my states of consciousness are immediately known to me. How does it happen that I pass beyond them to a transcendent reality and regard myself and my consciousness and its content as a dependent member of such an actual world?

This belief is rendered possible by what the ego experiences as a *willing* being. It becomes aware of its own strivings and their goal, and simultaneously recognizes the obstructions which are placed in their way. Its expectations of the future are disappointed by the reality, the current of its ideas is diverted from its spontaneous course, purposes are crossed, movements miss their aim. Such inner experiences are surely the primary conditions on which our division of the world into the ego and the non-ego depends. If they were entirely absent, the world would not be split up in this way at all. A merely presentative being, whose ideas are devoid of feeling, or a being whose will is absolutely realized, one to whom every willed idea is immediately presented as a perceived reality, would have no conception of an objective world existing outside of his own ideas. He would present his ideas and think his thoughts as a mathematician thinks his formulæ and figures.

The further development of the opposition between the ego and the non-ego in our perception of reality is, in the main, conditioned by the following facts:

(1) We distinguish our own body from other bodies. Our own body, which is immediately known to us by sense-perception, not otherwise than other bodies, necessarily comes to occupy a unique position, if only for the reason that its movements and contacts with other bodies are more immediately related to acts of will and feelings than the movements and contacts of other bodies. Furthermore, the perception of its own parts and movements forms a constant and identical background for the perception of all others.

(2) We distinguish between *possible* and *real* percepts. This, too, is a distinction which everybody learns to make. I see an object, then I close my eyes and do not see it. But I am convinced that I can at any moment see it again; my conviction is regularly verifiable by experiments. I leave my house or the town in which I reside; I see a thousand strange sights, and yet I am convinced that everything at home remains what it was; which means, I believe that, should I at any time change my position, I should be able again to see the same old objects. And when I return home this is found to be the case. The same remarks apply to the external world. There it is, ever ready to be reconstructed by perception. Thus I make a world out of

possible percepts, and the real percepts seem to comprise but an infinitesimal segment of the possible ones. Now these possible percepts constitute what in popular language is called the objective reality, while the real percepts are construed as the effects of this objective world upon the consciousness of the subject.

We may with J. S. Mill * explain the fact that the possible percepts preponderate over the real ones, about as follows : The possible percepts, or, in Kantian philosophy, the *phenomena*, are, as distinguished from the *sensations*, persistent and not dependent on volition. The real percepts are constantly changing, the content of consciousness is different for every given moment of time, and this change depends on my volition; each movement of the eye yields a different content. The possible percepts, however, the sensibilia or phenomena, are persistent and not dependent on volition. While I may at any instant cause the real percepts to disappear, the possible ones are, on the whole, constant. I can at any given moment stop perceiving the moon in the heavens, but I cannot in the same way remove the possibility of seeing it. This is why different subjects have the same possible percepts and the same connections between them, but not the same real ones; also, why the appearance of possible percepts is calculable and that of the real ones not. We may calculate the time when the moon becomes visible, that is, we may predict its rise, but we can never tell when and whether a particular individual will really see it. Hence all sciences inquire only into the possible percepts or the phenomena and their connections; they are not concerned with the contingent connections between real percepts in the individual consciousness: *Natural laws* are formulæ which express *the constant relations existing between phenomena*, as distinguished from *associations of ideas in the subjective consciousness*.

Thus arises the idea of an objective world. Consciousness is absolutely ignorant of this psychological process. It regards the corporeal world as an absolutely existent

* *An Examination of Sir W. Hamilton's Philosophy*, pp. 192 ff.

reality. Epistemological reflection alone leads to the view that the necessary correlate of such an objective world is a "consciousness in general," as Kant says, a constructing subject equipped with synthetic functions, and that we must presuppose behind the phenomenon, a being-in-itself, of which the phenomenon is the symbol. We have already hinted at the nature of this being: a self-existent inner life alone fulfils the conditions of the absolute being.

CHAPTER II.

THE PROBLEM OF THE ORIGIN OF KNOWLEDGE.

THE question concerning the origin of knowledge gives rise to the opposition between *Rationalism* and *Empiricism* or *Sensationalism*. Empiricism derives all knowledge from experience. Rationalism, on the other hand, asserts: Scientific knowledge cannot come from the senses at all; universality and necessity are essential to it; hence it is a product of the understanding.

I shall attempt to explain these theories and my attitude towards them in the form of a historical exposition.*

1. Rationalism.

The standpoint of common-sense in reference to our question—if it has any views on the subject at all—most nearly approaches sensualism : Our knowledge of things is derived from sense-perception.

As soon as philosophy rejects and opposes the popular conception of the universe, the rationalistic theory arises. Philosophy claims for itself an origin different from the one conceded to popular thought. It may be that the latter derives its knowledge about things from the senses, but scientific knowledge or philosophy in no wise springs from perception ; it is the product of thought or reason.

The great systems of Greek philosophy are unanimous on this point. However much they may differ concerning

---

*A. Riehl, *Der philosophische Kriticismus und seine Bedeutung für die positive Wissenschaft* offers an elaborate historical exposition and discussion of the problem. The reader will also find a brief sketch of the history of these systems in modern times, in my *Versuch einer Entwickelungsgeschichte der Kantischen Erkenntnisstheorie* (1875).

the nature of things, they are agreed that truth does not come from the senses. Heraclitus finds fault with the senses: "Eyes and ears are bad witnesses to men, if they have souls that understand not their language." He means that only those can learn anything from the senses who know how to interpret their testimony with critical understanding. The philosophy of the Eleatics is still more emphatic in its repudiation of the senses and opinion as sources of truth. The understanding alone furnishes us with truth; the senses produce a mere deceptive illusion; they present the One and the Real as a plurality, as moved, as originating and decaying. Zeno undertakes to prove by reason the inconceivability and hence the impossibility and unreality of the sensible world. The other two antipodes, Democritus and Plato, likewise agree that the understanding alone, not perception, leads to truth. To be sure; the senses see neither the atoms nor the ideas; these are seen by the understanding only, which penetrates through the manifoldness of phenomena to their ultimate ground, to the real reality.

The great systems of our modern philosophy are also rationalistic in their epistemology. Think of Descartes, Hobbes, Spinoza, and Leibniz. Mathematics is their starting-point. A mathematical physics, and ultimately a mathematical theory of the universe, is what they are driving at. It is evident, we can no more reach this by perception and experience than pure mathematics itself. Moreover, it is one of the aims of modern philosophy—at least in the opinion of some modern philosophers—like old scholasticism, to serve as a rational theology and to prove the existence of God and the immortality of the soul; a task for which experience is certainly inadequate. The rationalistic theory of knowledge thereby gains the reputation of orthodoxy, while empiricism is to this day suspected of heterodoxy. Even now the statement is frequently made, at least in Germany, that empiricism leads to materialism and atheism.

Rationalism is, therefore, the earliest form of a scientific theory of knowledge. It was created by the great metaphysical systems as the epistemological vindication of their claims. Empiricism is of later origin ; it arises as a crit-icism on the metaphysical systems and their epistemology.

Let me first outline the fundamental features of the ra-tionalistic theory. Its thesis is, let us say : All real or scientific knowledge is the product of the understanding; it is the result of an immanent evolution from *a priori* cer-tain principles that are not derived from perception or verifiable by experience. Mathematics serves as the pat-tern for this method. Two problems force themselves upon our attention, and their solution really constitutes the epistemology of rationalism : 1. How do we arrive at these first principles which form the absolute starting-points of knowledge ? 2. How does it happen that a system produced by the activity of pure reason yields us an objec-tive knowledge of reality ? For it is evidently the object of all sciences to tell us what reality is, and the harmony which exists between such an *a priori* system of thought and the real world is apparently not a matter of course but, when you come to think of it, a wonderful coincidence.

We may distinguish three fundamental forms of ration-alism according to the different answers that can be given to our two questions : *metaphysical, mathematical,* and *formal* rationalism. Plato, Spinoza, and Kant may stand as the representatives of these principal forms.

Metaphysical rationalism rests on the assumption that reality-in-itself is thought ; hence we can know it by pure thinking. It is Plato who, prepared by Eleatic specula-tion, was the first to make this conception the corner-stone of a great philosophical system. His thought is based on the conviction that the world of sense-perception is not the real world ; reality as such is an actual system of concepts or thoughts, a world of ideas. How do we reach a knowl-edge of it? Plato's answer is not really epistemological, but in line with his metaphysics. The soul is something that is in its original essence homogeneous with the real reality. Its real essence is thinking or spirit. The soul does not appear in its earthly guise as what it is in reality, as pure thought. Here its nature is obscured or corrupted by the admixture of sensuous elements, by perception and desire. The life on earth, however, is but a stage in its

being ; the soul itself existed before its incorporation, and
it will continue to exist after being separated from the
body. Its bodiless state is its real form ; here it comes
into immediate contact with the real reality ; it contemplates ideas, that is, thinks the actual thoughts. In the
body its thought is obscured by the senses. Or, as the
famous simile in the *Republic* says : As human beings, sit-
ting in a cave with their necks and legs chained and their
backs to the light, see nothing but the shadows which the
objects moving before the entrance throw upon the wall of
the den, so the soul dwells in the cave of the body and sees
all kinds of shadows coming to it from passing objects
through the openings of the body, through the eyes and
the ears. True, it has retained a faint trace of the real
thought, a reminiscence, as it were, of its former incorporeal
state when its vision was clear. And its mission in this
world is to do all it can to free thought from the senses,
which have buried it beneath falsehood and illusion. Mathematics and dialectics, the two great forms of conceptual
knowledge, are the means to this end.

I shall not discuss Aristotle's criticism of this rationalism, nor his attempt to found a theory of knowledge that
comes nearer to empiricism. Although Aristotle is so
severe and often unjust in his judgment of Plato, he has
not been able to offer anything in place of the latter's views.
His philosophy contains the rudiments of an empirical
theory, and these come from his observation, and also the
beginnings of a rationalistic theory which are rooted in his
syllogistic. But he makes no attempt to reconcile the two
thoughts. Let me, however, call to mind that the Platonic
conception has been revived in the speculative philosophy
of our century. We find the same fundamental conception
in Hegel: Reality as such is thought, an idea unfolding
itself with inner necessity. Perfect knowledge consists in
thinking the actual thoughts over again. In the dialectical
evolution of philosophical thinking the self-existent and
active absolute idea is repeated, or rather becomes conscious
of itself.

The *mathematical* rationalism of the seventeenth century
is another form of rationalism. It is distinguished from

382 PROBLEM OF THE ORIGIN OF KNOWLEDGE. [Book II.

Platonic rationalism in that it remains immanent. It
asserts : All sciences, particularly and above all the natural sciences, can and must adopt the method of mathematics; they must assume the form of a demonstrative
system deduced from principles. Descartes and Hobbes
agree in this fundamental presupposition; Spinoza attempted to apply it formally in his *Ethics ;* Leibniz, who
had already taken his stand in reference to the empirical
critique that had in the meanwhile sprung into prominence, sought to retain it with certain restrictions.

The following answer is given to the two questions proposed by rationalism (cf. p. 380). Descartes sometimes replies to the question concerning the value of the first principles of demonstrative knowledge, by saying: They are
innate ideas. The expression comes from Platonic philosophy. It is, however, only the old term without the old
meaning. Descartes does not advocate the doctrine of
pre-existence and recollection. This is what he means:
There are cognitive elements which are original products
of the intellect and do not need to be verified by experience. Mathematics is a proof of that. Definitions and
axioms constitute its principles; their truth does not depend
on perception and observation. The definitions of mathematics are concepts which the understanding assumes
unconditionally. The intellect is not determined by perception, but solely by its own functions, when it establishes
the definition of the circle and the tangent, of the power
and the logarithm. Hence axioms are propositions the
validity of which is not proved by experience; they are
recognized by the understanding as absolutely self-evident,
as soon as they are understood.

Now true science universally assumes this form. This
is particularly the case in physics, which is ultimately
nothing but a branch of mathematics. Descartes's philosophy is, above everything else, a system of thought that
aims to prove the possibility of a purely mathematical
physics. Hence the essence of corporeal nature is restricted
to pure extension; it has geometrical properties only, no
inner ones; hence it is subject to purely mathematical
treatment. *Corpus est res extensa:* that is a mathematical

definition, like the definitions of the angle or circle. The
same is true of the definition of the soul: *Mens est res (mere)
cogitans.* Axioms are added: *e.g.*, the proposition of the
conservation of substance: The quantity of matter is neither
augmented nor diminished; or the proposition of the conservation of energy: The quantity of motion is unchangeable; motion neither originates nor is lost, but is merely
transferred from body to body. On the basis of such
definitions and axioms, natural science is to be developed
as a demonstrative system of mechanics. The value of
perception is here fundamentally the same as in geometry:
it may give the first impulse to the formation of notions
and propositions. But demonstration alone constitutes a
real and perfect science.

We can now also answer the second question: How
shall we explain the harmony between such a system of
propositions developed in a purely immanent way and
reality? Descartes answers: These definitions resemble
mathematical concepts which are valid in themselves and
need no verification by experience. He embodies his
thought in a general proposition: What I perceive clearly
and distinctly is true. Every notion that is in itself clear
and distinct is valid, and its conceivability or possibility is
the guarantee of its validity. *Quidquid clare ac distincte
percipio, verum est;* this proposition clearly betrays its
mathematical origin.*

---

* In the third of the *Meditationes de prima philosophia* the proposition
has the appearance of being deduced from the *cogito ergo sum*. This is, of -
course, mere semblance. Indeed, the entire course of reasoning from absolute doubt to the absolute certainty of the *cogito ergo sum*, as well as the
deduction therefrom: the existence and veracity of God, which in turn is to
form the basis or the certainty of all scientific knowledge, is an after-
thought and an altogether gratuitous substruction for previously-established views. These previously-established views are: Mathematics is an
absolute science; compared with it, all previous sciences, especially metaphysics and scholastic physics, are uncertain, or rather no sciences at all.
They may, however, become such if they can be made mathematical. Since
Galileo's day this can be done for physics. The secret powers and entities
have been abandoned and are replaced by mathematical explanation and
calculation. Descartes finds that metaphysics, too, may, in a certain measure, become mathematical. Here, too, we may form certain concepts having absolute validity, *e.g.*, the notion of the most real being, of an *ens
realissimum sive perfectissimum*. Modern physics itself tends to the notion

This view is constantly carried out in the philosophical system of Spinoza. *Ethica more geometrico demonstrata* is the title of his principal work. He rigorously applies the mathematical method. All sciences, metaphysics, physics (outlined in a few propositions of the second book), the theory of knowledge, psychology, ethics with the fundamental notions of politics, are treated after the pattern of geometry. Each book begins with definitions and axioms; propositions and proofs, corollaries and scholia, follow. The whole of philosophy constitutes a system of necessary formulæ, deduced from necessary concepts and axioms. The answer to the questions concerning the harmony between this system and reality is given by Spinoza's metaphysics. The parallelism between the two attributes, thought and extension, is used as a basis for his epistemology: one and the same substance or all-real being reveals itself in the corporeal world and in the world of thought in a system of modifications. And for this reason the order and connection of the ideal world corresponds to the order and connection in the corporeal world. What appears in the latter as cause and effect is in the former ground and consequent: *sequi* and *causari* are fundamentally the same.*

2. Empiricism.

The second great school of modern philosophy, *English Empiricism*, subjects this mathematical rationalism to criticism. Locke and Hume are its chief representatives.

The fundamental conception of empiricism is: There are *two kinds of sciences, differing in nature and method*—purely *conceptual sciences*, like *mathematics*, and *objective sciences*, like physics and psychology. Rationalism errs in recognizing only *one* form of science, the mathematical, and in attempting to fashion all sciences after its pattern. That is an

---

of an absolute unity of reality. This conception is made the corner-stone of the systematic exposition. The object is clearly apparent.

* *Ethica*, II. 7: *Ordo et connexio idearum idem est ac ordo et connexio rerum.* We must add, however, that the psycho-physical parallelism between states of consciousness and nervous processes is here improperly transformed into an epistemological parallelism between the logical combinations of concepts and natural laws of motion.

impossible undertaking; the sciences dealing with matters
of fact, natural and mental sciences, wholly differ from
mathematics in content and method.*

It is characteristic of mathematics that it makes no
assertions concerning the existence and behavior of reality,
but deals solely with deductions from notions. Geometry
does not say : This figure is a circle ; this body is a sphere,
and its motion has the form of an ellipse but : Such and
such consequences follow from the definition of the circle
and the sine. Whoever accepts the definition must also
accept its deductions ; he is bound by logic to do so. It is
wholly immaterial whether or not anything exists corresponding to the notion.

The case is quite different in the other group of
sciences, which deal with objects. Physics and psychology aim to inform us how things act which exist independently of our notions. How can we know anything about
them? Empiricism answers : Only by experience. It is
absolutely impossible to discover from the notion of water
and of heat what will happen when the thermometer falls
to zero or rises to one hundred degrees; or to infer from
the concept of the body what will occur if it is deprived of
its support. Only by perception do we learn that it will
fall under such circumstances ; the concept does not help
us in the least. Not even the most perfect intellect, says
Hume, the intellect of Adam before the fall, could have
told him that if he should happen to fall into the water, he
would sink and be suffocated. Nay, it could not even reveal to him what would happen were a body in motion to
collide with one at rest. Nor can psychology deduce from
an absolute notion of the soul that it feels and desires,
reasons and infers, or foresee that air-waves will arouse a
sensation of sound, or pressure upon the eye, sensations of
light, or a blow in the face, a feeling of anger. All these
facts are known by experience only.

---

* The distinction between demonstrative and experimental knowledge
founded on perception is fundamental to the entire fourth book of Locke's
Essay, which is in reality the principal part of the work. The distinction
is, however, not accurately defined. The clear and logical exposition of
this difference forms the starting-point of Hume's *Enquiry* (Section IV and
Section XII, conclusion).

Locke began these reflections. He attempts to prove that all our notions are derived from experience. In the first book of the *Essay Concerning the Human Understanding* he undertakes to show, with hypercritical thoroughness, that men do not come into the world with innate ideas ; a fact of which perhaps no philosopher, least of all Descartes, needed to be apprised. The real opposition between them is a different one. Descartes claims that it is as possible to form notions in physics and psychology as in mathematics, the validity or truth of which is proved by their inner possibility. Locke denies it. The definition of the body : *corpus est res mere extensa,* or the definition : *mens est res mere cogitans,* may be logically possible ; it may be clearly and distinctly conceivable, but that by no means establishes its validity : we may have as clear and distinct a conception of a golden mountain. The truth of the notions of all sciences that deal with facts is based solely on the perception of such facts and connections. Hence it follows that the definitions of sciences of fact cannot be as fixed and final as mathematical concepts ; they may be enlarged and modified by further observation. Our notion of *gold* is the result of all previous observations concerning this body : it has such and such a color, a particular specific gravity, and reacts in a certain way upon mechanical, chemical, and thermal influences. Further observations may possibly discover new qualities. It is also possible that we may become acquainted with a body having all the qualities of gold but a somewhat higher or lower melting-point. We should in that event extend our notion sufficiently to admit this difference. The mathematical concept, however, is final : A figure in which the radii are not quite equal is not a circle ; a line that touches a circle at more than one point is not a tangent. The same remarks apply to the notions on which Descartes aims to base physics and psychology ; they are not final or mathematical, but provisional and empirical. Descartes explains : A body is a thing whose essence consists in extension, the soul a thing whose essence consists in states of consciousness (*cogitatio*), for I can clearly and distinctly conceive such a thing. Of course I can ; but should experience show that

this extended thing also thinks, at least occasionally, or
that this thinking being also sets bodies in motion, could
I not also conceive that? And in that case would it be
advisable to retain the above definitions? Evidently not.
For then they would be inadequate to explain actual facts.
Hence all concepts concerning matters of fact are provisional notions, they are constantly changing in order to fit
the facts yielded by observation. Such notions make a
demonstrative procedure like mathematics impossible.

Locke often insists that mathematics is the most perfect
form of knowledge. He deplores the fact that this kind of
knowledge (which outside of mathematics is possible only
in morals) is restricted to so narrow a field. Nevertheless
we must confess that the sciences of fact like physics,
chemistry, and psychology cannot be treated according to
the mathematical method ; observation and experiment are
necessary here.

Hume continued and completed these reflections. His
examination of the *notion of cause and effect* forms the
cardinal point in his brief and simple but thoughtful *Inquiry concerning Human Understanding.* The law of causality
had always been the chief support of rationalism. It was
supposed that the effect could be deduced from the cause ;
the relation existing between cause and effect is the
same as that existing between ground and consequent:
sequi = causari. Hume shows that this is an error.
Inference according to the law of causality is entirely different from concluding according to the logical law of contradiction. The relation between cause and effect is no
logical relation at all, discoverable by pure thought. In
physics and psychology such phenomena are said to be
causally related as invariably succeed each other in time.
The perception of succession in time is all that is really
observed here ; at any rate, an *inner connection* of phenomena, a necessity that binds them together, is not a
matter of observation. I perceive that a certain state
follows upon a given state ; I expect the same event to
succeed it the next time it occurs. Here we have the
beginning of the causal conception. We find it in animals ;
they too learn from experience, and in the manner indicated :

a certain succession is perceived in events; at the recur-
rence of the first, the second is expected or anticipated.
The function is more highly developed in man; not every
perceived succession leads us to expect its return; we
gradually learn to separate the constant causal relations
existing between phenomena from the accidental and dis-
soluble connections. But the principle is the same in
either case. It is absolutely impossible to discover the
effect from the notion of the cause by logical inference.
Take the simplest example. The motion of a body in a
given period of time is the cause of the same movement during the succeeding period. This is in no wise discoverable
by a logical inference. From the proposition that a certain
body moves with a certain velocity per second, and in a
certain direction, no logical conclusion follows, except
the falseness of its opposite. Nothing whatever can be
deduced as to what is going to happen during the *next* second. On the ground of previous observations, I *expect* this
body to pass through an equal space with the same velocity
and in the same direction, during the ensuing period of
time. But this expectation is not a *necessity of thought*, like
a mathematical proposition. It is also conceivable that the
movement should cease of its own accord, either suddenly
or gradually, or that it should turn off in any direction
whatever. Past experience has invariably taught us that
things behave in the manner stated in the law of inertia,
but it is not a logical necessity that the future should resemble the past. Moreover, says Hume,—and that is his
most general proposition,—there is absolutely no fact the
non-existence of which would not be conceivable or logically possible. The non-existence of any body, the invalidity of any natural law, is conceivable, for the non-existence of the entire world is conceivable.

Hence it follows: In the sciences concerning matters of
fact like physics and psychology there are no *truths that
are strictly universal and necessary.* These sciences contain
propositions that are *only probably universal.* Each one is
true with the tacit proviso: subject to correction by subsequent experience. The propositions of mathematics are
absolutely universal and necessary. No observation can

shake or change the proposition that the sum of the angles of a plane triangle is equal to two right angles; it is implied in the notions themselves as their logically necessary consequence. On the other hand, there is no proposition in physics or psychology that can be said to possess such necessity. Nor is the causal law itself an exception; the proposition that there is absolute regularity in the succession of natural phenomena has presumptive validity only. It is also conceivable or logically possible that phenomena should occur that stand in no relation whatever to all antecedent and all consequent phenomena. We should call such phenomena miracles. Hence miracles are undoubtedly possible, just as possible to thought as facts that may be explained by our laws of nature, *i.e.*, inserted into the natural connection of things according to rules. The question is not a question of possibility, but one of fact. Have facts been observed that would have to be regarded as miracles? Hume raises serious objections to the assertion. According to him the theory that the alleged miracles are explainable, if not physically, psychologically at least, has such great probability that it may be regarded as practically certain. It is a matter of such common experience that human testimony rests on voluntary or involuntary deception, that it seems much more plausible for us to explain an alleged miracle in this way than to abandon the fundamental principle of all natural science, the universal reign of law in nature. This presupposition is, of course, not logically necessary, but has been so often confirmed by facts and has, upon close observation, been so often verified even in the case of alleged miracles, that we have the right, on *a priori* grounds, to doubt new miracles.

That is the epistemology of empiricism. Kant opposes it and undertakes to restore rationalism, though of course with qualifications and restrictions.

3. The Formalistic Rationalism of Kant.

As has been said above, the question at stake in the controversy between rationalism and empiricism is: Do we possess an *a priori* or rational knowledge of objects? Ra-

tionalism answers in the affirmative: By pure thought we
reach an absolute knowledge of things that cannot be acquired through the senses. Empiricism denies the statement: We gain a knowledge of objects solely by perception, whence it follows that we have no absolute knowledge.

Kant's standpoint is conditioned by the following procedure: he takes what he regards as the correct half of
each of the two opposing theories and combines these
halves into a new theory. In opposition to Hume's empiricism he renews the old dogma of rationalism: *There is
a priori knowledge of objects.* In opposition to the rationalism of the Leibniz-Wolffian system he adds: but knowledge
of things *only as they appear, not as they are in themselves.*
The union of phenomenalism or idealism with rationalism is
the real characteristic feature of the Kantian epistemology.
Hitherto rationalism had always been realistic, while empiricism had become idealistic in Berkeley and Hume.

The first half of the *Critique of Pure Reason,* consisting
of the *Æsthetic* and *Analytic,* attempts to construct a new
epistemological system upon this basis. The second half,
the *Dialectic,* gives an elaborate exposition of the relation
of the new philosophy to the old metaphysics; it shows
the impossibility of a purely rational psychology, cosmology, and theology, the *impossibility,* if you please, of a
realistic rationalism, after the first half had shown the
possibility of a *phenomenalistic* rationalism. Let us begin
with a consideration of the first half, with the conditional
reconstruction of rationalism.

According to Hume, there are no universal and necessary judgments concerning matters of fact. All our natural
laws, the laws of mechanics as well as those of chemistry
and physiology, nay, the causal law itself, have presumptive universal validity only. That, says Kant, is complete
Skepticism. If Hume is right, real knowledge is no longer
possible; for universality and necessity distinguish knowledge from mere association of ideas, which even animals
have. Nay, Hume's skepticism is not confined to physics
and metaphysics, it necessarily includes mathematics also.
His arguments are thereby reduced *ad absurdum.* The
actual existence of this science shows the insufficiency of

the principles of empiricism. The question, therefore, simply is to show how such sciences are possible. How is pure mathematics, how is pure natural science, how is metaphysics possible? Or stating the question in a general formula : How are *synthetic judgments a priori possible?* That is, epistemologically, not psychologically, possible? In other words : How can propositions that *are not derived from experience* (judgments *a priori*) and are *not logical deductions* (not analytical propositions) possess the validity and the value of *objective knowledge* (synthetic judgments)?

That is Kant's problem. His answer is : Such propositions can have objective validity, only in case the *understanding itself creates the objects* of which it affirms these propositions ; it has an *a priori* knowledge of objects in so far as it produces them itself. This happens in mathematics. Its objects are pure intuitions constructed according to definition. The geometrician is able to describe the properties and relations of lines, angles, triangles, and circles in synthetic judgments *a priori*, because he creates the objects himself. In a certain sense the same is true of physics. The objects with which the physicist deals are natural phenomena ; in a measure, however, phenomena are the products of the subject to which they appear, and as such are conditioned, in their general form, by the nature and functions of the subject. Hence, in so far as we mean by nature the totality of phenomena,—and physics deals with nature in this sense only,—we can have an *a priori* knowledge of nature and of all natural objects—that is, as far as the general form of their phenomenality is concerned. On the other hand, there can be no *a priori* knowledge of nature, if we mean by nature an absolute reality that exists without any relation to the knowing subject. Of things as they are in themselves, independent of the subject, the intellect can, of course, know nothing *a priori*. Nor can it learn anything concerning them by the *a posteriori* method, for they would have to enter our consciousness or become phenomena before we could know anything of them. Hence if we mean by metaphysics what is usually meant, the knowledge of things-in-themselves, then it is not possible. It is possible only when it means nothing but "pure natural science," *i.e.*, a general phenomenology of nature.

This is Kant's rationalistic train of thought. It is presented in the briefest form in his *Prolegomena to every Future Metaphysics*, the treatise written in explanation and defence of the *Critique of Pure Reason*. In a certain sense this treatise most clearly reveals the object of Kant's thought : it accentuates his opposition to Hume. The reception with which the *Critique of Pure Reason* had met among his German contemporaries led Kant to write the book. The idealistic and skeptical features had attracted their attention ; they overlooked the rationalistic element. They simply noticed the opposition to their own mode of thinking, to the reigning system of the school ; its opposition to Hume's empiricism escaped their observation. The fact is, they were unacquainted with the latter. They did not permit Hume's skeptical reflections to shake their faith in the rational theology, cosmology, and psychology of the Wolffian system.

On the other hand, it must be confessed that Kant's original thought is somewhat distorted in the *Prolegomena*. By incidentally explaining mathematics and physics as actual and valid sciences that need no epistemological vindication whatever, he, of course, contradicts his original opinion. The starting-point of criticism is : There are such sciences, but their objective validity is endangered by Hume's skepticism. The problem is to save them, *i.e.*, to *prove* their *objective* validity. Their existence simply shows that certain propositions which claim to be *universal* and *necessary*, at the same time lay claim to *objective* validity. Take a proposition like the following : Matter is neither created nor destroyed. The proposition claims to be a universal and necessary judgment. If it is, it must be *a priori;* for experience gives us no universal and necessary knowledge. On that point Kant wholly agrees with Hume. On the other hand, it is a judgment that lays claim to objective validity, *i.e.*, affirms : Such a thing cannot happen *in reality*. It is not an analytical judgment—as, for instance, the proposition : Every body is extended ; the part is smaller than the whole—but a synthetical judgment, a propo-

sition predicating existence. The same may be said of
the proposition: Nothing occurs without a cause. It
claims to be both a universal and necessary judgment and a
judgment having objective validity. And this is also true of
the axioms of geometry; physicists unhesitatingly attribute
objective validity to them. They likewise presuppose that
the conclusions deduced from definitions and axioms, and
the calculations depending thereon, are not only true in
form, but also in reality; that the nature of the things is
mathematically knowable. How can this assumption be
established? How can it be proved that the propositions
affirming the conservation of matter and the universal reign
of law in nature are not merely, as Hume maintains, assumptions having presumably universal validity, but really
necessary and universal laws of nature?

Kant answers the question by revising the notion of experience in the manner indicated above. The popular view,
which is conceptually formulated in sensualistic theories,
understands by experience the passive reception of impressions from the real world. It regards the soul, to use
Locke's expression, as a piece of white paper, on which objects impress their characters. Of course, the paper cannot know *a priori* what signs it is going to receive. If the
soul is such a thing, and if experience consists in such a
process, then *a priori* knowledge, and with it universal and
necessary knowledge, are impossible. But the assumption is
false. Knowledge, even empirical knowledge, is not passively received from the external world: it is a product of
the spontaneous activity of the soul. Not, indeed, the
product of an absolutely spontaneous activity; the activity
is aroused by the environment. But "experience" can be
brought about only when the intelligence forms or fashions
the "affections." Experience is not a heap accidentally
jumbled together, a "conglomeration" of sensations, but a
system of phenomena combined according to principles.
Nature, the object of our experience, is conceived in this
way: as a unified system of facts governed by laws.

The fact that nature is more than a confused heap of sensations,—red, sweet, solid, liquid,—differing in quality and
quantity, is not the result of sensation or due to impres-

sions; it is the work of intelligence. The intelligence with its two aspects, sensibility and understanding, apprehends and forms, arranges and organizes the given manifold of impressions by means of its peculiar activities, and these we may designate as *functions of synthesis*, the comprehension of disconnected and manifold elements into a unity. Of course, the functions of the intelligence must everywhere be present in their product, experience, as the formal conditions of the same, and for that reason we may have an *a priori* knowledge of the form of nature. As we have an *a priori* knowledge of the shape of objects that are constructed according to the same pattern, so we can have *a priori* knowledge of the form of all products of human intelligence, *i.e.*, we know the form of nature and of all the objects therein.

From the uniformity of the manifold we may tell what in nature springs from the formative activity of the intelligence. Different parts of space are at different times filled with different forces. The qualities may change, but *space itself* with its determinations is everywhere and always the same, so that each part may be substituted for any other part. Similarly, *time* is everywhere and always the same, however different its content may be. So, too, the general form of reality is everywhere the same; there are many different changes and effects, but the *causal relation* is universally the same; it holds for every time and every place. There is likewise another fundamental schema of reality, the category of *substance and accident*, persistence and change.

Kant investigates the formal side of experience and everywhere attends to the constructive factors common to all experiences. He discovers two kinds of formal elements: he calls them *forms of intuition* and *forms of thought*. The two *forms of intuition* are *space* and *time*. Basing himself on formal logic and its table of judgments, he reduces the forms of thought (which he calls *categories*) to the round number of twelve. Space and time are, therefore, not actual realities, nor really existent arrangements of things-in-themselves, but subjective functions which synthesize the manifold sensational content. All sensations are arranged and unified in time-succession, so that each is simultaneous with every other or separated from it by some definite interval of time. All sensations of the external sense are inserted into the unified whole which we call the spatial world. Thus the unified perceived world of phenomena is produced by the functions of localization and temporalization, if we may invent these terms. And in the same way the functions of thought are forms of arranging our perceptions: forms of their arrangement in time. The general fundamental principle is: All phenomena are *a priori* conditioned by the rules which determine their relations *in time*. All phenomena, so the law of substantiality states in particular, contain a persistent element which constitutes the object itself and an element of change which is a mere determination of the object. The law of causality declares: Everything that occurs (or begins to be) presupposes something upon which it follows *according to a rule*. Kant finds it more difficult to demonstrate the remaining ten categories as constitutive elements of reality; most of them are mere makeshifts.

Let us now insert the theory of this new rationalism into our classification and say: Kant answers the question concerning the nature of the principles of rational knowledge as follows. They are modes of activity, synthetic functions, which the intelligence universally exercises and always exercises in the same way. The mathematical and physical axioms mentioned before are formulæ expressive of these functions and in so far principles of *a priori* knowledge. The functions are not innate; they are, like all functions, developed in the course of life, but they are not, on that account, carried into us from without by means of impressions; the impressions are simply the occasion of their development. This is the answer which had already suggested itself to Leibniz in his *New Essays concerning the Human Understanding*, which he opposed to Locke's *Essay*. *Nihil est in intellectu, quod non antea fuerit in sensu*, says empiricism, and rightly so; but we must add: *nisi intellectus ipse*. Everything is derived from experience, except the capacity for experience

This enables us to answer the second question: How can propositions that are not derived from experience still have objective validity? After many tiresome repetitions the *Transcendental Deduction,* which, it must be confessed, is by no means a model of accuracy and clearness, deduces them from the presuppositions already established: Propositions that express the synthetical functions of our sensibility and understanding, for that very reason possess the validity of laws of nature, in so far as we mean by nature what everybody actually means by the term: the totality of phenomena. Space and time being forms of our intuition are at the same time necessary forms of nature; nothing can be an object of our perception that does not exist in space and time. In the words of the first principle of experience, "the axiom of intuition," all phenomena are *extensive* quantities; and hence we might continue: Everything that can be predicated of extensity in general, its continuity and homogeneity, its illimitability and infinite divisibility, may also be affirmed of the real world. Or, whatever pure mathematics affirms of space and time relations is unconditionally true of all things that have spatiality and quantity. Likewise, whatever transcendental logic discovers concerning the nature of the understanding is true also of things in so far as they exist for the understanding. If the law of causality is a law of the pure understanding, it is for that very reason also a law of nature. "The understanding does not draw its laws from nature, but prescribes them to nature."

In the preface to the second edition of the *Critique,* Kant draws a striking comparison. He likens the revolution created by him in epistemology to the change produced in the astronomical conception of the universe by Copernicus. Prior to the days of Copernicus, the celestial phenomena were explained by the movements of the heavenly bodies around the earth. Copernicus offers a more simple explanation, assuming the motion to be in the observer. In a like manner, empiricism explained knowledge as the effect of objects on the intelligence. Kant, however, explains knowledge by assuming, "contrary to our senses," that objects are governed by our notions: Thought alone creates objects so far as the form is concerned. Hence it can, in so far, know them *a priori* and formulate its knowledge in universal and necessary propositions. The axioms of geometry, the law of causality, are necessarily and universally valid for all objects of experience.

The second thesis of this rationalism follows as a necessary consequence of the above. It asserts that there can be no rational knowledge in cases where objects are not determined by the understanding. The "things-in-themselves" are, of course, not subject to the synthetic functions of our intelligence, and hence metaphysics in the old sense, rational knowledge of absolute reality, is impossible. The elaboration of this idea, upon which the *Analytic* everywhere touches, forms the subject-matter of the second half of the Critique, the *Dialectic*. This part of the work, with its many almost unendurable imperfections of style and laborious expositions, shows that the attempts to employ the understanding and its forms of thought for the purpose of determining the nature of the things themselves in a rational psychology, cosmology, and theology were bound to fail. We cannot enter here upon a more detailed discussion of these points, nor consider the attempts made to regain for the "ideas," which are deprived of their constitutive validity, "regulative" value for the speculative reason and practical validity for the will.

But I should like to conclude my exposition by referring to a conception which is a characteristic of the Kantian system and with which Kant himself is acquainted, though he did not, to my knowledge, expressly formulate it anywhere. *Human* intelligence stands between *animal* and *divine* intelligence. The knowledge of *animals* consists of a "conglomeration of sensations," among which associative relations occasionally obtain. There is, however, no distinction made between subject and object, between the I and nature. The knowledge in question is not, therefore, objective, and hence not real knowledge at all, but a purely subjective train of ideas. Nor is *divine* knowledge objective according to our conceptions. The divine intellect creates reality by its thought; this is not opposed to it as something foreign or actual; the *intellectus archetypus* is "intuitive understanding"; its thoughts are actual concrete ideas, not abstract notions ; a human soul is a divine

398 PROBLEM OF THE ORIGIN OF KNOWLEDGE. [Book II.

"thought." The thinking of the creative artist is an illustration of this idea; as in him, so all thoughts bear an inner, æsthetical and teleological relation to each other in God. *Human* knowledge, however, is *objective* knowledge; it is the *conceptual interpretation* of something *that exists*. By means of the synthetical functions of intuition and thought peculiar to it, the human intelligence constructs unified systems of objects governed by laws, which we call nature, out of the given manifold of sensations. The objects are in form merely products of the understanding, but the understanding concedes independent existence to them and regards itself as an object among objects governed by natural laws.

4. Critical Remarks on Kant's Theory of Knowledge.

In criticising the Kantian theory, which was expounded in the preceding section and which lacks neither keenness nor depth, I shall state, as clearly and accurately as I know how, what, in my opinion, is untenable therein and then point out what it contains of permanent value.

I shall first let Hume, the chief object of attack in the *Critique*, defend his cause against Kant. Has Kant refuted the proposition, which is the climax of Hume's empiricism, that a knowledge of facts cannot be reached by pure reason, and hence that there are no absolutely universal and necessary judgments concerning facts, but only such as are probably universal? Has Kant, in opposition to Hume, really proved the possibility of universal and necessary propositions, *e.g.*, in natural science?

It was for a long time assumed in Germany that such is the case. I am not of the same opinion; I do not believe that Hume could be forced to acknowledge it. I shall let him defend his thesis against Kant.

In the first place, Hume would have refused to accept the line of argument followed in the *Prolegomena*, which was also introduced into the subsequent editions of the *Critique* itself, and which assumes that there are in pure mathematics and in natural science "real and at the same time pure truths *a priori* needing no proof." He would with justice have regarded it as a *petitio principii.* The existence of these sciences, he might have said, cannot, of course, be doubted; but the question is—and that is the very question asked by him—in what sense does objective validity appertain to their propositions? Indeed, he might have continued, in my opinion mathematics as such does not claim to possess objective validity at all. Geometry makes no assertions concerning reality. Whenever its propositions are employed to determine reality, *e.g.,* in astronomical calculations, they lose their apodictic character and become hypothetical. Provided physical space corresponds to geometric space and the measurements of distances and angles are correct, the moon is at such and such a distance from us, has such a size, such and such motion, etc. The propositions of trigonometry possess apodictic certainty, but no proposition in astronomy can claim it. The universality and necessity of pure mathematics depend on the fact that this science concerns itself wholly with notions. Physics, on the other hand, aims to supply us with knowledge of objective reality, thereby waiving all claims to universality and necessity—*i.e.,* in the strict sense of the term, for Hume too would, like every one else, concede probable validity to the laws of mechanics. Hence he would grant universality in the common acceptation of the term, only not the universality and necessity appertaining to mathematical propositions.

Kant once said that he had admitted metaphysics (that is, pure natural science) to the fellowship of mathematics. It could not in truth be in better company, only he should not have obliterated the essential difference existing between them. To that end, however, Kant invented the formula: *synthetic judgments a priori.* He embraces the pure mathematical and physical propositions under the ambiguous term "synthetic." By making such an indefinite and unsuitable distinction between "analytical and synthetical" judgments, he has removed the clear distinction between judgments concerning the relations of notions and judgments concerning the behavior of objects, and thereby hopelessly entangled the investigation. Propositions of physics are now regarded as analogous to those of *pure* mathematics. But this idea is not consistently carried out either. For the correct conception is always kept in view : the question is not, how is *pure*, but how is *applied*, mathematics possible? Thus especially in the *Transcendental Deduction of Mathematics*, which is found in the *Analytic* under the title " Axioms of Intuition." Here the real thought of Kant is clearly brought out : *Applied* mathematics is possible, because " the empirical intuition is possible only through the pure intuition (of space and time); and hence what geometry says of the latter is unconditionally true of the former, and therefore the evasive statement that sense-objects cannot conform to the rules of construction in space falls to the ground." The same reasoning is followed in the *Transcendental Deduction of Pure Natural Science.* The principles of the pure understanding have objective validity, because the empirical thinking of objects is possible only through pure thought.

If now, Hume might have continued, we examine Kant's essential proposition that knowledge *a priori*, and hence universal and necessary knowledge of facts, is possible through the *a priori* synthetical functions, which are not derived from experience, we shall find that it too is untenable. Even if we grant, as we most likely must, that there are such synthetical functions and that they play an important part in the construction of our world of experience, still serious objections may be urged against the Kantian view.

First, the question arises : How do we reach a knowledge of the synthetic functions ; do we get it *a priori* or by experience? Kant does not consider the question, and yet his entire undertaking will prove futile unless it be answered in the spirit of his philosophy. If we have no *a priori* knowledge of the functions—and I hardly know what that could mean even for adherents of the Kantian system—if we know of them only by experience, that is, by inner, anthropological experience, then the fundamental propositions in which the form of these functions is expressed would have empirical validity only. The assertions, Space and time are intuitive forms of human sensibility, The categories are intellectual forms of the human understanding, would then be generalizations of anthropology; and the axiomatic propositions which express the nature of our space-intuition or of the functions of our judgment as laws of reality would in the last analysis be propositions having empirical origin and empirical validity. The self-evident condition would attach to them: in so far as the synthetical functions remain identical. It would be conceivable that human beings or beings like human beings exist having other forms of intelligence, and then the intelligence itself might possibly change. Our descendants or even I myself might become equipped with different forms of conception. If, for example, my intuition were to change into a four-dimensional intuition of space, the axioms based on the old intuition of space would lose their objective validity. However improbable all that may appear to us, it is none the less conceivable, and hence we cannot prove the absolute universality and necessity of such principles. They would be valid with the proviso: so long and so far as these particular forms of space, time, and the categories are constructive factors of the world of phenomena.

In his *Neue Kritik der reinen Vernunft*, Fries raises the question which Kant evaded, and answers it in the sense of empiricism. Our knowledge of the formal elements is derived from experience only. The statement has been made that Fries corrupts Kant's thought; critical philosophy does not aim at a psychological proof of an anthropological fact, but at a transcendental inquiry into the possibility of experience. And that cannot be accomplished by observing what men actually do, but by reflecting upon what must be recognized in all knowledge as the necessary constituent, one that cannot be eliminated without destroying knowledge; we must investigate the axiomatic elements of knowledge. The synthetic principles are such elements; they express the nature of the intuitions of time and space, as well as of the forms of thought: unless we presuppose their validity, experience is utterly impossible.

Very true; that is what Kant aims at. But Hume would answer: That is just where the *petitio principii* comes in; I deny the axiomatic character of the causal law in the Kantian sense, and yet I regard experience as possible, such experience as we have in the sciences, not, however, experience as a system of absolutely necessary and universal propositions; we have propositions that are presumed to be universal and valid. For these the physicist really needs no other presupposition than the *presumptive* universality and validity of the transcendental principles. He may willingly grant, not only that a world is conceivable for which our causal law, for example, is not valid, but also that an event may at any moment occur in our world which cannot be explained according to the causal law—a movement, for instance, that is absolutely isolated and unrelated to all antecedent and succeeding movements. True, were the physicist to hit upon such an event, he would not cease to inquire into its cause and effect; hence he would not know or acknowledge it to be such an isolated fact. But it is conceivable that a movement should have neither a cause nor an effect. It is also conceivable that after having repeatedly endeavored to discover the cause and effect of certain phenomena and having failed, we should be gradually determined no longer to apply the category of causality to them. The same statements may be made of the axiomatic propositions concerning the nature of space. We presuppose that physical space is absolutely identical with geometrical space, that it is, like the latter, continuous and homogeneous. But we may also conceive that it is not. A physical space, for example, which is inwardly heterogeneous is conceivable. We assume that a movement will continue with the same velocity unless it meets with physical resistance; and whenever that does not take place, whenever the velocity of a body is diminished, we assume that it was influenced by certain physical forces. It is, however, conceivable that the assumption is false, that different spaces are of different permeability, that there are *metaphysical inequalities* in space. It is true, if any one were to suggest that we explain the retardation of a cosmical motion, for example, by such a hypothesis, we should not consent to it; we should insist that there are unknown forces at work, and our reasoning could hardly be shown to be erroneous. Nevertheless it is conceivable that we could be mistaken, and that is all that is necessary to destroy Kant's argument.

If, however, the counter-statements should be made that Kant has demonstrated that physical space is not different from geometrical space, that it is the purely subjective intuition of space in which the whole of nature is contained, we should reply as follows.

It is true, Kant assumes that space, time, and the categories are purely subjective factors of knowledge, and as such universally and necessarily applicable to whatever can become an object of the subject. But with what right? He himself afterwards explains all knowledge by means of two factors, the nature of the subject and the affections which the things produce in it. How can a sharp line of separation be drawn between the two? The product only, the world of ideas, is given; how is it possible to determine the factors from the product alone? Kant himself makes the assertion: It is absolutely impossible to deduce "particular laws of nature" from the pure understanding alone; we need "experience" for that. Well, if experience is needed for the law of gravitation, why not also for the law of causality? If "experience" is necessary for each particular localization—for geographical or astronomical localization, for example—why not for the formation of the idea of space itself? If, however, the nature of reality is a factor in the creation of the idea of space, then the same subject transplanted to a different world would produce a different form of intuition, one perhaps that is not at all comparable with our space. We may say the same of the forms of thought. The same subject placed in different surroundings would perhaps produce an entirely different notion of natural uniformity, or perhaps none at all. And hence the necessary conclusion would follow: There can be no absolutely universal and necessary judgments of facts. The principles would then be valid in all cases where the understanding finds a reality like ours, not, however, beyond that. We can conceive of a world that would not determine our intelligence to produce the law of gravi-

404 PROBLEM OF THE ORIGIN OF KNOWLEDGE. [Book II.

tation. So, too, a world is conceivable that would not give
rise to the law of causality in our intelligence.

In this way Hume might defend his theorem against
Kant : There are no universal and necessary propositions
concerning facts. And he might add: Should any one
consider such speculations on conceivability and possibility superfluous and say that, for the world in which we
happen to live, our intuition of space and our laws of
thought are adequate forms of conception, I, Hume, will
not deny it. It seems to me that Kant's "vindication of
the sciences " against skepticism is, to say the least,
equally superfluous. For all theoretical and practical purposes the conception of the causal law as the safest gen-
eralization of all our experiences is just as good as Kant's
a priori laws of thought. He would be as little inclined as
Kant to assume exceptions to the causal law. Against
alleged miracles he would, like the latter, urge the causal
law as an "axiomatic" proposition.

Hume would most likely also have called attention to
another fact that makes the value of the Kantian vindication wholly illusory. Kant himself confesses that the
knowledge of each *particular* causal relation is possible
only through experience. Herein he entirely agrees with
Hume; he does not at all share the view of the older
rationalism which believed that the particular effect could
in an "analytical" judgment be deduced from the notion
of the cause by a mere act of thought. Hence each particular causal relation, every natural law of our mechanics
and physics, is, even according to Kant, an empirical law,
and as such has no mathematical universality and necessity.
Only the causal law itself, the formula : Everything that
happens presupposes something upon which it follows
according to a rule, is said to be purely *a priori* and hence
universal and necessary. Well, very little would be gained
by that. We should simply know that every event regularly
succeeds *some other event.* Experience would have to tell
us which one it is, and even then it would always be possible to learn more from subsequent experience. True,
we would know : If such and such a relation of succession
derived from experience is a causal relation, then it is

necessary and universally valid ; but we could never be
absolutely certain that we have a real causal relation before us and not merely an accidental and contingent succession. Thus, for example, common-sense is disposed to
construct from its experiences a general law of nature :
The velocity of a falling body is dependent on its specific
weight. Physics corrects the formula; it is only conditionally valid : provided, namely, that the body falls through
a resistant medium. In case this condition is removed,
e.g., by the construction of a vacuum, all bodies fall with
equal velocity. Well, it is likewise conceivable that the
law of gravitation should be only conditionally true; that
the parts of ponderable matter gravitate towards each
other only on condition, *e.g.*, of the presence of an ether or
an electric tension. If it were possible to eliminate this
influence, the phenomena of gravitation would cease.
Even the law of the conservation of motion or of matter is
no exception to the rule. It is conceivable, *e.g.*, that matter
and motion are constantly destroyed, but that they are
constantly restored in equal measure by a cause unknown
to us, say by a transcendent being. In case the activity of
this being were to cease, we might reason, the loss would
be apparent. That is an utterly arbitrary notion, but it is
conceivable.

Hence, Hume might say, even if Kant has vindicated the
universal validity of the causal law, physics does not gain
anything by it; all its laws remain empirical laws having
presumptive universal validity only. This attempt at a
"vindication of the sciences" against skepticism, made
with so much ado, Hume might continue, seems to me to
yield rather modest, not to say scant, results.

Finally, however, Hume might have considered another
point in his criticism : The entire Kantian argument breaks
in two. Kant ought really to say what he says at the beginning: *particular* qualitatively-determined sensations
alone are given, whereas all *combination*, *all* arrangement,
is to be referred to the synthetic functions of the subject.
Through the forms of intuition and the categories, which
are but functions of synthesis and arrangement, each element is assigned its place in the whole of things. Kant,

however, afterwards recoiled from this consequence of his assumption. In the *Transcendental Deduction* he admits that our knowledge of the time-succession of events springs from "experience," that "experience" is essential to a knowledge of *particular* laws of nature. "The faculty of pure understanding, however, can by mere categories pre-scribe only such *a priori* laws to phenomena as govern *nature in general*, meaning thereby the uniformity of phe-nomena in space and time. Particular laws are concerned with empirically-determined (!) phenomena and cannot therefore be completely deduced from it. Experience must be added. . . ." This conclusion breaks the *Trans-cendental Deduction* in two. If "experience" can and must co-operate in determining the time-succession, where shall we draw the line? If the understanding needs "experi-ence" to make biological generalizations, chemical formulæ, and physical laws, why should not the same hold for the laws of causality and substantiality? Because they are universal and necessary? But that is the very point in question.

It is everywhere apparent how serious the break is, and how impossible it is to explain the unity of experience found in the sciences, by the pure intellectual concepts or the synthetic functions of the understanding and such "empirical determinations" of the phenomena. Read the *Transcendental Deduction* with its endless cumbersome repe-titions, where the conclusion invariably contradicts the be-ginning. First the assumption is made that synthesis is the product of the understanding, and then the proviso comes hobbling after : but *particular* synthesis springs from "experience," in which ambiguous notion the whole misery lies concealed. Note the attempts made to separate pure apperception and empirical association and then to unite them again, or the desperate endeavors in the chapter on the *Schematism of the Pure Concepts of the Understanding* to reduce the synthesis of thought to the sensuous synthesis of sensations in time or the no less desperate efforts of the *Prolegomena* (§ 20) to make "experience" out of "judgments of perception." I do not believe that anybody can boast of really being able to understand, *i.e.*, to think, these thoughts. We can understand them psychologically only, by disclosing the different impulses which pull the Kantian thought in different directions.

In regard to all this we may now say : Kant is quite right in maintaining that experience is not passively received, but a product of the sensibility and the understanding. We can also say : The intelligence itself produces nature, the totality of uniformly-connected phenomena. But, we must add, it produces it wholly in one and the same way, by observation and reflection. It has taken the human mind thousands of years to create nature, that is, the world as we now see it, by means of perception and reflection, explorations and philologico-historical research, by microscopic and telescopic observations and mathematical speculation, by physical experiments and conceptual deductions. There is not an item either in the constitution of the cosmos or in the inner uniformity of the course of nature that did not require the co-operation of observation and reflection. It is utterly impossible to make an absolute division between " empirical " and *a priori* elements. Even the causal law is an "empirical " law, not in the sense of being impressed upon the understanding from without, for that never happens, but in the sense that it presupposes observation as much as any law of chemistry or biology. The ground of our faith in the universal reign of law in nature is at bottom no other than the ground of our faith in the universal validity of the rule that every man has a father and a mother. Not an *a priori* necessity, but experience is its support. Of course, not ordinary experience, but scientific experience. Popular experience does not assume the universal validity of the causal law at all ; to this day it reckons with accidents and chances ; it has so often perceived absolute origination and decay that it sees nothing objectionable in these notions. It was science that first created the notion of natural uniformity. On what does it base its conviction ? On the fact, no doubt, that wherever it gained a deeper insight into things, it universally discovered causal connections or could show that so-called origin and decay were in truth but transitions from existing movements and substances to new forms. And

such experiences, a thousand times repeated, science formulates into axiomatic propositions which express the universal reign of law in nature, and says : Even in cases
where we do not yet know the cause or the law, it is present. If, however, science had never experienced the facts
just mentioned, such axioms would be out of the question.

This brings us to a point which I shall consider somewhat more in detail. Kant starts from a biological conception that was common in his day : The nature of living
beings is unchangeable. So, too, the forms of intuition
and thought are for him the constant endowments of our
intelligence.

Modern anthropology cannot concede this. There is
nothing absolutely stable in the organic world ; everything
in it is a growth and everything is changeable. The organization of the body, the nervous system, is the product
of a long series of transformations. Hence the same
remarks will also apply to the intellectual organization.
Space, time, and causality are not original, fixed possessions of human intelligence ; they were gradually developed
by the race in the course of its long life, just as they are
developed by the individual—developed, it is true, on the
ground of inherited dispositions and with the help of the
parental generation. This is most apparent in the case of
the causal conception of reality : the function is acquired
by the individual not otherwise than number and speech.
Hence it is that different individuals meet with different
success in the employment of the causal function. Some
do not get beyond the most immediate, practically-important
causal connections, while to many the notion of a strict and
universal reign of law in nature is wholly unknown.

We may not only trace the development of the causal
function in the individual, but may also outline its historical origin in the race. We find it in primitive form even
among the more highly developed animals ; they learn to
adapt their behavior to what occurs in the environment ;
experience makes them wiser. This is evidently due to
the fact that they remember the succession of events.
When the antecedent appears, the consequent is anticipated
by a kind of unintentional inference which determines the

practical behavior of the animal. And to some extent the converse of the inference is also drawn : The consequent is an object of desire; it calls the antecedent into consciousness as a means to an end. The dog that has been taught to beg by having his first performance rewarded with a fat morsel henceforth uses his art as the means to an end. The formula according to which he infers, even though he does not embody it in a proposition, is: The same antecedent is followed by the same consequent; if it does not always follow, it may at least always be expected.

Human inference is at first not different from this. Indeed, we may say that many persons never rise beyond it at all in principle, though they employ the process more extensively and with greater success than the most sagacious animal. Thus the whole of popular medicine, its pathology, therapeutics, and dietetics, consists of observed (be it of correctly or falsely observed) consequences. If you do thus or so, you will catch cold or get the fever; when you have the fever, you must sweat or take medicine. In some cases the need of a causal explanation is wholly satisfied with such connections. Nor will exceptions be taken if the remedy does not help in every case. The popular causal law does not require that; its formula is : As a rule, the same antecedent is followed by the same consequent; sometimes, however, it may happen otherwise. Indeed, this formula satisfies the most immediate needs; practical life has to do solely with such complicated connections as can be embraced only under rules which have exceptions, not under strictly universal laws : the peasant is concerned with the weather and such organic processes of life as cannot be calculated but only foreseen according to the formula in question, the mechanic with materials and tools which are never constructed exactly alike, the teacher and the official with human natures which, though they generally resemble one another, yet have their peculiarities and do not therefore react upon the same influences in the same way.

In fact we may say: It is really only a few centuries since science has arrived at a more exact formulation of the causal law. The Aristotelian philosophy is satisfied with a conception of causality that admits of exceptions which cannot be controlled; they are called accidents and are referred to the uncertain, indefinable, and lawless factor in nature, matter, whereas uniformity is peculiar to the other factor, conceptual essence. Hence, in so far as this disturbing element is present, science cannot get beyond the formula: " as a rule." Modern physics first consistently developed the notion of the uniformity of nature. The laws of mechanics have become the typical examples of all uniformity. It is owing to them that the idea of a strictly universal and absolute reign of law in all occurrences, in the outer as well as in the inner world, was first developed. Descartes applies the thought to the external world, especially to the biological domain; Hobbes and Spinoza, to the inner realm: volition and feeling obey absolute laws as well as the movements in the corporeal world.

How was the causal function developed in the human understanding? We may answer: By the evolution of the faculty to analyze complex facts into their components. The reasoning of animals, if we wish to designate their inferences by that name, consists in associating complex processes or perceptions. A horse that has once been well fed in a certain stable will, on passing along the same road after many years, turn into it again. In this case the entire surroundings are associated with the idea of good fodder. The same associations act in the case of man, only he does not obey them without hesitation; he first deliberates whether the same results can be expected to-day as before; whether the same man lives there, whether the same conditions obtain which caused him to be received so well at that time. The zoologist Möbius somewhere tells of the following experiment. A pike was placed on one side of a water-basin that had been divided into two separate compartments by a pane of glass; all kinds of little animals upon which the pike usually preys were placed in the adjoining space. The pike at once made for the animals, but instead of the expected morsel he received a smart blow from the glass. After several repetitions he finally learned

to give up the prey. A few weeks later the pane of glass
was removed and the pike was now free to move around
the other animals; he could not, however, be prevailed
upon to attack them. He had manifestly made a law
of nature for himself. To fall upon these animals results
in a blow on the jaws. A man would, under similar circumstances, try to analyze the complex occurrence into
its simple elements. He would say : The blow which you
receive is, perhaps, not a result of the nature of the prey,
but of some obstacle or other that is not visible to your
eyes. He would straightway attempt to discover the
nature of the obstacle by feeling around with his hand,
and then try to remove it or climb over it. A highly developed animal intelligence would have sufficed to bring
about the same result. But, as a rule, the behavior of
animals and the thoughts by which they are guided differ
from human conduct in this, that animals react upon complex situations or processes with stereotyped inferences
and acts. Human thought, and consequently human conduct, is more flexible ; it analyzes the phenomenon into its
essential factors and accidental circumstances and hence
separates real and constant sequences from accidental and
transitory combinations.

It is plain that this faculty is most intimately connected
with the characteristic which makes human thought
superior to animal thought : with *conceptual thinking.* The
nature of conceptual thought consists in resolving the perceptual complexus into its elements ; it consists in the inner
organization of the perception ; *analysis* and *synthesis* constitute the two sides of the process. The different elements of
the perception are isolated in the concept and then brought
into relation with each other again in the judgment. A
heavy stone will sink in water, wet wood will not burn ; a
judgment of perception as simple as this presupposes
enormous intellectual labor. The human eye does not see
more than that of the animal, but what remains an obscure
medley of perceptions in the animal consciousness is resolved into a plurality of components by the human intelligence and then recombined into a unified system. It
marks off the object for itself, then its quality, likewise its

movement; then it distinguishes in the movement its
direction and velocity; then it forms a judgment by combining all the elements of the entire occurrence into a
whole, into an organized whole in which each part has its
particular place.   It is evident that a knowledge of natural
laws was rendered possible only through such an organization of perceptions, and that presupposes keen analysis.
Only after the persistent substance and the transitory
process of motion were analyzed out of the perception of
a body in motion, and the direction then discriminated
from the motion itself, and after each of these elements
was relatively isolated, could the understanding rise to a
knowledge of the law of gravitation or the law of inertia.
The creation of the system of notions and categories which
finds objective expression in language, the thorough-going
articulation of reality, which corresponds to the articulation of speech—that is the enormous task which the human
mind performed before it could undertake the scientific
investigation of things.   At present each individual ac-
quires the results of the labors of countless generations
of ancestors, almost without exertion, within the first two
or three years of life, while the following two decades are
spent in mastering the improvements made in this system
of concepts by scientific thought.

The conditions of the development of man's theoretical
capacities are to be sought in his entire psycho-physical
make-up.   No doubt *the hand* plays a very significant part
in the evolution.   Man is not specially favored in the possession of sense-organs.   In the hand, however, he has a
wonderful instrument of inquiry.   It divides and joins
together objects and qualities or states in the real world,
it gives a body form, position, motion, and color, and deprives it of them.   How helplessly the quadrupeds stand
before the things, possessing, as they do, only one prehensile organ, the teeth !   No wonder the objects remain mute
in the presence of their understanding and seem to speak
to their stomachs only !   Note, on the other hand, that
even the little child experiments on objects with the hand,
how it turns them hither and thither, and looks at them,
sets them up and knocks them down, takes them apart and

joins them together. This practical analysis and synthesis which the hand employs on objects is repeated in the analysis and the synthesis which the understanding employs in perception. The concepts of the understanding correspond to the tools used by the hand. It has been rightly said that the characteristic which distinguishes man from the animals is his ability to make tools and to think in concepts. Indeed, there is an intimate connection between the two. Man acts upon percepts which the animal receives passively. His behavior is especially conditioned by the fact that he has a hand, which is ever ready to interfere with the course of events by experimenting on them. The experiment of the natural scientist is but an advance on the primitive experimentation of the hand of the child. And whoever has failed to handle things as a child will never become acquainted with them, even though he gather all the book-knowledge of the world in his head.

Let us now return to the subject under discussion and say : From the standpoint of the theory of evolution it is utterly impossible to speak of the absolute apriority of certain functions. Space, time, and the categories are as much products of evolution as eyes, ears, and brains. Like the latter, they now belong to the hereditary possessions of the individual, at least in a certain sense, as much so as our entire system of concepts, which is transmitted in language and which we are obliged to regard as the historical heritage of the individual. He finds himself in possession of it when he begins to think ; it is the *a priori* element, as it were, of the knowledge acquired by him in the course of a lifetime. Nor is it at all doubtful that his conception of the universe is invariably determined by this *a priori* element ; with the inherited forms of intuition and thought he apperceives whatever is presented to him. On the other hand, we do not, of course, believe that this mental endowment is *a priori* in the sense of constituting the essence of intelligence as a system of absolutely rigid forms that are wholly unrelated to reality ; we must say: All organs are developed by the contact of living beings with their environment and are adapted to their surroundings. The same is true of the most important and most

delicate of all organs, the intellect. Web-footed animals
could have been developed only in the vicinity of water and
by coming in constant contact with water ; ears could have
been evolved only in an environment that transmits sound-
waves. Similarly the inner forms of our intuition and
thought could have originated only in such an environment as our world offers. It is true, we cannot demonstrate the suitableness of the latter as we may in the case
of web-footed animals ; we cannot step outside of our ideal
world and compare it with the real world. However, if we
assume that the subject and its intelligence are developed
in an actual world, we cannot refrain from regarding the
world as a co-operative factor in the formation of the
intelligence.

Our conclusion would therefore be: Kant has not
accomplished the task at which the argument in the
Æsthetic and *Analytic* chiefly aims : he has not succeeded
in proving the possibility of a knowledge of facts by "pure
reason," and hence the possibility of strictly universal and
necessary judgments concerning facts. On this point
Hume's empiricism holds its own against Kant.

On the other hand, Kant's epistemology contains a
number of *valuable* and *permanent* elements, and these I
should like briefly to touch upon in conclusion.

Above all, it emphasizes the important truth that knowledge is not a collection of "impressions," but a product of
the spontaneous activity of the subject. Empiricism inclines to the erroneous view that the soul is originally a
piece of white paper on which objects inscribe their characters by means of the senses. This view runs through all
sensualistic and empiristic theories, from the sensualistic
materialism of antiquity, which assumed that minute corporeal images are separated from the surface of objects
like little membranes and wander into the sensorium, down
to the present time. Kant's theory shows the utter insufficiency of such a view, which makes of the subject a
passive receptacle for impressions. There is absolutely
nothing in our knowledge that wanders into the soul from
without. Even the mere sensation of light, sound, and
taste is not impressed upon it from without; it is created

by the soul when this comes in contact with the environment and is therefore simply its own product. Kant assumes this truth as a universally accepted fact. On the other hand, he insists that even the general forms of the sensuous-intuitive world, space and time, are arrangements spontaneously produced by the subject, not copies of an actually-existent empty space or empty time. Their reality consists solely in that active function of the subject which combines a plurality of sense-elements into the unity of a perception.

We cannot help but believe that reality as such, to which the subject bears an original and not further definable relation, is in some way or other the occasion of the nature of its presentation. We may ascribe an "intelligible" order to it to which our forms of intuition somehow correspond. But these forms of intuition are themselves not impressions, but creations of the subject; the bodies and their movements are phenomena.

This truth is even more apparent in the case of concepts. A concept is not a collection of impressions, a composite image, in which the common features are intensified, the dissimilar ones effaced, an image like that made on a photographic plate by repeatedly exposing the same to similar objects and thus mechanically producing the type of the physician or the preacher. The concepts exist only as the active function of conceiving a plurality of percepts. The matter is very plain when we consider more general concepts. We might possibly delude ourselves into believing that the notion of the apple is stored in the memory like a composite photograph, although even in this case it would be difficult to produce a "composite picture" of big and little, red and green, round and angular apples. But the impossibility of forming a composite picture of fruit in general, representing apples and cherries and nuts and figs, etc., is quite apparent. And think of the composite picture of a product or a body or an object in general, or of the general image of color, form, size, velocity, direction, unity, plurality, reality, possibility, negation! It is plain that concepts like these cannot be produced by a kind of photographic process; they do not exist at all in the form of intuitive images, but only as conceptual activities, as mental operations dealing with a multitude of possible percepts, in which the word or some other sign serves as a substitute for the idea. Of course, such notions could not exist without percepts; and their sole importance consists in the fact that the percepts exist which we conceive or command by means of them.

We shall therefore say: All knowledge is an activity of the subject, and as such *a priori*. Certainly not *a priori* in the sense of being an absolutely isolated inner process. The activity of the intelligence is, like all activity, partially determined by the nature of the objects towards which it is directed. Sensations are activities of the subject provoked by the environment. The stimulus helps to determine the quality of the sensation; the sensation in turn stimulates the subject to produce the perception, the perception becomes a stimulus for the formation of the conceptual system. We can therefore also say: All knowledge is *a posteriori;* this is as true of the highest categories as of the most primitive sensations. And that is essentially Kant's meaning. There is no real knowledge that does not contain both an *a priori* and an *a posteriori* element. Percepts without concepts are blind, concepts without percepts are empty. But he persisted in ascribing pure and absolute apriority to certain elements, simply in order to save the universality and necessity, as well as the objective validity, of certain propositions, "the synthetical principles of the pure understanding."

From this another conclusion follows. We shall say with Kant and with all rationalists, beginning with the very first Greek philosophers: Scientific knowledge is not derived from the senses, but from the understanding; it is produced, not by perception, but by conceptual thought. Of course, philosophical empiricism needs no instruction on this point. Hume and J. S. Mill knew perfectly well the respective parts taken by the senses and by thought in science. Hume would not have written a theory of knowledge, nor Mill a system of the inductive method, had they believed that the eyes and the ears are the real organs of scientific knowledge; and Bacon is not an empiricist in the sense of having been the first to call the attention of his contemporaries to the fact that they would have to open their eyes if they would know anything of objects. On the contrary, he points out that it is not enough to gather observations. True, that too must be done, but it is a mere prelude to the real scientific work, the *inductio vera.* Imperfect induction, the *inductio per enumerationem simplicem,* contents itself with enumerating a few cases and then drawing from them a general law. Bacon prided himself on having discovered a method by which to draw real, universally valid judgments from particular observations, *i.e.*, a method for creating science. Whether or not he succeeded in his undertaking is a different question; at any rate, he had a correct conception of the problem.

Indeed, only the most superficial reflection can rest in the belief that scientific knowledge is derived from perception. Not the senses but the understanding made Copernicus the founder of modern astronomy and Galileo the founder of modern natural science. Nay, one might say in the spirit of Plato: Only by destroying the illusions of sense did they advance to the truth. The geocentric conception, the Aristotelian distinction between light and heavy bodies, the former of which tend upwards, the latter downwards, in proportion to their weight, seems much more plausible to the senses or to the man who does not go beyond them, than the doctrine of modern science. The same is true of the proposition of Aristotelian mechanics : The movements caused by external forces cease of their own accord when the velocity communicated by the impact is exhausted. Daily " experience " proves this. It is the thought which transcends perception that leads to new views, not, of course, without drawing perception or observation into its service. Thought resolves the manifold movements of rise and fall, of projection and impact, which old physics, relying on perception, simply accepted as absolute facts, into their component parts. Thus it explains the real motion of an impelled body by the coöperation of the tendency to persist and the resistance which the body has constantly to overcome ; it explains the real falling motion, whether it be motion upwards or downwards, by the general tendency of bodies to gravitate and to persist, which acts in coöperation with the static tendency of the medium. Thus Newton resolved the heavenly movements, explaining them by the coöperation of an original tangential motion and the tendency to gravitation. The old cosmology had simply formulated the perceptions as they offered themselves to the senses: The motion of the heavenly bodies is the simple, uniform, eternal circular motion.*

Hence science is universally found to be the result of reflection which has emancipated itself from sense-perception. In observation or in the experiment, perception becomes an indispensable but altogether secondary factor. The more developed science becomes, the less important is the part played by perception. The biological sciences at present very plainly exemplify the diminished importance of perception. Physiology and the theory of evolution have begun to transform the old " descriptive " sciences, which gathered perceptions, into systems of thought. Thus we may say even of Darwin's theory that it is " contrary to sense " (*widersinnisch*) in the same sense in which Kant once applied the term to the Copernican theory; it contradicts the truth of the perception that the specific type is constant. Even history manifests such a tendency to change from what it was, *i.e.*, a mere collection of percepts (recollections and testimonies), into a system of evident truths. The beginning has been made by the doctrine of the laws of economic life, and its influence on the development of historical science is apparently increasing rapidly. The laws of political economy evidently did not arise from a collection of percepts, but were discovered by deductive thought. Nay, we may go a step farther and say: Historical research does not acquire its truths by gather-

---

* Lotze, *Logik*, p. 585 (English Translation edited by B. Bosanquet, vol. II. p. 314): "It was not by the testimony of repeated perceptions that they (the principles of mechanics) were discovered and reduced to the exact form of a law; it was by an operation of thought, apprehending with the clearness of immediate vision the self-evident law in an instance where it is presented in its purity." Then self-evidence, he goes on to say (p. 596, Eng. trans. p. 329), "must no longer be called logical but *æsthetic*, and will accordingly find the touchstone of its validity no longer in the unthinkableness, but in the plain absurdity, of its contradictory."

ing testimony ; whoever has no *a priori* knowledge of what
has taken place cannot be taught by the evidence; unless
you know how to seek, you will find nothing; unless you
know how to ask, the sources will give no answer, but will
overwhelm you with a confused mass of rumors and opinions. He alone can make inquiries who knows what the
subject is about. Old Heraclitus was quite right when he
declared: Polymathy will not beget understanding.

In conclusion let me call to mind the cardinal thought
in the Kantian philosophy: *Knowledge is a function of the
subject, but not the only and not the most important one.* Its
object is to serve us as a practical guide through the world,
and it realizes this end. It is not, however, given to us,
nor is it adequate, as a means of penetrating absolutely into
the inner essence of reality, of resolving the world into
thoughts, so to speak. Hume agrees with Kant on this
point: An absolute knowledge of reality is impossible. —
That was the error of old rationalism or dogmatism : it believed that both the dignity of man and the final goal of
life consisted in knowledge. Kant subjects this overweening scientific pride, which both the philosophy of the
school and scholastic theology share, to the most crushing
criticism : there is no science of the absolute or suprasensuous. The absolute and suprasensuous exists, but it transcends the sphere of possible knowledge. Critical reflection shows us that our knowledge is confined to the domain
of the sensuous, to possible experience; it also shows us,
on the other hand, that our world of experience is not the
world of things-in-themselves. Our theoretical reason takes
us so far.

Practical reason takes us a step farther, as does every
philosophy that does not restrict itself to the theoretical
speculation on nature, but contemplates man from the
point of view of his vocation. And such a philosophy alone
is philosophy in the highest sense, philosophy in its world-
definition, as distinguished from the scholastic definition of
the term. It shows us that the vocation and dignity of
man is not ultimately rooted in knowledge, but in the volitional side of his nature. Here also lie the deepest roots
of our being ; in conscience, in the consciousness of the

moral law, we become aware of our real essence. We possess the immediate certainty that the real essence of our being is grounded on reality itself, that we belong, not to nature as it appears to the senses and the understanding, but to absolute reality itself, and therefore come to believe in the absolute teleological order of things, in a moral world-order, of which the natural order is but an external reflection. In religion the spirit posits what it regards as the highest and best, as the emanation of the final source of reality, and conceives reality as the phenomenon of a realm of ends, as the creation of God and the sphere of his activity. It is an aberration of the mind to hold afterwards that faith can be proved and forced upon the intellect. This error gives rise to a reaction, to the negative dogmatism of materialistic atheism. The critical philosophy reveals the impossibility both of a positive and a negative dogmatism. In doing that it demonstrates the possibility of faith, of a faith that is grounded solely on the will and needs no proof: I could not live, I could not breathe and move freely in a world that is nothing but an enormous senseless and soulless machine; hence I cannot believe that it is such a machine; hence I believe that it is the revelation of an all-wise and all-good God, even though my eyes fail to see him and my understanding comprehend him not.

APPENDIX.

THE PROBLEMS OF ETHICS.*

It is a fact that man's actions are determined by motives which exist in the form of purposes, *i.e.*, as ideas of a good to be attained by action. Thus the question arises : What is *the final aim* or *the highest good* for the sake of which everything else is desired? *Hedonism* answers : *Pleasure ;* it is for this that everything else is desired. This view is opposed by another theory, which does not seek the highest good in subjective feelings, but in an *objective* content of life, or, since life is activity, in a *specific mode* of life. Permit me to call this view *energism*.

It is also a fact that human beings *judge* the behavior and acts of others as well as of themselves. They judge by means of the predicates *good* and *bad*. A man's conduct and disposition arouse feelings of *approval* or *disapproval* in the spectator; when these feelings become habitual, feelings of admiration or contempt arise. When such emotions are referred to our own self and our past behavior, they are called feelings of remorse or pangs of conscience, or, conversely, self-respect and peace of conscience. When they refer to possible future actions, we call them feelings of duty or feelings of obligation. That phase of our nature by means of which we judge of our volitions and acts is called *conscience*.

The question arises : What occasions such a judgment

---

* The following suggestions are intended to indicate the position occupied by ethical inquiries rather than to give an elaborate exposition of the same. The reader who is interested in my views on these subjects will find a detailed account of them in my *System der Ethik* (3d ed., 1894).

which at first sight appears to be wholly independent of
my judgment concerning what is useful or harmful?
What is the standard by which we measure the *moral* worth
of dispositions and actions? This question, too, may be
answered in two ways: (1) The moral law, which everybody harbors within himself, is the standard of moral
worth; an act is good when the will is determined by a regard for the moral law. (2) The effect of the act upon the
welfare of all whom it reaches is the standard. This constitutes the distinction between *formalistic* and *teleological*
moral philosophy.

The antithesis between hedonism and energism is fundamental to the Greek systems of morality. Aristippus and
Epicurus belong to the former, Plato, Aristotle, and the
Stoa to the latter school. In modern philosophy it is above
all the adherents of English empiricism and analytical
psychology who incline to hedonism. Bentham and James
Mill are its most consistent representatives. Psychological analysis, they find, reveals the fact that all action is,
without exception, determined by the motive to procure
pleasure and to avoid pain. The necessary goal of human
volition is accordingly to obtain a maximum of pleasure
and a minimum of pain. Different forms of energism are
advanced by Hobbes, Spinoza, Shaftesbury, Leibniz, and
Wolff: self-preservation and self-realization, the freedom
of the rational self in real thought, the harmonious development and exercise of all our powers, perfection—these
are some of the principles advanced by the theory. The
evolutionistic ethics of modern times accepts this view:
A specific type of life and the exercise of the same is the
real aim of all life and striving.

I believe that energism is in the right. Analytical
psychology is in error when it holds that the *idea of pleasure*
is the constant motive of human volition. It is a false
theory of willing that bases it exclusively on feelings of
pleasure and pain. It is not true that a feeling of pleasure
is first aroused by the food or sexual function, and that
after the pleasure has once been experienced it is anticipated in the future, and that the impulses spring from the
expected pleasure. Nor is it true that feelings of pain are

first removed by the exercise of these functions, and that a permanent impulse is thereby created. No, the impulse is an original determination of the being; it arises in consciousness, not as pain, but as a felt craving, as a desire or a love for a particular mode of action; and a feeling of pleasure appears only when the impulse is realized, while a feeling of pain ensues when it is obstructed. Unless the impulse existed, pleasure and pain would be out of the question. The same may be said of the higher impulses; the impulses to specific action, to run and to leap, to play and to work, to fight and to rule, to think and to write poetry, make themselves felt in life at the proper time without being preceded by feelings of pain, the removal of which is the end desired. Nor are feelings of pleasure presented in idea as the goal of the activity. Accordingly we say: The goal at which the will aims does not consist in a maximum of pleasurable feelings, but in the normal exercise of the vital functions for which the species is predisposed. In the case of man the mode of life is on the whole determined by the nature of the historical unity from which the individual evolves as a member. Here the objective content of life, after which the will strives, also enters into consciousness with the progressive evolution of presentation; the type of life becomes a conscious ideal of life. The will is directed upon some particular objective form of existence and activity; it is attracted by the life of the warrior, of the investigator, of the saint, of the wife and mother, of the sister of charity; and room is left for individual differences. The realization of the goal is followed by satisfaction; discontent and inner discord follow failure.

The problem of ethics, therefore, is to set forth in general outlines the form of life for which human nature is predisposed. Of course, ethics cannot give a concrete exposition of the content of life or of the ideal desired by the individual; that is the business of creative nature and in a certain sense of art. Science confines itself to describing the general forms within which alone a perfect human life is possible, one that realizes and permanently satisfies the human will. This task is performed in the doctrine of virtues and duties, the concrete form of which is determined by people and times. Hence ethics is related to life as grammar is to language, æsthetics to art, dietetics to bodily life; it outlines the form of the possible and the allowable, and these forms may be filled with different contents. The perfect is like the beautiful, not a uniform type; it consists of an infinite variety of individual creations. Ethics will explain moral evil or the bad as medicinal dietetics explains disturbances, weaknesses, and malformations. The latter occurrences are regarded as the results of external obstructions and disturbances, that are contrary to the tendency of the disposition to develop normally. Similarly, ethics will refer the evil and the bad, not to the real volition of the being itself, which is to be regarded as tending to develop normally and to make for human perfection, but to unfavorable conditions of development, in consequence of which the predisposition is dwarfed and deformed. That evil is really contrary to the real nature of the will, that the desire of the bad man to do the will of God is essential to his being, is proved by the fact, ethics will add, that wickedness is invariably accompanied by inward dissatisfaction. This is the reaction of the fundamental will against particular momentary desires or against hypertrophically developed impulses, which coerce it, as it were. The dietetic method to be pursued is thereby prescribed: unfavorable conditions which occasioned such deformities must be removed and the original purpose of the will strengthened by removing excrescences and otherwise encouraging it.

We now turn to the opposition existing between *teleological* and *formalistic* moral philosophy. The former view is common to Greek philosophy. The Greeks are agreed that all distinctions regarding the worth of moral modes of conduct ultimately depend on the different effects which the different modes of conduct tend to produce; all of them explain ethics as the science of the highest good, which they all define as eudæmonism. The other theory is more acceptable to the moral philosophy favored by Christianity: Good and evil are determined, not by referring the act to an end, but by measuring it by an absolutely valid law, the law of God, which the church teaches. The first epoch of modern philosophy returns to

the teleological mode of treatment. We discover it in
Spinoza and Wolff, in Shaftesbury and Hume. With Kant
a strong reaction begins against " eudæmonistic " ethics in
favor of formalistic ethics, the after-effects of which are
felt in German philosophy to this day. Indeed, there is
something very convincing about formalistic moral philosophy : an act is good or bad, not because of its effects ; it
is good or bad in and for itself. Falsehood and deceit are
bad in themselves, without regard to their effects, and so
too honesty and self-control are good in themselves. Or
in Kant's words : A good will is the only thing that is good
in and for itself ; it has absolute worth, wholly regardless
of what it accomplishes and how it succeeds in the world.
There is some truth in the assertion, but we cannot stop
here. The statement is made : It is right to act justly and
wrong to act unjustly, regardless of the real effects of the
act ; the disposition and not the effect, which is always uncertain, decides. To be sure, we shall say, the disposition
which prompted a particular act alone decides its moral
worth. But could we speak of justice and injustice at all
if the actions of men had and could have no effects whatever upon the welfare of others ? Apparently not. Then
can the value of conduct be wholly and in every respect
independent of its effects ? Should we still call wrong-
doing bad and reprehensible even if, by virtue of its nature,
it never had harmful but only favorable influences upon
the welfare of all the parties concerned ? If it lay in the
nature of falsehood to promote the interest of the deceived
one and to gain confidence for the liar, would lying still be
bad ? Is this judgment like an axiomatic proposition, or
like a judgment of perception, for which no reason whatever can be assigned ? Or can a reason be assigned why
it is better to be moderate and prudent, just and truthful,
peaceful and benevolent, than the opposite ?

I believe that there is a reason, a reason which the
experience of all nations sets forth in thousands of proverbs : Falsehood, injustice, and excess are ruinous ; they
are the bane of individuals as well as of nations. And,
conversely, justice and prudence are means of salvation.
Indeed, to grant that acts have effects on welfare and then

to deny that such effects determine their value somewhat
resembles the teleophobia mentioned before, which says:
We see because we have eyes; but we do not have eyes
that we may see. So, too, in this case: Virtues preserve
life, vices destroy it, but their moral worth does not depend on this.

The problem of ethics consists in applying the teleological view in detail, and in showing how life, human-
mental life, is preserved and promoted by virtuous deeds,
but impeded and destroyed by vice. Honesty is good;
theft in every shape and form is bad, for theft injures first
the life of the aggrieved person then also that of the
thief; it deprives him of the blessings of labor, for thieves
do not work. Finally, it destroys the security of property and hence the desire to acquire it; for nations whose
property-rights are insecure become impoverished. Property, however, is the fundamemtal condition of all higher
development in human-mental life. Thus veracity is good
and falsehood bad, because in addition to the disturbances
which it produces within the narrowest circles, the deception of the offended person, the isolation of the liar, it has
the secondary effect of destroying the confidence of men in
general. Confidence, however, is the fundamental condition of human social life, and without society there can be
no real human life. Similarly, adultery and licentiousness are reprehensible, because they ruin individuals and
tend to destroy healthy family life, the root of all healthy
human life; and, conversely, to live a pure and chaste
life in word and in deed is good, because it preserves life
in the physical and spiritual sense. And so it is everywhere : certain modes of conduct are good in so far as
they have the tendency to preserve and to augment human
goods, others are reprehensible and bad, because they tend
to destroy the conditions of a wholesome, beautiful, and
spiritual human life. In so far now as welfare is accompanied by feelings of satisfaction, decline and ruin, by feelings of pain, we may also say: Virtue is the road to
happiness, vice to unhappiness. Pleasure, so Aristotle declares, follows the realizatiom of the act as an unintended
secondary effect.

Let me add a few remarks in order to protect this view against misunderstandings and objections. The confusion which prevails here seems to me to be essentially due to the fact that we do not distinguish between the dual judgment to which every act gives rise : the *subjective* judgment concerning the moral worth of the will, which is expressed in the act, and the *objective* judgment concerning the worth of the act as such. The former considers the disposition only : an act is morally good when it springs from a good will, *i.e.*, one determined by the consciousness of duty, be its effects what they may. But ethics does not deal solely and preferably with such judgments. To be sure, it must say with Kant, and insist on it, that the moral worth of a man does not depend on what he accomplishes and how he succeeds in the world, but on the faithfulness with which he does what he feels and recognizes to be his duty. Its real business, however, is to ascertain the *objective* worth of acts and modes of *conduct*. And this is not dependent on the disposition. The theft of Crispinus, to use an old scholastic example, springs from a good will and is in so far a good deed ; yet it is at the same time a reprehensible mode of action, because theft as such, independently of the intentions of the thief, undermines the institution of property. Moreover, the judgment of the disposition of the subject is ultimately based on teleological considerations ; a good will is, in the last analysis, good because it is good for something, because it tends to produce such behavior and action as has objective worth, *i.e.*, leads to the perfection of human life.

I further remark that the standard with which moral philosophy measures the value of modes of conduct neither is nor can be also *the motive* of action. The real motives of action are inclinations, habits, principles, definite concrete aims, ideas of what is dutiful and proper. This is and always will be the case. The general intention to promote the welfare of the human race will never become the motive of conduct ; it cannot be, if only for the reason that the welfare of the human race cannot be concretely presented to consciousness ; furthermore, because we can never calculate the relation of the effects of a particular act to such an ultimate end. Every act has an infinite number of effects; even the direct effects which an act has on the agent and his surroundings are incalculable, much more so its indirect effects; think of the effect of example, habit, and heredity! If, before reaching a decision, we should have to figure out all the possible favorable and unfavorable effects of a deed, we should never act. Hence the process is abbreviated; acts are as a rule *automatic reactions*, which are released, without much calculation, by circumstances, by the occasion. The factors just mentioned, inclinations and habits, customs and principles, decide the form of the reaction. Hence the great importance to life of forming by practice the right automatic acts, *i.e.*, such as are on the whole teleological or make for welfare.

And in this connection it is worthy of note that the collective bodies of which individuals are the members, that nations show the same immanent purposiveness common to all organic beings and develop automatic forms of reaction for the solution of certain problems of life. They create *customs* (*Sitten*). By these we mean all such modes of action and behavior as are binding upon the members of a people, including the legal forms. The individuals are thereby relieved of the impossible task of calculating the effects. They now act as custom and law prescribe, and hence are spared the uncertainty of the calculation before the act, as well as the uncertainty appertaining to the effects following the act. They have at all events acted as it behooves just and "moral" men to act under such circumstances. As instincts save animals the trouble of considering and calculating the acts that are useful and essential to the preservation of life, so customs save man the same trouble. In the former case, the inherited forms of reaction determine the activity universally conducing to the preservation of the individual and the species. In the latter case customs (*Sitten*) which are based on inherited instincts and developed by education produce a similar result. There is as little foreknowledge of the purposiveness of the customary act in the one case as in the other. The natural man knows the custom; in this respect he is superior to the animal which knows nothing of the instinct; but he does not know why the custom is valid; it exists in him as objective, not as subjective, reason. It is only on reflection, which reaches its highest development in ethics, that the teleological necessity of custom is understood.

From what has gone before we may determine the nature of *conscience.* Conscience is originally nothing but the knowledge of custom. The individual knows what mode of behavior, *e.g.*, towards the opposite sex, is enjoined upon him by custom. From his earliest childhood it has been impressed upon him by his education, by the opinions of society concerning what is decent and indecent, by laws and punishments, finally by religious commandments, how he *ought* to behave. He compares the reality with this obligation, the norm which is always present and absolutely binding; it admonishes him, it impels him, it warns and punishes. The obligation is not something foreign to his own will; he himself wills that the norm be valid, that custom be obeyed; he invariably demands that others do so; indeed it is his will that the community, the historical organism to which he belongs, preserve itself and live. Only accidentally and occasionally does a conflict occur between the obligation and the momentary desire, the isolated craving. True, it is then that we are most conscious of the obligation, and hence it might appear as though the opposition between duty and inclination were essential to morality.

Conscience assumes another form on a higher stage of development. Corresponding to the individualization of mental life it here becomes an individual ideal of life, which even antagonizes custom. That has happened in all great reformations of moral-religious life, and there is no conflict as hard and tragic as this: in battling for a higher morality to oppose the popular morality of the times and to be judged by it. Jesus and his disciples fought this fight: custom and law, the temple and the sabbath, are not the highest; the kingdom of God is higher. And for that reason the citizen of the kingdom of God rises above the law.

INDEX.

A.

Academy, 340.
Actio ad distans, 212 ff.
Activities, 354 ff.
Agnostic monism, 48, 60.
Agrippa of Nettesheim, 107 note.
Albertus Magnus, 31.
Analysis and synthesis, 411 ff.
Analytical judgments, 399.
Anaxagoras, his teleology, 154 ff.
Ancestor-worship, 267 f., 274.
Animism. See Fetishism.
Anthropomorphic theism, 149 ff., 160, 207, 218, 291 f. See also Theism.
Anthropomorphism, 226,255 ff., 258, 270 ff., 273 f., 276.
A posteriori knowledge, 391, 416.
A priori knowledge, 16, 380, 389 ff., 398 ff., 413 f., 416.
Aristippus, 422.
Aristotle, 6, 22, 31, 41, 45, 56, 101, 106, 154 f., 209, 219 f., 232, 235, 314, 339, 360, 363, 381, 410, 422, 426; his definition of philosophy, 17, 22; his idealism, 93; his ontology, 56; his teleology, 154 f.; his theology, 28 f.
Association, 218 f., 376, 410 f.
Astral souls, 106.
Atheism, 14, 246 f., 292 f., 305 f.
Atom, 131 f., 208 ff.
Atomism, 48, 149 ff.; ancient, 339; critique of, 207 ff.
Augustine, 249, 289, 313.
Automatic movements, 89, 190.
Automaton, 96.

B.

Bacon, Francis, 157, 416 f.; his conception of philosophy, 23.
Baer, K. E. v., 218 note, 222, 225, 229.
Belief in God, 158 ff.; origin of, 273 ff.

Bender, W., 251 note.
Beneke, 60.
Bentham, 422.
Berkeley, 390; his idealism, 60; on perception, 348.
Böhme, J., 265.
Bopp, 196.
Brahman, 284 f.
Brain, 63 ff., 84 f., 134.
Bruchmann, 198.
Bruno, 5, 235.
Büchner, L., 67 note, 80 f., 86, 100, 266, 324.
Buddhism, 177.
Bunsen, 320 note.

C.

Cartesians, 96, 143.
Categories, 322, 351, 394 ff., 400 ff., 413 f.
Causality, 145, 205, 211 ff., 351, 387 f., 390, 394 ff., 402 ff.; development of, in man, 408 ff.; and finality, 218 ff.
Choice, 115.
Christianity, 7, 15, 177 f., 247 ff., 261, 287 f., 326 ff., 424; its teleology of history, 178.
Church, relation of, to philosophy and science, 7, 13, 159.
Common-sense, its ontology, 53 f.; its conception of soul, 53 f., 357 f., 364; and idealism, 111.
Comte, 13, 27, 267, 315 f., 332, 340.
Concept, 415.
Conception and understanding, 373 f.
Conceptual thinking, 411, 416 f.
Conscience, 202, 419, 421, 429.
Consciousness, 61 ff., 120 ff., 127, 140 ff., 359; evolution of, 119 f.; explanation of, 79; relation of soul to, 120 ff.
Contradiction, law of, 215, 384, 387.
Copernicus, 417; and Kant, 396 f.
Cosmic organization, 147 f.

www.ingramcontent.com/pod-product-compliance
Lightning Source LLC
Chambersburg PA
CBHW022020110726
47901CB00006B/1606